Philosophies of Place

EDITED BY

Peter D. Hershock and Roger T. Ames

Philosophies of Place

An Intercultural Conversation

University of Hawai'i Press
and East-West Philosophers' Conference

HONOLULU

The editors gratefully acknowledge the long-standing and magnanimous support of the Hung Wo and Elizabeth Lau Ching Foundation and the Uehiro Foundation on Ethics and Education (Tokyo). The generous sponsorship of the following organizations and individuals is also greatly appreciated: Diamond Head Memorial Park; Alexander and Baldwin, Inc.; the K. J. Luke Foundation; Warren and Carolyn Luke; the Chan Foundation (Vancouver); Professor Barbara B. Smith; Mr. and Mrs. Gulab Watumull; the James and Juanita Wo Foundation; and Roger and Bonnie Ames. Over the years, the East-West Philosophers' Conference and book series have benefited tremendously from their generous contributions.

Printed in the United States of America

Library of Congress Cataloging-in-Publication Data

Names: Hershock, Peter D., editor. | Ames, Roger T., editor.
Title: Philosophies of place : an intercultural conversation / edited by
    Peter D. Hershock and Roger T. Ames.
Description: Honolulu : University of Hawai'i Press : East-West Philosophers'
    Conference, [2019] | Includes bibliographical references and index.
Identifiers: LCCN 2018047509 | ISBN 9780824876586 (cloth ; alk. paper)
Subjects: LCSH: Place (Philosophy)
Classification: LCC B105.P53 P45 2019 | DDC 114—dc23
LC record available at https://lccn.loc.gov/2018047509

ISBN: 9780824892364 (paperback)

Contents

Philosophies of Place

Introduction

Peter D. Hershock and Roger T. Ames

Humanity takes up space. In this, humanity is no different from other species. Humanity also purposefully transforms space but, once again, is not unique in doing so. Other species also reshape the spaces they occupy to serve their purposes: birds create nests, bees create hives, and beavers create dams. What seems to be uniquely human is the disposition to qualitatively transform spaces into places that are charged with distinctive kinds of intergenerational significance.

Think, for example, of the felt difference between a house as domestic space and a home as familial place, or of that between the summit of a mountain one has just climbed for the first time and the "same" ancient rock thrust up into the sky, but haloed and hallowed now by ancestral narratives of spiritual communion between the celestial and terrestrial realms. It is, perhaps, a uniquely human creativity that imbues spaces, both natural and built, with a fifth dimension of depth—a dimension, not of quantifiably passing time, but of qualitatively pervading histories.

Contemporary philosophical uses of the word "place" cover considerable conceptual ground, centered on a distinction between "space" and "place" that was formalized by geographer-philosopher Yi-Fu Tuan, who suggested that "place incorporates the experiences and aspirations of a people" over the course of their moral and aesthetic engagement with sites and locations.[1] Building on this distinction, we might say that spaces are openings for different kinds of presence—physical, emotional, cognitive, dramatic, spiritual, and so on. Places emerge through fusions of different ways of being present over time—a meaning-infusing layering of relationships and experiences that saturates a locale with distinctively collaborative patterns of significance. Place implies sustainably appreciated and enhanced relational quality.

This angle of philosophical approach to issues of place, however, is emblematic of what Edward S. Casey has succinctly argued are specifically Western (though ostensibly "universal") convictions about the primacy of absolute space and time that emerged coevally with the progressive dominance of the scientific imagination.[2] In John Locke's notable formulation, places are logically posterior "modifications" of space—functionally defined "sites" hewn by human agency out of the infinite dimensions of cosmic space and time. According to Casey, the reappearance of place in Western philosophy has been by way of the body—that is, by way of a turn away from abstract and a priori reasoning and back toward phenomenal experience and recognition of the primacy of emplaced being.[3]

This affirmation of the primacy of the emplaced, lived body in human experience resonates with contemporary theories of enactive cognition or awareness.[4] A key facet of the enactive approach to understanding cognition is that sentience should not be identified with or defined by gathering sensory information about the world that is used to build representations of existing circumstances on the basis of which courses of action or response are subsequently formulated. Rather, sentient being consists in dynamic, meaning-generating processes of *enacting worlds*.[5] That is, emplacement occurs synthetically among the full range of *relational* domains out of which we can abstract individual living beings and their lived and living environments. And, for us humans, these domains encompass always ongoing and reflexively evolving cultural, social, economic, and political dynamics.

To be "in place" is thus to be intimately and irreducibly related. And it is thus not surprising that anthropological studies of place and indigeneity served as key points of departure for Casey's philosophical approach to reestablishing the primacy of place. For many indigenous peoples, their relations with "place" traditionally have been so intimate that to be forced off their lands (or out of their waters) is to be forced out of themselves—to be cut off from part of what makes them who they are. Thus, Native Hawaiians regard place as a distinctive pattern of mutually enfolding relationships among people, nature, and the supernatural world—an interweaving of spiritual, physical, ancestral, and sociocultural relations, practices, and traditions.[6] In a very real sense, the genealogies of Native Hawaiians and other indigenous peoples are ultimately narratives of emplacement.

Sustaining such an intimately familial relationship with place is seemingly at odds with the superficial engagements with lived environments that are fostered by the commercialization of real estate, by the adventitious mobility normalized by contemporary globalization processes, and by the homogenization of urban and suburban spaces by global capital—all of which contribute to a pervasive nullification of place and to the deepening experience and acceptance of placelessness.[7] And indeed, being cosmopolitan has come to be identified by many as a readiness and capacity for being "at home" anywhere—a readiness and capacity that critics might deride as evidence of failing to realize that no place truly belongs to us unless we belong to it in turn. But in fact, contemporary urban residents can and do develop deep senses of a dynamic and recursive relationship between *who* they are and *where* they are. This is certainly true for many residents of New York City and Shanghai, to pick just two global cities in which personal identities are intimately bound up with place.

Moreover, while it is possible and perhaps imperative to call critical attention to the attenuated relational bandwidth at which sociality is now being realized through social media and other virtual domains, these media and domains are nevertheless experienced by their most avid users *as* meeting places. As such, they are as properly topics of any comprehensive philosophy of place as are the natural/cultural environs of indigenous peoples. Is it possible in virtual places to realize other than merely virtual relations of mutual belonging? If, for so-called digital natives—the "indigenous" peoples of Internet-mediated worlds—all times, locales, material goods, cultural products, and people are effectively "equidistant," are they then truly capable of attending to and acting in the "fifth dimension" of qualitatively deepening and intimately shared histories that would be crucial to the emergence of cyber-places and not just electively populating cyberspace?

If, indeed, the place-making propensities of humanity find expression in dynamic and ongoing enactments of meaning, then they must be seen from the outset as having been inseparable from formulating and answering questions about our place in the world: the place of "humanity," of "my people," and of "me" personally. One result historically of these questions has been the crafting of complexly imagined cosmologies and narratives of "promised lands" and "paradises" beyond the horizons of current experience. The Garden of Eden invoked by the Judeo-Christian-Islamic account of human origins has been a place of real and continued significance for more than two thousand years in spite of being spatially inaccessible—a place from which humanity fell into confusion and conflict. In contrast, Tao Yuanming's story of the Peach Blossom Land, composed in 421 during a period of social and political disruption across the Chinese heartlands and still invoked today throughout the Chinese cultural world, envisions an extraordinary place of peace and tranquility hidden within the mundane world, accessible only by narrow accident—a place into which people have retreated in eras of disorder and violence and abided thereafter in ever-blossoming harmony.

As illustrated by these disparate visions of paradisal places—and of damning falls from grace and of salvific retreat into vibrantly shared oases—our human propensities for generating meaning can be at odds with one another. What can and should *take place* is open to contestation. Another result, then, of questions about our places in the world has been concerns about positional inequalities in social, economic, and political space and what governs or justifies them. Although we are all situated beings, we are clearly not always situated humanely or in ways that guarantee equivalent opportunities for participation and contribution. One response to these concerns about equity and justice has been the crafting of utopias—literally, non-places—as means to establishing trajectories of hope that might transport us out of access-and-opportunity-denying places and onto common ground for realizing conditions of dignity for all. Another, more recent response has been the crafting of "places of difference"—heterotopias—in which impulses to universality and commonality are consciously resisted in favor of cultivating capacities for and commitments to sustaining relationally enriching places in which each of us can have a distinctive, contributory share.

In sum, we might say, then, that places emerge or are enacted through the sustainably shared practices of mutually responsive and mutually vulnerable agents and that our places are as numerous in kind as we are divergent in the patterns of values, intentions, and actions through which we articulate who we are, how we are, and why we are precisely as and where we are. If we can speak intelligibly about *the* philosophy of place, it is perhaps only in the sense that we can speak about *the* rain forest ecology—as something always adaptively expressive of apt differentiation. Accepting this understanding of emplacement speaks both to the epistemic value of embracing philosophically disparate approaches to place, and to the merits of struggling with significantly recursive questions about the place(s) of philosophy itself.

The Present Volume

In keeping with these reflections on the meanings of approaching place philosophically, the contributions that have been partnered in the present volume are purposely wide-ranging and have been grouped as ensembles addressing one of five topics: conversations of place in intercultural philosophy; the critical interplay of place and personal identity; personhood and environmental emplacement; shared places of politics and religion; and the emotionally emplaced body.

Part I: Conversations of Place in Intercultural Philosophy

The contributions included in this section express a shared (but by no means common) conviction that discussions of globalization and cosmopolitanism belong crucially to any contemporary philosophy of place. Stanley Cavell has drawn a useful distinction between *conversations-about* justice and *conversations-of* justice.[8] The former discourse places justice in the position of discursive object, while the latter places it in that of discursive subject. Blending this contrast with Jean-Luc Nancy's incisive distinction between the coercive potential of the "common" and the contributory nature of the "shared,"[9] we can say that in conversations *about* place, place is a common concern; in conversations *of* place, place is something not-yet-given and in the emergence of which we each can have a distinctive contributory share. The contributions in this section thus do not explicitly talk about place but, rather, allow the voicing of place concerns in considerations of the meaning of philosophy in the context of contemporary scales and scopes of globalization.

The lead piece, by David Wong and Marion Hourdequin, addresses the meaning of cosmopolitanism in connection with the growing recognition that contemporary challenges like climate change, migration, and humanitarian intervention require concerted and coordinated action across national and cultural boundaries—action undertaken and sustained by putatively cosmopolitan members of a single moral community. Yet, they argue, it is not at all clear what cosmopolitanism is in a world of increasingly complex global interdependencies. Drawing on Confucian and Daoist sources, they forward a conception of cosmopolitanism that is rooted in face-to-face encounters and that valorizes difference as the basis of mutual contribution.

The following three chapters critically link the prospects of freeing philosophy from cultural and conceptual dualisms with the prospects for truly global conversations of place. Steven Burik makes use of Heideggerian and Daoist resources to argue against the need to choose between "provincialism" and "cosmopolitanism" as subject positions from which to engage in comparative philosophy, and then to argue for the possibility of a middle path of nondualistic comparison. In a complementary fashion, beginning with the recognition that philosophy always takes place in specific locales, Britta Saal investigates the processual place of the "inter" in intercultural philosophy. Drawing on insights from philosophies taking place in Europe, the Americas, and Africa, she argues for a relational conception of the place of intercultural philosophy. Next, John Krummel explores the experiential horizons of engagement with places of pilgrimage and ethical and ontological implications that are coeval with the opening of such places in authentic face-to-face encounters with others, both human and otherwise. In this conversation of place, Krummel includes both Japanese and German interlocutors who—as contemporary philosophers—are differently intent on disclosing places of experienced otherness that lie beyond humanly constructed semantic fields.

In the final chapter in this section, James Buchanan acknowledges the challenges noted by Wong and Hourdequin but questions whether any of the great ethical traditions of the past is adequate to frame responses to them in light of the complex, nonlinear ways in which these challenges emerge and are manifest. In contrast to ethical traditions that begin within the proximate horizons of specific experiences, traditions, and communities, Buchanan calls for a more platially extensive ethics—an ethics of exercising responsibility in a world of complex global systems in which "the seemingly simple act innocently done," such as turning on a light switch, can affect the lives of people continents away.

Part II: The Critical Interplay of Place and Personal Identity

Among the key insights of the philosophy of place is that the relationship between self and place is one not merely of mutual influence but of "constitutive coingredience," so that "there is no place without self and no self without place."[10] In this section, Joshua Stoll and Meera Baindur approach the constitutive coingredience of self and place from two very different perspectives. Beginning with the conceptual problem of other mind—a problem that asks how we bridge the gap between first- and third-person ascriptions of mental properties—Stoll works out from within the debates between Indian Buddhist, Nyāya-Vaiśeṣika, and Kaśmīr Śaiva traditions to argue that we can negotiate the space between witnessing the experiences of others and inhabiting experiences as our own, because the self is originally no-self in the sense of being always already decentered by societal emplacement. Engaging with feminist construals of relational autonomy, he asserts that the place of encountering another in mutual recognition is one that emerges, not because our minds or experiences are somehow the same, but precisely because they are different—an actuality, Stoll maintains, that we are apprised of because we are each different in responding to the ways in which society differentiates among us.

Seeing the roots of self-identity as societal or relational is crucial to Baindur's searching examination of place-related personal identity in the matrix of traditional Indian thought and contemporary society. Through an examination of place-related terms in Indian thought, Baindur argues that not only do location-based identities influence social relations and ethical norms, but they also establish zones of inclusion and exclusion. With caste and gender as focal concerns, she goes on to carefully articulate how the displacements and dislocations mandated by traditional caste and gender hierarchies are also, if always ambiguously, given within spaces of soteriological opportunity for deliberately leaving one's societally determined place and identity to seek other positions and eligibilities.

Part III: Personhood and Environmental Emplacement

Considerations about relationship between place and identity are taken up once again in this section of the book, but specifically in terms of the relationship between persons and environments. Michael Hemmingsen takes as his point of departure questions about animal subjectivity and how the answers to those questions reflect certain positions or places from which to engage in moral discourse. As Hemmingsen notes, many indigenous peoples accord to animals depths of subjective awareness and intentionality that are parallel to, though not necessarily the same as, those enjoyed by humans. Often it is by appeal to the sociality of relations made possible by these shared depths of awareness and intentionality that indigenous populations argue on behalf of what (in contemporary global discourse) is referred to as natural resource conservation—an appeal that "works" only to the extent that we accept the validity of their claims about animal subjectivity and what it implies regarding moral considerability. Hemmingsen asserts that such an appeal is valid, not factually but literally, as an instance of what he terms "ecological truth"—a truth that occurs in an epistemic space shared with other than human species.

Justas Kučinskas and Naglis Kardelis broaden the relational horizons of the reciprocal influences taking place between humans and their environs by exploring the thought of the Lithuanian philosopher Arvydas Šliogeris and his approach to "philotopy," or the love of particular places. In contrast with Yi-Fu Tuan's comparable notion of "topophilia," or the human love of place, Šliogeris focuses, not on emotional connections dependent on human cultural, historical, or instrumental projections onto living environments, but on connections fused directly with natural places in their natural (rather than human) specificity. It is ultimately such a shift of attention, Kučinskas and Kardelis argue, that is needed in order to forge locally effective responses to global environmental challenges.

Hemmingsen, Kučinskas, and Kardelis seemingly agree in regarding place as a source of other-than-human contributions to knowledge and emotion as relational phenomena and, by implication, in entertaining the possibility of not just learning about place but also learning from and learning with place. Rein Raud fleshes out this possibility by thinking through Dōgen's notion of landscape or environment as scripture. As Raud eloquently contends, Dōgen's claim was not that a particular natural environment or place "becomes" scriptural because it has been inscribed from without by some agent or power external to it. Rather, the availability of a meaningful experience of reality is, for Dōgen, in itself a linguistic phenomenon. Accordingly, he sees his praxis not as an overcoming of our immediate reality but as an engagement with it in order to develop an unmediated relation to what surrounds us. Doing so is to eschew seeing each of the things among which we find ourselves emplaced as allowing access to some hidden, ultimate reality and to see instead that the irreducible dynamism of each thing is itself an assertion of ultimate reality. The interplay of things around us is scriptural, not as a conversation about enlightenment, but as a conversation of enlightenment.

Part IV: Shared Places of Politics and Religion

One of the core characteristics of Western modernities has been the separations of "church" and "state" and of the "private" and the "public" spheres. While the precise location of the boundaries between these paired spaces has been subject to contestation, the necessity of their bifurcation as a safeguard against one half of the pair subsuming the other has for the most part been taken as given. Yet this clear bifurcation is a historical artifact rather than a natural or conceptual fact. The four chapters in this section seek philosophically significant insights through exploring places—in imperial China, in Meiji Japan, in colonial India, and in contemporary Palestine—where politics and religion are intimately blended.

Albert Welter undertakes a comparison of the now globally prevalent notions of public place and private space with traditional Chinese conceptions of a continuous and harmonious (if often contested) relational terrain that is structured in terms of privilege differentials determined by proximity to the "inner" or "central" places of imperial authority. Although he focuses on the place of Buddhist monastic institutions in imperial China, Welter's concerns are not primarily historical. Rather, he is concerned to see how Chinese secularism and the imperial administration of religion continue to shape practices in the People's Republic of China and to raise philosophically probing questions about whether the Chinese emplacement of the private/religious sphere within the public/political opens distinctive prospects for conceiving and realizing post-Weberian modernities.

Nakajima Takahiro likewise focuses on the blending of political and religious places in Buddhist institutions, but here in the context of a rapidly modernizing Japan at the end of the nineteenth century and through the first half of the twentieth. But rather than the politics of national or imperial authority, Nakajima is interested in the place of religion in the politics of everyday life and the dynamics of social engagement. Working through the biographies of three leading exponents of rethinking the place of religion in Japanese society—Suzuki Daisetz, Chikazumi Jōkan, and Miyazawa Kenji—Nakajima engages their different attempts to articulate in practice a form of religiosity beyond modern interiority: a restoration of religion to the public sphere, not as a support for Japanese nationalism, but as a support for social transformation.

Social transformation is also at the heart of Bindu Puri's investigation of the relationship between place and justice. Taking as her point of departure the divergent convictions of Gandhi and Ambedkar regarding the importance of universal access to religious space in building national unity during India's sovereignty struggles, Puri undertakes an incisive study of the complex interdependence among the place(s) of religion, caste, and political consciousness. Her conclusion, deftly argued, is that a blending of sacred and theoretical spaces that is resolutely sensitive to differences in experience is needed to sustain the redefinition of oppressively emplaced selves in ways that also erase circles of suspicion.

In the final contribution to this section, Michael Myers directs attention to one of the planet's most profoundly contested sites of oppression and suspicion—the land claimed by both Israeli Jews and Palestinian Arabs. Invoking Tuan's space/place distinction as a hermeneutical device, Myers' chapter is crafted around a chorus of four distinct voices, those of Raja Shehadeh, a Palestinian attorney and activist; the Palestinian philosopher Sari Nusseibeh; Chaim Gans, an Israeli professor of law; and the writer and Holocaust survivor Primo Levi. What emerges through this chorus is a deep appreciation of the justified claims of belonging made by both Palestinian Arabs and Israeli Jews to their rights to live in a single, confined, and contested space or land—a single space that is justly occupied by two peoples as two different places. Rather than seeing this as a condition of ownership stalemate, however, Myers embraces the legitimacy of opposing Israeli and Palestinian claims and argues the merits of refraining from *choosing between* their different aspirations for homeland and embracing instead their correlation.

Part V: The Emotionally Emplaced Body

The concerns raised in the previous section about the place of religion in public life, about access to sacred space, about the ownership of humiliation due to caste, gender, or ethnicity, and about rights to a homeland combine to make clear that the human transformation of spaces into places is unavoidably embodied and suffused with emotion. The four chapters in this final section, by Ilana Maymind, Carl Helsing, Lara Mitias, and Kathleen Higgins, focus specifically on the emotional dimension of emplacement.

Evincing important resonances with Michael Myers' contribution, Ilana Maymind begins with reflections on the Roman conception of exile as a substitute for death and Theodor Adorno's definition of exile as "life in suspension," each of which suggests that to be exiled is to be cut off from possibilities for active moral community. Maymind argues, instead, for seeing exile as (at least potentially) a place for deepening empathy. Through careful readings of selected works by the Japanese Buddhist monk Shinran (1173–1263) and the Sephardic Jewish philosopher Moses Maimonides (1135–1204), Maymind builds a case for seeing how the adversities of life in exile can foster experiences of strangeness that are conducive to the acceptance and appreciation of difference and, thus, a readiness to engage others, not on the basis of inherited norms and exclusive mores, but rather in ways that are both tolerantly inclusive and deeply ethical.

Carl Helsing is similarly concerned with the origins of the moral and ethical life, but he turns for resources to Mencius—to Mengzi. After first exploring Mengzi's leading metaphor of the four sprouts or seeds (*siduan*) as a source of insight into the structure of emotional-moral experience, Helsing turns toward considerations of the conditions needed for healthy emotional growth and activity. As his careful reading of Mengzi reveals, emotional maturation depends on living in a healthy social environment that depends in turn on maintaining a sustainable relationship with the material resources of the natural environment. The general insight thus afforded, Helsing maintains, is as applicable today as in pre-Qin China: any practically valid moral psychology must take into account the interdependence of poverty and material duress, mental health, and emotional maturation. Realizing places of exemplary moral conduct requires structural, material equilibrium.

Lara M. Mitias emphasizes the role of the lived and living body in phenomenologies of place. Using the work of Edward Casey and Nishida Kitarō (1870–1945), Mitias argues that, given the similar descriptions of place in both accounts, the body-mind complex should be considered preeminently platial. Casey argues that in addition to our many postmodern displacements, we are, in modern times, alienated from "place" itself. But since our places are phenomenologically and ontologically primordial, he urges a renewed sense of lived and living places and our "getting back into place." To develop these ideas, Mitias turns to Nishida's conception of *basho* (place). On her reading, Nishida's *basho* enables us to overcome subject-object dualisms and a false sense of self that characterize ordinary experience. This overcoming entails a return to the lived and living body as our ultimate and most primordial place—as the actual place in which the dualities of subjects and objects, minds and bodies, thoughts and feelings, are dissolved and yet from which these same oppositions can be abstracted. Any sense of being-in-place, she concludes, must be based intimately on this, our own most fundamental place.

The place of intimacy is the ultimate concern of this volume's final contribution, by Kathleen Higgins—ultimate, most elementally, in focusing on the experience of grief in the absence or evacuation of place that is caused by death. Insofar as the dead are nowhere to be found, they are "no place." And yet, death is not utopia for those surviving the dead. The bereaved, Higgins writes, are not just confronted with a loved one's absence; they are also confronted with the physical remains of the dead, for which a place must be found and revered among the living. As she points out, while how this is done varies from culture to culture, it almost invariably includes participating in rituals that enable *caring properly* for the deceased. And, as Higgins insists, when it is engaged in authentically, caring for and considering the dead becomes a "live" relationship—a place of continued and invaluable emotional growth.

The eighteen contributions contained in this volume do not present a unified vision of the significance of place. Neither do they afford anything like a comprehensive or even fully representative survey of perspectives on place. What this volume does present, however, is strong and coherent evidence of the diversity and inexhaustibility of meaning that is opened by the perhaps uniquely human disposition to qualitatively transform spaces into places.

NOTES

1. Yi-Fu Tuan, *Space and Place: The Perspective of Experience* (Minneapolis: University of Minnesota Press, 1977).

2. Edward S. Casey, "How to Get from Space to Place in a Fairly Short Stretch of Time: Phenomenological Prolegomena," in *Senses of Place*, ed. Steven Feld and Keith H. Basso (Santa Fe, NM: School of American Research Press, 1997), 13–42.

3. Edward S. Casey, *The Fate of Place: A Philosophical History* (Berkeley: University of California Press, 1997).

4. See, e.g., Francisco J. Varela, Evan Thompson, and Elinor Rosch, *The Embodied Mind: Cognitive Science and Human Experience* (Cambridge: MIT Press, 1991); and Daniel D. Hutto and Erik Myin, *Radicalizing Enactivism: Basic Minds without Content* (Cambridge, MA: MIT Press, 2013).

5. John Stewart, Olivier Gapenne, and Ezequiel A. Di Paolo (eds.), *Enaction: Toward a New Paradigm for Cognitive Science*, ed. (Cambridge, MA: MIT Press, 2011).

6. Shawn Malia Kanaʻiaupuni and Nolan Malone, "This Land Is My Land: The Role of Place in Native Hawaiian Identity," *Hūlili: Multidisciplinary Research on Hawaiian Well-Being* 3, no. 1 (2006): 281–307.

7. E. C. Relph, *Place and Placelessness* (London: Pion, 1976). See also Robert Freestone and Edgar Liu, eds., *Place and Placelessness Revisited* (New York: Routledge, 2016).

8. Stanley Cavell, *Conditions Handsome and Unhandsome: The Constitution of Emersonian Perfectionism* (Chicago: University of Chicago Press, 1991).

9. Jean-Luc Nancy, *Being Singular Plural*, trans. Robert D. Richardson and Anne E. O'Byrne (Stanford, CA: Stanford University Press, 2000).

10. Casey, *Fate of Place*, 684.

PART I

CONVERSATIONS OF PLACE IN INTERCULTURAL PHILOSOPHY

Hiding the World in the World   1

A CASE FOR COSMOPOLITANISM BASED IN THE *ZHUANGZI*

David B. Wong and Marion Hourdequin

As a species, we have long been both settled and mobile, with some of us rooted in place and others more migratory. Mobility is not a new feature of human life; however, contemporary forms of mobility diminish geographical, cultural, and ecological rootedness and bring together people with many diverse ways of life. This cultural interchange offers both challenges and opportunities: challenges as people encounter unfamiliar contexts and navigate values and perspectives that differ radically from their own; and opportunities as new perspectives can generate new insights and possibilities for living well together.

Along with this cultural exchange, there are significant pressures to reach common moral understanding on issues such as climate change, migration, humanitarian intervention, and responses to poverty. Global discourse is no longer governed exclusively by international political realism, and moral reasons are frequently invoked in international debates. In light of these contexts, many believe that we should view the world as a single moral community—we should be cosmopolitans—but precisely what this entails remains subject to debate.

Do the Confucian *Analects* and the early Daoist text, the *Zhuangzi*, offer resources relevant to the contexts just described and to understanding what forms contemporary cosmopolitanism might take? The first, theoretical/textual portion of this chapter answers affirmatively, showing how insights can be gleaned from both traditions and how these insights complement one another. The *Analects* illustrates the importance of certain forms of rootedness and connection for moral personhood, suggesting that cosmopolitanism needs to make space for sustained relations and take seriously the significance of culture. On the other hand, the *Zhuangzi* cautions against fixating too strongly on a single outlook and casts doubt on claims of a single, uniquely correct moral point of view. The second part of the chapter considers the relevance of these perspectives for contemporary debates over cosmopolitanism and human rights. There we critique approaches that place too much weight on a universal moral minimum and show how both Confucian and Zhuangian insights may inform a genuinely multicultural cosmopolitanism.

Confucian Perspectives on Tradition, Change, and Cosmopolitanism

How might Confucianism, as represented in the *Analects*, respond to the circumstances of the world today? Mobility and globalization are both associated with novelty, flux, and instability, whereas Confucius as presented in the *Analects* is famous for his reverence for tradition and hesitancy to embrace social change.[1] Morality, from the Confucian point of view, is possible only through certain stable forms of social organization that structure relationships within and outside the family and across generations. Thus, Confucianism would seem to favor strongly rooted moral identities and to criticize forms of mobility and globalization that undermine tradition and the stability it can provide. Even moral cosmopolitanism—though in some ways resonant with the Confucian virtue of *ren*, with its emphasis on extending concern outward from family to all persons—may chafe if based on a thin "moral minimum" that overlooks the distinct characteristics of particular persons or overlooks the importance of special relations in favor of a more impartial point of view. Nevertheless, early Confucianism generally, and the *Analects* in particular, offers important insights for developing a contemporary cosmopolitanism that takes seriously the importance of attachment, culture, and history.

Continuity and Change

The cosmopolitan view of the world as a single moral community and the frequently associated view of moral relations as relations among abstract (though morally significant) individuals give little weight to time, place, and history. However, place—understood in terms of social, cultural, and historical location—plays an important role in early Confucianism. In the Confucian *Analects*, morality is grounded in tradition and ritual, and the mythical sage-kings as well as the harmonious society of the Western Zhou dynasty serve as important models for reform.

Confucius questions radical changes to rituals and, as a response to moral—or infrastructural—degradation, recommends revitalizing rather than rebuilding from the ground up. For example, Confucius praises Min Ziqian, who, in commenting on the construction of a new treasury in Lu, asks, "Why not simply restore it? Why must it be rebuilt?"[2] Elsewhere, Confucius embraces change but emphasizes continuity through change: a silk cap may be exchanged for a linen one, because this is "frugal," but another innovation—bowing at the top of the steps rather than at the bottom when approaching a ruler—is rejected, for it fails to preserve the ritual's underlying purpose of showing respect and deference.[3]

Confucius' emphasis on tradition is far from blind adherence to the past, but the *Analects* as a whole reflects the view that harmonious social life must be grounded in certain common practices and understandings, embedded in ritual. Reinventing these patterns of coexistence from scratch would not only disrupt contemporary relationships but also fail to acknowledge the intergenerational dimensions of human moral life. Thus, Confucian rootedness allows for change but seeks meaning-preserving change, through which important forms of continuity are maintained.

The themes of continuity and rootedness emerge also in relation to the family. For Confucius, sustained relationships in the family provide the starting point for moral self-cultivation. The parent-child relation, in particular, is pivotal. Through this relation, children, as subjects of caring attention, ideally experience love, concern, and support for their growth and development. Parents thus model *ren* 仁, or humaneness. The parent-child relationship also teaches reciprocity. The parent offers care and support, and the child shows respect and gratitude. Later in life, as parents age, grown children provide care. These familial relations teach certain moral attitudes and emotions yet are also structured through rituals and etiquette, or *li* 禮.

Rituals, Roles, and the Structure of Moral Space

Rituals structure moral space and, in combination with various social roles, embed us within a broader network of human relations. In the Confucian family, one's role defines one's responsibilities and the appropriate ways in which to act (*Analects* 1.2, 2.5, 2.7, 2.8, 4.19, 4.21, 12.11). A similar logic operates in society at large: interactions are shaped by rituals that reflect and acknowledge social roles, express key moral attitudes and emotions, and facilitate harmonious social life (*Analects* 1.12, 2.3, 8.2, 12.1, 13.3, 13.4). Interestingly, the *li* both provide cultural rootedness—through particular, culturally specific ways of structuring social interaction—and enable successful social interactions beyond close family and friends. The moral sensitivity established in the family can carry through to many other contexts. For this reason, Confucius suggests, the person who is truly *ren* can live among those who are uncultivated and, in doing so, transform them (*Analects* 9.14).[4]

For Confucius, *ren* can transcend the physical distance between the center of the empire and its borderlands, as well as the moral distance between the *junzi* 君子, or exemplary person, and the so-called Nine Barbarian Tribes of the East. Confucius frequently stresses the idea of moral distance, and he invokes physical distance primarily to illustrate the power of *ren* to extend beyond family and immediate community:

> If in word you are conscientious and trustworthy and in deed singleminded and reverent, then even in the lands of the barbarians you will go forward without obstruction. But if you fail to be conscientious and trustworthy in word or to be singleminded and reverent in deed, then can you be sure of going forward without obstruction even in your own neighborhood?[5]

Without *ren*, even the most local and intimate of relations will fail;[6] with it, harmony within the empire can be restored.

Thus, virtue can overcome spatial distance, and mobility, in itself, does not appear problematic. However, there are caveats. The sustenance of certain important relations and the fulfilment of key responsibilities may require limits on extended travel or distant moves: "While your parents are alive, you should not go too far afield in your travels. If you do, your whereabouts should always be known."[7] Moreover, Confucius criticizes those who distance themselves from society altogether. Once, when traveling, Confucius and Zilu encounter a man who has retreated to the countryside to escape the corruption and travails of the state. Confucius remarks: "One cannot associate with birds and beasts. Am I not a member of this human race? Who, then, is there for me to associate with?"[8] Although *physical* distance has limited moral significance for Confucius, the *social* distance this recluse has created between himself and others is problematic. This idea carries through *Analects* as a whole, which emphasizes the importance of embeddedness in society and persistence through difficulty rather than withdrawal or escapism (see, e.g., 18.7, 14.38).[9] Confucian moral personhood is fundamentally social: morality requires social engagement and cultural understanding, and *ren* is a virtue that locates persons in relation to family, society, history, tradition, and an intergenerational community.[10]

Given these considerations, mobility may be problematic if it disrupts the lasting relationships central to moral personhood. Relatedly, the Confucian commitment to meaning-preserving change in the *li* constrains the nature and pace of cultural change—and this, in turn, may be in tension with contemporary forms of mobility that result in rapid cultural loss, because they deprive people of the social scaffolding needed to sustain moral life. Confucianism therefore rules out forms of cosmopolitanism that sever sustained connections or treat cultures as costumes to be donned and discarded at will.

Confucian Cosmopolitanism?

Despite these caveats, Confucianism may support specific forms of cosmopolitanism, such as a rooted cosmopolitanism that rejects thin, abstract conceptions of persons as unattached "citizens of the world."[11] Philip J. Ivanhoe describes a rooted, Confucian cosmopolitanism,[12] and his approach echoes that of geographers David Seamon and Jacob Sowers, who argue, "An empathetic and compassionate understanding of the worlds beyond our own places may be best grounded in a love of a particular place to which I myself belong. In this way, we may recognize that what we need in our everyday world has parallels in the worlds of others."[13] A rooted Confucian cosmopolitanism would acknowledge the importance of thick, relationally grounded identities yet encourage individuals to venture out to encounter, interact with, and acknowledge others beyond their home communities.

In Ivanhoe's elaboration of this view, "a cosmopolitan is not a citizen of nowhere but *an interested guest or visitor* of various cultures and ways of life who is comfortable around the world."[14] This rooted Confucian cosmopolitanism takes seriously "the irreducible pluralism that one finds among the traditions of the world" and does not treat culture as mere "window dressing."[15] In engaging with others, Ivanhoe's Confucian cosmopolitans defer judgment, and they use encounters with difference to prompt reflection on their home culture. In its most robust form, Ivanhoe contends, Confucian cosmopolitanism extends compassionate concern to all persons, recommending that we "[regard] all within the four seas as brothers" (*Analects* 12.5).[16] The Confucian cosmopolitan is thus grounded in a particular culture yet approaches other cultures with humility, humaneness, and polite inquisitiveness, and concern for others transcends cultural boundaries.[17]

Ivanhoe's approach is promising insofar as it goes, but two concerns linger. First, an adequate Confucian cosmopolitanism needs to avoid parochialism, and this seems to require an interpretation of the *Analects* that downplays the ethnocentrism that at times emerges in the text.[18] Although the Confucius of the *Analects* expresses faith in the capacity of *ren* to transform even distant barbarians, he seems to assume that those lacking the *li* are inevitably uncivilized. So although all humans can develop virtue, it is an explicitly culturally rooted conception of virtue that the *Analects* seems to portray. To address this concern, we might set aside the implicit assumption of cultural superiority and take from the text the more general claim that rituals and traditions of some kind or another are critical to both individual moral development and broader social harmonies. This makes space for the affirmation of pluralism that Ivanhoe favors.

However, there is another related but deeper concern regarding the nature of engagement with other cultures and values. The *Analects* clearly contains important resources for the development of a rooted cosmopolitanism that supports respectful interaction with difference, as Ivanhoe explains. But should the cosmopolitan remain merely an "interested guest or visitor" of other cultures? Or might other cultures, forms of life, and ethical outlooks enter into our own lives in more transformative ways? And how might cosmopolitanism take seriously the insight that thick relations and cultures matter, without presupposing that any particular culture should generalize to all? Ivanhoe's Confucian cosmopolitanism offers ways of relating to others with different cultural backgrounds and perspectives, but neither his contemporary Confucian cosmopolitanism nor classical Confucianism itself develops the possibility of a more thoroughgoing multicultural cosmopolitanism.[19] For this, we turn to Zhuangzi.

Hiding Our Boats

The sixth chapter ("Da zongshi" 大宗師 [Great and venerated teacher]) of the *Zhuangzi* begins with fishers trying to hide their boats or nets to keep them safe. But a strongman comes in the night and takes them. Rather than hiding what is precious to us in the world, we are invited to hide the world in the world, so that we would have nothing to lose.[20] That is, if we embrace the whole world and all its transformations, then we can wander (*you* 遊) everywhere and not get lost.

The strongmen who steal the precious include not only death but also powerful social and economic forces upsetting the traditional matrices that make for stable relationships and cultural rootedness. Fewer jobs are full-time and stable, prompting people to move to where the better jobs are.[21] Rising divorce rates have created families that are constellations of different relationships.[22] Increasing immigration, political persecution, and frequent international travel contribute to a growing number of bicultural and binational families that reflect the whole world rather than a small part of it. It is not unusual now for families to construct their own cultures by combining elements from plural traditions.[23] To "hide the world in the world" amidst such change and heterogeneity is to see opportunities to find value in new places and new relationships, to construct and reconstruct our cultural roots. We may feel what we have lost through change for as long as we live, but other parts of ourselves can be resilient and move beyond the mourning.

Finding Value in Changing Places with Others

The title of the first chapter of the *Zhuangzi*, "Xiao yao you" 逍遙遊, may be taken as a recommendation—to go "wandering round and about," not necessarily from place to place in a literal sense but in our minds and hearts, to change places with others who have different perspectives and to discover new sources of value. This chapter begins with an invitation to take seriously the transformation of things (*wu hua* 物化), the only constant of the world. A huge fish, Kun 鯤, transforms into a huge bird, Peng 鵬, that sets off a six-month gale when she takes flight. When we look up to where Peng is, all we see is blue-green, but is that the sky's proper color or just the result of its being so far away? After all, Peng sees the same thing when she looks down to where we are. The story brings home the relativity of perceptual perspective to the scale of creatures and how they are able to move about in their environments. Each species perceives things that other species do not, but it typically is not aware of its own limitations.

The Zhuangian skeptical stance is not doctrinal. The intention is not to establish that we know nothing but, rather, to open us to new possibilities of what might become new knowledge and insight, though discoveries are never immune to questioning in turn, especially when they calcify into received wisdom. This is the point of the story about Huizi and the gourds. Huizi, Zhuangzi's friend and philosophical sparring partner, grows some seeds that turn into huge gourds. When he tries to put them to some use, he finds that they are not sturdy enough to be water containers and are too big to be ladles. Huizi gives up, smashing them to pieces. Zhuangzi chastises his friend for failing to see that he could lash the big gourds "together like big buoys" and then "go floating on the rivers and lakes instead of worrying that they were too big to dip into anything." His friend's mind is full of underbrush, Zhuangzi declares.[24] Huizi was so wedded to his ideas of how to use the gourds to *hold* water that he could not think of using them to *float upon* water.

The underbrush in Huizi's mind is made up of language and concepts, which enable us to selectively abstract from the potentially overwhelming flow of experience and to focus on resources in the world that satisfy our needs. Their abstracting function is indispensable but also limiting. We tend to rely on what has worked for us in the past, even if the present has significantly changed. We tend to focus on what we already want instead of what we might want if only we were open to encountering it. Our concepts and language, which reflect our past experience and desires, push the familiar into the foreground of perception and other valuable things into the blurry background. Because we tend not to be aware of the limitations of our perspectives, the *Zhuangzi* questions all those who take their perspectives to be the measure of right and wrong.

The Limitations of Moral Perspectives

Among those taken to be in need of corrective therapy are Confucians, who hold that the degree and nature of one's concern for others should vary with one's relationship to them (e.g., more is owed to family members), and Mohists, who hold that impartial and equal concern is owed to all. Each calls right what the other calls wrong, and each calls wrong what the other calls right. The *Zhuangzi* is skeptical of the power of argument to resolve the differences between those who, like Mohists and Confucians, insist on their rights and wrongs.

It is in accord with a Zhuangian perspective that even if one starts out with a view of what is right and wrong, one should be able to see why others can hold very different views. Every coherent ethic cuts out something of genuine value. Each ethic, in defining what is right, also requires what is wrong according to some other coherent and viable ethic. More generally, the *Zhuangzi* seeks to undermine the assumption that our own perspectives on value are uniquely correct, not by discrediting them, but by undermining their claim to have exhausted what there is to see and value, and this involves opening our minds to perspectives other than our own. Thus we are not disabused of the notion that our moral codes embody real values. The *Zhuangzi*'s constructive skepticism holds that typical normative perspectives go astray in claiming an exclusive and comprehensive insight into value, and while it does not deny that our current perspectives are based on genuine values, it also encourages us to expand our view of what other perspectives have a similar status.[25]

Recognizing the worth of other ways of life can and often should have a deeper and wider effect on one's original moral perspective. If one genuinely appreciates the use of gourds to make tubs to float around in, one is unlikely to remain the sort of person who smashes them when one fails to use them as water dippers. One should sometimes go beyond acceptance of the new toward incorporating it into one's perspective. One need not, and often cannot, try to incorporate an entirely different way of life. One can seek to affirm certain values underlying that other way of life by balancing one's efforts to realize them in relation to values one already affirms. One can strive to create and maintain the stable relationships and shared culture that make for robust moral identities, while one remains open to change through recognition of the value of other ways of life. One can be rooted and cosmopolitan—though in ways that are different from those suggested by the rooted Confucian cosmopolitanism described above. If one is open to such a possibility, then one must be ready to make one's value commitments open-ended and flexible, to leave them to a certain degree indeterminate with respect to what values are affirmed and what the relationship of priority is among those values in case of conflict. This is where Zhuangzi seems to depart from Confucius and from contemporary Confucian cosmopolitans who, on the one hand, recommend engagement with other cultures through the model of an interested visitor who interacts politely and respectfully with difference but, on the other hand, do not mention, much less encourage, the possibility of transformative encounters. In the next section we deepen our characterization of Zhuangian cosmopolitanism by contrasting it with those versions of cosmopolitanism that have garnered the most attention in the philosophical literature.

Existing Forms of Cosmopolitanism: The Problem of Parochialism and the Limitations of a "Moral Minimum" Approach

Under its broadest definition, cosmopolitanism argues for a moral community of all human beings.[26] The more radical forms hold that all fundamental moral duties are owed to human beings as such and that duties to those with whom we are locally attached have no more weight unless justified by reasoning from the fundamental duties to all. The fundamental duties might be derived from a consequentialist ethic[27] or from an ethic that specifies universal rights.[28] These radical forms of cosmopolitanism are not hospitable to Zhuangian roaming, because they elevate one kind of value to the highest place and are usually rooted in and confined to one tradition of ethical thinking. They thus fail to overcome the problem of parochialism, described above.

Moderate, liberal cosmopolitans allow for more pluralism, attempting to avoid the problem of parochialism. They think "that there are many values worth living by and that you cannot live by all of them," as Kwame Anthony Appiah puts it, adding, "So we hope and expect that different people and different societies will embody different values."[29] For Appiah, however, there is a kind of moral minimum that bounds the pluralism: the "core moral ideas" increasingly embodied in "our" conception of basic human rights, including "needs for health, food, shelter, education," "certain options" everyone ought to have: "to seek sexual satisfaction with consenting partners; to have children if they wish to; to move from place to place; to express and share ideas; to help manage their societies; to exercise their imaginations." Finally, people need protection from "needless pain, unwarranted contempt, [and] the mutilation of their bodies."[30]

We do not disagree with the idea of a moral minimum, but it is important to acknowledge two potentially significant concerns, based on the discussion of Confucianism and Zhuangzi above. From a Confucian perspective, one might worry that a moral minimum approach is too "thin" and fails to capture the importance of cultural rootedness, along with its particular attachments, practices, and value commitments. A moral minimum may fail to take any particular thick perspective, such as Confucianism, seriously. Zhuangzi adds the concerns that the idea of "moral minimum"—embodied, for example, in human rights—should not be used either to mask the complexity that lurks behind it or merely to make a safe space for difference. Zhuangzi encourages encounters and exchange among diverse perspectives and values, embracing the interaction between and consideration of multiple rich perspectives.

Both concerns are bound up with the deep-seated nature of value differences, a feature of such differences that Appiah himself acknowledges. These deep differences will effectively limit the power of his proposed moral minimum to bring about real and practical consensus, even among reasonable people of good faith. Although moral concepts, even "thickish" ones such as courage, cruelty, and politeness, will appear in the moral vocabularies of different cultures, Appiah concedes that shared understanding on a general level will not prevent cultures from disagreeing over how to apply those concepts to particular cases. He further concedes that people may share values but disagree as to what weight to give to them.[31] These value differences apply to Appiah's core ideas such as "health," "education," "freedom of expression," and "helping to manage one's society." Many of them, such as "helping to manage one's society," are specified at such an abstract level that they inevitably will receive very different interpretations. The extent to which one ought to be able to express and share one's ideas and to exercise one's imagination will be limited by cultures in different ways. Finally, in different cultures the needs and options that Appiah specifies will be prioritized differently.

We do not mean to diminish the importance of any of the values Appiah mentions. But calling them human rights is often a rhetorical move to confer on them an unassailable status that masks the serious debates that take place over how to interpret and prioritize them relative to other values.[32] To take these things seriously requires going beyond a surface nod to their universal appeal. We must discuss them in relation to the different circumstances of different societies—for example, identifying what kind and level of education are important for members of a society given its current forms of social and economic organization.

The dominant forms of cosmopolitanism, then, are motivated by a desire to provide a "safe" place for people to act on their different cultural traditions—to live and let live—as long as everyone respects a moral minimum. While there are acts and practices that clearly fall outside a genuine moral minimum, such as torture and suppression of peaceful dissent, the language of human rights characteristically is expanded way beyond uncontroversial boundaries. Dominant forms of cosmopolitanism have become unproductive for two reasons. First, the language of human rights is often used so as to imply that what they protect is an object of universal, reasonable consensus when the situation may be more complicated. Often calls to defend human rights are rhetorically effective only among an audience of the previously converted. Second, providing a safe space for cultural difference in a live-and-let-live fashion is to let go of the opportunity of encouraging mutual learning across such difference. These two disadvantages interact to aggravate the situation. Assuming that we already know what the moral minimum is inhibits intercultural exchange on what it might or might not be. A form of cosmopolitanism in the Zhuangian spirit would recognize what we do not yet know and take a stance of openness to what we might learn from others.

Zhuangian Cosmopolitanism in Application: Considering Human Rights in a Confucian Context

In the first part of this chapter, we acknowledged the strength of a Confucian ethic that upholds the value of community and relationship as healthy places in which viable moral identities can grow. Can such a rooted, relational Confucian ethic be compatible with the recognition of human rights? And how might a Zhuangian cosmopolitanism shed light on this question?

To defend one's rights is often taken to mean protecting one's vital interests against others. This combative stance is often justified, but when embedded in one's habitual moral language for conceptualizing and describing one's entire moral life, it encourages one to presume that there is fundamental and inevitable conflict between one's vital interests and those of others. Confucianism, with the high value it places on harmony (*he* 和) and its conception of human fulfilment as lying in relationship with others, promotes a conciliating and accommodating approach to putative conflicts of interest.[33] For example, such an approach bids people to reconsider what truly is at stake for them and whether they might find a way to satisfy the interests of all concerned—if not simultaneously, then perhaps over a period of time.

This tension between the tendency of rights advocacy to accept conflict and the Confucian values of harmony and relationship is not a logical contradiction, but it is a real one nevertheless. It becomes real, not because of any abstract definition one might give of what it is to have a right, but because of a nexus of assumptions and particular uses that have come to be associated with rights language. At the same time, it must be noted that different societies, even different communities in the same society, vary in the content they assign to this nexus. In the United States, for example, rights language is most likely, among all the most developed countries, to carry with it the presumption that individuals' interests fundamentally and inevitably conflict, while this is not as true in the country immediately north, Canada.

So a Confucian ethicist would have reason to be cautious in appropriating rights language but might also have reason to be discriminating about the different associations such language carries from place to place. A more positive reason for considering the appropriation of rights language lies in the recognition that satisfactorily implementing a conciliating and accommodating approach to apparent conflicts of interest can require more skill and wisdom than is possessed by the relevant parties. The ability to think of a course of action that in the situation at hand reconciles apparently competing interests lies very much at the heart of the ideal of the Confucian *junzi* 君子, or exemplary person. It is an ideal very much worth striving for. But what shall we do in the meantime, when there are not enough such exemplary people around to resolve conflicts of interest in wise and skillful ways? How should we address the very real tendencies of those in positions of power to perceive what is in their personal interests as identical with what is in the interest of the community and to be more likely to err in this direction the longer they remain in power? One possibility for thinking about how to mitigate the tension between rights and relationships is to think of rights as providing prima facie or defeasible protections, with the burden of justification on those who would set them aside for the sake of harmony and relationship. This holds true especially for rights to freely criticize those in power.

It might be thought that rights language is simply too different in its philosophical and cultural origins from Confucianism to make viable the kind of appropriation we have just proposed. But accepting this notion is to neglect the rich and complex history of the evolution of rights language. Consider the Universal Declaration of Human Rights (UDHR), which was proclaimed by the United Nations General Assembly in 1948.[34] It famously lists an array of rights that range from civil and political rights, such as those to freedom of expression and of assembly, to social and economic rights, such as those to social security, to work, and to rest and leisure. The declaration provides no theoretical foundation for these rights, no specific interpretation of what they mean, and no weighting in case of conflict.

This omission was intentional, and a key figure in this decision was P. C. Chang, born and raised in China, holding bachelor's, master's, and PhD degrees from Clark University and Columbia University, and adherent to the philosophies of John Dewey and the early Confucians and neo-Confucians. Chang was China's chief resident delegate to the United Nations in the early postwar years and served as vice-chair, under Eleanor Roosevelt, of the UN Commission on Human Rights, which drafted the UDHR. Sumner Twiss, from a reading of Chang's speeches and records of the deliberations during the declaration's drafting,[35] points to Chang's role in arguing for omission of any metaphysically controversial grounding and for relying instead on a growing consensus on the rights that should be recognized, as reflected by many of the world's constitutions, in spite of differences in philosophy and ideology in how to justify the consensus.[36]

Despite omitting a metaphysical grounding for rights, Chang did bring some substantive moral beliefs to his interpretation and formulation of human rights. Article 1 of the UDHR reads, "All human beings are born free and equal in dignity and rights. They are endowed with reason and conscience and should act towards one another in a spirit of brotherhood." The reference to "conscience" appears to have derived from Chang's efforts to include a reference to the Confucian value of *ren* 仁. Chang translated *ren* as "two-men-mindedness," taking his cue from the composition of the word from the characters for "two" and "persons." He understood *ren* as realizing one's humanity through the kindly and respectful treatment of others and connected this idea with the Article 1 phrase "spirit of brotherhood."

He regarded the first sentence of Article 1, with its emphasis on rights, as well balanced by the second sentence, with its emphasis on conscience that prompts actions in the spirit of brotherhood.[37] Chang also characterized the first sentence of Article 29 as reiterating not only a necessary balance between rights and duties but also their interdependence:[38] "Everyone has duties to the community in which alone the free and full development of his personality is possible."

While there is no concept of rights in the works by the Confucians and neo-Confucians Chang cited, there is arguably in *Mencius* a concept of individual human dignity. In 6A10, Mencius asserts that a wayfarer will reject even at the risk of death a basketful of rice and a bowlful of soup when offered contemptuously.[39] A beggar will not demean himself by taking them if they have been trampled on. In each case, the man is plausibly construed as defending his dignity. Mencius holds that such reactions emerge from one of the inborn beginnings of goodness—in this case, the disposition to regard certain acts as shameful—and the defense of human dignity includes the disposition to reject demeaning treatment. Moreover, it includes the disposition to regard treating others in a demeaning way as shameful (2A6). More positively, defending human dignity is the disposition to *jing* 敬, or to respect others, to take them seriously. Such dispositions, both feeling and thinking at the same time, can grow into the ethical excellence of righteousness, *yi* 義, which is a dedication to act on what is right (in implicit contrast to a commitment to act on the motive of personal profit). In the contemporary terms of ethical theory, the Mencian basis for moral agency, the inborn beginnings of goodness, is the source of human dignity.

It is crucial to understanding Mencius, and Chang, that these inborn beginnings of goodness are only beginnings. They require nurturing through education, through the provision of opportunity for secure livelihood that will afford people the physical and psychic resources to develop their beginnings and, through the personal effort of each person, to develop his or her beginnings. In Confucianism, the basis of dignity for the individual also confers responsibility on that same person to develop it, to learn how to care for and respect others. It also depends on those in a position to help that person, especially those with great power to shape the political and social environment. That is why, in 1A7, Mencius clearly holds King Xuan responsible for realizing these conditions for his people, and if he does not, Mencius says, there will be no dissoluteness, depravity, deviance, or excess to which people will not succumb. A king who creates poverty and punishes people for the crimes they commit under these conditions is a king who entraps his own people. This emphasis on secure livelihood as a precondition for ethical growth that results in realization of one's humanity provides an important rationale for the economic and social rights listed in the UDHR.

We have highlighted a particular moment in the origination of human rights language and P. C. Chang's role in that moment in order to contrast it with the way the use of rights language has evolved. Chang died in 1957, and he would have had reason to celebrate the ubiquity of human rights as a language of moral critique and reform, as well as the prominence of the human rights movement. He would have had reason to celebrate the human rights movement's successes, primarily in defending people from oppressive governments. He might not have been so happy at seeing the "happy balance" he envisioned shift so decisively to civil and political rights, to the relative neglect of economic and social rights. This example, however, illustrates the shifting ground that a moral minimum can provide. As previously noted, the concept of human rights is specified at a very general and abstract level so as to minimize controversy, and this allows for the movement to protect and enforce human rights to take an array of different forms, and for the forms it does take to be influenced by the most powerful nations, such as the United States, with its history of greater concern for and action on behalf of civil and political rights.

The most prominent international nongovernmental organizations associated with human rights defense have been Amnesty International and Human Rights Watch, and it has only been since the 1990s that these influential organizations have taken on economic and social rights as an important part of their mandate.[40] As Makau Mutua has observed, civil and political rights still enjoy a normative privilege, while for most states economic and social rights have the status of desirable goals.[41]

Mutua argues that a certain way of thinking about human rights, embodied in a guiding metaphor, has narrowed the field of ethical vision. The metaphor is that of savages, victims, and saviors. Savages are those who violate human rights, and they are quite often states operating from repressive cultural agendas. The victims are powerless innocents. The saviors are the better angels who restrain the savages and protect the innocents from tyranny.[42] Even when economic and social rights are the issue, we are often guided by this metaphor to look for savages who ravage humanity, such as multinational corporations and the operators of sweatshops, whether they are turning out T-shirts or smartphones. There undoubtedly are cases that fit the metaphor well. Yet there are many other cases in which indifference, neglect, and omission play major causal roles in bringing about catastrophe and misery. A report by the United Nations Children's Fund (UNICEF) ranks the United States as thirty-fourth among thirty-five developed countries (second only to Romania) in terms of the percentage of children living in relative poverty.[43] The roots of such problems cannot be addressed by merely looking about for the "savages" who perpetrated this outcome, as the prosecutorial model of human rights advocacy encourages us to do.

We need to think more deeply and seriously about alternatives to structures and institutions that provide not only too many incentives for exploitation but too many opportunities for neglect and omission. We need to think about what is owed to children, and to think about it in a way that recognizes the importance of a "secure livelihood" for the development of their humanity.

Otherwise, our thinking reflects a sort of blindness that is precisely the sort of thing the *Zhuangzi* warns us against, where what we are able to see is deeply shaped by what we think we "know." If we continue to use rights language to try to remedy this kind of blindness, we need to use it in such a way that brings a better balance between rights as claims on others to protect one's vital interests, on the one hand, and the recognition of duties to others and to community, on the other. We need to emphasize responsibilities to provide the conditions for Mencian secure livelihoods and identify these conditions as necessary for the development of moral agency.

Toward a Genuinely Multicultural Cosmopolitanism

The type of contribution that P. C. Chang made to the drafting of the UDHR points the way to a different kind of cosmopolitanism, one that does not presuppose a definite moral minimum that can be prescribed across the board. We do not dismiss a priori the possibility of such a minimum, but it has to be earned, through serious examination of what different cultural traditions of thought have said, not just as a nod to accepting human diversity. We need to take what great traditions of moral thought have said, extract what we see of value in them, and adapt them to our circumstances. More important than being able to declare that a truly definite, universal moral minimum has been found, we think, is to deal effectively with cases on which there is a wide consensus—or at least a consensus that is in reach through some work—that crucial interests have been harmed. We need to think of new uses for the gourds.

There are strong arguments for acknowledging that people cannot meaningfully exercise their civil and political rights without the fulfilment of some crucial social and economic interests. As Mencius suggested, people's minds will be preoccupied with the means to subsist as long as they are impoverished. And even when people have the psychic resources to press for change, gross inequality can render their voices ineffective. In the United States, Martin Gilens has studied the policy preferences of Americans of different income levels and compares these preferences with the actual decisions of the president and the Congress.[44] In cases where their preferences diverge from those in the top 10 percent income level, the affluent prevail in getting their preferences enacted. Unsurprisingly, the affluent are disproportionately active in the political process and in making campaign donations.

But our responsibilities to each other do not need to be dragged back to the forefront of our attention merely on the grounds that rights imply or require them. They can be brought back to the forefront because rights language has received a kind of interpretation that has narrowed the focus of our attention.

That interpretation is most easily and effectively deployed when there are identifiable agents against whom rights can be claimed and who can be blamed and held responsible if they violate those rights. That is why rights are so easily understood through the metaphor of savages, victims, and saviors.

One benefit of turning the focus back to responsibilities is that instead of making stern calls to honor rights, we have the opportunity to call people to greater fulfilment. As P. C. Chang tried to point out to his fellow committee members, to affirm and to act on our responsibilities to each other is not just to do our duty but also to realize our humanity in relationship to each other, our two-person-mindedness. To point out what is gained by everyone if the needs of the worst off are addressed is surely to provide stronger motivation to those who have greater responsibilities.

The task of producing morally competent people is labor-intensive, and the major part of it must be done face-to-face and among people who have come to know and trust one another. This is the Confucian truth that must be acknowledged by cosmopolitans if they wish to realize a moral community of any size. The challenge is to combine the need for rootedness with the diversity that is increasingly inevitable and desirable. We have deployed Zhuangzi's teachings to elucidate how difference is beneficial. None of us should pretend that we have a specific and definite set of rights that govern our relationships with different others. To be a true cosmopolitan is to be prepared to learn from these different others. It is to acknowledge and to act upon the dynamic and unfinished nature of mutual learning across cultural traditions.

NOTES

1. Some have suggested that Confucius simply equates morality with tradition or convention (see Chad D. Hansen, *A Daoist Theory of Chinese Thought: A Philosophical Interpretation* [New York: Oxford University Press, 1992. Even if one thinks this latter view is too strong (see Marion Hourdequin, "Tradition and Morality in the Analects: A Reply to Hansen," *Journal of Chinese Philosophy* 31, no. 4 [2004]: 517–533), Confucius clearly does emphasize the role of tradition, ritual, and exemplars from the past in moral self-cultivation.

2. D. C. Lau, trans., *Analects* (London: Penguin, 1979) 11.14, 108.

3. Lau, *Analects* 9.3, 96.

4. This idea is reiterated in *Analects* 16.1, where Confucius comments: "When distant subjects are unsubmissive one cultivates one's moral quality in order to attract them, and once they have come one makes them content" (Lau, 139). This contrasts with a more combative approach, which Confucius criticizes: "Instead, you propose to resort to the use of arms within the state itself. I am afraid that Chi-sun's worries lie not in Chuan Yu but within the walls of his palace" (ibid.). In this passage, Confucius is responding to the Chi family's plan to subdue Chuan Yu through the use of force, and he emphasizes the idea

that a virtuous leader can more effectively quell a rebellion than an aggressive army. A harmonious state begins with virtuous rulers: if the people are unruly, one should look first "within the walls of [one's] palace" to find the source of the problem.

5. Lau, *Analects* 15.6, 132–133.

6. See, e.g., *Analects* 9.31, which suggests that relationships can transcend physical location: "He did not really think of her. If he did, there is no such thing as being far away" (Lau, 100).

7. Lau, *Analects* 4.19, 74.

8. Lau, *Analects* 18.6, 150.

9. Note that Confucius remains open to multiple forms and degrees of engagement with society. For example, *Analects* 8.13 suggests that one should leave a corrupt state; and taking up an official position may be appropriate in some instances and not in others (Lau, *Analects* 2.21, 3.24).

10. Henry Rosemont Jr., "Rights-Bearing Individuals and Role-Bearing Persons," in *Rules, Rituals, and Responsibilities: Essays Dedicated to Herbert Fingarette*, ed. Mary I. Bockover (LaSalle, IL: Open Court Press, 1991), 71–101.

11. Philip J. Ivanhoe, "Confucian Cosmopolitanism," *Journal of Religious Ethics* 42, no. 1 (2014): 22–44.

12. Ibid.

13. David Seamon and Jacob Sowers, "Place and Placelessness (1976): Edward Relph," in *Key Texts in Human Geography*, ed. Phil Hubbard, Rob Kitchen, and Gill Valentine (London: Sage, 2008), 50.

14. Ivanhoe, "Confucian Cosmopolitanism," 34 (emphasis added).

15. Ibid., 34, 28.

16. Quoted in ibid., 37.

17. Ivanhoe, "Confucian Cosmopolitanism," 37.

18. See *Analects* 3.5 and 9.14, translated by Sor-hoon Tan in "Cosmopolitan Confucian Cultures: Suggestions for Future Research and Practice," *International Communication of Chinese Culture* 2, no. 3 (2015): 159–180.

19. Like Ivanhoe, Robert Neville ("Dimensions of Contemporary Confucian Cosmopolitanism," *Journal of Chinese Philosophy* 39, no. 4 [2012]: 594–613) offers an important and insightful view of Confucian cosmopolitanism. Although we lack space to discuss Neville's account in detail here, he describes cosmopolitanism as "the trait of a culture whose members interact well with people of different cultures" (594) and argues that cosmopolitanism can be an individual virtue as well (particularly where the more widespread cultural trait is lacking). Neville identifies a number of key resources in the Confucian tradition that support this trait of interacting thoughtfully with diverse others. However, neither Ivanhoe nor Neville considers the kinds of transformative engagement with deep differences that we discuss in relation to Zhuangzi in the next section of this chapter.

20. Chinese text consulted is from the Chinese Text Project, http://ctext.org/zhuangzi. Translation consulted is by Paul Kjellberg in *Readings in Classical Chinese Philosophy*, 2nd ed. (Kindle), ed. Philip J. Ivanhoe and Bryan W. Van Norden (Indianapolis: Hackett, 2011).

21. A report from the International Labour Organization, a United Nations agency dealing in labor issues, analyzed employment patterns in more than 180 countries at all levels of development and found that employment patterns had changed considerably in the decade preceding 2015. Full-time, stable employment contracts represented less than one in four jobs. Fewer than 45 percent of wage and salaried workers were employed on a full-time, permanent basis, and even that share appeared to be declining (International Labour Organization, *World Employment and Social Outlook 2015* [Geneva: International Labour

Office, 2015], 13, http://www.ilo.org/wcmsp5/groups/public/---dgreports/---dcomm
/---publ/documents/publication/wcms_368626.pdf).

22. The German sociologists Ulrich Beck and Elisabeth Beck-Gernsheim have called
our attention to "the increasing fragility of such categories as class and social status, gender
roles, family, neighbourhood[,] etc." See Beck and Beck-Gernsheim, *Individualization:
Institutionalized Individualism and Its Social and Political Consequences*, Kindle edition
(London: Sage, 2002), Kindle locations 362–363. "Even parenthood, the core of family
life, is beginning to disintegrate under conditions of divorce. Families can be constellations
of very different relationships" (ibid., locations 3910–3911).

23. As Beck and Beck-Gernsheim observe, "Today in every marriage, different life-
styles, values, ways of thinking and communicating, rituals and everyday routines have to
be fitted together in one family world" (ibid., locations 1964–1965). "Each couple goes
its own way, seeks its own forms," perhaps choosing one cultural tradition in its entirety
or combining elements from different traditions, perhaps testing out various options and
switching around (ibid., location 1975). This does not mean that family ties will be less
important, since less can be taken for granted about obligations to kin: "New rules of solidarity and loyalty become necessary" (ibid., location 2046).

24. Kjellberg, in Ivanhoe and Van Norden, *Readings*, 213.

25. In a sense, Zhuangzi encourages us to recognize two distinct but interacting perspectives on moral values and on that which we value more generally (including our lives,
our human form, our relationships, and so on). On the one hand, there is the rooted perspective in which we hold particular values and recognize certain attachments (to family,
friends, place, culture, etc.) as important. Yet on the other hand, we can see that our own
particular attachments and values reflect just one perspective and just one set of attachments and values among many. What's more, we can see that our own attachments and
values are both contingent and transitory. This does not mean they are not worth caring
about, but it does challenge the notion that they are the *only* values and attachments worth
caring about or that our values have a special, unique status in relation to those of others.
Acknowledging and embracing both perspectives may open us to considering and appreciating forms of value other than those with which we begin.

26. H. C. Baldry, *The Unity of Mankind in Greek Thought* (Cambridge: Cambridge
University Press, 1965), 122; Martha C. Nussbaum, "Patriotism and Cosmopolitanism,"
Boston Review (1994), 3, http://bostonreview.net/martha-nussbaum-patriotism-and
-cosmopolitanism; Catherine Lu, "The One and Many Faces of Cosmopolitanism,"
Journal of Political Philosophy 8, no. 2 (2000): 245.

27. See Peter Singer, "Famine, Affluence, and Morality," *Philosophy and Public Affairs*
1, no. 1 (1972): 229–243.

28. See, e.g., Thomas W. Pogge, "Cosmopolitanism and Sovereignty," *Ethics* 103, no. 1
(1992): 48–49.

29. Kwame Anthony Appiah, *Cosmopolitanism: Ethics in a World of Strangers*, Kindle
edition (New York: W. W. Norton and Co., 2010), Kindle locations 2187–2189.

30. Ibid., locations 2443–2447.

31. Ibid., locations 1123–1124.

32. The specification of a particular conception of rights as constituting a moral
minimum—though motivated in part by the goal of avoiding imposition of parochial
values on others—often ignores competing conceptions and may therefore generate a new
form of parochialism.

33. Cf. Chenyang Li, *The Confucian Philosophy of Harmony* (New York: Routledge,
2014).

34. United Nations General Assembly, Universal Declaration of Human Rights
(1948), http://www.ohchr.org/EN/UDHR/Documents/UDHR_Translations/eng.pdf.

35. See Sumner B. Twiss, "Confucian Contributions to the Universal Declaration of Human Rights: A Historical and Philosophical Perspective," in *The World Religions after September 11*, ed. Arvind Sharma (Minneapolis: Fortress Press, 2011), 1:154–173.

36. The basis for his conclusions include *Economic and Social Council Official Records, Second Year* (United Nations General Assembly, 4th Session, 28 February–29 March 1947, with Supplements 1–10 [Lake Success, NY: United Nations, 1947], 111); *Official Records of the Third Session of the General Assembly* (United Nations General Assembly, Part I, Social, Humanitarian and Cultural Questions, Third Committee, Summary Records of Meetings, 21 September–8 December 1948, with Annexes [Lake Success, NY: United Nations, 1948], 87).

37. *Official Records of the Third Session of the General Assembly*, 98.

38. Twiss, "Confucian Contributions," 166.

39. Irene Bloom and Philip J. Ivanhoe, trans., *Mencius* (New York: Columbia University Press, 2011). All other references to Mencius also from this source.

40. Makau Mutua, *Human Rights Standards: Hegemony, Law, and Politics* (Albany: State University of New York Press, 2016), 142–146.

41. Ibid., 146.

42. Makau Mutua, *Human Rights: A Political and Cultural Critique* (Philadelphia: University of Pennsylvania Press, 2002).

43. "Relative poverty" is defined as "living in a household whose income, when adjusted for family size and composition, is less than 50% of the median income for the country in which they live" (UNICEF Innocenti Research Centre, "Measuring Child Poverty," *Innocenti Report Card 10*, 3, https://www.unicef-irc.org/publications/pdf/rc10 _eng.pdf).

44. Martin Gilens, *Affluence and Influence: Economic Inequality and Political Power in America* (New York: Russell Sage, 2013), 1.

Between Local and Global

2

The Place of Comparative Philosophy
through Heidegger and Daoism

Steven Burik

Monotonization of the world. Strong spiritual impression of all travels
of the last years, despite the individual happiness: a pale drab of monotonization of the world. Everything is becoming similar in its outward
appearances, levelling out in a uniform cultural scheme. The individual
customs of peoples are wearing off, the way of dress is becoming uniform, ethics international. Ever more nations seem fused together, people
living and working in the same way, cities looking alike. Ever more the
fine aroma of the particularity of cultures evaporates, ever more vengeful
the colours peel off, and beneath the cracked layers of varnish the steel-
coloured pistons of the mechanical bustle, the modern world-machine,
become visible.

—*Stefan Zweig*

The wisest, because they have a full view of far and near, do not belittle
the smaller or make much of the greater, knowing that measuring has no
limit.

—Zhuangzi, *chapter 17*

It is often argued that comparative philosophy is afflicted by an inherent contradiction. For in order to be truly comparative, it needs to assume some overarching position with regard to the thinkers or thoughts under comparison, to
somehow stand above or beyond what is being compared. In other words, it
must transcend the things under comparison. If the comparative philosopher
does not undertake at least the transcendence of her own culture, then she is in
danger of imposing her own standards on foreign ways of thought. So comparative philosophy needs to show some form of what I designate here as "cosmopolitanism." Other notions in this category, which I use loosely, are globalism,

34

globalization, or universalism. The *Oxford English Dictionary* defines "cosmopolitan" as "belonging to all parts of the world; not restricted to any one country or its inhabitants," and as "having the characteristics which arise from, or are suited to, a range over many different countries; free from national limitations or attachments."[1] It is clear from these definitions that being cosmopolitan is supposed to be something shared, something *not specific* to different cultures. A cosmopolitan is someone who has transcended her own narrow perspectives and is, at least to a certain extent, globalized, a global citizen.

Yet we know that being free from one's *own* culturally colored perspective need not mean that one is also free from *any* perspective or that one now shares "global" perspectives. However, this is often how a cosmopolitan is understood: as a citizen of the world, a globalized person. Proponents of universal character traits of thinking and philosophy are especially attracted to such an understanding, and we can see from the definition above that being "cosmopolitan" is perceived as something positive. The freedom from "national limitations" is conventionally understood to be beneficial. It is in this way that things such as globalization, the loss of provincial thinking, and freedom from cultural obstacles are understood as progressive.

Between Provincialism and Cosmopolitanism, between Being at Home and *Unheimlichkeit*, between Localism and Globalization

Within comparative philosophy, in order to make meaningful comparisons, one does have to stand outside one's own culture and not be limited to narrow ways of thinking. So, in many ways, one has to display (at least to some extent) a form of this kind of cosmopolitan or global thinking. On the other hand, and this is where I perceive a potential and specific problem for comparative philosophy, in its practice comparative philosophy should display a form of cosmopolitanism that should reflect what is often considered its exact opposite—namely, a certain form of what may be called provincialism or localism, if we understand different cultures as having different ways of doing philosophy. One definition of "provincial" important in the present context is this: "having or suggestive of the outlook, tastes, character, etc., associated with or attributed to inhabitants of a province or the provinces; esp. (depreciative) parochial or narrow-minded; lacking in education, culture, or sophistication."[2] If the claims of comparative philosophy are to be taken seriously, then we would need to display an appreciation of different ways of thinking as practiced or originated in different parts of the world and, more importantly, as tightly connected to particular cultural environments. But as we can glean from this definition, provincialism, as the opposite of cosmopolitanism, is often seen as a negative trait. It is basically understood as an unwillingness to see the bigger picture, due to being stuck in one's own way of thinking or in one's feeling threatened by the bigger picture. So it seems that comparative philosophy is caught between a rock and a hard place: either we are stuck in our own cultural prejudices and remain provincial, or we transcend those prejudices to become globalized or universalized. But this latter option entails either finding some place from which we can be totally objective, which is unlikely to happen, or thinking that our own provincial approach and our own categories are somehow valid for the rest of the world as well.

Can we use notions of place in order to alleviate the apparent contradiction between these two positions, both of which seem necessary, to (re)shape comparative philosophy? Is it possible to see comparative philosophy as occupying some viable middle ground or a third position? This chapter argues for the importance of "place" for comparative philosophy in two ways. First, through a comparison of provincial or local versus cosmopolitan/globalized thinking, using Heidegger and Daoism, I hope to show that thinking in these terms may not be very productive for comparative philosophy, or at least how we may need to understand them differently from these traditional understandings. Second, and related to this, I look at how Heidegger perceives notions of inside and outside, homely and foreign/unhomely (*Unheimlichkeit*), as relational and not as dichotomies or dualities. I then compare these findings to the Daoist tradition, using mainly Zhuangzi—who also prefers to argue in a nondualistic and nonhierarchical way—and explore how this nondualistic thinking affects how we perceive the goals and ideas of comparative philosophy. I aim to show how reading Heidegger and Zhuangzi helps us understand that in the mainstream Western history of philosophy there is almost always some form of dualism at work, and a closely related hierarchy is usually the outcome of this dualism (hence, for example, the positive views on cosmopolitanism and the negative views on provincialism). My aim is to use Heidegger and Zhuangzi to overcome that dualistic way of thinking. And this is exactly why comparative philosophy might find it unhelpful to think of itself in terms of either provincial/local or global/universal, because hierarchies have always been attached to these terms. Through the Daoists, and through Zhuangzi in particular, we may be able to find more complementary ways of understanding these dichotomies, or at least be able to see them both as necessary parts of the same system, and perhaps even to suggest ways of overcoming them.

A related notion that needs thinking through in this context is that of "home." Is asking whether or how comparative philosophy might bring us closer to our home as human beings a viable question when comparative philosophy seemingly promotes the cosmopolitan ideal of homelessness or rootlessness? Or should comparative philosophy be directed, not to bringing us closer to home, but rather to understanding how different ways of thinking result in building different homes? However one chooses to answer these questions, it still seems the case that practicing comparative philosophy includes some form of actively leaving one's home, one's own way of thought, and actively reaching out to other forms of thought. How can this leaving home be understood as bringing us closer to "home"? Can we even think that there is such a thing as humankind's "home"? Do cosmopolitanism and globalization necessarily mean the loss of rootedness, or can comparative philosophy build a bridge to preserve the local in the global? Can we argue that provinciality or local thinking, although usually understood in a disapproving fashion with negative connotations, has a positive meaning as well? I will argue that it does, if it is understood as standing for an attack on the idea of universality in the form of Western philosophy's dominance over other ways of thought. "Provincial" would then mean a challenge to the dominance and universal pretence of the traditional Western way of doing philosophy.

It is evident why the dominant tradition, as such, would want to discredit "provincial" thought, since "provincial" does not tally with its universalist tendencies and ideals. Rethinking provinciality would amount to a reinsertion of humans into their environment, into their place and surroundings, into the world, instead of the long-dominant approach of situating humans outside of their physical reality and environment (think of the dualisms of mind-body, ideas-matter, and reality-appearance and their hierarchical valuation).

Also, and connected to this, in comparative philosophy notions of inside and outside are very important. However, these notions of inside and outside need to be rethought comparatively. One of the main tasks of comparative philosophy as I see it is to recognize the complicated nature of our notions of inside and outside, since they often reflect the dualistic way of thinking that predominates in traditional Western philosophy, and to admit that this has not been conducive to understanding profoundly different ways of thought. Thus, attitudes about insiders and outsiders, about the inside and the outside, and about the home and the foreign or unhomely need to be challenged or rethought. For example, there is the now well-known debate about whether or not Chinese thought is "philosophy." In this debate, some think that Chinese philosophy must (and can) live up to the dominant trends and scientific rigor perceived to be hallmarks of Western philosophy. Others, more sympathetic to Chinese thought, argue that Chinese philosophy neither needs to nor should want to be philosophy, because "philosophy" historically has rested on a way of thinking that has always excluded anything unlike itself and, as such, represents only a small part of "thinking." Those less friendly to Chinese thought argue precisely that Chinese thought simply does not count as philosophy, because "philosophy" involves a very specific way of asking and answering already-established questions. Although this description of the debate is somewhat simplistic, it is useful in making the point that the debate is, in fact, based on ideas of inside and outside, of home and foreign, of universal and local. And, to me, this is a first indication that, at best, these notions will prove unconducive to dialogue and mutual understanding. In contrast, I will argue that in both Heidegger and Daoism we find insights about the value of, at the same time, both leaving home and not leaving home and of perceiving inside and outside as the same without being identical. Heidegger in this context talks about a "gathering" as keeping or preserving a belonging-together through difference, and Zhuangzi discredits those who think in terms of "this" or "that."

I will first look at Heidegger's thinking on "place" and his ideas with regard to the concepts of provincialism and globalization. I will then move on to Daoism and argue that ideas crucial to the *Daodejing*, but even more so the *Zhuangzi*, accord well with Heidegger's position. Lastly, I consider how these findings complicate the dichotomy of global and local in ways useful for comparative philosophy.

Heidegger on Place and Provincialism

The importance that Heidegger attaches to the notion of "place" should not be underestimated. In fact, he himself has said that within the journey of his thinking, "place" occupies the last and thus arguably most important position:

> With *Being and Time* . . . the "question of Being" . . . concerns the question of being qua being. It becomes thematic in *Being and Time* under the name of "the question of the meaning [*Sinn*] of being." Later this formulation was given up in favour of that of "the question of the truth of being," and finally in favour of that of "the question concerning the place or location of being" [*Ortschaft des Seins*], from which the name topology of being arose [*Topologie des Seins*]. Three terms which succeed one another and at the same time indicate three steps along the way of thinking: MEANING—TRUTH—PLACE (τοποσ).[3]

I will not delve very deeply here into how Heidegger understands the notion of "place" itself but will instead focus on how he thinks in terms of localized thinking, or, in other words, how Heidegger is a provincial and situational thinker. When I affirm this, I am not going against what Heidegger himself says. In fact, Heidegger has gladly acknowledged his provincial approach and his preference for the Black Forest in his *Aus der Erfahrung des Denkens*, where, in a piece called "Why Do We Stay in the Provinces?" he states that his entire work "is intimately rooted in and guided by the world of these mountains and peasants."[4] In other places too, Heidegger comes across as a thinker of a provincial and nostalgic nature: in his ruminations on the Black Forest farmhouse in "Building Dwelling Thinking"; in his thoughts on the peasant woman's shoes portrayed in a Van Gogh painting, discussed in *The Origin of the Work of Art*; and in what are generally perceived as his rants against technology. In relation to this, Heidegger has spoken extensively of ideas of proximity or neighborhood, which all sound rather provincial. "Neighborhood means: dwelling in nearness."[5] Such an attitude seems already present in his early work. In *Being and Time*, for example, among his key concepts are *Befindlichkeit* and *Geworfenheit*, both of which connect to the phenomenological finding oneself in a world; *Dasein*, or being-there, in a place; *Stimmung*, as mood; and *Mit-sein*, *Bei-sein*, or being-with, in-the-presence-of, understood as always finding oneself connected to other people and places. All of these notions indicate the situatedness of Heidegger's thought.

This emphasis should lead us to believe that Heidegger is not a proponent of global thought. In fact, he has argued:

> The frantic abolition of all distances brings no nearness; for nearness does not consist in shortness of distance. What is least remote from us in point of distance, by virtue of its picture on film or its sound on the radio, can remain far from us. What is incalculably far from us in point of distance can be near to us. Short distance is not in itself nearness, nor is great distance remoteness.[6]

So it is not really physical distance that concerns Heidegger but, rather, the mind-set of seeing everything as equally accessible, which brings about its exact opposite: "Everything gets lumped together into uniform distancelessness."[7] Nearness and farness are both annihilated in globalization. Some may say that this is a good thing, and it may well be, but, in thinking, it is this uniformity that Heidegger argues against as containing a loss of diversity, and it is this uniformity that can be understood as a threat inherent in cosmopolitanism because cosmopolitanism includes a reduction of differences to uniform standards not informed by cultural specificities, those same differences that comparative philosophy is supposed to celebrate.

The objection may be (and has been) raised that Heidegger is just a nostalgic thinker who longs for the good old days. And, in many ways, such an objection can also be levied against Daoists, as we shall see later. They are all, it might be said, peasant boys afraid of the big city and new development, unable and unwilling to understand and use new technologies, eager for the good old days. But this would be a sadly mistaken and shallow view. To be sure, Heidegger is not a big fan of cities or of technology. The common misconception, though, is that he is against these things when he actually is *not*. Rather, he warns against possible dangers if the ways of thinking connected to cosmopolitanism—or technology, for that matter—were to become dominant in such a way that we are left no exit, trapped in one very particular mode of thought where we can no longer even conceive of other ways of thinking. The trap of "cosmopolitanism" traditionally understood is that it imposes, under the guise of objectivity and freedom from oppressive cultural obstacles, a very specific view of the world and humanity's place in it as the only correct view.

So, although not a keen cosmopolitan, Heidegger has in fact argued for the "polis" as the site of aboding, the site of historical unfolding: "Perhaps the *polis* is that realm and locale around which everything question-worthy and uncanny turns in an exceptional sense."[8] This positive understanding of the polis is also found in the *Introduction to Metaphysics*, where "polis" is understood as "the site [*Stätte*], the Here, within which and as which being-here is historically": "The polis is the site of history [*Geschichtsstätte*], the Here, *in* which, *out of* which, and *for* which history happens."[9] What I wish to make clear is that while Heidegger is not a globalist, he is also not on the other side of the dichotomy of global and local. Rather, his thinking seeks to complicate the dichotomy by pointing to an understanding of the polis that is not the usual one. To be sure, the metro-polis is not really what Heidegger would see as a proper polis. Heidegger does, however, talk about the polis as a "pole" around which things gather. Referring to the polis, he says that "what is essential in the historical being of human beings resides in the pole-like relatedness of everything to this site of abode."[10] As such, the polis fits in with his understanding of the "gathering in difference" mentioned earlier, which is one of Heidegger's wider key concerns. For our purposes, we can say that in terms of actual people gathering in different places, maybe our abode is indeed everywhere, cosmo-politan. But not every abode is or should be the same, and in every abode the history of thought may unfold differently. This understanding of "cosmopolitan," as dwelling differently in different abodes all over our world, is one Heidegger could affirm.

Heidegger's engagement with Hölderlin can bring us further useful clues here. Florian Vetsch has compiled three steps of the intercultural *Auseinandersetzung* based on what Heidegger took to be crucial in intercultural encounters and what Heidegger himself deduced from Hölderlin:[11]

1. Before his departure to the foreign, the future wanderer is still caught in his own surroundings.
2. The journey begins, and the wanderer encounters the foreign.
3. The wanderer returns, but remains thoughtful of the foreign; in this something new shows itself.[12]

First of all, it must be noted that these notions of "home" and "homelessness," and "wanderer" and "foreign," are largely to be understood metaphorically. As most of us know, Heidegger himself was not much of a traveler. But the list of steps goes to show that, for Heidegger, the *Auseinandersetzung* with foreign ways of thought, at which he did make certain concerted attempts, has two aims. The first is a learning of what the foreign has to offer. To establish this, the "self" has to (temporarily) forget its own, not in the sense of losing oneself in a taking over of "other" habits and ideas, but in the sense of opening up a space for different ideas to be allowed access. If we remain closed, any "wandering" will be futile. We must somehow transcend our own views. As Heidegger puts it, "Where it remains only a matter of refuting, or even of annihilating the foreign, what necessarily gets lost is the possibility of a passage through the foreign, and thereby the possibility of a return home into one's own, and thereby that which is one's own itself."[13] This is the second aim of the *Auseinandersetzung*. The passage through the foreign is crucial for an understanding of what is one's own. But, again, the "wandering" has to be of a very specific character because "only where the foreign is known and acknowledged in its essential oppositional character [*Gegensätzlichkeit*] does there exist the possibility of a genuine relationship [*Beziehung*], that is, of a uniting that is not a confused mixing but a conjoining in distinction [*Unterscheidung*]."[14] It is thus not a matter of learning another culture as a "sum of learnable data,"[15] which you can then take home and mix into your own cultural practices, but one of learning to see another culture as a living, historically moving, open-ended totality, which is not readily at one's disposal but is always open to renewed conversation. This is what the *Auseinandersetzung* is about. Thus, the relation between different cultures is literally a never-ending story. In terms of the vocabulary used earlier, we move from provincial to cosmopolitan, from local to global, or at least from our own into a different culture. What is most important, however, is to be able to move back to the local and apply what was learned, including the realization that the dialogue among localities is open-ended. Our new understanding of "cosmopolitan" may facilitate such a realization, whereas the traditional one cannot.

It is also vital to fully understand the complexity of the relation between the "own" or "homely" and the "other," "foreign," or "unhomely" as it unfolds in Heidegger's *Hölderlin's Hymn "The Ister."* It has been noted that the *Auseinandersetzung* is not meant to be a mere appropriation or incorporation of the other. The other *as* other is not to be overcome in this way; it is the encounter *itself* that matters, so that "the law of the encounter [*Auseinandersetzung*] between the foreign and one's own is the fundamental truth of history."[16] The "coming home" is not a return to a kind of safe haven; it is precisely *in* the encounter itself that the "wanderer" finds herself. Again, the transcending of one's own culture is not understood as standing above all cultures, or as being totally free from culture, or even necessarily as standing *above* those under comparison. The transcending is an opening up to difference as a lasting opening. We could also say that the third step of the intercultural encounter is not so much a return to one's own but a lingering in the encounter, a taking home of the encounter, to remain in the *Auseinandersetzung*. This is where "something new" happens. As Heidegger says, "What is worthy of poetizing in this poetic work is nothing other than becoming homely in being unhomely."[17] And elsewhere in the same volume, he says, "The appropriation of one's own *is* only as the encounter [*Auseinandersetzung*] and guest-like dialogue with the foreign."[18]

I am sure many of us have experienced that one develops a much keener eye for one's own tradition by being exposed to other traditions, both in positive and negative terms. But is this what Heidegger intends when he says that in the third step "something new" happens? How should we understand this "something new"? Have we, through this exposure, transcended both cultures into a position from where we objectively look down on both? Would not that assumption instead indicate some kind of arrogance worse than the colonial arrogance? As mentioned, I do not believe Heidegger sees it this way. In fact, I would argue that he understands that the process involves an awareness of the futility of trying to transcend every standpoint in such a way and that any unity between the homely and the unhomely, or between the self and the other, the own and the foreign, can exist only as the ongoing conversation *between* the two.

In other places in the *Ister* work, Heidegger talks about the unity of journeying and locality [*Ortschaft*] through the metaphor of the river, which is both moving and in one place.[19] But we know that "unity" in Heidegger is never a superficial oneness. As Heidegger puts it, "'Unity' here meaning only that we can come to experience the ground of their originary and reciprocally counterturning belonging-together [*gegenwendige Zusammengehörigkeit*]."[20] Elsewhere, in many other works, he discusses the same ideas in the form of a "gathering in difference." That this "gathering" is connected to notions of "place" is clear; for example, in *Aus der Erfahrung des Denkens*, Heidegger states, "Place always opens a region, when gathering things into their belonging together into it."[21] The function of place is "preserving, the gathering of things in their belonging together."[22] As we shall see later, this ties in with Ames and Hall's ideas of field and focus. The region is the field, and the place is the focus where the field is gathered.

Coming back to our ideas of local and global, or provincial and cosmopolitan, we now understand that the cosmopolitan viewpoint, as traditionally understood, is really the universalist position in disguise. I have argued that Heidegger, first appearances to the contrary, does not stand purely for the provincial side of this dichotomy but offers valuable ways to mediate the two and understand them differently. Another way of seeing this is that, in line with Heidegger, we should not understand "cosmopolitan" as an overarching position. Rather, we should understand it as a position that, on the one hand, recognizes that it itself still involves a very specific viewpoint but, on the other hand, also at least has the benefit of seeing different standpoints as compatible. And this obviously brings me to Zhuangzi.

Daoism (Zhuangzi) as Provincial?

I think most people will not have a problem with me arguing for the idea that in Daoism generally, and in the *Zhuangzi* in particular, there is a situatedness to our being and that this means that the provincial or local affinity is also present. We have only to think of chapter 80 of the *Daodejing*, where people are told that in the best scenario they stay in their own place, or chapter 47, which argues that to know, one does not have to actually go anywhere. "Venture not beyond your doors to know the world. . . . The farther one goes, the less one knows."[23] In the context of my argument here, this is definitely an appeal for localized living and against the traps of the big city or court. And the sages are supposed to follow the localized perspective, for they have to "take the thoughts and feelings of the common people as their own."[24] This ties in with the field and focus ideas of Ames and Hall: "The emphasis in this Daoist epistemology of feeling, then, is neither the external environs as an object of knowledge nor the solitary knower as subject, but upon the site at which the act of knowing takes place, and the range and quality of relationships that constitute this site."[25] Or, as they put it a bit later in the same work, "Knowledge entails proximity."[26] Field and focus ideas of knowledge relate people intimately to their surroundings. Knowing is always from a place, from a perspective. The trick is to understand that no single perspective (your own, for example) is necessarily better than any other perspective and that we cannot really escape the idea of perspective totally: "Knowledge is not the subjective representation of some objective reality, but a quality of the local experience itself."[27] And again: "A fully responsive appreciation of the local redirects us back to unmediated feeling as the real site of efficacious knowing and living."[28]

The *Zhuangzi* also seems to have this preference for a kind of local thinking, where knowledge is situational. Although there is a lot of metaphorical roaming around, the *Zhuangzi* never actually advises us to go travelling and see different cultures to broaden our perspective. In fact, although this is not its concern, it advises against this kind of thought in a roundabout way, asserting that things do not thrive when taken out of their natural environment (see, for example, chapter 2 on the natural place for different creatures) and that the natural environments for humans are the agricultural village and the family, not the court with its trappings and artificial rules.[29]

Although the *Zhuangzi*'s inner chapters do not mention this simple local thinking much and do display a genuine preference for people who have escaped the confines of their narrow-minded environs, such escapes are complicated by Zhuangzi as escapes on the level of viewpoints themselves (I will come back to this later). In other chapters, we do find much more evidence of the preference for this local situatedness and the accompanying distaste for the traps of court and of technology. For example, in the story of the well-sweep in chapter 12, Zhuangzi shows that it is better to stay close to nature and that ways of thinking that untie people from their immediate environment are not to be applauded.

Similarly, and quite naturally, the primitivist chapters 8, 9, and 10 display a preference for a simple lifestyle close to nature, in harmony with how nature works. In chapter 10 the exhortation to stay in your village and lead a local existence is repeated from the *Daodejing*. This advice is not to discard technology per se but to discard a lifestyle that adheres to technology and becomes dependent on it. The understanding is that such a lifestyle is not good: "We disturb the brightness of the sun and moon above, dissipate the quintessences in the mountains and rivers below, interrupt the round of the four seasons in between; of the very insects which creep on the ground or flit above it, not one is not losing its nature. How utterly the lust for knowledge has disordered the world!"[30]

Although I realize that this view is most present in the primitivist chapters, I do think that the *Zhuangzi* as a whole can be seen as advocating small communities where people live in harmony with each other and with nature. And there is also another way in which this situatedness plays out in the *Zhuangzi*: all the references about localized skills seem to point in this direction. People function best when they are intelligently engaged in practices in localities they know well. Think of Cook Ding in chapter 3 or the swimmer, the bell-stand maker, and other examples in chapter 19. In each case, we see absorption in a local situation with full attention, rather than the abstraction from it.

The same idea is also supported by the passages in the *Zhuangzi* where people who have been enlightened with Daoist insights prefer to stay at home and practice a simple kind of life rather than commit to serve in government. Liezi, in chapter 7, after concluding that he did not yet know *dao*, goes home and leads a simple life. Bozheng Zigao, in chapter 12, returns to plowing his fields because the *dao* went missing in his times. And Zhuangzi himself, in chapter 17, cannot be bothered with the administration of Chu and, in the famous "happiness of the fish" passage, declares that he knows the fish swimming in their natural environment are happy from his own, particular perspective on the bridge above them.

All this points, even if sometimes indirectly or by analogy, to a preference for not having to leave the local lifestyle and for a situational understanding of humans as intricately tied to a place, as rooted in place. Yet it is important to understand that this local lifestyle is not the same as that of those who are usually derogatorily referred to as "the stupid peasants." The local situatedness and rootedness of Daoist sages and their preference for it is *not* in ignorance of, but rather in full awareness of, the alternatives. It is, to come back to Heidegger, represented by one who prefers the local as the more conducive site of being, after having experienced its other, the global.

Yet at the same time, as we know all too well, it also seems that Zhuangzi at least condemns the local viewpoint as biased or unhelpful. And he does this quite frequently. In chapter 1, for example, the fact that the people of Sung were not able to see the extended use of their salve, outside of their own community and their own applications, makes them (and by extension Huizi too) narrowminded. Also in the first chapter, the little birds cannot compete with the big bird Peng. And again, in chapter 2, Zhuangzi discusses the viewpoints of *shi* (correct) and *fei* (wrong) and how they are relative to one's partial perspective. There are more such examples, but what I find most telling is that although Zhuangzi does accord a preference for the larger or more encompassing view, he always immediately makes it clear that this larger view should still be understood as being just that, a larger perspective, which in the end suffers from the same shortcomings. In fact, in chapter 17, in the "Autumn Floods" dialogue, the virtues of small or specialized creatures are specifically lauded for being able to do what the "bigger" creatures cannot, bringing us back full circle to an appreciation of both:

> A beam or a pillar can be used to batter down a city wall, but it is no good for stopping up a little hole—this refers to a difference in function. Thoroughbreds like Qiji and Hualiu could gallop a thousand *li* in one day, but when it came to catching rats they were no match for the wildcat or the weasel—this refers to a difference in skill. The horned owl catches fleas at night and can spot the tip of a hair, but when daylight comes, no matter how wide it opens its eyes, it cannot see a mound or a hill—this refers to a difference in nature. Now do you say that you are going to make Right your master and do away with Wrong, or make Order your master and do away with Disorder? If you do, then you have not understood the principle of heaven and earth or the nature of the ten thousand things. This is like saying that you are going to make Heaven your master and do away with Earth, or make Yin your master and do away with Yang. Obviously it is impossible.[31]

Applying these findings to our concerns about the global or cosmopolitan versus the local or provincial, it would then seem that Zhuangzi is both on the side of the global and on the side of the local. He makes it quite clear that the "local" views of the little birds in chapter 1 and the frog in the well in the "Autumn Floods" chapter do not measure up to the more "global" views of the bird Peng and the Turtle of the East Sea, respectively. And it is beyond doubt that Zhuangzi regards the Confucian and Mohist ideas as provincial in a way, as stuck in a limited viewpoint to be overcome. Thus, he advocates letting go of the confines of the Confucian and Mohist moral settings. Yet exactly such a view that sees the global as hierarchically above the local is always instantly complicated by Zhuangzi. In chapter 1, he makes it clear that even Liezi's flying on the clouds is still just a view, larger but still dependent. And in the "Autumn Floods" chapter, after praising the smaller, the local, for being able to see and do what the larger, the global, cannot, he comes to the conclusion that "the wisest, because they have a full view of far and near, do not belittle the smaller or make much of the greater, knowing that measuring has no limit."[32] Also of special importance here is chapter 6, where the dichotomy between what is of *tian* (the celestial) and what is of man is questioned and found to be unhelpful: "Someone in whom neither Heaven nor man is victor over the other, this is what is meant by the True Man."[33]

This means that, at least by analogy with our vocabulary, Zhuangzi is an advocate of "provincial" thinking, if "provincial" is now understood as a criticism of the traditional understanding of "global" or "cosmopolitan." Although Zhuangzi obviously never spoke about cosmopolitanism, by extension we could say that in advocating for both the smaller *and* the larger views, he seeks to overcome the traditional global/local distinction altogether and tries to replace it with a different kind of thinking. It is that kind of thinking that may be able to shed some light on what comparative philosophy, being in the same predicament, should focus on. This different kind of thinking is not beyond cultures but recognizes the inevitability of always coming from somewhere in any engagement among different cultures. To me, this move is similar to Heidegger's returning home, where we actively engage with the foreign from a particular perspective but are always aware of that perspective and what it does, fully aware of the fact that "between" should not mean "beyond" or "above" but should instead consist in an openness and willingness to entertain difference.

Similar analogies can be found with regards to the other notions in Heidegger that were discussed earlier, those of inside and outside and of home and unhomely. Like the terminology of cosmopolitan and provincial, the terminology of inside and outside or of home and unhomely does not really occur with the Daoists, but there are still analogies to be found. In chapter 2 of the *Daodejing*, for example, it is said that "determinacy (*you*) and indeterminacy (*wu*) give rise to each other, difficult and easy complement each other, long and short set each other off, high and low complete each other . . ."[34] Something similar is repeated in chapter 40 and in many other chapters, and these instances show that we cannot have one side of a pair without the other. In chapter 59 the ruler is urged to find a way in which "none can discern your limit," because then "you can preside over the realm."[35] I take this passage to mean that the ruler must see himself or herself as continuous with the state and not as opposite to it. This kind of thinking is present throughout the *Daodejing*, which advises us to see contraries, not as opposites and definitely not in hierarchical fashion, but as two poles of a single spectrum, thus denying the strict dichotomy and hierarchy that are inherent in thinking in such terms as inside and outside.

With respect to the *Zhuangzi*, numerous passages in the inner chapters display a similar challenge to the perceived dichotomies involved. For example, in chapter 2 there are the exhortations not to perceive the heart-mind (*xin*) as central and the rest of the body as peripheral, not to hold on to artificial distinctions between *shi* (that's it) and *fei* (that's not), but to let "both alternatives proceed."[36] The sages of old had recognized that this distinction-making process between *shi* and *fei* was at the root of all problems:

> The men of old, their knowledge had arrived at something: at what had it arrived?
> There were some who thought there had not yet begun to be things—the utmost,

the exhaustive, there is no more to add. The next thought there were things but there had not yet begun to be borders. The next thought there were borders to them but there had not yet begun to be "That's it, that's not." The lighting up of "That's it, that's not" is the reason why the Way is flawed.[37]

Not making distinctions, and seeing continuity rather than opposition, is a hallmark of Zhuangzi, who even goes so far as to assert that saying that the *wanwu* (the ten thousand things) and himself are one goes in the wrong direction, for it adds the saying of it to the original oneness. Because "the Way has never had borders,"[38] distinguishing what is inside from what is outside is always complicated.

A similar thing is presented in chapter 6, where making a distinction between your boat and the place where you hide it will result in the loss of your boat when it is stolen, but making no such distinction between what is mine and the rest, between the boat and the world, avoids this problem. A last example, in the same chapter, is the famous story of Hundun, who by being "gifted" the power to make distinctions lost his life.

As mentioned earlier, I do not wish to claim that Daoism attaches much importance to the notions of local and global or of cosmopolitanism and provincialism. Such notions are obviously Western in origin and were not of direct concern to classical Daoist thinkers. Yet I have noted enough similarities in the form of analogies that show how the Daoists were indeed concerned with undoing such dichotomies in general, and I hope to have shown how these analogies apply successfully to our problematic here.

Although the notions of global and local, cosmopolitan and provincial, and inside and outside seem to present a problem for comparative philosophy, I think that in fact the problem lies mostly in the traditional, dichotomous understandings of such terms. Thinking with Heidegger and Zhuangzi, we can see the complications implicit in these terms and how they rest on each other for meaning. We can then come to a different understanding of terms like "cosmopolitan" and "provincial" and use them in different ways to our advantage. Both Heidegger and the Daoists seek to understand the situatedness of our existence and knowledge as positive, without thereby falling into the dichotomy and hence into the hierarchy. We must understand both positions as not only different but also complementary, and it would be wise to heed the following from the *Daxue*: "There is no such thing as healthy branches when the root is rotten."[39] If you are not locally involved and do not understand your own perspective, then you will have lost the root. Cosmopolitanism as traditionally understood is the loss of roots, and the branches by themselves are not healthy. No global thinking, without local thinking at its roots, can keep us tied to the world. When cosmopolitanism is understood as entertaining an openness and appreciation for the ongoing diversity of different ways of thought, and when provincialism is understood as the recognition of always coming from a certain perspective and of reinserting human beings into their environment, instead of abstracting them from it as has been done in the traditional Western history of philosophy, then we may be in a better position to do comparative philosophy without falling into self-defeating dichotomies.

For comparative philosophy itself, this means that although we may never be able to escape personal and cultural perspectives, we can certainly escape the patently false ones, the small ones. Acknowledging that this is so need not lead us into a pernicious relativism, however, since it entails also acknowledging the indispensability of such "small views" in certain scenarios. For comparative philosophy, this means that it might be more fruitful to return to the idea of intercultural philosophy, which may be a better description of what we do. "Intercultural" philosophy has the benefit of acknowledging that we do work from one culture to the other, and while we must certainly "transcend" our own cultural views, it is impossible to ever really stand completely outside of those things under comparison. This means we do not need to pretend to be objective or to conceive of "comparative" philosophy in ways that implicitly entail promoting some overarching position.

On a more practical level, I hope that this chapter can contribute to a better understanding of political issues involving globalization. As traditionally understood, globalization has the potential to render all things the same, fostering an unbiased stance toward specific cultures by eliding the particularities of their differences. Globalization is thus thought to make one cosmopolitan. But this idea of cosmopolitanism is the traditional one, where cultural differences are supposed to be overcome. In fact, this has not happened. Instead of sameness, globalization has fostered an embrace of the equality of all differences, so that it can be argued that everyone now considers all opinions to be equally important, and so that cultural biases are now displayed as valuable in their own right. This is, at least partly, what enables some of the global problems that we face today—including terrorism, global warming, and increasing inequalities in many areas—to be justified under the guise of rightfully respected "differences." The dream of the traditional cosmopolitan is a metropolis where everyone gets along together because they have all overcome their cultural specificities. But our reality continues to be one of places wherein different viewpoints compete for attention and supremacy and wherein the notion of difference is exploited in many ways. And as Zhuangzi noted, this is not really viable.

Our reconsideration of terms may assist in understanding things differently. "Cosmopolitan" should really mean that one is in constant conversation with what is other and that one is constantly seeking to deepen understandings of other cultures rather than to overcome them. And "provincial" should not be seen as necessarily opposed to this sense of "cosmopolitanism" but instead should be understood as the realistic starting point of our conversations—a place wherein we do not deny our own differences from others but celebrate them together when possible and discuss their merits and demerits when necessary. May comparative or intercultural philosophy help us in these endeavors.

NOTES

Epigraph 1: Stefan Zweig, *Gesammelte Werke in Einzelbänden: Zeiten und Schicksale* (Frankfurt: S. Fischer Verlag, 1990), 30 (my translation). *Epigraph 2: Zhuangzi*, chap. 17, trans. A. C. Graham in *Chuang-tzú; The Inner Chapters* (Indianapolis: Hackett, 2001), 145–146.

1. *Oxford English Dictionary Online*, s.v. "cosmopolitan," http://www.oed.com.

2. Ibid., s.v. "provincial."

3. Martin Heidegger, *Four Seminars*, trans. Andrew Mitchell and François Raffoul (Bloomington: Indiana University Press, 2004), 47.

4. Martin Heidegger, *Aus der Erfahrung des Denkens (Gesamtausgabe*, vol. 13) (Frankfurt: Vittorio Klostermann, 1983), 11 (my translation).

5. Martin Heidegger, *On the Way to Language*, trans. Peter D. Hertz (New York: Harper and Row, 1971), 93.

6. Martin Heidegger, *Poetry, Language, Thought*, trans. Albert Hofstadter (New York: Harper and Row, 1971), 163.

7. Ibid., 164.

8. Martin Heidegger, *Hölderlin's Hymn "The Ister,"* trans. William McNeill and Julia Davis (Bloomington: Indiana University Press, 1996), 81.

9. Martin Heidegger, *Introduction to Metaphysics*, trans. Gregory Fried and Richard Polt (New Haven, CT: Yale University Press, 2000), 162.

10. Heidegger, *Hölderlin's Hymn*, 82.

11. The German *Auseinandersetzung* has such diverse meanings as "argument," "examination," "discussion," "encounter," "confrontation," and "dialogue." The most common translation for Heidegger's works is "con-frontation," with the hyphen indicating that Heidegger uses the term to denote the coming together in difference of what belongs together. I shall indicate where the term is used in translated quotations, but I prefer to use the German word to keep the full range of meanings that Heidegger is aiming for.

12. Florian Vetsch, *Martin Heideggers Angang der interkulturellen Auseinandersetzung* (Würzburg: Königshausen und Neumann, 1992), 68 (my translation).

13. Heidegger, *Hölderlin's Hymn*, 54.

14. Ibid.

15. Vetsch, *Martin Heideggers Angang*, 80 (my translation).

16. Heidegger, *Hölderlin's Hymn*, 49.

17. Ibid., 121.

18. Ibid., 142 (italics in the original).

19. Ibid., 142, 166.

20. Ibid., 68.

21. Heidegger, *Aus der Erfahrung*, 207 (my translation).

22. Ibid., 207–208 (my translation).

23. Roger T. Ames and David L. Hall, *Daodejing: Making This Life Significant* (New York: Ballantine Books, 2003), 150.

24. Ibid., 153.

25. Ibid., 108.

26. Ibid., 109.

27. Ibid., 150.

28. Ibid., 203.

29. One of the only ideas that Zhuangzi shares with the Confucians is the naturalness of familial love and ties. See, e.g., chapter 4, where the "Daoist" Confucius says that "a child's love of his parents cannot be dispelled from the heart" (Graham, *Chuang-tzŭ*, 70), or chapter 18, where Zhuangzi assumes that the "skull" may possibly be in the state it is in because it brought shame to its family (ibid., 124).

30. Ibid., 210.

31. Burton Watson, *Zhuangzi: Basic Writings* (New York: Columbia University Press, 2003), 103.

32. Graham, *Chuang-tzŭ*, 145–146.

33. Ibid., 85.

34. Ames and Hall, *Daodejing*, 80.

35. Ibid., 169.

36. Graham, *Chuang-tzŭ*, 54.

37. Ibid.

38. Ibid., 57.

39. Quoted in Ames and Hall, *Daodejing*, 162.

About the *Taking Place* of *Inter*cultural Philosophy as Polylogue

3

Britta Saal

In the course of the so-called spatial turn within the humanities and social sciences, space has become a metaphor for cultural dynamics.[1] Thinking spatially thus entails awareness of the cultural aspects of globalization as well as the manifold localities taking part in it. With the emergence of comparative philosophy in the first half of the twentieth century, and especially of intercultural philosophy in the late 1980s, it has been claimed that philosophy can no longer be equated with European philosophy and that philosophies of different kinds have emerged in different cultural places across the planet. Moreover, intercultural philosophy involves recognizing a plurality of philosophies and philosophical places in the global space but also implies—by the prefix "inter-"—a dynamic and active realm of encounter and exchange.

Considering now the rising philosophical interest and engagement with place as well as space, the leading questions for the following reflections are "Where, in which *place* in this inter-space, does intercultural philosophy take place?" and "How does it *take* place?" To answer these questions, I will first deal with two specific notions: the "situated unsituatedness" (*orthafte Ortlosigkeit*) of philosophy, coined by the Indian-German philosopher Ram Adhar Mall, and the project of "philosophy-in-place," formulated by the Canadian philosopher Bruce Janz with reference especially to the African context. I will then reflect on the *inter*-space before elaborating on the processual notion of "taking place" to denote *inter*cultural philosophy, first and foremost, as an activity marked by a processual and common practice.

Intercultural Philosophy and Place

By stressing active encounter and mutual exchange, as well as negotiation, intercultural philosophy claims to be a new orientation in philosophy. In the words of Ram Adhar Mall, one of the founders of intercultural philosophy, "An intercultural philosophical orientation pleads for unity without uniformity. It is not

51

a matter of unity in diversity but 'unity in the face of diversity.' "[2] That means that there never can be any absolutist position claiming to possess *the* one and only truth. Intercultural philosophy enables us, rather, "to critically and sympathetically examine one philosophical tradition from the point of view of the other and vice versa. In a certain sense, the phrase 'intercultural philosophy' is tautological, for philosophy is by its very nature intercultural."[3]

In this context, Mall speaks about the "situated unsituatedness" (*orthafte Ortlosigkeit*) of philosophy.[4] By introducing this term, Mall stresses the simultaneity of placelyness (*Orthaftigkeit*) on the one hand and placelessness (*Ortlosigkeit*) on the other. That means philosophy is always at the same time culturally embedded and yet never limited to any specific cultural place: "Philosophy is undoubtedly born in particular cultures and thus is local in character, but it is not exhausted in any one of its manifold local manifestations."[5] By "philosophy," Mall refers here to the so-called *philosophia perennis*, the everlasting and eternal truth—that is, *the one and only* philosophy that exists in all cultures and is not limited by time and space.[6] The problem, according to Mall, arises out of the fact that, despite its universal inclusiveness, "the claim to possess philosophia perennis has been explicitly or implicitly made in nearly all traditions."[7] But the *philosophia perennis* is rather placeless and, at the same time, only appears embedded in different cultural places: "The one perennial philosophy . . . does not have one mother tongue; it is polylingual."[8] Thus, philosophy can be found in every culture, but no philosophy from any culture is the one for all.[9]

Even though Mall refers to the idea of a universal *philosophia perennis*, he doesn't mean that it is always "one and the same" in the many traditions. Indeed, he rejects this kind of ontological, metaphysical, and ideological assumption.[10] The universality of philosophy in Mall's sense consists in philosophy's being an activity undertaken and sustained in so many places in the world. But, of course, this activity does not look the same everywhere. On the contrary, the *questions* that are asked—or not asked—philosophically reveal philosophy's cultural contextuality and embeddedness. Thus, whenever specific questions are asked, we can cross-culturally speak about philosophy.[11] Against this background, situatedness (in the sense of having a place, or being "placely") corresponds to diversity and plurality, while unsituatedness (in the sense of having no place, or being "placeless") corresponds to universality.[12] Wherever the idea of philosophia perennis takes concrete shape by a specific way of questioning, it is situated—placely. But since it never can be identified with any of those shapes, it is unsituated—placeless.[13]

Philosophy-in-Place

Referring to the African philosophical context, Bruce Janz, who sometimes is referred to as an "African philosopher,"[14] also stresses the importance of place by talking about the "platiality" of philosophy. For him, a platial orientation is opposed to a spatial orientation in philosophy, with the latter identified with efforts to establish and defend "an intellectual territory."[15] A platial orientation, in contrast, is aware of the constitutive meaning of a concrete place and of a specific lifeworld in the creation of philosophical concepts.[16] The shift from spatiality to platiality means turning away from asking only general or "universal" questions and generating, instead, new questions in reference to particular discourses and conditions within a particular place.[17]

But why does place matter? And why it should matter especially in Africa? At the very beginning of his book *Philosophy in an African Place*, Janz includes a quotation from Jacques Derrida, which I requote here in an abbreviated fashion: " 'Where does the question of the right to philosophy take place?' . . . Where does it find today its most appropriate place?"[18] These questions evince two aspects of long-dominant views of philosophy, each of which points in the direction of answers to the question of why place matters. The first aspect refers to the long-lasting European point of view that takes for granted that the real *one and only* philosophy resides in the place of Europe. The second aspect, concerning Africa, refers to the equally long-lasting European point of view, also taken for granted, that there is *no* philosophy in the place of Africa. In short, Africa has been completely excluded from the "realm of philosophy"; and any African right to have a philosophy and to take part in the philosophical project has been denied. The right to determine these declarations has been taken by the Europeans from a self-asserted position of (political and economic) power and thus took place in Europe. This is why "the history of African philosophy has been the history of struggle to find a place, or to claim a place, or to assert the entitlement to a place."[19] For this reason, reflections about Africa as an "appropriate place" of philosophy—one of Janz' main projects[20]—are really relevant.[21]

The shift from a spatial to a platial orientation in philosophy corresponds in the African case to the shift from asking very general questions like "Is there an African reason?" or "What is the *Africanness* of African philosophy?" to more lifeworld-concerning questions like "How is the concept of reason formed and deployed in thought-lives in Africa?" or "How is tradition transmitted in an African world?"[22] According to Janz, the (spatial) quest for metaphysical grounding—presented in the big question, "What is African philosophy?"— "has distracted scholars from moving to a more creative and less defensive posture, one which can truly examine the interesting and useful ideas that might come from the sages, from the proverbs, or from the academy."[23] Instead, attempts to answer the metaphysical grounding question have resulted in a tendency to focus on the "tradition." And, as a result, African philosophers have tended to view each other's writings as writings *about* philosophy but not as philosophy itself.[24] Therefore, it is necessary to generate new insights for one's own purpose.[25]

In short, the basic assumption of a "philosophy-in-place" in Janz' sense is that "philosophy always comes from a place" and therefore "thinking in place is . . . ultimately unavoidable."[26] And since, throughout the world, existence is reflected upon and questioned, any cultural population "*must* have some level of philosophy."[27] Janz is convinced "that philosophy must attend to the conditions in which its *questions* arise, and that this attention does not diminish philosophy's traditional . . . striving for universals."[28] Again we are reminded of the importance of questions and the role they play in conceptualizing philosophy. But in contrast to Mall, Janz makes clear that asking the big metaphysical question of "What is philosophy?"—which is the same as asking, "What is the philosophia perennis?"—is finally self-undermining, because "those who might be able to ask it are already immersed in a tradition."[29]

This leads us back to the topic of intercultural philosophy. Both Mall and Janz stress the importance of place and the activity of questioning. The difference between them lies in how they deal with the connecting or encounter element. While Mall introduces the notion of unsituatedness, by which he aims to conserve the idea of unity in the face of particularity and tries to overcome the dichotomy between universality and particularity, Janz turns away from any kind of metaphysical questioning. Janz does still ask the "central question of philosophy," but, recalling Derrida's question, he asks what it is exactly within "any given culture, that a person feels the need to use philosophical reason to analyze or reflect": How does philosophical reasoning emerge? Where does it come from?"[30] These questions are real platial questions, since they are asked in the face of the respective place. And it is from these places that Janz deals with the problem of the common ground, "how (or whether) those places can *relate* to each other": "This is vastly different from the European starting point, which assumes that philosophy has a universal character, and that Africa simply has to measure up."[31] Consequently, the common ground does not exist as such but needs to be negotiated and, thus, builds on an understanding of philosophy as *activity*. In this sense, intercultural philosophy is about the *taking shape* of philosophies in different cultural places as well as, at the same time, about the *taking place* of doing philosophy *in between* these places.

The *Inter*-space

Considering the platiality of philosophy and how the very notion "intercultural" points to a space (as indicated by the prefix "inter-"), my questions are now: Where is intercultural philosophy to be located? Where, in which *place* in this *inter*-space, does intercultural philosophy take place? How does it *take* place? And what does doing philosophy in this intercultural place mean?

The prefix "inter-," on the one hand, seems to be contradictory to place, because it denotes an in-between *space*. On the other hand, however, the term "intercultural" overcomes this contradiction by denoting a space between cultural *places*. This is to say, in the inter-space, place occurs in the plural, as places that are always implied and referred to as distinct. Thus, the plurality of places and space are mutually constitutive. Given the plurality of places, the space-in-between (the "inter-") is not a particular space and does not differ from *the* space but, rather, points to an encounter activity. The "inter-" in this sense is a meeting space of places in relation.

Concerning the two basic factors of the "inter-" (relationality and activity), Michel de Certeau describes the relationship between space and place in a short but very illuminative way: "Space is a practiced place."[32] Without going into Certeau's theory in great detail, I will focus on how he defines space and place, and the main implication that follows from these definitions. For Certeau, a place as such—for example, a street or a text in the sense of a sign system—doesn't have any inherent meaning. It is an "order" for the distribution of elements concerning their relational coexistence: "It thus excludes the possibility of two things being in the same location."[33] Every element has its "proper" place—an "instantaneous configuration of positions" that involves an "indication of stability."[34] The meaning, then, is produced by actors—for example, people walking on the street or reading a text, who, by their activities, create relations between places and thereby transform activity of relating into a space: "Space is composed of intersections of mobile elements. It is in a sense actuated by the ensemble of movements deployed within it. . . . [I]t has thus none of the univocity or stability of a 'proper.'"[35] In short, according to Certeau, space is not given as such but, rather, opens up through the place-connecting activity carried out by actors.

From this perspective, "cultures"—in the sense of communities sharing some connecting cultural elements—can be identified on a map as cultural places but are at the same time already spaces in which cultural meanings have been and are being continuously produced. Taking a look at such variable identity movements in the global context, we can analyze these by referring to Certeau's "law of the 'proper,'" which rules in the place.[36] The more a cultural community asserts its *own* identity in a culturalistic way, the more it becomes a stable and immobile particular cultural place and cuts off the relation to space— that is, its own cultural space as well as the global intercultural space. It is identified but not actualized.[37] The alternative would be, not to reject identity, but to be aware of the basically dynamic structure of culture on the local as well as on the global level. In this sense, cultures are cultural spaces-in-place.

The intercultural philosophical relationship could be characterized, then, as follows: cultural subjects from places *in the plural* create the space of intercultural encounter through their *relational* philosophical activities. To stress the relational aspects of encounter, exchange, negotiation, conversation, and so forth, I would propose distinguishing between inter*cultural* and *inter*cultural. While inter*cultural* refers more to the multiple cultural places and philosophies-in-places, *inter*cultural refers primarily to the mutual conversational activity between these philosophies-in-places and the creation of a new philosophizing space-in-place. This space of *inter*cultural encounter is itself a meeting-place of active philosophizing. Place thus becomes an event-place, which has the form of a "taking place."[38] In this sense, *inter*cultural philosophy as an activity *takes place* as a "polylogue," as this term is used by the Austrian philosopher Franz Martin Wimmer.[39]

As mentioned earlier, philosophical thinking is formed by the *questions* that arise in *places* that guide the *directions* of the respective ways of philosophical thinking. *Inter*cultural philosophical thinking goes a step further, since its place is not a particular, previously existing place but always a place consisting in, and only in, a process of taking place. Place here becomes an encounter space-in-place. This encounter space-in-place, then, guides and inspires new questions. In encountering *inter*-space, this place emerges in the very moment when the polylogue takes place as a relational philosophical interaction between thinkers of different cultural places. In short, *inter*cultural philosophizing in the form of a polylogue takes *place* in relation to the *inter*-space and starts from a place that arises in the very moment of *taking* it.

The *Taking Place*

To further elaborate this *inter*cultural philosophical activity of *taking place*, I'd like to start with some interlingual thoughts. The expression "taking place" is commonly used to denote a planned or scheduled, more or less specific event, while "happen" refers to an unplanned or accidental event. In German there is a similar relation between the verbs *geschehen* (happen) and *stattfinden* (take place). The word *statt* in the abridged version of *eine Statt finden* in Old High German means *Stelle* or *Ort* (place). So, in the English as well as in the German case, there is a reference to place when describing the happening of a specific event. But there is also a very interesting difference. In German, this place is *found* and thus refers to a mediating process in which the subject and the object become fitting, while in English the place is *taken*, which refers to a very active process led by the subject. It is exactly in this—in my eyes—very fruitful tension between *finding* and *taking* (a) place that I would like to locate the following reflections.

Coming-to-the-World

In his Frankfurt lectures in 1988[40] and in his book *Eurotaoismus* from 1989,[41] Peter Sloterdijk coined the notion of "coming-to-the-world" (*Zurweltkommen*).

This notion in German usually describes the event of a child being born. Correspondingly, the notion used by Sloterdijk refers to the very moment at the beginning of our life, when the newborn *finds* and *takes* his or her *place* somewhere in the world. This notion denotes a becoming-place, since the place for the child is not yet there but comes into existence only when his or her birth *takes* (his or her) place. It is an event-place.

Sloterdijk introduces the notion of coming-to-the-world as the metaphoric basis for a poetics of beginning. What happens by birth, according to Sloterdijk, is at first the "fastening to the openness" (*Anheftung ans Offene*)—since the child comes from the enclosed inside of the mother's womb to the outside— and only after that the "connection to the world" (*Anbindung an die Welt*).[42] That is to say, at the very beginning the born one does not yet have any notion of the world and is not yet disturbed by any preconceptions. However, human beings are born into language and also political communities, which serve, according to Sloterdijk, as "systems to disappropriate the born one from the openness."[43] What follows is a "tattoo . . . with the patterns of the particular national language,"[44] which frequently leads to a linguistic "dissemination force" (*Weitergabegewalt*) marked by fixed conceptions.[45] To overcome this, Sloterdijk recalls the liberating potential of language in the form of "free speech" (*Freispruch*).[46] For free speech to unfold, a second birth is necessary in the form of a "de-connection" (*Ent-Bindung*) from the language community.[47] Free speech, in the form of a free and critical conversation, is possible when we leave the fixed boundaries marked by "linguistic boundedness" (*Sprachgebundenheit*) or by "speaking nationality" (*sprechende Nationalität*).[48] We then have to recall as a priori the basic condition of natality shared by all human beings. Sloterdijk speaks here also about the need to turn from inter*nationality* to inter*natality*, whereby "internatality" means the "joint knowledge [*Mitwissen*] about the coming-to-the-world of the other under his or her own conditions."[49] By this, multilingualism could become a "medium of the de-connection from national language force."[50]

The coming-to-the-world, thus, describes the possibility to begin creating the world. This refers to the state—or, better yet, the process—that immediately precedes the beginning of humanly shared lives. It is the moment in between the free and open space and particular cultural places. It is the moment just before taking a place, where there is still freedom and where the *inter*cultural inter-space opens. The common ground of *inter*natality opens possibilities for creating this space by means of a free and critical language—by an *inter*cultural polylogue—that goes beyond a particular, culturally bound language. In this sense, *inter*culturality as coming-to-the-world refers to this potential and the possibility to leave—not to quit—"our" places in favor of meeting in a new place and coming to the world together by beginning to create it anew. By this, Sloterdijk adds a third simultaneous event-moment in addition to event-moments of *finding* and *taking* (a) place: the *coming*.

Acting in the World-between-People

The idea of new-beginning is basic for the thought of Hannah Arendt. In fact, Sloterdijk is clearly building on her thoughts about birth, natality, and beginning, even though he mentions her work only in passing. One reason for his mentioning her only in passing might be Sloterdijk's fundamentally different focus, showing a strong distrust for the political and being concerned instead primarily with the literary-aesthetical potential of language.[51] For Arendt, in contrast, the political is precisely the realm where the world is created. The political here is neither meant to be the topic of political sciences nor meant to be identical with politics but, rather, is seen as the execution, or the *taking place*, of human interactions. "The world," Arendt says in her speech about Lessing in 1959, "lies between people."[52] It is here, in this in-between of the world as an event-place, where speaking and acting and, thus, the origin of the political are located.

Arendt's theory of action is based on two fundamental conditions—natality and plurality—that mark the connection between "the capacity of beginning something anew" and "taking an initiative."[53] As we have seen, Sloterdijk refers not so much to plurality but especially to the condition of natality and connects it with language and literature. His focus is on the event of leaving the mother's womb and the accompanying situation of openness—that is, the not-yet-boundedness from where we can start to *speak* freely. Arendt, on the other hand, refers to natality as a beginning through acting in a place—that is, the very moment when we start to *act*—and it is in this moment that the fact of being born is confirmed. For Arendt, the condition of plurality is essential here, because action depends on the plurality of human beings, who are all born as individuals, in order to begin taking place.[54]

Arendt and Sloterdijk both provide very fruitful bases for an understanding of philosophy as an active and processual thinking—or, in other words, as an event in the form of *taking place* (*Vollzug*)—by stressing slightly different, but equally important, event-aspects of beginning. Arendt's work, however, offers notions like "plurality" and "inter-action" as well as "in-between" and "web of human relationships," which advance us a bit further in terms of intercultural thinking. Concerning the in-between, Arendt makes an interesting distinction between the first (objective) in-between (which refers to the worldly, objective reality) and the second (subjective) in-between (which refers to human beings directly). The first in-between is created by the people—in plurality—who "constitute . . . something which *inter-est[s]*"[55] Simultaneously, while acting and speaking about these inter-ests, the individual agents uncover themselves by unavoidably bringing in something personal or, in other words, showing something specific from one's place. This second in-between Arendt calls the "'web' of human relationships" to denote its intangible but nevertheless real quality.[56]

Given this inter-human relationship, Arendt speaks very clearly about the political importance of friendship. In her speech about Lessing, she remarks: "For the world is not humane just because it is made by human beings, and it does not become humane just because the human voice sounds in it, but only when it has become the object of discourse. . . . We humanize what is going on in the world and in ourselves only by speaking of it, and in the course of speaking of it we learn to be human."[57] What she stresses here is that it is by discourse that we humanize the world. We make the world human, by speaking of it as humans. The "faculty of action," in the sense of beginning something new, "interferes" and "interrupts" the course of the world and human affairs, which—without ever being interrupted—would lead to ruin and destruction of everything human.[58] Drawing from the above, I suggest seeing the *inter*cultural philosophical polylogue precisely as a discourse in this sense. The common global world becomes human only when it is talked about and thereby created through the *inter*cultural plurality of humans and their critical and free speech.

Temporal Positioning

This emphasis on the humanizing aspect of discourse and the huge potential of political speech and action is confirmed especially in postcolonial contexts. In the multiple movements of empowerment, it is the action and the voice of the suppressed or subalterns who enter the stage to take part in shaping the world—a world from which they have been excluded for a long time. Thinkers like Frantz Fanon, Homi Bhabha, and Stuart Hall speak from places confronting a history of suppression. Even though they stress the dangers of nationalist or other forms of ideological exploitation of liberation slogans in the frame of identity discourses and independence struggles, they nevertheless try to introduce a discursive space of political agency.

In this context, Stuart Hall points out that, for political agency and self-confident action, identity is necessary. Hall is very much aware of the dilemmas that identity discourses and political agency are facing in marginalized contexts. On the one hand, there is often an all-too-easy identification with some ideology and, just as often, an application of the same mechanisms of exclusion that the subaltern is being confronted with by the dominating group. On the other hand, identity enables one to take a political standpoint, a position, in the global power structure. This is why Hall does not like to give up identity fully. But it is important to understand identity not as fixed or stable but, rather, as a processual formation shaped by differences.

For example, Hall considers that as long as one is confronted with the racist structures of exclusion, injustice, and marginalization in the context of liberation struggles and antiracist resistance, a counter-identification in the sense of an "imagined political new-identification" like "black identity"[59] is a necessary first step toward self-confidence.[60] Hall calls this "Identity Politics One." But because this "black" counter-identity still contains too much suppression—of, for example, the particular experiences of Asian people, the problem of gender inequalities, and the general social exclusion and discrimination that also affect white people—the first stage of identity politics finally needs to be exceeded.[61] Since the problem arises with a fixed understanding of identity, Hall stresses that identity is learned.[62] In Hall's words, identity is not "one" but is always "complexly composed" and "historically constructed." Identity is "never in the same *place* but always *positional*."[63] In the process of learning identity, one has to develop an awareness that every identity consists, in fact, of many social and cultural identities.

This is the basis for the second-degree identity politics of positioning.[64] Here positioning means the formation of a processual identity in and through differences. To make this point clear, Hall refers to Jacques Derrida's *différance* but is going one step beyond it by inserting "temporary 'break[s]'" into the infinite interplay of differences.[65] Since meaning, according to Hall, is constituted only in moments of break, the "'cut[s]' of identity"—the positionings—are not contradicting but, rather, specifying the *différance*.[66] The danger of misunderstanding appears only when these positionings are conceived as stable and permanent, even though they are hybrid, dynamic, and temporal. The taken position is never everlasting.

Following Hall, positioning appears as the process of creating temporal places from which one speaks. Those places are absolutely necessary for action—especially for political action in the sense used by Hannah Arendt. For Arendt, action takes place in the public space in between people. Taking a place, a position, a standpoint from where one speaks and acts, is basically necessary and even more important to stress in suppressed contexts. What is at stake here is *taking* a place for playing an active part in global discourse. This is why Hall defends the need to rescue a particular notion of identity in the form of positioning. The way Hall determines this notion is a perfect example of how taking a place takes place. Coming from somewhere, we choose a temporal position by which we can temporarily be identified and from which we can start to move, to speak, to act. In this way, Hall also stresses the processual event-character of places in the form of temporal positioning and pleads for beginning anew by taking a place in the in-between and thereby taking part in creating the world. I therefore would say that Hall, in accordance with Arendt, is implementing on the political level exactly what Sloterdijk thinks—in a very poetical way—is possible only in literature: "The free breath *takes positions* by inhaling and vacates them by exhaling. . . . Poems and other free said things are little breathing ships that expose themselves into the openness. This is the reason why free words are more important than big ones."[67]

As I hope the preceding reflections have shown, building on the assumption that philosophy is fundamentally platial does not necessarily lead to divisive relativism. Rather, what connects us is precisely the plurality of human beings, places, and cultures. Although born in different places, we can always begin anew by taking positions and, thus, come-to-the-world and act together in the *inter*cultural space. Plurality and natality are the preconditions for creating the world by acting, thinking, and speaking together. This creative and processual shaping of the world *takes place* in-between people. The "world" appears here, simultaneously, as both a *space* in-between and as an event-*place*. Expanding the words of Certeau in an intercultural direction, we can say that the worldly *inter*cultural in-between space is a practiced place.

Thinking in this event-place in-between is, I think, fundamentally *relational* and exceeds categorization as either universal or particular. Relationality here means being aware at once of particular cultural places and of the *inter*-space—the *inter*cultural connection, entanglement, and encounter of these places. According to this view, the main links between particular elements are not any kind of universals but, rather, are the *relations* between them. Starting from here, we might find commons[68] that are not fixed universals "from above" but the results of open, dynamic, and creative processes of encounter, exchange, and negotiation.

Finally, in relation to Mall's "situated unsituatedness" of philosophy and Janz' "philosophy-in-place," I suggest that the very active "taking place" of the *inter*cultural philosophical polylogue is marked by the conditions of natality, plurality, processuality, and relationality. In this sense, *inter*cultural philosophical thinking means coming-to-the-world, finding and taking temporal positions, and thus acting and creating the world together. *Inter*cultural philosophy therefore *is* not, but *takes place* first and foremost as an activity marked by an open attitude and a common practice between people in-between cultural spaces-in-place.

NOTES

1. Doris Bachmann-Medick, *Cultural Turns: Neuorientierungen in den Kulturwissenschaften* (Reinbek: Rowohlt, 2007), 297.
2. Ram Adhar Mall, "Intercultural Philosophy: A Conceptual Clarification," *Confluence: Online Journal of World Philosophies* 1 (2014): 69.
3. Ibid., 71.

4. Ibid.

5. Ram Adhar Mall, *Intercultural Philosophy* (Lanham, MD: Rowman and Littlefield, 2000), 4.

6. Ibid., 29.

7. Ibid.

8. Ibid., 10.

9. Ibid., 14–15.

10. Mall, "Intercultural Philosophy," 69.

11. Ram Adhar Mall, "Zur 'orthaften Ortlosigkeit' der philosophischen Rationalität: Eine interkulturelle Orientierung," in *Kreativität: XX. Deutscher Kongreß für Philosophie*, ed. Günther Abel (Hamburg: Meiner, 2006), 516.

12. Mall, *Intercultural Philosophy*, 15.

13. Ram Adhar Mall, *Indische Philosophie—Vom Denkweg zum Lebensweg: Eine interkulturelle Perspektive* (Freiburg: Verlag Karl Alber, 2015), 35.

14. Jonathan O. Chimakonam, "Conversational Philosophy as a New School of Thought in African Philosophy: A Conversation with Bruce Janz on the Concept of 'Philosophical Space,'" *Confluence: Online Journal of World Philosophies* 3 (2015): 31.

15. Bruce B. Janz, *Philosophy in an African Place* (Lanham, MD: Lexington Books, 2009), 213.

16. Ibid.

17. Ibid., 214.

18. Ibid., 1. The quotation is taken from Jacques Derrida, "Of the Humanities and the Philosophical Discipline: The Right to Philosophy from the Cosmopolitical Point of View," *Surfaces* IV.310 (1994): 1, http://pum.umontreal.ca/revues/surfaces/vol4/derrida .html.

19. Janz, *Philosophy in an African Place*, 1.

20. Ibid., 23.

21. In this context, I would briefly like to mention that there is a very vital and promising new movement in African philosophy, inaugurated by the so-called Calabar School of Philosophy and referred to by one of the leading figures, Jonathan O. Chimakonam, as "conversational philosophy." By this he means "the rigorous engagement of individual African philosophers with one another, or their works, in the creation of critical narratives using an African mode of thought." Consequently, in reference to Janz, Chimakonam sees African philosophy as "a platial enterprise commanding phenomenological preoccupations." See Chimakonam, "Conversational Philosophy," 22. See also Jonathan O. Chimakonam, ed., *Atuolu Omalu: Some Unanswered Questions in Contemporary African Philosophy* (Lanham, MD: University Press of America, 2015).

22. Janz, *Philosophy in an African Place*, 214.

23. Ibid., 26.

24. Ibid.

25. Ibid., 25.

26. Ibid., 5–6.

27. Ibid., 219 (emphasis added).

28. Ibid., 2 (emphasis added).

29. Ibid., 3.

30. Ibid., 4.

31. Ibid., 14 (emphasis added).

32. Michel de Certeau, *The Practice of Everyday Life* (Berkeley: University of California Press, 1984), 117.

33. Ibid.

34. Ibid.

35. Ibid.

36. Ibid.

37. Ibid., 118.

38. See also Rob Shields, who refers to Michel Serres. Rob Shields, "Can Place Prehend Philosophy?," in *Philosophie des Ortes: Reflexionen zum Spatial Turn in den Sozial- und Kulturwissenschaften*, ed. Annika Schlitte, Thomas Hünefeldt, Daniel Romic, and Joost van Loon (Bielefeld: Transcript Verlag, 2014), 112, 118.

39. According to Wimmer, a polylogue between representatives from as many cultural traditions as possible is "a conversation between *many* about one topic" and thus goes further than a dialogue, which is, literally speaking, a conversation between just two. Franz Martin Wimmer, *Interkulturelle Philosophie* (Vienna: WUV/UTB, 2004), 67n27 (my translation).

40. Peter Sloterdijk, *Zur Welt kommen—Zur Sprache kommen: Frankfurter Vorlesungen* (Frankfurt: Suhrkamp, 1988).

41. Peter Sloterdijk, *Eurotaoismus: Zur Kritik der politischen Kinetik* (Frankfurt: Suhrkamp, 1989).

42. Sloterdijk, *Zur Welt kommen*, 111. All translations of quotations from this book are mine.

43. Ibid., 155.

44. Ibid., 157.

45. Ibid., 153, 156.

46. The German word *Freispruch* is normally used in the juridical context and means "acquittal," or "the verdict of not guilty." Sloterdijk's very unconventional use has, thus, in German a very interesting resonance.

47. In German there are two words denoting birth. The first is the notion *Geburt*, which refers to the process of the child being born and takes thus the perspective of the child; Sloterdijk uses this term to denote the child's liberation. The second is the notion *Entbindung*, which refers to the process of disconnecting the umbilical cord and takes thus the perspective of the mother—in Sloterdijk's sense, her liberation.

48. Sloterdijk, *Zur Welt kommen*, 160.

49. Ibid.

50. Ibid.

51. Another reason might be the different spelling of the German word for natality. In *Eurotaoismus*, Sloterdijk uses the term *Geburtlichkeit* in reference to Hans Saner, who uses the same word in his book about the philosophical meaning of birth (Hans Saner, *Geburt und Phantasie* [Basel: Lenos, 1977], 128n64). Saner mentions his reference to Arendt's term *Gebürtlichkeit* (with an umlaut) in a footnote but omits the umlaut for a more common reading. Furthermore, it is remarkable that both men mention their—metaphorically speaking—"mother of philosophical thought" only in footnotes. As a reason, one can consider the will of both to initiate and develop(!) a philosophy of natality by themselves. Nevertheless, Hannah Arendt has to be regarded as the founder of a philosophy of birth.

52. Hannah Arendt, "On Humanity in Dark Times: Thoughts about Lessing," trans. Clara and Richard Winston, in *Men in Dark Times* (San Diego: Harcourt Brace, 1968), 4.

53. Hannah Arendt, *The Human Condition*, 2nd ed. (Chicago: University of Chicago Press, 1998), 9, 177.

54. Ibid., 8.

55. Ibid., 182.

56. Ibid., 182–183.

57. Arendt, "On Humanity," 24–25.

58. Arendt, *Human Condition*, 246.

59. Hall mentions elsewhere that the collective black identity is marked by a paradox: It was not a common origin but the shared historical experience of deportation and slavery that has been the unifying power. This shared experience was enough to create a unity

after the peoples of different origins lost their particular pasts. See Stuart Hall, "Cultural Identity and Diaspora," in *Colonial Discourse and Post-Colonial Theory: A Reader*, ed. Patrick Williams and Laura Chrisman (New York: Columbia University Press, 1994), 396.

60. Stuart Hall, "Old and New Identities, Old and New Ethnicities," in *Culture, Globalization and the World System*, ed. Anthony D. King (London: Macmillan, 1991), 52.

61. Ibid., 56–57.

62. Ibid., 55.

63. Ibid., 57 (emphasis added).

64. Stuart Hall developed his identity politics of positioning from the late 1980s on, and especially during the 1990s.

65. Hall, "Cultural Identity and Diaspora," 397.

66. Ibid.

67. Sloterdijk, *Zur Welt kommen*, 174–175 (emphasis added).

68. Concerning the notion of the "common," see Michael Hardt and Antonio Negri, *Commonwealth* (Cambridge, MA: Harvard University Press, 2011).

Place and Horizon 4

John W. M. Krummel

Wherever we are, we are *emplaced*, delimited by a horizon—not only literally but metaphorically, both semantically and ontologically. As we look in every direction, there is the horizon defining our world. Literally, this is the line demarcating the upper and lower hemispheres. The two surfaces—heaven and earth—meet at the horizon, constituting the finite space surrounding us.[1] As German phenomenologist Otto Bollnow emphasized, concrete human space is thus always finite: beyond every particular border or limit—of a room or building—there is the horizon (*Horizont*), in Greek meaning "that which bounds or limits" (*das Umgrenzende*).[2]

But this line is not immovable; it appears always in correlation to us so that as we move, it moves, and the farther we advance, the farther the horizon retreats. While it unfolds space for us, we can never step beyond it to its other side. Yet the horizon necessarily belongs to the world. Without a horizon, nothing will cohere. But it is not a thing in the world. On the one hand, it opens the place of spatial unfolding for us, and on the other hand, it bounds it. Kyoto School philosopher Ueda Shizuteru 上田閑照 thus states that the horizon opens and limits.[3] The later Heidegger—for example, in *Zur Sache des Denkens* (On time and being)—preferred to no longer use the Husserlian terminology of the horizon but still had something similar in mind when speaking of the clearing (*Lichtung*) as the "openness [*Offenheit*] that grants a possible letting-appear and showing."[4] The space of meaning thus opened nevertheless implies uncanniness that escapes our grasp. In this chapter, I examine and develop this idea and unpack its ontological and ethical implications, especially in our contemporary situation, where we encounter a plurality of others and find ourselves in the vast expanse of the universe. To do so, I make use of ideas found in some contemporary German and Japanese thinkers—Martin Heidegger, Karl Jaspers, Otto Bollnow, Günter Figal, Bernhard Waldenfels, Nishida Kitarō, and Ueda Shizuteru, among others—but the prime purpose is to develop our own phenomenological understanding of place in relation to horizon and alterity.

Our emplacement within a horizon is not just literal or geographical but also has figurative or metaphorical meaning. Bollnow, for example, notices that there is a horizon for the world of the intellect that gives one a particular perspective or worldview.[5] Such intellectual perspectives with distinct horizons are not one but many. They not only are individual but also can be of a collective, such as of a nation or people or of an age. And knowledge in general has a horizon. Karl Jaspers states that we always live within the horizon of our knowledge.[6] We strive to get beyond that horizon but can never attain a standpoint where the limiting horizon disappears in order to survey the *whole* of reality, without horizon. No matter how far the horizon is expanded, the object is within the particular range of the possible, and its other side is beyond the known. Or if we surpass one particular horizon, we find another horizon surrounding the previous one. We secure no standpoint from which to survey the whole of being.[7] Every mode of knowledge in that sense is inadequate insofar as it is confined to a particular *mode* of reality.[8] Every horizon points to a further horizon, and Jaspers (in both *Reason and Existence* of 1935 and *Philosophy of Existence* of 1937) had this situation in mind when he spoke of "the encompassing" or "the embracing" (*das Umgreifende*), which he proposed as what transcends and comprehensively envelops every possible horizon, while always seeming to *recede* from us—akin to Heidegger's notion of the clearing or the regioning (*Gegnen*)—to make each relative horizon possible from yonder. For Jaspers this is the unknowable "whole as the most extreme, self-supporting ground of being."[9]

I think the most important and general aspect of a horizon in its figurative or metaphorical sense is that it is semantic; it constitutes a world of meanings. The world we inhabit is meaningful, and every place within it is loaded with specific meanings, differentiated in distinct ways, such as preferred and avoided areas, and so forth.[10] These significances and meanings fill our experience of space, overlapping the space of the physical world. This semantic dimension of space is what Günter Figal calls hermeneutical space.[11] For Figal, in his book *Gegenständlichkeit* (Objectivity), that hermeneutical space consists of the lifeworld (in Husserl's sense) together with the thing-world,[12] the latter being the space of things to be de-removed.[13] Ueda likewise believes that the world for us is a semantic space wherein events occur as bearing meaning as they pass through a linguistic framework whereby they can be articulated and understood.[14] The danger for Ueda, however, is that this language world can become a great birdcage in which we become entrapped. Humankind orders its space, assigning things their place and position, linked in meaningful connections, integrating them into the surrounding cosmos.[15] In Heidegger's *Sein und Zeit* (Being and time), things are linked together within an overreaching area, or "region" (*Gegend*), for practical purposes. Experienced space in general thus represents a meaningfully structured totality of places.

What is clear is that such space constituting the meaningful world as a whole has a horizon. In distinction from abstract mathematical space, which is homogeneous and infinite, concrete lived space as such is heterogeneous and finite, demarcated by a horizon. And within that space, order demarcates that distinction between possibilities and impossibilities, excluding the possibility of the institution of new orders—such an institution can happen only from *beyond* the horizon and cannot be anticipated from within. Through the process of ordering, things—inanimate, living, plants, animals, humans, natural, artificial, and so on—are demarcated from one another, and each is delimited from its surroundings and defined as what it is. The *cosmos* as the totality of such things embodies *order as such*.[16] Space is thus articulated through processes of differentiation within the *cosmos qua order*, assigning each being its suitable place. Thereby, each thing can show itself *as something X* within the semantic context of the world.[17] Space as such within the horizon is oriented in correspondence with meanings and accordingly heterogeneous. Mathematical homogeneous space, phenomenologically speaking, can only be derivative of that semantic heterogeneity. But the space of meanings as a whole—the world—in itself is demarcated by its horizon from the asemantic, from nonmeaning. As Ueda notes, place by definition is finite, delimited, demarcated. We are inevitably delimited in our being-in-the-world, our emplacement, by the horizon as such.

For Nishida Kitarō 西田幾多郎, the starting point was that to be is to be emplaced. In the initial formulations of his theory of place (*basho* 場所) in 1926, his concern was primarily epistemological, and his attention was turned inward to the workings of consciousness and the depths of self-awareness that unfolds and points to the place of pure experience preceding the subject-object split. Place was positioned to underlie the field of consciousness (*ishiki no ba* 意識の場) in permitting the interrelationship of form and matter, concepts and sensation.[18] Within that place, all beings can be emplaced to be objectified and taken up as the subject (*shugo* 主語) of a statement. That is, beings have meaning, identified as X, within the *place* of the self. Having considered the self in such platial terms, Nishida turns his attention *outward* in the 1930s to the social and historical world (*shakaiteki rekishiteki sekai* 社会的歴史的世界) as the medium (*baikaisha* 媒介者) wherein the epistemological subject comes to know his or her object and wherein free subjects can interrelate as I and thou, self and other. The self that is platial, irreducible to any particular *thing*, is thus opened to the place *wherein* it is emplaced. The I self-aware that "I am a teacher" is thus opened to that place—the context—wherein teacher and students are co-emplaced and coexist.[19] And place, in Ueda's reading of Nishida, in each case as a concrete semantic place is juxtaposed with other places, which are multilayered, one upon another.[20] On this basis the multilayeredness and co-being of multiple places converge in the world (*sekai* 世界) as the final comprehensive place.[21]

Our emplacement within the world that is necessarily horizoned seems to be an essential feature of our existence. As Bollnow states, the horizon belongs inseparably to humans; we only live within it and can never escape its bond.[22] The horizon is then ontological. And while many philosophers, most notably Kant and Heidegger (of *Being and Time*), have underscored the experience of time as an essential condition of our finite transcendence, this horizonal structure of our being-in-the-world in itself seems to indicate an essential spatiality as constitutive of our way of being.[23] Heidegger does work out the spatiality of human existence in *Being and Time* when he says, "The subject, being-(t)here, if well understood ontologically, is spatial [*räumlich*]."[24] He recognized that humans are conditioned by their comportments in relation to the surrounding space, which he discusses in terms of "being-in" (*In-Sein*) (in "being-in-the-world" [*In-der-Welt-sein*]) as an *existentiale* of our "being-(t)here."[25] He viewed the world that we are thrown into, and simultaneously project, as the semantic context—network of meanings—for our comportments to beings hermeneutically discovered within it. Things thus discovered are positioned in their spatiality as handy or available (*zuhanden*) in reference to our own spatiality as being-in-the-world through their "de-distancing" or "de-removing" (*Entfernung*) and our "orientation" or "directionality" (*Ausrichtung*).[26] In the end, Heidegger buries this spatial analysis under the primacy of temporality as the ultimate condition of our spatiality. But Bollnow, taking off from Heidegger and extending his spatial analysis further, argues that the horizon "belongs to the transcendental condition of the human being-in-the-world [*transzendentalen Verfassung des menschlichen In-der-Welt-seins*]" and as such belongs inseparably to the spatiality of human existence.[27]

Ueda, in his 1992 work *Basho: Nijū sekai naisonzai* (Place: Being-in-the-twofold-world), contributes to our understanding of this ontological spatiality vis-à-vis the horizon in his analysis of the duplicity of the world as on the one hand demarcating a realm of determinacy, a semantic space that constitutes the world, and as on the other hand pointing to its *other* on its other side, the exteriority escaping that demarcation or delimitation of the world. The horizon opens space but also binds it. This binding points to the *other* side, which as Ueda states is the fundamental negation of *this* side, an indeterminacy *beyond* the horizon whereby the horizon and everything within it is *determined, determinate, de-limited*. As its unknown "other side"—"the other side of the horizon" (*chihei no kanata* 地平の彼方)—it constitutes the restriction of the possibility of the horizon itself.[28] Every horizon emerges from its yonder and disappears into its yonder.[29] It draws a boundary whereby an *inside* is separated from the *outside*, the *alien* or *strange*.[30] That *other* to the horizon is thus indispensable to its structure.[31] In that sense the horizon, while emplacing us within the familiar, the homely, points beyond itself to the unknown, the unfamiliar—the wilderness beyond the *polis*, the *chaos* beyond the *cosmos*—what ontologically is a nothing, or semantically without meaning, an *excess* irreducible to semantic or ontological determination. Hence, place at the limit-point of its horizon implies the interface of meaning and a-meaning, *nomos* and anomie, order and chaos, principles and *anarché*, or in Nishidian terms being (*yū* 有) and nothing (*mu* 無), in Heideggerian terms unconcealment (*Unverborgenheit*) and concealment (*Verborgenheit*). We are set *on the inside of* the horizon, at home in our familiar environment, but facing outward, we are surrounded by the unfamiliar, the uncanny. Our emplacement is thus twofold: *in* the world but facing *out to* what lies beyond the horizon. And we might say that this difference between in and out, own and other, set by the horizon, as the process of "originary difference" or "primordial distinction,"[32] proves to be the very *institution* (*Stiftung*) of the world. In facing that horizon, we stand "as on the brink of an abyss," filled within infinite possibilities.[33]

In relation to the horizon itself and its primal distinction, difference in general implies a certain spatiality, its most elemental form being the here-there distinction, implicit in all forms of *other*-ing. Figal, questioning whether the experience of time is truly primary, argues that the finitude of our being-in-the-world is first discerned from the fact that we live in space, wherein our finite transcendence is animated by our confrontation with the *exteriority* of entities—*Gegenstand*, in the literal sense of something standing (*stehen*) *against* (*gegen*) me, resisting me, as *other*. Our experience of things along with ourselves is guided by a hermeneutical space enabling our interpretation and understanding of them. For Figal, the world is the whole of this hermeneutical space encompassing the human sphere of meaning, values, norms, but also the sphere of things that comes into tension with the former. We create the world of meaning in our encounter with things and the realm of things simultaneously sustains and limits our creation of meaning. The implication is that things, as literally "standing-against" us, are indicative of an excess or alterity to the horizon of meaning. Space for Figal entails expanse and removal (*Entfernung*: distance, absence),[34] the latter whereby things show themselves as *other* than me. Things are at a remove because they do not yet belong to the "proximity of things as one's own or as things familiar."[35]

In a certain sense, Immanuel Kant had already recognized this alterity of things in terms of an "exteriority" that precedes cognition when he spoke of objects represented as "outside" (*außer*) and of the reference of sensations to something "'outside' of oneself."[36] Self-consciousness is made possible by this reference to something as *outside*. What is indicated here in our mode of existence as finite and receptive, coming into contact with things *other* than ourselves,[37] is a precognitive spatiality that, according to Figal, is no longer to be conceived as a priori. It is the space in which one locates oneself to traverse toward the other.[38] This space releases our impulse to *de-remove* (or "de-distance") (*ent-fernen* from *Ent-fernung*), integrate, order, appropriate, them into the network of proximate things, bring them into the horizon. Human existence is thus spatial, moving in the expanse between there and here. Exteriority is always implied as an unrestricted remove ("distance") in all relations of space.[39] And the proximity of the surrounding world is due only to remove as such;[40] it points to its *other* preceding any thematization. The fact that we are emplaced, in-the-world, de-limited by a horizon, in our semantic field, necessarily implies that exteriority, the *other*, the *not* to our place, lying beyond the horizon, on its *other* side.

We can also speak of this other in terms of a happening bursting into our horizon from the outside at the limit of our world. The alien (*fremd*) as event (*Ereignis, événement*) interrupts familiar formations and makes its appearance as *extra*-ordinary, failing to be identified as something meaningful within the semantic framework on this side of the horizon. In its excess it is irreducible to any sense given within the framework and diverts from any such meaningfulness to disturb, disrupt, or interfere.[41] But in doing so, it inspires curiosity and wonder, provoking new institutions or foundings (*Stiftungen*) of an order, inaugurating or disclosing new fields of sense, establishing new meanings or new symbolic orders. Entering our lifeworld unsummoned, unexpected, it affects us, provokes sense, but without itself having sense, without itself finding its place within the given order, without functioning as a part of what it makes possible.[42] In our receptivity—Waldenfels calls this *pathos*—that *other*, not yet our own, not at our disposal, senseless and goalless, *happens to* us, overcoming, stirring, surprising us, disturbing our projects, arriving from *elsewhere* as a "limit phenomenon" or "hyperphenomenon."[43] An example might be cancer that creeps onto us from nowhere. Even if we are able to eventually ascribe to that happening some significance and identify it as something X within our world (an "accomplishment of sense"), this always implies, as a *heterogenesis*, a certain hiatus or temporal-spatial gap—a *diastasis*, as Waldenfels calls it—from its originary event, a *primal forgetting (Urvergessen)* of its exteriority to the horizon as an appropriation that comes too late but nonetheless overshadows that primal alterity.[44] For example, we can locate and date the founding of Rome or the birth of Christ or the Buddha, the fall of the Berlin Wall or the attack on the World Trade Center (which we now designate "9/11"), and register it within the existing order proceeding from it, but the event itself is outside the horizon it inaugurates.[45] In *itself (sich)* it is always *more than* and *other than* what it seems to be, *more than* what can be subsumed to a rule.[46] Its uniqueness as singular is an *excess* to what can be meaningfully placed within the horizon. Its happening was anonymously *given*, whereby—as Heidegger says—"there is/ it gives (*es gibt*)" order or truth. Despite that hiatus, we cannot deny the alterity that meaning covers over and that, as Figal shows, belongs to even the most familiar things of everyday as their *other* side. In that sense the *other* as *beyond* the horizon of our familiar meaningful world is not just *over there but also here in our very midst.*

Moreover, if self-reference requires alien-reference, no one is merely who they are; alienness begins in one's own home.[47] Even our own embodied self is not at all transparent to us; our body is filled with riddles, first and foremost birth and death as limit events that happen *to me* as a patient rather than as their agent.[48] In that sense we are never absolute owners of ourselves. Our own identity originates from *beyond* the horizon. As liminal beings we partake in a "liminal alienness."[49] Even one's thoughts and ideas *come to* oneself; they sound their voices in one's mind, of which one cannot take possession.[50] Counter to Descartes's postulation of the *cogito ergo sum*, Nietzsche recognized an "it" of "it thinks" (*Es denkt*) behind our thoughts,[51] Merleau-Ponty spoke of an "it" in "it perceives" (*on perçoit*),[52] and of course there is Freud's "Es" (Id) operating in our unconscious.[53] Nishida, for example, acknowledged an alterity that he called "absolute other" (*zettai no ta* 絶対の他) within the depths of the self.[54] And Dōgen 道元 as well had famously stated in his *Genjōkōan*, "To study one's self is to forget one's self; to forget one's self is to be confirmed by all things in the universe."[55] Our situation "here" in the world is filled with a "not-here," an *other* that has always already invaded from beyond the horizon, permeating our familiar environment. Just as one is never completely in possession of oneself, one can never feel completely at home in one's tribe, nation, or house.[56] We are never master of our own house, because we cannot keep the uncanny away.[57] The alien as a *xenos topos* (alien place) underlies our world and being, our proper *oikeios topos* (home place).[58] As Waldenfels states, alienness is not only beyond the given order as its *other side* but also found on *this side* of order; in preceding and exceeding order, the *extra*-ordinary permeates order with *infra*-ordinary roots.[59] Surrounding us in both space and time—exceeding the horizon of the world and encompassing birth and death—it permeates meaning and being, self and world.

Hence, it is not only being-toward-death or temporality that shapes our horizon but, more primordially, *being-toward-other* and its spatiality that shapes the horizon and our being as liminal beings. Contrary to what Heidegger argued in 1927, if our relationship to the horizon shapes the unfolding of the world, our being-toward-other would be just as constitutive as—or even more so than—our being-toward-death. The horizon points to an alterity of which death is only one instance—as Peter Berger (in *Sacred Canopy*) noticed when he took death as a phenomenon of *anomie* in relation to *nomos*.[60] Even Heidegger, after 1930, moves away from the primacy of time to recognize the ontological significance of alterity in the clearing (*Lichtung*) of being as indicated in his notion of the "turning" (*Kehre*).[61]

The horizon in these senses—as Ueda argues—is twofold, facing within and without. The horizon's *beyond*, as discontinuous with what is on this side of it, is the world's fundamental negation—a-meaning, nonbeing. Ordinarily we are concerned with, taken by, what appears *upon* the horizon, *within* the world, and we forget that there is the dark other side of the horizon.[62] We can be aware of this darkness only as limits to our light, but we cannot directly shine our light upon it. That is our situation. Whether one speaks of place or of horizon, no matter how multilayered, by definition it is limited, de-limited by what is exterior to the place, what is beyond the horizon. That exteriority or alterity as such constitutes the very condition for the horizon's possibility. And the expanse that exteriority implies is undelimitable. As Ueda states, place entails in its own delimited emplacement an unlimited or unbounded open-ness (*unendliche Offenheit*; *mugen no hirake* 無限の開け) wherein it is emplaced.[63] The world as a comprehensive semantic space, the whole frame of meanings, within which are implicated innumerable semantic interconnections, is delim-ited, finite, emplaced within the boundless open that exceeds the bounds of sense/meaning.[64] Jaspers, in his discussion of the encompassing, also spoke of an "open, horizonless realm encompassing all horizons."[65] But that excess or alterity also permeates the world on this side of the horizon. Our emplacement is a being-in-the-world-in-the-abyss, the abyssal expanse that envelops *both* this side of the horizon—the meaningful world—*and* the other side of the horizon that exceeds meaning.

In ontological terms, in terms of "something that is," that exteriority is a *nothing*, although Jaspers and Heidegger also named that nothing *Sein*, which in its withdrawal makes beings possible. Waldenfels has suggestively related the sense of absence of the alien—what Figal calls "remove"—to the Chinese con-cept of nothingness (*wu* 無), as distinct from a mere negative predication with the particle "not" (*bu* 不), by evoking darkness and emptiness.[66] The nothing in this sense opens the space for the horizon, allowing for the world to be set up. Heidegger in *Was ist Metaphysik?* (What is metaphysics?) states that only by being held-out into the nothing (*sich in das Nichts hineinhält*) can the human being-(t)here (*Dasein*) be open and relate to beings.[67] The wholeness of beings as a whole—world as world (*Welt als Welt*) as the coherence of beings—can be such only by being determined, delimited, by the nothing.[68] Thus in being *in* the world, our "(t)here" is "held-out-into-the-nothing." And, as Ueda explains, the various meanings of being "as . . . (X)" are birthed not only from their contextual interrelations but also from a certain symphony with its surround-ing empty space akin to how the margins shape a text.[69] The world, on the one hand, is the semantic field as a whole, the totality of networks of significances, whereby things *are* with meaning. But, on the other hand, the world is manifest as such, through its horizon, in its delimitation from an undelimitable nothing. While the world on this side of its horizon is limited, bound, and hence coher-ent, the nothing on the other side of the horizon continues on into the endless open, surrounding and enveloping what lies within it and permeating it as an underlying emptiness. In Ueda's formulation, the world is thus emplaced in the nothing. For Bollnow, this is a "free space" (*freie Raum*) or "infinitely open space" (*unendlich offene Raum*), transcending and surrounding the environing space (*Umraum*) of our experience.[70] Ueda also calls this the "open expanse" (*kokū* 虚空) that envelops the horizon, both its interior side and its exterior side, and he equates it with Nishida's place of absolute nothing (*zettai mu no basho* 絶対無の場所).[71] In being "thrown into the world," we are thus thrown into "the nothing of the world," the nothing that delimits the world.[72] And thus "being-(t)here is emplaced in the world emplaced in the nothing" (*gensonzai wa, mu ni oitearu sekai ni oitearu* 現存在は無においてある世界においてある).[73] Since the world is emplaced in the boundless open, our existence is "emplaced in the world emplaced in the endless open [*mugen no hirake*]" or emplaced in the "world/open expanse" (*sekai/kokū* 世界/虚空).[74] Ueda calls this situation being-in-the-twofold-world (*nijū sekai naisonzai* 二重世界内存在): we are in the everyday life-world of significances that is itself emplaced in the open expanse enveloping that world.[75] For Bollnow, humans are thus a part of, and are supported in, the great encompassing space (*großen umfassenden Raum*).[76] While being-in-the-world, we thus also ex-sist (*datsu-ji* 脱自)—that is, as nonsubstantial ex-sistences[77]—in that unbounded openness.[78] From out of that nothing, the world determines itself, as Nishida stated, and the world worlds, as Heidegger stated. The nothing as such is the inexhaustibility, excess, *of being itself* that is not only on the *other* side of the horizon but also permeates and surrounds us and—as Jaspers stated about the reality of any individual thing—permits unlimited interpretation and reinterpretation.[79]

And that nothing beyond the horizon as an excess beyond order is also *chaos.* Since ancient times, connections have been made among chaos, nothing, and the indeterminate expanse. According to Mircea Eliade in *Das Heilige und das Profane* (The sacred and the profane), the space of the world, the *cosmos* as comprehending all, as conceived in ancient myths was a finite space, but surrounding that ordered universe is the unknown and indeterminate space that is no longer a cosmos but a chaos.[80] For Hesiod (in the *Theogony*),[81] *chaos* (χάος) is *where* cosmic ordering takes place and has this sense of an indeterminate openness[82] that makes room for determinations, an idea that later evolves into the etymologically related concept of *chōra* (χώρα). We might note that in the meantime the ancient Chinese also viewed *chaos* (*hundun* 混沌) qua nothing (*wu* 無) as the source of cosmic ordering, which centuries later then evolved into the Kyoto School's notion of the nothing as the place of the world, as we see in Nishida. As in the Mahayana saying, true emptiness is wondrous being. And yet we forget this primal chaos as our concerns are directed toward the intraworldly (beings, ordered with meaning)—that is, what lies on this side of the horizon, in contrast to which it is but nothing. The nothing becomes concealed, hidden, by what is—beings—that it allows to manifest.[83] The task of philosophy might then be to open us up to, remind us of, this "breadth and depth," a wondrous but hidden excess.

But because of its abyssal nature and incomprehensibleness, providing no secure ground—leaving us with the sense of losing hold or losing horizon— our response when we are forced to confront the nothing, as Heidegger recognized, is anxiety (*Angst*).[84] What primordially and directly opens the world as delimited by the nothing, for Heidegger, is anxiety.[85] While understanding (*Verstehen*) discloses the world in accordance with its meaningfulness (the semantic network of intraworldly things), anxiety discloses the world's wholeness by exposing the nothing delimiting that wholeness.[86] In anxiety, we are exposed to the nothing, and thus: "The totality of relations . . . discovered within the world . . . [,] as a whole, is without significance. The world has the character of complete meaninglessness."[87] After the revolution in spatial consciousness started by the discoveries of Copernicus and Columbus, Pascal (in *Pensées*) wrote that "the eternal silence of these infinite spaces fills me with dread."[88] Focusing on these words, Bollnow suggests how we come to be gradually dominated by "the sense of being lost [*Gefühl der Verlorenheit*], the ultimate loneliness [*letzten Verlorenheit*] . . . in this space."[89] But Ueda suggests that this is due to these spaces being experienced strictly from within the bounds of the familiar.[90] Ueda argues that the nothing disclosed through anxiety is only how it becomes manifest initially to one who has forgotten the nothing that envelops and delimits the world to begin with.[91] Anxiety's disclosure of the nothing thus demands a further conversion to its more originary disclosure as one's very "(t)here."[92] When toward the end of *What Is Metaphysics?* Heidegger speaks of "letting oneself free into the nothing" (*das Sichloslassen in das Nichts*), Ueda interprets this to mean entering without reserve into the nothing, whereby one breaks through the mood of anxiety and the originary disclosure of the nothing becomes the (t)here of one's being-(t)here. For Ueda, this anticipates a leaping turn in the later Heidegger from the anxiety when exposed to the nothing to "releasement" (*Gelassenheit*) that sets one free into the nothing,[93] involving a qualitative leap from the understanding of the semantic interconnections— of the intraworldly, on *this side* of the horizon—to the *other* that embraces and exceeds that interconnectivity. Bollnow adds to this a suggestive claim, citing Gaston Bachelard's *La poétique de l'espace* (The poetics of space), that even space, despite its infinity, in its concrete experience retains the character of a sheltering hollow space (*eines bergenden Hohlraums*), whereby "the world is a nest" (*le monde est un nid*).[94] For Bollnow, the issue is to allow oneself to trust and be supported in that greater space (*große Raum*), exterior to one's home, whereby it loses its menacing character and becomes a sheltering space (*bergenden Raum*), wherein one dwells.[95] Just as one might dwell in a house, one dwells more comprehensively in space: one finds oneself in it, moves in it, and is a part of it, *is* it. Once we see this, we realize we are supported and sheltered by it.[96] We do not have to feel anxious, once we see that we dwell within the open expanse enveloping both the world and its other and that both sides of the horizon are necessary for our being. In Dōgen's terms, it is the water fish swim, the sky birds fly.[97]

Nevertheless, it is due to this expanse in excess to any meaning we ascribe to things or would project upon the world—the implicit necessity of its alterity as *other*, *exterior* to the horizon—that the horizon cannot simply be confined to the sphere of transcendental subjectivity. This is so, even if it is the case that the horizon always moves with oneself and as such "belongs to the transcendental condition of the human being-in-the-world."[98] For that alterity as such is eternally hidden from and beyond the subject's reach, and the expanse encompassing that alterity also encompasses the self as that *wherein* it is amidst things encountered as *other*. We cannot deny the alterity in our very midst in the things of what Figal calls the thing-world as the resistant *other* side of our lifeworld of meaningful appropriations. The later (post-1930) Heidegger, as alluded to above, attempts to move beyond any residual transcendentalism of being-(t)here by emphasizing releasement as ontological, taking place from the side of being itself that humans can only let-be. We are reminded of Dōgen's famous saying: "To practice and realize all things by conveying one's self to them is illusion; for all things to advance forward and authenticate the self is enlightenment."[99]

During the 1940s, Heidegger describes this sense of letting in spatial terms as the regioning or regionalizing (*Gegnen*) that occurs from beyond the horizon. He also speaks of the worlding of the world as no longer simply an existential constituent of humankind's being-in-the-world. Nishida, in the 1930s and 1940s, having turned his attention outward and no longer exclusively focusing on the interiority of the self-aware individual, analogously goes on to speak of the place of absolute nothing as determining itself in the world of which human individuals are expressions even as they are co-constituents. Perhaps in response to any misgivings concerning the transcendentalist implications of the phenomenological term "horizon," Ueda supplements this term with the expression, using a fraction symbol, "world/open expanse." The point seems to be that the world in which we *are* is itself amidst an open expanse that exceeds the world within the horizon while encompassing its other side, whereby the twofold horizon is at the same time nullified within the onefold of the open expanse. But he also eventually comes to accompany this by using the fraction in reverse as "open expanse/world," as if to express how the open expanse not only is outside of the world but penetrates and permeates it throughout. Returning to Dōgen's metaphor momentarily, in his terms this might be the water through which fish swim without seeking to exit it.[100] The point still is to look beyond one's myopic view onto the other side of the horizon, to see the open expanse permeating into this side of the horizon, to recognize, as Dōgen put it, that even "green mountains always walk" (青山常運歩).[101]

In its contact with that unassimilable or irreducible excess beyond, the horizon's line of demarcation at the interface between being and nothing is itself contingent, in flux, and unpredictable. In pointing to the alterity of the *beyond*, it is itself altering. The world facing alterity at its horizon is in alteration. The horizon that constitutes our place or world, entailing *both* finitude within *and* openness beyond, entails alterity and alteration. The place determined within its horizon will thus always be provisional, despite any appearance or claims to the contrary. The order of the world is never complete. Its determination is indeterminate. And yet, despite, and because of that inherent indeterminacy, the horizon is necessary for human existence, which requires meaning, coherence, order.[102] The horizon "prevents one from getting lost, and gives one the means to determine one's situation."[103] Humanity requires space, but that space must be defined, determined, and delimited from without and ordered within. The structured space regulates our movements toward the *outside* and back to our *inside*, back and forth, in our day-to-day living.

Bollnow explains how the system of spatial relationships is structured from our dwelling outward: one goes forth from one's home, exposes oneself to the dangers of a potentially hostile world to perform errands, fulfil tasks, or achieve some goal and then returns to rest in the shelter of one's dwelling.[104] The dwelling place is the organizational center to which the places one goes are spatially related; and when one moves to a new dwelling place, the world is reconstructed anew around that new home.[105] In this organizational spatial structuring of one's world, the horizon not only provides a limit but opens a field for one's vision and movement in space.[106] And in this opening of a field of movement, we might be enticed to expand our horizons and to seek our lost home in the distance when we feel lost in the busyness of everyday life and are no longer "at home" in our home or feel alienated by it.[107] It is then that the chaos or the nothing is attractive. In pointing to the *other* side, the unbounded expanse, the horizon, uncovers our homelessness and entices us to seek where we belong in the vast and fading distance. By wandering out, we break out of the stratification, rigidity, of our home. It is a release from narrowness,[108] whereby one gains contact with the deeper purposeless (un)ground of one's life—for as Meister Eckhart says, in the depths of one's being, life is without why—and one experiences rejuvenation.[109]

Through contact with the nothing, one broadens the horizon and revitalizes one's world and one's life. And so humans are both wanderers and dwellers, centered and eccentric.[110] For Bollnow, our inner health depends on the equilibrium of these two sides.[111] But it is also the case that such rejuvenation may occur unexpectedly as a fundamental experience at the very edge of the horizon, where in its unpredictability it opens a vista into the dark and unassimilable expanse on the other side, in a qualitative rupture that breaks us out of the familiar world, evoking in one a prelinguistic, preintellectual response of astonishment or wonder, *thaumazein*.[112] And in response, vis-à-vis that expanse, we are called to a journey, to wander, to make our homelessness home. As a liminal being, the human, despite being finite, being bounded, "is not locked in by fixed boundaries."[113] Our home is constructed and deconstructed amidst this perpetual homelessness.

To depict this homelessness, Heidegger uses the motif of the river (*der Strom*) from Hölderlin's poetry, with its ever-flowing nature wherein one must set up a place (*Ort*) for one's poetic dwelling. While the river provides the locality of the place (*die Ortschaft des Ortes*) where one belongs, where one is homely (*heimisch*),[114] Heidegger also understands the river in terms of humanity's "journeying" (*Wanderschaft*) as "ever on the way." The river flows on, continuously establishing distinctive places for human dwelling.[115] The abode (*Aufenthalt*) that dwelling (*wohnen*) takes is thus a "lingering" or "whiling" (*Verweilen*) in the midst of journeying.[116] That is, possibilities are released in the spatializing alignment and realignment of boundaries, horizons, to permit a rest—for a "while." The river's journeying (*Wanderschaft*) and its locality (*Ortschaft*) of place (*Ort*) are in dynamic tension: the river is *both* the place where humanity makes its home *and* the journeying whereby humanity searches for and establishes its home.[117] This simultaneity of journeying and locality means, for Heidegger, humanity's "becoming-homely" (*Heimischwerden*) in its very "being-unhomely" (*Unheimischsein*).

This journeying entails a homeless wandering *into* the *other*, whereby we are torn onward upon the river's path, out of the habitual, out of our *own* selves, and into a "foreign land."[118] Ownness, the home, the native, is to be discovered only via and vis-à-vis the other, the homeless, the foreign (*fremd*).[119] Places and their horizons are thus never completely stabilized, for the river continuously flows as the "bearer" of a yet-to-be-unveiled "meaning" (*Bedeutung*) for human dwelling.[120] "Homecoming" is thus in a dynamic correlation with our "exile." The two features of the river—locality and journeying—are inextricably linked so that even in being at home, we are in fact perpetually homeless, wandering, journeying to discover anew our "home" upon the vast open expanse. "Poetic dwelling," for Heidegger (in his reading of Hölderlin), is this becoming-homely (*Heimischwerden*) in being-unhomely (*Unheimischsein*), being "at home" *precisely in* this homelessness.[121] Only thus do we attain our ownmost (authentic) being-at-home. It calls for us to recognize our contingency or finitude vis-à-vis the horizon, and its contingency and its *beyond*, amidst the open expanse.

That is one possible approach to the globalization of the world amidst the expanse that destabilizes our world in the face of the diversity of *other* worlds. Today we face the reality of a multiplicity of intercultural worlds varying historically and geographically.[122] Globalization provokes the anxiety we feel in the face of the other. Before the global relativization of the spatial order of the cosmos, as with Columbus' "discovery" of America, each nation considered its country to be the center.[123] With the rounding of the earth's surface into a sphere, the secure ground of a distinctive center had been lost, so that we can no longer believe that the place where our people reside is the world's center.[124] But it is also the case that throughout human history, "home-worlds" have been transformed into "alien-worlds"—and vice versa—through migrations, conquests, deportations.[125] So Kristeva says, "We are all aliens."[126] And yet, as Nietzsche (in *Thoughts out of Season*, or *Untimely Meditations*) recognized, there is health, strength, and productivity only within a certain horizon drawn around oneself.[127] The forming of a horizon to shape our world becomes a creative task. For Bollnow, this means the right balance between assimilation and acquisition of the foreign. Ueda adds that the world of multiplicity needs to be brought together via "mutual critique and mutual supplementation between . . . traditions."[128] What is to be resisted is the superficial, but thoroughgoing, homogenization brought on by globalization cementing uniformity over differences.[129] The better route, for Ueda, is a keen awareness and experience of the reciprocal heterogeneity between different cultural modes of being, as exemplified in the encounter of Zen and philosophy in Nishida.[130] As we open our horizons to the rich diversity of ways of being—opening to *other horizons* as the *horizons of others*—we can encounter others likewise expanding their horizons, meeting in mutual enrichment without an erasure of difference. No longer with a privileged center but also precluding the suffocation of diversity under uniformity, we need to acknowledge a polycentric world ultimately made possible by the open expanse beyond horizons.

Neither can the human world, the *polis*, ignore its surrounding wilderness, the wild, the nonhuman *other* beyond the space of ordered utility. Of course, even the landscape beyond the urban-technical areas is humanly structured, with planted gardens, tilled fields, and so on. But at the limits of human development, the truly untouched landscape opens up, no longer shaped by human desires, where space is no longer organized according to our needs.[131] This was implied by the originary sense of the Greek *chōra*, prior to Plato's appropriation of the term, that Nishida drew inspiration from for his idea of place. But if we think of Nishida's conception of the place of absolute nothing, the pre-Platonic sense of *chōra* and its etymological link to Hesiod's *chaos* from the *Theogony*—*chōra* that in turn is derived from the verb *chainō* for "opening"—may be closer to what Nishida had in mind. The ancient Athenians, for example, understood *chōra*—variously translated as place, space, land, country, earth, field, territory, and area—to be the region called Attica.[132] The ancient Greeks took *chōra* in its everyday usage as the land or country surrounding the city or town, providing their habitat, the concrete terrain or region wherein they dwell and constituting their landscape.[133] On this basis Augustin Berque, for example, interprets *chōra* as designating the immeasurable opening that constitutes our concrete milieu upon the earth.[134] One's environing conditions extend beyond the world and into the earth in this sense of the nonhuman other.

In 1935, in "Der Ursprung des Kunstwerkes" (The origin of the work of art), Heidegger speaks of the primal strife (*Urstreit*) between earth (*Erde*) and world (*Welt*) that clears space.[135] Even while supporting the world, the earth refuses its ways in its "a-historical and pre-cultivated materiality."[136] That resistance—like a horizon—opens while defining the space of human significations, the world. During the 1940s, Heidegger also had drawn inspiration from the notion of *chōra*[137] in developing his understanding of the "region" (*Gegend*) that surrounds us while withdrawing in a "regioning" (*Gegnen*) to clear space for our dwelling.[138] The sense of withdrawal attests to an alterity that slips away from our grasp, while in the same move making room for the presencing of things in our grasp. It is the alterity lying on the *other* side of, or *beyond*, the horizon upon which our world on this side of the horizon is contingent. It is the boundless *apeiron*, the yawning *chaos*, from out of which—but also *in* which yet in *distinction* to which—*cosmos*, world, is erected.

The earth as such is also a planet surrounded by outer space. Perhaps even more profound than Columbus' "discovery" is the discovery made in astronomy vis-à-vis the space of the heavens. Copernicus' discovery collapsed the closed space of the Ptolemaic universe, moving the central point from the earth to the sun while bursting through the firmament of allegedly fixed stars. As Nietzsche saw, we now know that the earth wanders through the vast empty universe as if not even hinged upon its sun, straying through infinite nothingness (*unendliches Nichts*) and empty space (*leere Raum*).[139] The vastness of the opened expanse exceeds even that encountered by Columbus. The findings of both Columbus and Copernicus led to a revolution in our experience of space, rupturing our sense of finite closed space to open up the expanse.[140] Not only can no country be privileged over others,[141] but neither can the earth be privileged over the rest of the universe. In this vast expanse, we feel uprooted and homeless. But Bollnow defined dwelling as being at home in a place, being rooted in it and belonging to it, decisive in our relationship to the world.[142] Homelessness then sets the task for humanity to find the center for its own space, a home we must *create* ourselves. To attain healthy stability amidst the expanse requires the building of a specific area, wherein we can move and dwell. In building a home, we carve "a hollow space for dwelling out of the environment,"[143] a cosmos in the chaos. The point of the river metaphor for Heidegger was to learn to be "at home" in one's "homelessness." But Heidegger, in "Bauen, Wohnen, Denken" (Building dwelling thinking), also stated that "to be a human being means . . . to dwell" (Mensch sein heißt . . . wohnen) and that humankind needs to learn how to dwell (*das Wohnen*), which also involves building (*bauen*).[144] Dwelling then entails a dynamism involving homeless wandering, building, and being-at-home.

Nishida expressed his love for the sea, feeling that "the infinite moves through the sea," and Nishitani Keiji also expressed how he felt that "the sky is the infinite made visible." In both Nishida's and Nishitani's sentiments here concerning the sea or sky, Ueda sees the boundless open (*hirake*), disclosing itself in their experiences.[145] And it is within that open expanse to which the horizon opens, surrounding all horizons of intelligibility, the regioning or clearing or encompassing of ever-receding horizons and unfolding alterities, as emplacing East and West, North and South, that any genuine dialogue between distinct cultural-linguistic worlds or "houses of being,"[146] as well as healthy co-dwelling with our ecological surroundings, would have to take place. This dialogue or conversation may constitute, or unfold, what Nishida called a "world of worlds" or "multi-world" (*sekaiteki sekai* 世界的世界), wherein what Bret Davis calls a *diatopical* conversation between different cultural-linguistic *topoi* can occur. This would give further disclosure—or formation?—to the expanse as what Nishida spoke of as the deeper root from which spring the branches of East and West.[147] It is also *in* that open expanse, beyond all humanly constructed semantic fields, that we step *out* of our egos in ex-sistence (*datsu-ji* 脱自) and that an authentic face-to-face encounter can occur between free individuals.[148] The same goes for our encounter with nonhuman others. The point is also to build out of that free space for our co-being and co-dwelling. Dwelling today, in addition to the dynamism of homeless wandering, building, and being-at-home, necessitates negotiating with a polycentric world—world(s) of multiple horizons—(un)grounded upon the open expanse. The horizonality of our emplacement entails alterity. This means finitude and requires, on our part, humility and openness.

NOTES

1. Otto Friedrich Bollnow, *Mensch und Raum* (Stuttgart: W. Kohlhammer Verlag, 1963), 48; Bollnow, *Human Space*, trans. Christine Shuttleworth (London: Hyphen Press, 2011), 48.

2. Bollnow, *Mensch und Raum*, 74; and *Human Space*, 72.

3. Ueda Shizuteru, *Basho: Nijū sekai naisonzai* (Tokyo: Kōbundō, 1992), 85–86.

4. Martin Heidegger, *Zur Sache des Denkens* (Tübingen: Max Niemeyer Verlag, 1988), 71; Heidegger, *On Time and Being*, trans. Joan Stambaugh (New York: Harper and Row, 1972), 65.

5. Bollnow, *Mensch und Raum*, 79; and *Human Space*, 76–77.

6. Karl Jaspers, *Philosophy of Existence*, trans. Richard F. Grabay (Philadelphia: University of Pennsylvania Press, 1971), 17.

7. Karl Jaspers, *Reason and Existenz: Five Lectures*, trans. William Earle (New York: Noonday Press, 1955), 52.

8. Jaspers, *Philosophy of Existence*, 68.

9. Jaspers, *Reason and Existenz*, 52. See also Jaspers, *Philosophy of Existence*, 18.

10. Bollnow, *Mensch und Raum*, 69; and *Human Space*, 67.

11. Günter Figal, *Objectivity: The Hermeneutical and Philosophy*, trans. Theodore D. George (Albany: State University of New York Press, 2010), 144.

12. Ibid., 152.

13. The fact that these things are to be "de-removed" means that they are "removed" in that they are distant or *other*. What this means and the significance of the "thing-world" and "de-removal" are discussed in the text that follows and in note 26.

14. See Ueda Shizuteru, *Nishida Kitarō o yomu* (Tokyo: Iwanami shoten, 1991), 101–102.

15. See Bollnow, *Mensch und Raum*, 31; and *Human Space*, 31–32.

16. And "order" is one meaning of the ancient Greek term *kosmos*.

17. The so-called lifeworld itself might be thus divided into a plurality of contexts, of specific particular worlds, professional worlds (*Sonderwelten, Berufswelten*). On this, see Bernhard Waldenfels, *The Question of the Other* (Hong Kong: Chinese University Press, 2007), 112–113. Another example of the demarcation of space would be the different ways in which towns are ordered or structured, giving them distinct "senses." Waldenfels discusses how there are traditional European towns surrounding a public place (e.g., agora, forum, market) or centered on a church or town hall; noncentered towns like Kyoto, divided into many temple districts; American town-landscapes spread out like a carpet; and harbor towns like Hong Kong, which grew from a small land strip between rocky hills and the coast to become an assembly of skyscrapers. See ibid., 117.

18. See Nishida Kitarō, "Basho," in *Nishida Kitarō zenshū* (Tokyo: Iwanami shoten, 2003), 3:415–477; and Nishida, "Basho," in *Place and Dialectic: Two Essays by Nishida Kitarō*, trans. John W. M. Krummel and Shigenori Nagatomo (New York: Oxford University Press, 2012), 49–102.

19. Ueda, *Nishida Kitarō o yomu*, 319.

20. See ibid., 314.

21. See ibid., 373.

22. Bollnow, *Mensch und Raum*, 76; and *Human Space*, 74.

23. By "finite transcendence," I mean human *existence*, or what Heidegger calls "being-(t)here" (*Dasein*) in its relation and comportment to beings (entities, objects) while precluding its own reduction to mere entities or objects.

24. Martin Heidegger, *Sein und Zeit* (Tübingen: Max Niemeyer Verlag, 1993), 111.

25. Ibid., 54. An *existentiale* for Heidegger is a characteristic of human existence or being-(t)here (*Dasein*) as revealed in its analysis, a characteristic constitutive of humans' existential structure.

26. Things become available/handy for Heidegger through "de-distancing/de-removing" (*Ent-fernung*) together with "orientation/directionality" (*Ausrichtung*). The former (de-removing) is an important concept in Günter Figal's own attempt to construct a philosophy of hermeneutical space. According to Figal, in "de-removing," the human being-(t)here attempts to bring into its proximity what does not but should belong into its familiar world, its horizon. See Figal, *Objectivity*, 134–135.

27. Bollnow, *Mensch und Raum*, 76; and *Human Space*, 74.

28. Ueda, *Nishida Kitarō o yomu*, 97.

29. Ibid., 101.

30. In different degrees, this can entail the politics of inclusion (*Eingrenzung*) and exclusion (*Ausgrenzung*), as discussed extensively by Waldenfels in his *Question of the Other* (e.g., 7).

31. Ueda, *Nishida Kitarō o yomu*, 93.

32. See Waldenfels, *Question of the Other*, 16; Bernhard Waldenfels, *Phenomenology of the Alien: Basic Concepts*, trans. Alexander Kozin and Tanja Stähler (Evanston, IL: Northwestern University Press, 2011), 75–76.

33. Immanuel Kant, *Werke in sechs Bänden*, vol. 6: *Schriften zur Anthropologie, Geschichtsphilosophie, Politik und Pädagogik*, ed. Wilhelm Weischedel (Frankfurt: Insel-Verlag, 1964), 89.

34. Figal, *Objectivity*, 129.

35. Ibid., 138.

36. Immanuel Kant, *Kritik der reinen Vernunft* (Hamburg: Felix Meiner Verlag, 1993), A22/B37.

37. See Karl Ameriks, *Interpreting Kant's "Critiques"* (New York: Oxford University Press, 2003), 26.

38. Figal, *Objectivity*, 141–142.

39. Ibid., 142.

40. Ibid., 136.

41. See Waldenfels, *Phenomenology of the Alien*, 81. Waldenfels explains that *fremd* has the sense of being *exterior* in contrast to being interior, and this exteriority of the alien is noticeable also in the meanings of ξένον, *externum, extraneum, étranger, stranger, foreign*, and the Chinese *wài* 外 (*gai* in Japanese). See Waldenfels, *Question of the Other*, 130n10; and *Phenomenology of the Alien*, 71.

42. See Waldenfels, *Question of the Other*, 2, 31, 104; and *Phenomenology of the Alien*, 32, 41.

43. See Waldenfels, *Question of the Other*, 22, 34, 74; and *Phenomenology of the Alien*, 4, 6, 8, 26–27, 32.

44. See Waldenfels, *Question of the Other*, ix, 50–51, 63; and *Phenomenology of the Alien*, 24. Waldenfels gives the example of the traffic accident taken from Robert Musil's novel *The Man without Qualities* as an unexpected event that breaks the flow of things, taking us by surprise. Only after the fact does an onlooker from among the crowd drawn to the aftermath turn the tragic event into something "orderly" with meaning and conforming to rules through his explanation of what just happened to a woman by making use of the statistics of road accidents in America and transforming the accident into a technical issue. Thereby he "normalizes" the incident. See Robert Musil, *The Man without Qualities* [*Der Mann ohne Eigenschaften*] (Hamburg: Rowohlt, 1952), 10–11; Musil, *The Man without Qualities*, trans. Sophie Wilkins (New York: Alfred A. Knopf, 1995), 4–5). See also Waldenfels, *Question of the Other*, 37; and *Phenomenology of the Alien*, 24–25.

45. See Waldenfels, *Question of the Other*, 42, 122.

46. See ibid., 39.

47. Waldenfels, *Phenomenology of the Alien*, 16–17.

48. See Maurice Merleau-Ponty, *Phénoménologie de la perception* (Paris: Gallimard, 1945), 249–250; Merleau-Ponty, *Phenomenology of Perception*, trans. Colin Smith (London: Routledge, 1962), 215–216; Waldenfels, *Question of the Other*, 45, 68. Some cases of suicide in that sense may be attempts to bring agency into the event of death—i.e., to appropriate it and make it one's *own*. On the other hand, birth is never experienced by its subject and never a matter of free choice.

49. Waldenfels, *Question of the Other*, 13.

50. See ibid., 15.

51. See Friedrich Nietzsche, *Jenseits von Gut und Böse*, in *Sämtliche Werke Kritische Studienausgabe*, vol. 5 (Berlin: Walter de Gruyter; Munich: Deutscher Taschenbuch Verlag, 1980), 31, §17; Nietzsche, *Beyond Good and Evil*, trans. Walter Kaufmann (New York: Random House, 1966), 24, §17.

52. Merleau-Ponty, *Phénoménologie de la perception*, 249; and *Phenomenology of Perception*, 215. The published English translation renders *on perçoit* as "one perceives."

53. See Waldenfels, *Question of the Other*, 45–46, 134nn6–7.

54. See Nishida Kitarō, *Nishida Kitarō zenshū* (Tokyo: Iwanami shoten, 2002), 5:305–306.

55. Dōgen, *Genjōkōan*, in *Shōbōgenzō*, vol. 1, ed. Mizuno Yaoko (Tokyo: Iwanami shoten, 1990), 54; *The Heart of Dōgen's "Shōbōgenzō,"* trans. Norman Waddell and Masao Abe (Albany: State University of New York Press, 2002), 41. The translation has been slightly altered.

56. See Waldenfels, *Question of the Other*, 15.

57. Ibid., 4; Waldenfels, *Phenomenology of the Alien*, 77. David Lynch's films, such as *Lost Highway* and *Mulholland Drive*, and his TV series *Twin Peaks* depict quite well this sense of how the home can be alien.

58. Waldenfels, *Question of the Other*, 126. Waldenfels suggests this opens the horizon to a series of what Foucault calls *heterotopias*. See Michel Foucault, *Les mots et les choses: Une archéologie des sciences humaines* (Paris: Gallimard, 1966), 9; Foucault, *The Order of Things: An Archaeology of the Human Sciences* (New York: Random House, 1970), xviii.

59. See Waldenfels, *Question of the Other*, 13, 14.

60. Peter Berger, *The Sacred Canopy: Elements of a Sociological Theory of Religion* (New York: Random House, 1967), 23.

61. *Kehre* ought not to be understood simplistically as a period in Heidegger's oeuvre when he shifts from the early to the later standpoints, as many commentators still do. On this, see John W. M. Krummel, "Spatiality in the Later Heidegger: Turning—Clearing—Letting," *Existentia* 16 (2006): 405–424; Parvis Emad and Kenneth Maly, introduction to Martin Heidegger, *Contributions to Philosophy (from Enowning)* (Bloomington: Indiana University Press, 1999); Charles E. Scott, Susan Schoenbohm, Daniela Vallega-Neu, and Alejandro Vallega, eds., *Companion to Heidegger's "Contributions to Philosophy"* (Bloomington: Indiana University Press, 2001); and Friedrich-Wilhelm von Hermann, *Wege ins Ereignis: Zu Heideggers "Beiträgen zur Philosophie"* (Frankfurt: Klostermann, 1994). See also Heidegger's own 1962 letter to William Richardson, included as the preface in William J. Richardson, *Heidegger: Through Phenomenology to Thought* (New York: Fordham University Press, 2003, 1963).

62. Ueda, *Nishida Kitarō o yomu*, 375.

63. Ibid., 313–314, 322.

64. See ibid., 374.

65. Jaspers, *Philosophy of Existence*, 26.

66. See Waldenfels, *Question of the Other*, 130n14.

67. Martin Heidegger, *Wegmarken (Gesamtausgabe*, vol. 9) (Frankfurt: Vittorio Klostermann, 1976), 121; Heidegger, *Pathmarks*, ed. William McNeill (Cambridge: Cambridge University Press, 1998), 96.

68. Ueda, *Nishida Kitarō o yomu*, 50.

69. Ibid., 101–102.

70. Bollnow, *Mensch und Raum*, 303; and *Human Space*, 282.

71. Ueda, *Nishida Kitarō o yomu*, 106. Or if lying within the horizon are beings and beyond it is the nothing, we might call it an anontological space for encompassing being and nonbeing, as I have suggested in my other writings.

72. Ibid., 56.

73. Ibid., 51.

74. Ibid., 283.

75. Ibid., 34–37; Ueda Shizuteru, "Jitsuzon to kozon, soshite *genius loci*," in *Ueda Shizuteru shū dai kyū maki: Kokū/sekai* (Tokyo: Iwanami shoten, 2002), 324ff.

76. Bollnow, *Mensch und Raum*, 304; and *Human Space*, 283.

77. *Datsu-ji* literally means "escaping or exiting the self in the sense of the ego." Ueda's sense is that we are not static substances, as we might assume in the everyday lifeworld.

78. Ueda, *Nishida Kitarō o yomu*, 194.

79. See Jaspers, *Philosophy of Existence*, 67.

80. Mircea Eliade, *Das Heilige und das Profane* (Hamburg: Rowohlt, 1957), 18; Eliade, *The Sacred and the Profane: The Nature of Religion*, trans. Willard R. Trask (New York: Harcourt Brace Jovanovich, 1959), 29.

81. See Hesiod, *"Theogony" and "Works and Days,"* trans. M. L. West (New York: Oxford University Press, 2008), esp. 6–7.

82. The Greek *chaos* is derived from the verb *chainō* (χαίνω) for "opening."

83. Ueda, *Nishida Kitarō o yomu*, 52.

84. Waldenfels seems to suggest that both agoraphobia and claustrophobia are cases of this sense of losing horizon. See Waldenfels, *Phenomenology of the Alien*, 66. In that sense, one might argue that they are derivative effects of anxiety in the face of the nothing.

85. Heidegger, *Sein und Zeit*, 187.

86. Ueda, *Nishida Kitarō o yomu*, 55–56.

87. Heidegger, *Sein und Zeit*, 186 (see also 343).

88. Blaise Pascal, *Pensées* (London: Penguin Books, 1995), 206, §201.

89. Bollnow, *Mensch und Raum*, 86; and *Human Space*, 84.

90. Ueda, *Nishida Kitarō o yomu*, 95.

91. Ibid., 56–57.

92. Ibid., 54.

93. Ibid., 64.

94. Gaston Bachelard, *La poétique de l'espace* (Paris: Presses Universitaires de France, 1958), 102–104; Bachelard, *The Poetics of Space*, trans. Maria Jolas (Boston: Beacon Press, 1969), 103–104; Bollnow, *Mensch und Raum*, 302; Bollnow, *Human Space*, 281–282.

95. Bollnow, *Mensch und Raum*, 310; and *Human Space*, 288–289.

96. Bollnow, *Mensch und Raum*, 304; and *Human Space*, 283.

97. Dōgen, *Genjōkōan*, 58; and *Heart of Dōgen's "Shōbōgenzō,"* 43.

98. Bollnow, *Mensch und Raum*, 76; and *Human Space*, 74.

99. Dōgen, *Genjōkōan*, 54; and *Heart of Dōgen's "Shōbōgenzō,"* 40. Translation slightly altered.

100. Dōgen, *Genjōkōan*, 58; and *Heart of Dōgen's "Shōbōgenzō,"* 43.

101. Dōgen, *Sansuikyō*, in *Shōbōgenzō*, vol. 2, ed. Mizuno Yaoko (Tokyo: Iwanami shoten, 1990), 184; Dōgen, "Dōgen's 'Mountains and Waters Are *Sūtras*' (*Sansui-kyō*)," trans. Graham Parkes, in *Buddhist Philosophy: Essential Readings*, ed. William Edelglass and Jay L. Garfield (New York: Oxford University Press, 2009), 87.

102. See Bollnow, *Mensch und Raum*, 80; and *Human Space*, 77.

103. Bollnow, *Mensch und Raum*, 80; and *Human Space*, 78.

104. Bollnow, *Mensch und Raum*, 58, 137–138 (see also 58–59); and *Human Space*, 57, 132 (see also 57–58).

105. Bollnow, *Mensch und Raum*, 58–59; and *Human Space*, 57–59.

106. Bollnow, *Mensch und Raum*, 75; and *Human Space*, 73.

107. Bollnow, *Mensch und Raum*, 94; and *Human Space*, 91–92.

108. Bollnow, *Mensch und Raum*, 117; and *Human Space*, 112.

109. Bollnow, *Mensch und Raum*, 119; and *Human Space*, 115.

110. Bollnow, *Mensch und Raum*, 104; and *Human Space*, 101.

111. Bollnow, *Mensch und Raum*, 138; and *Human Space*, 132.

112. Hence if philosophy is born out of anxiety for some like Epicurus, for others like Plato it is born out of wonder. For Rudolf Otto, religion emerges out of the experience of the *tremendum et fascinans* (terrifying and fascinating). For Waldenfels, all of these are affects of the alien. See Waldenfels, *Phenomenology of the Alien*, 81.

113. Ibid., 8.

114. Martin Heidegger, *Hölderlins Hymne "Der Ister"* (*Gesamtausgabe*, vol. 53) (Frankfurt: Vittorio Klostermann, 1984), 23; *Hölderlin's Hymn "The Ister,"* trans. William McNeill and Julia Davis (Bloomington: Indiana University Press, 1996a), 21.

115. Heidegger, *Hölderlins Hymne*, 23–24; and *Hölderlin's Hymn*, 20–21.

116. Heidegger, *Hölderlins Hymne*, 23; and *Hölderlin's Hymn*, 20.

117. Heidegger, *Hölderlins Hymne*, 35–36, 39, 178; and *Hölderlin's Hymn*, 30–31, 33, 142.

118. Heidegger, *Hölderlins Hymne*, 32; and *Hölderlin's Hymn*, 28.

119. Martin Heidegger, *Erläuterungen zu Hölderlins Dichtung* (Frankfurt: Vittorio Klostermann, 1996b), 96; Heidegger, *Elucidations of Hölderlin's Poetry*, trans. Keith Hoeller (Amherst, NY: Humanity Books, 2000), 119.

120. Heidegger, *Hölderlins Hymne*, 16; and *Hölderlin's Hymn*, 15.

121. See Heidegger, *Hölderlins Hymne*, 67, 166, 173, 178, 184; and *Hölderlin's Hymn*, 54, 133, 138–139, 142, 148.

122. Waldenfels, *Question of the Other*, 112.

123. Citing Eliade and Grönbech, Bollnow reminds us how old Iran saw its land, Airyanam Vaejah, as set in the middle of the world; the Chinese viewed their country, Zhongguo 中国, as the country of the center; the ancient Germans regarded Midgard as the world's center; and even nomadic peoples of Australia carried their sacred pole with them as the center to erect wherever they settled in their wanderings. See Eliade, *Heilige und das Profane*, 20, 24; Eliade, *Sacred and the Profane*, 32–33, 40; Wilhelm Grönbech, *Kultur und Religion der Germanen* (Stuttgart: W. Kohlhammer Verlag, 1954), 2:183; Bollnow, *Mensch und Raum*, 60–61; Bollnow, *Human Space*, 59–60.

124. Bollnow, *Mensch und Raum*, 84; and *Human Space*, 82.

125. Waldenfels, *Phenomenology of the Alien*, 80. Waldenfels also quotes the character Ulrich from Musil's *Man without Qualities*: "Anyone who really loved his country should never think his own country the best" (Musil, *Mann ohne Eigenschaften*, 18–19; Musil, *Man without Qualities*, 13; Waldenfels, *Phenomenology of the Alien*, 11).

126. Julia Kristeva, *Etrangers à nous-mêmes* (Paris: Gallimard, 1988), 209 (see also 284); Kristeva, *Strangers to Ourselves*, trans. Leon S. Roudiez (New York: Columbia University Press, 1991), 192. See also Waldenfels, *Phenomenology of the Alien*, 80.

127. Friedrich Nietzsche, *Thoughts out of Season*, part 2, trans. by Adrian Collins, in *The Complete Works of Friedrich Nietzsche* (Edinburgh: T. N. Foulis, 1909), 5:10.

128. Ueda Shizuteru, "Contributions to Dialogue with the Kyoto School," in *Japanese and Continental Philosophy*, ed. Bret W. Davis, Brian Schroeder, and Jason M. Wirth (Bloomington: Indiana University Press, 2011), 19–32.

129. Ueda (ibid., 30) states that its thickness corresponds to its hollowness. One might see this in the consumer and pop (pseudo-) culture that appears to permeate differences.

130. Ueda, *Nishida Kitarō o yomu*, 176–177.

131. See Bollnow, *Mensch und Raum*, 213; and *Human Space*, 200–201.

132. Augustin Berque, *Fūdogaku josetsu—bunka o futatabi shizen ni, shizen o futatabi bunka ni* [Introduction to museology: From culture back to nature and from nature back to culture], trans. Nakayama Gen (Tokyo: Chikuma shobō, 2002a), 49.

133. Ibid., 40, 41n22, 43n24; Augustin Berque, "Overcoming Modernity, Yesterday and Today," *Journal of East Asian Studies* 1, no. 1 (2002b): 94, 101nn20–21. Berque refers to Pradeau, Brisson, and Boutot, all of whom take *chōra* as a milieu or field of relations— e.g., Jean-François Pradeau, "Être quelque part, occuper une place: *Topos et chōra* dans le Timée," *Les Études philosophiques* 3 (1995), 396; Alain Boutot, *Heidegger et Platon: Le problème du nihilisme* (Paris: Presses Universitaires de France, 1987), 131, 222; and Luc Brisson, *Le même et l'autre dans la structure ontologique du* Timée *de Platon: Un commentaire systématique du* Timée *de Platon* (Sankt Augustin: Academia Verlag, 1994). See also Berque, *Fūdogaku josetsu*. 32, 38; and "Overcoming Modernity," 94–95.

134. Augustin Berque, "The Choretic Work of History," *Semiotica: Journal of the International Association of Semiotic Studies*, no. 175 (2009): 165; Berque, "*Where Is Knowledge? (In the Mediate Data of the Unconscious)*," paper presented at the

International Conference on Knowledge and Place, Sōka University, December 9–10, 2000, http://pweb.ens-lsh.fr/omilhaud/berque_knowledge.doc, 6, 8–9, 8n73. In a variety of works, Berque (e.g., *Fūdogaku josetsu*, 163–164) goes on to develop his understanding of *chōra* in terms of our eco-techno-symbolic milieu. That is to say, the technological and symbolic systems on the side of humanity and the ecological system on the side of nature—since humankind lives on earth—co-constitute the existential field of things, such as a pencil, making possible its meaningful being. The human being as such opens out into a common eco-techno-symbolic milieu, taking *milieu* as this relationship of human society to space and nature. "Milieu" in this sense is both natural and cultural, subjective and objective, collective and individual. As Berque puts it, "The whole of human milieux forms the ecumene [*écoumène*], which is the relationship of humankind with the earth" ("Research Agenda on the History of Disurbanity—Hypotheses and First Data," *International Journal of Urban Studies* 5, no. 1 [2001], 1). See also Augustin Berque, *Japan: Nature, Artifice and Japanese Culture*, trans. Ros Schwartz (Northamptonshire, UK: Pilkington Press, 1997), 9, 99, 116–117, 226.

135. Martin Heidegger, "Der Ursprung der Kunstwerkes," in *Holzwege* (Frankfurt: Vittorio Klostermann, 2003), 48–50; Heidegger, "The Origin of the Work of Art," in *Off the Beaten Track*, trans. Julian Young and Kenneth Haynes (Cambridge: Cambridge University Press, 2002), 36–37.

136. Edward S. Casey, "Heidegger in and out of Place," in *Heidegger: A Centenary Appraisal* (Pittsburgh: Duquesne University Press, 1990), 80–81.

137. See Heidegger's 1944 Heraclitus lecture *Logik: Heraklits Lehre vom Logos* [Logic: Heraclitus' doctrine of Logos] (*Gesamtausgabe*, vol. 55) (Frankfurt: Vittorio Klostermann, 1979); and his 1944–1945 *Zur Erörterung der Gelassenheit* [Toward a discussion of releasement], which appears in *Gelassenheit* (Pfullingen: Günther Neske, 1959) and in *Aus der Erfahrung des Denkens, 1910–1976* (*Gesamtausgabe*, vol. 13) (Frankfurt: Vittorio Klostermann, 1983). The English translation of the last one is "Conversation on a Country Path about Thinking," in *Discourse on Thinking* (New York: Harper and Row, 1966).

138. Heidegger came to understand "region" in terms of a "regioning" (or "regionalizing," *Gegnen*) activity, on the basis of, or at least in conjunction with, a renewed understanding of Plato's *chōra* while explicitly distinguishing it from the phenomenological—or more specifically, Husserlian—notion of a "horizon" (*Horizont*). In his 1953 parenthetical remark in *Einführung in die Metaphysik* [Introduction to metaphysics], Heidegger also suggests *chōra* to be what *withdraws* to make-room for the presencing of things. See Martin Heidegger, *Einführung in die Metaphysik* (Frankfurt: Vittorio Klostermann, 1983), 51; Heidegger, *Introduction to Metaphysics*, trans. Ralph Manheim (New Haven, CT: Yale University Press, 1987), 66; Heidegger, *Introduction to Metaphysics*, trans. Gregory Fried and Richard Polt (New Haven, CT: Yale University Press, 2000), 70). On this topic of *chōra* in Heidegger, see John W. M. Krummel, "Chōra in Heidegger and Nishida," *Studia Phaenomenologica* 16 (2016): 489–518.

139. Friedrich Nietzsche, *Die fröhliche Wissenschaft*, in *Friedrich Nietzsche Sämtliche Werke: Kritische Studienausgabe*, vol. 3 (Berlin: Walter de Gruyter; Munich: Deutscher Taschenbuch Verlag, 1980), 481, §125; Nietzsche, *The Gay Science*, trans. Thomas Common (Mineola, NY: Dover, 2006), 90, §125.

140. See Bollnow, *Mensch und Raum*, 85–86; and *Human Space*, 84.

141. Bollnow, *Mensch und Raum*, 123; and *Human Space*, 119.

142. Bollnow, *Mensch und Raum*, 125–126; and *Human Space*, 121–122.

143. Bollnow, *Mensch und Raum*, 267; and *Human Space*, 249.

144. Martin Heidegger, *Vorträge und Aufsätze* (Pfullingen: Günther Neske, 1954), 147, 162; Heidegger, *Poetry, Language, Thought*, trans. Albert Hofstadter (New York: Harper and Row, 1971), 147, 161.

145. Ueda Shizuteru, *Keiken to jikaku: Nishida tetsugaku no "basho" o motomete* (Tokyo: Iwanami shoten, 1994), 19.

146. This phrase, "house of being" (*Haus des Seins*), appears in Heidegger's "Dialogue on Language," in *Unterwegs zur Sprache* (*Gesamtausgabe*, vol. 12) (Frankfurt: Vittorio Klostermann, 1985), 85, 105–107; *On the Way to Language*, trans. Peter D. Hertz (New York: Harper and Row, 1971), 5, 21–22. See also Heidegger, *Wegmarken*, 313; and *Pathmarks*, 239.

147. See Nishida Kitarō, *Nishida Kitarō zenshū*, vol. 9 (Tokyo: Iwanami shoten, 2004), 80; and *Nishida Kitarō zenshū*, vol. 13 (Tokyo: Iwanami shoten, 2005), 19–20.

148. See Ueda, *Nishida Kitarō o yomu*, 194.

The Proximate and the Distant　　　**5**

James Buchanan

The question that concerns us in this chapter is the ethical dimension of place. The experience of place does not always entail an ethical dimension, but ethics always depends on a relationship to place or the proximate. Ethical theories such as those of Aristotle and Confucius are platial and are relatively adequate only for what I will call the proximate. Just as the experience of place itself begins to disintegrate with the introduction of the distant, our ability to apply the moral principles that are effective in the proximate begins to disintegrate as we introduce the distant. The more fundamental problem is that the distant is always already present in the proximate, potentially rendering even the seemingly simplest ethical decisions problematic.

I will first draw on the work of Edward Casey, Martin Heidegger, and Yi-Fu Tuan, attempting to bring out some of the moral and ethical implications of their reflections on place. Using Aristotle and Confucius as examples of platial ethics, I contend that these (and arguably all of the great ethical systems) are relatively adequate only as proximate ethics and are less relatively adequate as we introduce the distant. Finally, drawing on systems theory, I argue that the proximate is always already displaced by the complexity of the spatial and temporal distant, which raises questions of the relative adequacy of our ethical traditions in an age of global and generational systems.

Space and Place

In writings such as *The Fate of Place: A Philosophical History* and "Between Geography and Philosophy: What Does It Mean to Be in the Place-World?"[1] Edward Casey focuses on place as "experienced" (by human beings), while space "discourages experiential explorations."[2] According to Casey, space is "the encompassing volumetric void in which things . . . are positioned," whereas place is "the immediate environment of my lived body—an arena of action that is at once physical and historical, social and cultural."[3] Casey would not deny that we experience space but insists that both the depth and the nature of that experience is fundamentally different from those of place. It is this difference that transforms experientially "thin" space into experientially "thick" place.

Casey explores the experience of place in terms of self, body, and landscape. As he says, "The self has to do with the agency and identity of the geographical subject; body is what links this self to lived place in its sensible and perceptible features; and landscape is the presented layout of a set of places, not their mere accumulation but their sensuous self-presentation as a whole."[4] Self as both agency and identity are always embodied and located; both are equally critical parts of a complex system of self, body, and landscape that comprise key dimensions of what I call the proximate.

As Casey argues, "The relationship between self and place is not just one of reciprocal influence . . . but also, more radically, of constitutive coingredience: each is essential to the other. In effect there is *no place without self and no self without place*."[5] Thus there is also no identity or agency without place.

While Casey's philosophical history deals with space and place throughout the Western philosophical tradition, it is in the work of Martin Heidegger that he finds the most salient reflections. According to Casey, Heidegger, with his critique of Western metaphysics and particularly of the transcendental ego of Husserl, is not just a philosopher of time but our most significant modern philosopher of place. For Heidegger, Dasein is that self which interprets the world through engagement. For early Heidegger, this engagement was interpreted in terms of temporality, but in his later writings he came to understand that temporality is always in place, or platial. In *Being and Time*, Heidegger uses the example of the skilled craftsman who simultaneously finds himself and his world in the process of engagement with the place of the workshop and the processes of work that takes place. Self and place are intertwined and mutually constitutive in the world of work. The whole workshop becomes a complex web of relations that brings into being both the world and the worker. The worker is always already located in place. Casey notes, "When Heidegger remarks that 'our concernful absorption in whatever work-world lies closest to us has a function of discovering,' he means that this absorption helps us to discover our own being-in-the-world and not just the external destination."[6]

What makes Heidegger's experience of place a moral relationship are his ideas of authenticity and care. Heidegger's claim is that Dasein is that being for which "Being is an issue." That issue is ontological and moral. There is an "anxiety" about our being that comes from and reveals to us our being unto death. Taking this anxiety seriously ought to result in concernful being as care and authenticity. To live authentically is both to discover one's being and to take responsibility for that being. Only in so doing do we give our lives meaning. Authenticity is ultimately about the relationships through which we manifest care for our world.

Casey maintains that Heidegger "seizes on 'closeness' (*die Nähe*) as the most salient characteristic of the spatiality of the ready-to-hand in its familiarity."[7] It is the relationship between "closeness" (what I call the proximate) and responsibility that interests us. Heidegger is clear that place is "limit": "Within a limit, room is made and thus place. To lack limit is to lack place, and conversely: not to be in place is to be unlimited. A limit is a positive power within which place is made."[8] As Heidegger puts it, "Limit and end are that wherewith a being begins to be."[9] Limit, according to Heidegger, is "not that at which something stops but, as the Greeks recognized, that from which something *begins its presencing*."[10]

While Casey and Heidegger use the term "limit" as key to place, I prefer the idea of limit/horizon.[11] The term "horizon" holds within it both limit and openness. This term also allows us to draw on the work of Hans-Georg Gadamer and his use of "horizon" hermeneutically. Gadamer's claim that all interpretation is prejudiced or perspectival is to claim that it is platial or horizonal. Place is horizonal, and horizon is platial. The proximate, as limit and place, is a horizon within which the self as moral self exists. The question that haunts the proximate and the proximate moral self is, how far can we extend that horizon before the understanding and principles of that place begin to disintegrate into the spatially and temporally distant?

Yi-Fu Tuan in his many works on space and place, including *Space and Place: The Perspective of Experience* and *Humanist Geography: An Individual's Search for Meaning*,[12] describes himself as a humanist geographer: "Insofar as I am a humanist, I focus on the individual—individualism being a child of humanism. Insofar as I am a geographer, I focus on community and place—the social and material dimensions of living."[13] The tension, and it is an ethical tension, in all of Tuan's writing has been between these two dimensions, which we all inhabit. He admits that they are often at odds with one another. He also struggles with the question of scale. Only at scale can the humanist and the geographer be integrated into a relatively unified self. Scale in Tuan relates to limit in Heidegger. Unlimited scale results in the world of what he calls cosmopolites: individuals who freely associate beyond the limits of their community. The lack of limit means that the cosmopolite faces the challenge of "sustaining neighborly commitment and care."[14] While cosmopolitanism promotes individual excellence and the highest level of achievement, it also has the effect of a corresponding loss of community.

Tuan's question of scale is critical to my own moral concerns. Beyond what scale or limit do both moral agency and identity begin to disintegrate, to dissipate into a thinning distant? Can the cosmopolite be a moral agent? Certainly we would have to answer affirmatively. But the question is at what scale and in what way does that morality express itself? At what point does the worldly commitment of the cosmopolitan move beyond his or her capacity to apply moral principles to the real-world ethical decisions that, though still complex, are possible at the level of the proximate of community?

From the work of Heidegger, Casey, and Tuan, three key dimensions of place as they relate to an ethics of place or the proximate emerge. First, all describe place in terms of relationality. What transforms space into place is the difference and depth of human experience. It is this relational experience or relationality that is critical. Space, we recall, "discourages experiential explorations"; it is a relational "void." Place is meaningful place in proportion to the depth of our sense of relation to it and within it. We become ourselves in that complex set of relationships that constitutes place. One important dimension of questions of relationality is that, ultimately, they all ought to be moral questions.

Second, place must be understood in terms of limit/horizon. Unlike space, place is limited or horizonal. Place is always relatively proximate. As place becomes less proximate, it "thins," possibly to the point that place becomes the ambiguous void of space. As place thins, so does our sense of identity and agency. This thinning of identity and agency is a moral thinning as well.

Third, inherent in all of their work is the question of responsibility. Because of the depth of relationality within the limit/horizon of space, we are able to understand ourselves as moral agents with the capacity of ethical decision making. It is the sense of responsibility that shapes the relationships that constitute place. My agency and identity are dependent on being able to take responsibility for my being. Like identity and agency, responsibility is horizonal. As limit approaches unlimit, the question of responsibility must be reframed as the question of response-ability—literally, our ability to be responsive or responsible due to the thinning of the place as it moves from the proximate to the distant.

Proximate Ethics: Place in Aristotle and Confucius

A body of thought has developed around the ethics of place. The majority of this has been connected to ecological thought. Writers such as Timothy Beatley, Kristy Manning, Mick Smith, Ian Billick, Mary Price, and Michael Northcott have all built their environmental ethics upon a connection to place.[15] All of this body of thought owes much to Wendell Berry, who has written about the experience of place with an unsurpassed eloquence. Although none of these writers develops a phenomenology of place such as we find with Heidegger or Casey, their concerns are also relationality, limit/horizon, and responsibility. There is a strong moral focus in the writings of ecology of place that extends our sense of being in the world beyond the workshop to our relationship to nature and the importance of a sense of responsibility because of and to that relationship. Our relationship to nature also becomes an arena in which the question of the limit/horizon of responsibility is present as we are now confronted with complex global and generational ecological issues such as climate change, or what Elizabeth Kolbert has recently called "the sixth extinction."[16] Does our experience of ecological place, as the proximate, help us in the global and generational ethical decisions with which we are faced? And if so, how?

The underlying premise of this last question, which has been asked in various forms above, is the claim that all of the great ethical traditions are relatively adequate only as proximate ethics and thus become relatively less adequate when the complexity of spatial and temporal distance is introduced. Further, I assert that these spatial and temporal distances are always already inherent and present in the proximate. As I will put it below, all place is always already displaced. This becomes the basis of the profound moral quandary in which we find ourselves in the twenty-first century.

Before we address this last idea, a brief analysis of the platial dimensions of two traditions will be helpful. Here I focus on the Aristotelian and Confucian traditions. Both of these traditions are examples of platial or proximate ethics. While both are "communitarian," they have universal claims and ambitions that seek to transcend the proximate. My ultimate question will be whether or not they are able to transcend the proximate, and, if so, how?

Both Aristotle and Confucius are virtue-based ethical systems. In contrast to deontological or consequentialist theories, they are less concerned with claims of universal principles than with questions of character and habits that are fundamental to living the good life. We are not virtuous in a relational vacuum; we manifest virtue in place or in the proximate. Virtue is always relational, conditioned by limit/horizon and an expression of responsibility. We do not raise questions of virtue or character in space; we raise them only in place.

Casey has looked at Aristotle's *Physics* to explore the importance of place in his writing. He summarizes the importance of place for Aristotle by saying, "For Aristotle, *where* something is constitutes a basic metaphysical category. Except for the extraordinary cases of the Unmoved Mover and the heavens . . . taken as a single whole, every perishable sublunar substance . . . is place-bound, having its own 'proper place.'"[17] But place is equally important in Aristotle's ethical writings, such as the *Nicomachean Ethics* and the *Politics*.

In the *Physics*, space surrounds or contains. It is the "first unchangeable limit . . . of that which surrounds."[18] Ethically, that which surrounds or contains us is first and foremost the polis. Aristotle acknowledges the importance of the family as a context for moral development, but the polis is ultimately the more important place. Both the family and the polis are the proximate place of virtue. I am not kind or courageous except in a space of engagement with others—in other words, in a place. Virtues are limits both because they can manifest only within a place such as a community or polis and because no one is simply virtuous—instead we engage in virtuous acts. Each act of virtue is a limit/horizonal act. We are always only as virtuous as our last act. This limit of virtue is expressed also by the doctrine of the mean. The doctrine of the mean is the recognition of the limit/horizon of every act of virtue and states that this recognition is a necessary part of the act of being virtuous. Aristotle claims that virtues should be ends-in-themselves, but at the same time he recognizes that they would be irrelevant in the social vacuum of space and thus they are really always ends-in-place. Heidegger draws on Aristotle when he says that the polis is "the place, the there, wherein and as which historical being-there is" and that it is "the historical place . . . , the there *in* which, *out* of which, and *for* which history happens."[19] Heidegger and Aristotle agree that ethics happens only in history and that history happens only in that place we call the polis.

Likewise, the key intellectual virtue—*phronesis*, or practical wisdom—is platial. This is the intellectual virtue that challenges us to reason well relative to every particular situation. While the case can be made that, for Aristotle, *phronesis* works toward the ultimate goal of theoretical reason, in terms of virtue and character *phronesis* is the more important of the intellectual virtues. *Phronesis* is the form of reasoning that is active in the polis, that essential place of virtue. While theoretical reason relates to the ultimate or universal, *phronesis* is reasoning in the proximate.

The appropriation of Aristotle by contemporary philosophers such as Alasdair MacIntyre, Michael Sandel, Michael Walzer, Hans-Georg Gadamer, Stanley Hauerwas, and Charles Taylor brings them into the discussion of the ethics of place. The so-called liberal-communitarian debate hinges on issues of identity and agency and makes clear the importance of place for the communitarians. For the liberals (e.g., John Rawls), the self is autonomous to the extent that the fundamental character we must assume is that we are each a bundle of self-interests. Justice is a procedural issue through which we manage the conflict of self-interests in a fair way. For the communitarians, identity and agency are embedded in community, webs of interlocution, or thick association. Identity and agency are constituted by place. As Sandel puts it,

> To say that the members of a society are bound by a sense of community is not simply to say that a great many of them profess communitarian sentiments and pursue communitarian aims, but rather that they conceive their identity . . . as defined to some extent by the community of which they are a part. For them, community describes not just what they *have* as fellow citizens but also what they *are*, . . . not merely an attribute but a constituent of their identity.[20]

Ontologically we are bound to place. Thus, the chief virtue of the polis, justice, is always communal or platial. For Aristotle and the communitarians, agency and identity are constituted only in the proximate—as relational, as limit/horizon and responsibility.

Confucianism is often described in terms of an ethics of roles. Roles make sense only in a context and change as contexts change. Context or place begins with the proximate and then extends outward. Role works most adequately in direct relationship to the relative proximate of place. In the *Analects* (*Lunyu*), the basic moral community is the family and, in particular, the extended family. The extended family, as understood by Confucius, is not a group of individuals but more accurately a place filled with a variety of relationships, roles, and responsibilities. While the central virtues of *ren* and *li* are learned in family (the proximate), Confucius also has them operative throughout the five cardinal relations even as he is clear that responsibility is greater in direct proportion to relative proximity.

Li (translated as rite, propriety, decorum) helps us understand the relationality of place by observing that all relations have a structure. Recognizing the fact of structure and the need of structure in all interactions allows for a community to determine what is and is not appropriate structure. *Li* as structure is also limit. "Anything goes" does not apply in human interactions, but neither is structured relationality necessarily a formality that stifles all spontaneity. Knowing and respecting the limits of every interaction allows for a field of engagement that defines place in terms of purpose and participation. Space, as experienced, is not structured. Place, as experienced, is always structured. As Casey pointed out, "To lack limit is to lack place."

But, for Confucius, *li* is not just structure but must be appropriate structure. *Ren* (translated as benevolence, compassion, humanity, reciprocity) is what transforms *li* as mere structured space into moral place. Roger Ames' translation of *ren* as reciprocity expresses the relationality of *ren* as a fully platial virtue. Within the structure of *li* we need honesty (*yi*), wisdom (*zhi*), and integrity (*xin*), but above all we need *ren*. *Ren* is that profound sense of relationality, connection, and responsibility that is necessary to transform a *li* situation into an ethical encounter, one characterized by something analogous to Heidegger's care and authenticity. Ames says that "ritual propriety requires personalization and participation."[21] *Li*, again in Ames' interpretation, is "ritualized awareness" of the "familiar": "'Familiar' is a deliberate choice of a term . . . because it shares the same root as, and thus evokes the notion of 'family' which . . . is at the center of the Confucian socio-religious experience."[22] The familiar is place, and place is the proximate as relationality, limit/horizon, and responsibility.

It is *ren* that "charges" *li* and prevents it from becoming a manifestation of power relations or being reduced to an empty formalism. This is a critical insight because in it is Confucius' recognition that experience of place need not be moral and that agency and identity within place need not be moral. Place is space experienced. Moral place is space experienced in a way that we would judge to be "good." We both learn and practice virtue best in the hierarchy of the proximate. According to Ames' reading of Confucius, "Because *jen* [*ren*] always entails the application of personal judgment to the concrete circumstances of environing persons, it follows that one is most fully constituted by those relationships nearest at hand."[23] Confucius makes it clear that there is a hierarchy of responsibility based on the proximate. *Analects* 13.18 is the classic example of the priority of the proximate:

> The Duke of Sheh informed Confucius, saying, "Among us here there are those who may be styled upright in their conduct. If their father has stolen a sheep, they will bear witness to the fact." Confucius said, "Among us, in our part of the country, those who are upright are different from this. The father conceals the misconduct of the son, and the son conceals the misconduct of the father. Uprightness is to be found in this."

Whether it is the polis of Aristotle or the extended family in Confucius, place (as the proximate) is the key to both the development and the practice of virtue. This is not an ethics of place in the ecological sense but an ethics of place and the proximate as social. Virtues are the questions we must take into every social encounter. These are platial questions that are best asked and responded to in the proximate. Our question, again, is what happens morally when place is displaced? What happens when we introduce spatial and temporal distance into the equation? To consider this, we turn to systems theory.

Systems Theory

The term "systems philosophy" was first used by Ervin Laszlo in his book *Introduction to Systems Philosophy*.[24] Around the same time, Ludwig von Bertalanffy published his *General System Theory*.[25] Since these original attempts to conceptualize systems, a growing body of work has developed that has applied the theory to science, medicine, business, ecology, design, legal studies, innovation, and community and also includes a number of interesting studies that have compared systems philosophy with ancient Chinese and Indian philosophies.[26] According to Bertalanffy, general systems theory deals with "models, principles, and laws that apply to generalized systems or their subclasses, irrespective of their particular kind, the nature of their component elements, and the relations or 'forces' between them" and is "a theory, not of systems of a more or less special kind, but of universal principles applying to systems in general."[27]

Laszlo presents systems philosophy as a new worldview. His claim is that the holistic vision of the systems sciences is a necessary scientific and moral corrective to the mechanistic worldview of post-Cartesian modernity. The Cartesian worldview analyzes the world in terms of its "intricate but replaceable machine-like parts."[28] It is atomistic and individualistic and is based on a series of dualisms beginning with the thinking subject and the extended subject (Descartes's *res cogitans* and *res extensa*). The modern atomistic or mechanistic mode of thought is linear, and the method of analysis emphasizes linear chains of cause and effect moving from the part to the whole.[29] Fritjof Capra describes one criterion of systems thinking in this way:

> Living systems are integrated wholes whose properties cannot be reduced to those of smaller parts. Their essential, or "systemic," properties . . . arise from the "organizing relations" of the parts—that is, from a configuration of ordered relationships that is characteristic of that particular class of . . . systems. Systems properties are destroyed when a system is dissected into isolated elements.[30]

With systems, we move constantly between parts and wholes. Every part of the system works in feedback loops; thus, changes at any level mean changes at every level of the system. Systems thinking focuses on the dynamic processes of relationality. Quantum physics, as an example of systems thinking, has shown us that there are really no parts at all, only complex webs of relationship. The world is no longer a collection of objects in relationship, but objects themselves are understood as networks of relationship. As Capra puts it, "the boundaries of the discernible patterns ('objects') are secondary" to the webs of relationality.[31] Note that boundaries, or limit/horizon, are now in question in ways in which our previous analysis of place and the proximate could not accommodate. While we might be able to speak of discrete systems, such as a particular ecosystem, we also understand that every ecosystem is systemically part of increasingly complex systems ad infinitum. With systems, we acknowledge particular relationality, but because of the inherent holism, we are always already beyond limit/horizon. This raises questions of place, proximity, and responsibility in radically new ways.

A systems approach focuses our attention on dynamic patterns and structures and the way in which feedback loops both reinforce and change those. It forces us to become aware of patterns and structures that are constitutive of our relationships and thus of our identity and agency, challenging us to understand them in increasingly complex ways. The awareness itself becomes part of the system and inevitably creates its own feedback loops that change the patterns and structures. Feedback loops are as simple as a thermostat in your house and as complex as global supply chains, the Gaia system of planetary relations, or the intergenerational implications of genetic engineering. Recognizing how seemingly simple patterns in our lives become structures (institutionalized or unconsciously repetitive patterns) and how structures exist in reinforcing feedback loops with worldviews is a key part of what systems thinking challenges us to consider.

Systems theory also claims that systems self-organize. All living systems (and any system that involves human interaction is a living system) organize as patterns and structures. Because of the complex of feedback processes, systems self-organize and reorganize constantly. The mechanistic worldview understood living systems as substance or form. Substance can be measured and quantified.

Systems, as relational patterns, cannot be definitively quantified; they must be mapped. At the same time, we realize that the map is dynamic, in constant flux. Systems are best represented as dynamic relational networks operating between parts and ever increasingly complex wholes and back to parts. The first and most obvious property of any network is its nonlinearity. Relationality is no longer reducible to linear chains of cause and effect. Relationality as network is nonlinear. Instead of cause and effect, systems thinkers speak about "emergence." The dynamic nature of systems means that new patterns constantly emerge.

When systems are applied to agency and identity, ontologically relational being is understood as dynamic networks or patterns. Human being is the constantly changing emergence as those relationships. Ontologically, there is nothing beyond or a priori to this relationality. To say that we self-organize is not to say that we consciously emerge as relational patterns, though consciousness plays an important role in emergence. Rather, it is to say that the emergence of patterns and structures is always an outcome of complex relationality.

From a systems perspective, virtue would be seen as emergence and pattern. Rather than being seen as behaviors or character traits, virtues are first questions that are posed within dynamic relational horizons that emerge as patterns within other complex patterns. This is not inconsistent with either Aristotle or Confucius. Virtue is dynamic in that it is the question within every encounter and whatever emerges from that questioning, which always returns to another questioning in looping nonlinearity. Virtue is always in an interrogative mode. We should take the classic virtues of Plato (courage, justice, temperance, and prudence) or those of Confucius (*ren*, *li*, *yi*, *zhi*, *xin*), not as character traits exemplified by paradigmatic figures, but as types of pattern questions that a paradigmatic figure asks of every new relational encounter. The virtuous act is whatever emerges from the questioning of that encounter. The relative adequacy of the questioning and the response is in direct relationship to the proximity within which we judge it.

The problems begin to emerge for place with systems thinking's introduction of complexity as an unavoidable dimension. The recognition that all situations, regardless of how proximate, are complicated is not a new idea. The idea that every relational encounter is complex, and potentially infinitely so, is a new concept and one that throws into question both limit/horizon and responsibility. Complexity theory developed as a way to understand the nonlinear dimension of systems. Complexity means that, scientifically, we can aspire no longer to Cartesian certainty but only to approximation as that relates to self-organization and emergence.

Prior to systems theory, our conceptions of space were linear. Place, as space experienced through linear worldviews, was also linear. With systems, place and proximity are also thrown into question. Place emerges as complex relationality, complex limit/horizon, and complex responsibility. Further, systems theory understands that these dimensions exist as complex systems. Place is displaced by the always already present distant in the complexity. Said in a slightly different way, the distant is always already inherent in the proximate; thus, place is always already displaced.

Place, the Proximate, and Complexity: Responsibility and Response-Ability

Although system theory developed first within science, it is equally relevant for understanding our social and moral universe. To ask our moral questions relative to complex patterns rather than to individual events and to play those implications out as far as we are able can radically alter the ways in which we engage those moral principles developed in and for the proximate. As with science, ethically we move from the proximate to the approximate. Every ethical decision becomes a wager into an abyss of complexity. The seemingly simple becomes the infinitely complex, just as the linear becomes the nonlinear. Within a systems worldview, the experiences of space that transform it into place become complex networks and patterns that are inherently displacing in their complexity. While this displacement has experiential implications, it is the implications for the application of moral principles in ethical decision-making that are more critical.

Morally, systems philosophy and complexity challenge the ways in which we think about relationality, limit/horizon and responsibility. Agency and identity can no longer be tied only to place and the proximate. Morality ceases to be a bundle of principles or virtues. All must be rethought in terms of complexity in nonlinear ways. The ethics of place, ecologically or socially, is displaced. The moral principle becomes an emergent approximation, and the ethical decision becomes the moral wager.

Though place and the proximate are where our moral identity and agency are both formed and primarily expressed (as noted above), our experience of place need not be moral. For the moral agent, every experience of place demands the type of moral questioning we find in Aristotle or Confucius. Space as relationality and limit/horizon demands of the moral agent a response. The initial form of the response is the moral interrogative, which characterizes virtue. Morality is first the demands we place upon ourselves to ask the moral question, but it is also the response that I have called the moral wager. Just as systems puts into question limit/horizon and the proximate, so it also puts responsibility into question.

Let me demonstrate the problem of responsibility with a practical example to make experientially clear the inherent complexity of the proximate moral space. I call this "the seemingly simple act innocently done." I can give only the barest outline of this idea here, but I hope that it will suffice to demonstrate the point that we all recognize at some level that even the most mundane activities are inherently part of complex systems and thus morally complex. It also exemplifies how the distant is always already present in the proximate and thus the displacement of place.

The seemingly simple act innocently done is any act I do with a linear expectation of some commodity. Every morning I walk into my home office and do these two seemingly simple acts. I turn on a light, and I turn on my computer. All I want from these seemingly simple acts are commodities—light and word processing. This is my modern equivalent of Heidegger's workshop. For Heidegger, this act of engagement allows us to "discover" our own being-in-the world. As Casey points out, it "helps us to grasp the particular place we are in as the particular person who we are."[32] Place and self, as has been noted, are integrally related. Casey goes on to point out, "It would follow that thinned-out places are those in which the densely enmeshed infrastructures of the kind Heidegger discerns are missing . . . lacking the rigor and substance of thickly lived places."[33]

While, experientially, the place (my office) may maintain its density, systems thinking forces me morally to recognize the "thinning" of the place-experience of the seemingly simple act by the displacement of complexity. We might understand this moral thinning in two ways. Albert Borgmann, in his *Technology and the Character of Contemporary Life*, speaks about the "device paradigm" and about "the foreground of technology."[34] Borgmann distinguishes between a "thing" and a "device." While he does not use "density" or "thinness" in his description, the terms can effectively be applied to his distinction between a thing and a device. A "thing" for Borgmann has density. His example is the wood-burning stove or hearth. The hearth was the center of the home that not only gathered the family for the warmth but also gathered them in all of the activities associated with keeping the fire supplied with wood and burning. The hearth is a complex system, but in our terms it is relatively proximate in terms of relationality and limit/horizon. The activities—through which family members might go and chop wood, build and maintain the fire, and gather there—are all relatively direct and proximate. The family members can take a more or less direct responsibility for all of these. Borgmann's description of the "thing" is consistent with Casey's description of the density of the experience of place or Heidegger's description of the workshop.

Borgmann's example of a "device" is the central heating system, which has replaced the hearth in the modern home. Here the focus has shifted from the experience of the place (which Borgmann calls "focal" things and practices) to the commodity. "The machinery makes no demands on our skill, strength, or attention, and it is less demanding the less it makes its presence felt. . . . The emphasis lies on the commodious way in which devices make goods and services available."[35] With the device there is a distinct division between the means and the ends. Borgmann observes that "in the progress of technology, the machinery of a device has therefore a tendency to become concealed or to shrink."[36]

The device paradigm introduces new levels of complexity into any place, because distance and displacement are concealed by the shift from the focus on the active engagement with the "thing" to the focus only on the foreground of the commodity. The foreground of the seemingly simple act innocently done conceals a background of infinite complexity. The light and my computer still function as tools for work; thus, there is still an experience of place. I sit at my desk and write. The familiarity of that place is constitutive in dense and substantive ways, and it is also quite possible that the work that I do in that place is, at many levels, ethical. However, if we broaden our focus, it is the awareness of the background of what it takes to deliver that light and that computing power that can disintegrate the proximate and displace the experience of that place.

There has always been a foreground and a background to technology. Even in Heidegger's workshop, the tools were made somewhere beyond the workshop, and the workman could have made himself aware of this had he chosen to do so. The difference, and this is the critical difference, is that we are the first generations that can no longer feign ignorance of the background of the technologies that deliver the commodities we desire. Understanding the light switch as a complex system, we see first our relationship to it as in that foreground that desires the commodity. However, if we attend only to the construction of the switch box and trace that out in detail, we find that it is composed of dozens of parts made of dozens of materials. Looking deeper into the supply chains consisting of resource harvesting and transportation, manufacturing, wholesale and retail marketing, and so on, we very quickly find ourselves in a complex world of global technology, global markets, and global politics, replete with complex global and generational ethical issues. And thus far we have looked only at the switch box. There are systems within systems connected with the seemingly simple act innocently done. Although I may not readily acknowledge it, my seemingly simple act innocently done is no longer simple or innocent. The proximate, about which the philosophical and religious ethical traditions can offer relatively adequate guidance, has been transfigured into a complex system where the presence of the complex distant has altered my confidence in the possibility of the virtuous act that was relatively adequate in the proximate. That act has not become morally ambiguous. It has become a wager into the abyss.

One way to think about the issue is to return to Tuan's concern with scale. Are the virtues or the principles we find in our major moral theories scalable such that they can provide guidance when we recognize the complex systemic dimensions of every action? Hans Jonas, in his book *The Imperative of Responsibility*, argues that "modern technology has introduced actions of such novel scale, objects, and consequences that the framework of former ethics can no longer contain them."[37] Not only is it the case that most of the ethical issues with which we are faced are either directly the result of technology or involve technological processes in some way, but because of what Jacques Ellul refers to as the "systemic dimension" of technology (technology tends to become inter-linking systems),[38] these issues require that we think in totally new ways. Due to the awesome power and interconnection of technology, we now must think globally and generationally about every seemingly simple act.[39]

Awareness of this level of complexity—and again our generation is the first generation that can no longer hide from this awareness—changes the question of responsibility into one of response-ability. Are we even capable of factoring such complexity into any or all of the hundreds of seemingly simple acts we do daily? Are we able to be responsive to a complexity that challenges relational-ity by exploding limit/horizon beyond our ability to even really experience it? To co-opt Casey's terminology, have we left the dense experience of place and entered into a moral space of the void? The danger of this awareness of what can seem like an overwhelming complexity is that it can lead to a kind of moral cata-tonia in which we are unable or unwilling to make the moral wager.

Having a deeper understanding of the phenomenology of place and reflect-ing on morality as platial or experientially proximate help us think about the great ethical traditions and appreciate their importance in new ways. They help us understand identity, moral agency, and their formation. At the same time, if we contextualize these reflections in the complexity of systems that are now undeniably global and generational, questions arise about their value beyond the proximate.

That we have entered into a new era of the moral wager, the morally approx-imate, and moral ambiguity unlike any before seems to me to be undeniable. But it is equally undeniable that we must not allow the inherent complexity of even the seemingly simple act to overwhelm us to the point that we no longer feel compelled to make the moral wager. It is that deep, authentic, concernful engagement with place and the proximate that has the power to shape our moral identity and to motivate us as moral agents. It is that engagement in the proxi-mate that will ultimately compel us to continue to ask the moral question and to make the moral wager even in the face of complexity and ambiguity. It is in the proximate that we will develop a strong sense of moral principles and moral questions. How we apply these in ethical decision-making in light of complex-ity is the new question.

If virtue and character are always operative in an interrogative mode, the admission of a new understanding of the complex systemic dimension in the background of every question demands that the limit/horizon of the questions themselves must change. We can no longer be morally satisfied with what works only proximately; we must learn to think in more complex, nonlinear ways even as we acknowledge that past a certain point we are entering realms of such high levels of ambiguity that no firm or certain ethical decision is any longer possible. Living in the openness of complex systems, learning to see and think about increasingly complex patterns, and then—as soon as we humbly make our moral wager—beginning the process of rethinking the questions and responses anew is the new challenge. There is an imperative of responsibility, proximately and distantly. Ultimately, it will be how well we manage the ongoing struggle between the proximate and the distant, and between the seemingly simple and the complex, that will help us understand that all moral wagers, in the end, are not only wagers into the abyss but also wagers of hope.

NOTES

1. Edward S. Casey, *The Fate of Place: A Philosophical History* (Berkeley: University of California Press, 1998); Edward S. Casey, "Between Geography and Philosophy: What Does It Mean to Be in the Place-World?," *Annals of the Association of American Geographers* 91, no. 4 (2001): 683–693.

2. Casey, "Between Geography and Philosophy," 683.

3. Ibid.

4. Ibid.

5. Ibid., 684 (italics in the original).

6. Ibid., 684.

7. Casey, *Fate of Place*, 261.

8. Ibid., 262.

9. Quoted in ibid., 262.

10. Quoted in ibid., 262 (italics in the original).

11. Thanks to Peter Hershock for the suggestion that "limit" lacked the openness I was seeking, thus leading me to opt for "horizon."

12. Yi-Fu Tuan, *Space and Place: The Perspective of Experience* (Minneapolis: University of Minnesota Press, 1977); Yi-Fu Tuan, *Humanist Geography: An Individual's Search for Meaning* (Staunton, VA: George F. Thompson, 2012).

13. Tuan, *Humanist Geography*, 4.

14. Ibid.

15. Timothy Beatley and Kristy Manning, *The Ecology of Place: Planning for Environment, Economy, and Community* (Washington, DC: Island Press, 1997); Mick Smith, *An Ethics of Place: Radical Ecology, Postmodernity, and Social Theory* (Albany: State University of New York Press, 2001); Ian Billick and Mary V. Price, *The Ecology of Place* (Chicago: University of Chicago Press, 2010); Michael S. Northcott, *Place, Ecology and the Sacred: The Moral Geography of Sustainable Communities* (London: Bloomsbury, 2015).

16. Elizabeth Kolbert, *The Sixth Extinction: An Unnatural History* (New York: Henry Holt, 2014).

17. Casey, *Fate of Place*, 50.

18. Aristotle 212a, 20–21, quoted in Casey, *Fate of Place*, 55.

19. Quoted in Casey, *Fate of Place*, 262 (italics in the original).

20. Michael J. Sandel, *Liberalism and the Limits of Justice* (Cambridge: Cambridge University Press, 1982), 150 (italics in the original).

21. Roger T. Ames, "Observing Ritual 'Propriety (*li* 禮)' as Focusing the 'Familiar' in the Affairs of the Day," *Dao: A Journal of Comparative Philosophy* 1, no. 2 (June 2002): 145.

22. Ibid., 148.

23. David L. Hall and Roger T. Ames, *Thinking Through Confucius* (Albany: State University of New York Press, 1987), 120.

24. Ervin Laszlo, *Introduction to Systems Philosophy* (New York: Harper Torchbooks, 1972).

25. Ludwig von Bertalanffy, *General System Theory: Foundations, Development, Applications* (New York: George Braziller, 1973).

26. Fritjof Capra, *The Tao of Physics: An Exploration of the Parallels between Modern Physics and Eastern Mysticism* (Boston: Shambhala, 1999); Gary Zukav, *The Dancing Wu Li Masters: An Overview of the New Physics* (New York: William Morrow, 1979).

27. Bertalanffy, *General System Theory*, 32.

28. Ervin Laszlo, *The Systems View of the World: A Holistic Vision for Our Time* (Cresskill, NJ: Hampton Press, 1996), 10.

29. For a brief but good synopsis of this, see ibid., 10–13.

30. Fritjof Capra, *The Web of Life: A New Scientific Understanding of Living Systems* (New York: Anchor Books, 1996), 36.

31. Ibid., 37.

32. Casey, "Between Geography and Philosophy," 684.

33. Ibid.

34. Albert Borgmann, *Technology and the Character of Contemporary Life: A Philosophical Inquiry* (Chicago: University of Chicago Press, 1984), 48–57.

35. Ibid., 42.

36. Ibid.

37. Hans Jonas, *The Imperative of Responsibility: In Search of an Ethics for the Technological Age* (Chicago: University of Chicago Press, 1984), 6.

38. Jacques Ellul, *The Technological System* (New York: Continuum, 1980).

39. Also see Peter D. Hershock, *Reinventing the Wheel: A Buddhist Response to the Information Age* (Albany: State University of New York Press, 1999).

PART II

THE CRITICAL INTERPLAY OF PLACE AND PERSONAL IDENTITY

Where Is My Mind?

ON THE EMPLACEMENT OF SELF BY OTHERS

Joshua Stoll

6

What does it take to be a first-person realist, to admit the reality of what Jonardon Ganeri calls a first-person stance as opposed to a first-person perspective? In other words, what does it take to make sense of the idea that I own my experiences—my intentions, perceptions, desires, actions, beliefs, and so on—that is, that I inhabit and engage with these experiences rather than merely witness or observe them as happening to me? Curiously, this question can hardly be answered without recourse to first-persons who aren't me. For attempts at establishing "real subjects," "real selves"—attempts at establishing the sense of ownership an "I" has over his or her mental life in the sense that I *am* this mental life—cannot do so adequately without navigating the potential pitfalls of solipsism.

One way to put this is to say that, in order to understand how I am the owner of my life-experiences, I must also be capable of making sense of how the semantics of self-ascriptions for mental terms deliver the same meanings of those terms in other-ascriptions; so that the term "pain," for example, means precisely the same thing when I say that "I am in pain" and when I am aware that "You are in pain." There is a notorious gap here between first-person accounts of mentality and third-person accounts of mentality: given that I only ever have such a sense of ownership over myself, how can I understand that you have such a sense of ownership over yourself? This is what has been called the conceptual problem of other minds. Ganeri proposes that bridging the gap requires "a certain conception of self" that explains the manner in which a mind and a body are related.[1] Ganeri also suggests that, on the other hand, if we can't answer the conceptual problem, we will be left with an attenuated theory of self. That is, if we can't say how first- and third-person ascriptions of mentality are semantically equivalent, we may be left with a conception of self that, like a wave in a roiling ocean, cannot be individuated. And so there would be no way to distinguish myself from you.

However, I propose that such ontological questions as how mental and physical pieces of the universe fit together cannot be approached without having recourse to an investigation of axiological issues having to do with the way in which selves are emplaced in societal structures. To this end, I will discuss Ganeri's approach to selfhood—what he calls a kind of "ownership view"—and the manner in which it may avoid the conceptual solipsism and attenuation discussed above. Such an approach, however, is itself wanting: though it has room for social effects on the experience of oneself as oneself, such effects are not particularly articulated. Indeed, insofar as the place of the self in social space is not articulated, we will still be left with an attenuated self that must face up to the conceptual problem of other minds. I will suggest, through a discussion of the embodiment of subjective space as well as the intersectional identity of subjectivity decentered by societal emplacement, that the more pressing and primary problem with regard to the sense of oneself as oneself is not that of how we are extensionally the *same* as others. Rather, it is a set of problems having to do with understanding the manners in which we are *different* from each other and our responsiveness to the ways society, and the individuals with whom we share society, differentiate us—that is, to the ways in which we are socially situated. In order for there to be a first-person stance (a sense of engaged inhabitation or ownership with respect to experience), we must always already be seconded by others—that is to say, placed among the array of social possibilities.

Buddhist No-Selfism (*Anātmavāda*): Setting up Ganeri's View

Ganeri suggests that a strong, naturalistic theory of the first-person stance must do at least two things: it must answer the question "What am I?" as well as the question "Which one am I?" However, if we answer the former question in a way that denies the possibility of answering the second question, the result is that we leave no room for understanding how I am not the only "self" in existence. This is what Ganeri calls an attenuated theory of self. It is closely related to the conceptual problem of other minds. Indeed, it is the other side of the coin. If I cannot individuate myself from you, if I can't tell whether this next episode of experience is mine rather than someone else's, how can I possibly understand that you are really the sort of entity I am—namely, a self? In other words, if there is no answer to "Which one am I?" then there certainly can't be an answer to "Are your pains like my pains?"

It is this dilemma that Ganeri puts to Buddhist reflexivism of the sort proposed by Dharmakīrti. Following the line of thought initiated by the seminal Buddhist logician Dignāga, Dharmakīrti considers subjective experience to be reflexive. Each moment of experience has two inseparable and irreducible aspects (*ākāra*): subjective and objective. It is this dual-aspect of consciousness that allows one to be self-aware (*svasaṃvedana*), since, for each moment of conscious, objective experience, there is prereflective, implicit awareness of that object-awareness. A more robust, reflective self-awareness can thus be had when the subject-aspect (*grāhakākāra*) is taken by a later conscious event as an object-aspect (*grāhyākāra*). However, such forms of self-awareness are not awareness of a substantial self (*ātman*), since they are merely moments (*kṣaṇāḥ*) of the causal psychophysical stream of experience (*santāna*) that is conventionally designated as one's "self." Taking up or appropriating (*upādāna*) such self-awareness is, for these Buddhists, an error, an illusion, since this would imply determinate identity conditions for individuating discrete psychophysical streams. But this would be like trying to find determinate identity conditions with which to individuate waves in a body of water; and there is no determinate answer to the question "Is this wave the same as the last one?" Thus, if we are to answer the question "What am I?" in this Buddhist fashion—the answer being "a causal stream of psychophysical elements"—then it seems that there is no answer to the question "Which one am I?" Solipsism would ensue.

Dharmakīrti, sensing this difficulty, argued that another's stream of experience (*santanāntara*) is inferable. Our only access to the minds of others, he argued, is by "observing the purposeful actions outside ourselves" and inferring, based on this, that since I did not produce those actions, another mind-stream must have.[2] That is, since I am aware that before my actions there is a certain desire to act, I can assume—according to Dharmakīrti—that some internal mental state such as a desire is the cause of an act. And since I do occasionally experience actions that are not the results of my desires, I can infer that another's desire was responsible for the action that I did not cause.

It is worth noting here that while this sounds like the classic argument from analogy found in John Stuart Mill, the structure of the inference is slightly different. The emphasis of Mill's argument is more about my experiences tout court, while, as Jeremy Henkel points out, Dharmakīrti's argument is more about a general causal relationship between mind and body.[3] The analogical argument has the following general structure:

> I exist.
> There is a certain correlation between my behavior and my mental processes.
> Other bodies display behavior similar to what I find myself displaying.
> Therefore, another mind underlies those behavioral displays.

Dharmakīrti's argument, on the other hand, has something more like the following structure:

> I experience behavioral actions.
> Not all actions I experience are produced by me.
> All actions are caused by mind.
> The action that I experience as not mine must be caused by another mind.

Here reference is first made to my experience of something objective—in the sense of experienced but not caused by me—rather than to my own particular existence and ability to cause events in the world, as the argument from analogy does. Next, it is noted that any action that I do not cause must still be caused by some mind, since action is, so to speak, the embodiment of mind. Thus, there must be at least one mind out there that is not my mind.

However, since Dharmakīrti suggested that the only evidence we have of the minds of others is representations or ideas (*vijñāpti*) of external signs (set up in the dual-aspect mode discussed above), one can ask why such representations must be caused by an alternate consciousness. Aren't objective representations dependent for their presentation on the subjective aspect of experience such that the cause of something that appears externally is just an internal trace (*vāsana*) that remains from previous experiences? Isn't there, as Dharmakīrti famously suggested, a lack of distinction between blue itself and the perception of blue? Wouldn't there then be a lack of distinction between your bodily gesticulations and my perceptions of your bodily gesticulations? If so, why assume that some other mind-stream external to the series I identify with caused those particular gesticulations? Dharmakīrti replies (rather dogmatically, as R. K. Sharma points out[4]) by suggesting that if such gesticulations had no cause, then by the invariable concomitance found between one's own action and intent, no presentation of purposive action *in general* can be said to have a cause.[5]

But as the eminent Kaśmīr Śaiva polymath Abhinavagupta explains, such a generalization can't be invariably concomitant. One can't establish, based on one's own experiences with the connection between desires and actions, that such a connection is necessary or invariable, and thus generalizable across all instances of action. It is at best contingent, and to put forth an inference to the effect that the connection is necessary would be to beg the question. For the whole inference to another's mind rests on the assumption that the other has a desire, say, to speak—and this already implies the other's existence.[6] Dharmakīrti might reply that when one desires to speak, one also desires to be heard. So that in each desire to speak there is both the subjective "I wish to be heard" and the objective "I hear her speak"; and action thus always comes with the awareness, as Sartre aptly points out, that others might be witnessing it.

This movement toward being aware of the presence of others as knowers of actions, however, does not necessarily save Dharmakīrti, for as Abhinavagupta puts it, "It is not universally true that the effect of the subjective is the objective; because there are exceptions."[7] Isabelle Ratié gives a suitable example: "I can very well wish to be heard and yet not be heard."[8] Abhinavagupta goes on to point out—in a way rather similar to that of Ratnakīrti, also a Buddhist reflexivist of the Yogācāra tradition—that the inference faces a dilemma. For the very idea of another stream of experiences is incoherent if all we can be aware of are reflexively self-aware representations. If you were to exist, there would have to be a notable difference between your mind and mine—for if there were identity, we would both simply be me. But what mark of difference is there? For a difference to be manifest, it would have to occur in my experience, lest no mark of difference be *present*. And because it occurs in my experience, I would take such a *presentation* as my own, as reflexively constituted, as *representation*. However, the difference is to be sought between my mind and another's. And if I could note the experience of another reflexively as I could my own, that person's experience would just be mine. Were you, qua your first-person reflexive experiences, manifest to my experience, there would be no difference between my mind and yours. Either Dharmakīrti admits solipsism or he admits that there are entities that exist independent of one's own mind-stream. He can't accept the latter without compromising one of the central tenets of his philosophy. And if he accepts the former, the very notion of another would make no sense. Thus, since the very idea of another's life-experiences collapses under analysis, there is no way of telling when a moment of experience is mine or not (attenuation). Indeed, it would not make sense for there to be experiences that aren't mine (conceptual problem).

Ganeri's Ownership View

Ganeri suggests that avoiding the dilemma that Dharmakīrti faces requires a conception of selfhood that distinguishes between the ways in which mental properties are exemplified (the question "What?") and the manner in which a set of mental properties are individuated from another set ("Which one?"). What I am—the owner of a certain set of experiences—is a place (*ādhāra*) in which mental properties inhere or through which they are exemplified: I am a "metaphysical location" for my experiences.[9] But I am *this* particular set of experiences—*this particular owner, right here*—because of the normative responsiveness of my embodiment. My body is the ground or base (*āśraya*) upon which my ownership of experience supervenes. Whereas *ownership* is thus a matter of psychic interconnections in the depths of my mental life, my mental life is individuated due to the manner in which my body normatively responds to these psychic depths. Thus, I am my desires and preferences because, as Ganeri puts it, in respect of them, there is autonomy;[10] but my autonomy, being mine and not yours, is expressed in the manner in which my body moves in the hodological spaces provided by these preferences and desires. We can get a better picture of the ontological relation between the place that exemplifies my mental life and the base upon which my mental life supervenes by noting three interrelated dimensions of selfhood distinguished by Ganeri: the immersive self; the under-self, or procedural self; and the participant self.

    The immersive self is a phenomenological sense of mineness. It is the feeling of being present, of not just bearing witness to one's own mental life but taking it up as one's own and thus living it. Such an experience requires some manner in which my sense of ownership tags each moment of my mental life so as to indicate of an experience that "This is mine." Ganeri points out that this can be accounted for in purely subjective terms as well as in terms of embodiment—the body-subject (*corps sujet*), in Merleau-Ponty's turn of phrase. Ganeri turns to Vasubandhu for an account of such subjective immersion. This Buddhist thinker, one of the founders of the Yogācāra tradition, accounts for a continuing sense of oneself as oneself (*manovijñāna*) in his discussions of what he calls the afflicted mind (*kliṣṭmanas*) and the repository consciousness (*ālayavijñāna*). The repository consciousness acts as a base (*āśraya*) that can be accessed in a first-personal, prereflective manner in order to retrieve traces of previous experiences that are tagged as "mine." Since these tags are, according to Vasubandhu, nonliteral, the appropriation of these tagged experiences as a sense of ownership delivered is an error, and so such minds are said to be afflicted (*kliṣṭi*). It is because of this move to an error theory of selfhood—combined with a neglect for the distinction between place (*ādhāra*) and base (*āśraya*), between a sense of ownership and individuation (for a sense of ownership is always misplaced, according to the Buddhists)—that Ganeri prefers the embodied version of immersion.

In embodied immersion, the phenomenological sense of mineness is delimited by the boundaries of the body on which it supervenes, and so it can be given precise identity conditions. However, we must be careful here as Ganeri adamantly argues against any identification of selfhood itself with the body itself. He adduces five kinds of arguments for the distinction between selfhood and bodyhood. While we cannot get into all five of these arguments here, the gist is that mental properties cannot be properties of the body, since the manner in which they are exemplified differs from the manner in which physical objects exemplify physical properties. We can see this clearly in arguments from self-reference—namely, in Śaṅkara Miśra's reply to an argument by the Cārvāka materialists. These materialists claimed that the self just is the body, since we can say of ourselves "I am bulky." However, Śaṅkara Miśra argues that such use is metaphorical, since "even someone whose eyes are closed thinks 'I . . .'"[11] The reason that such metaphorical uses are applicable is grounded, Śaṅkara Miśra suggests, in the manner in which the sense of I-ness (*ahaṃtva*) is superimposed on the body. The idea is that the body is the region throughout which the self—the experience of ownership—occurs, the body here *belonging to* myself, enacting or expressing my mentality by individuating the experiences and actions I am engaged with from those I am not.

The body also participates in procedurally monitoring my experiences, unconsciously regulating experiential awareness so as to prompt impulses toward action (*prayatana*). Here Ganeri puts forth his primary claim to the "metaphysical dependence" between the disparate ontological fields of selfhood and physicality. This procedural self, or underself, is the unique access we seem to have as regards our past experiences, and it is regulated by the body's normative responses to immersion insofar as it is regulated by the embodied subject's history—it is what Ganeri calls our "deep psyche." Still, the self is not the body, since the properties it exemplifies cannot be exemplified by physical entities alone. Thus, whereas the self is the exemplifying or individual cause (*samavāyikāraṇa*) of my mental life, my body is my mental life's feature cause (*asamavāyikāraṇa*). In other words, the self is an agent (*kartṛ*) who can prompt action by exemplifying properties proper to the history that is featured in an embodied subject's course of life. That is, the self as agent is the individual who experiences mental or psychological episodes that supervene on, and so are featured in but not exemplified by, a body's responsiveness.

Finally, the participant self is the terminus of the impetus for action (*prayatana*). This is the aspect of self that does not merely feel a sense of mineness or monitor the experiences that fall under this mineness, but engages with or otherwise enlists one's own experiences to the end of the kinds of action one is to perform. It is the active aspect of self that utilizes a sense of presence, regulated by background experiences, in order to act. Ganeri suggests that the participant self, through emotional prompts, unifies the self as a singular experience of ownership: emotions provide a hodological space for action, wherein immersive embodiment provides for experiences that are compared and contrasted so as to prompt impulses toward action and thus a sense of engagement or inhabitation in the expression of one's satisfactions and dissatisfactions.

Thus, in Ganeri's naturalistic account of real selves, owners of experience have at least four aspects:

1. Real selves are normative: we are responsive to valences embodied, in part in the responsiveness of the body to its physical environment but also, as humans, no less so to our social environment. Thus, insofar as selfhood is normative, it is a place for the ownership of commitments, intentions, and preferences; the self consists in continuing dispositions of endorsement, whereby each owned state has the potential to make normative demands on other owned states, implying an autonomous capacity to move through hodological space in particular ways given certain backgrounds.

2. Real selves are embodied: we have the ability to be responsive to and engage with inhabited states of mind, particularly emotions as the connection between immersive experience, unconscious monitoring mechanisms of one's mental life, and participation in that mental life by inhabiting and engaging one's experiences rather than merely witnessing them.

3. Real selves are thus owned: I am the mentality that is inhabited and thus owned by my selfhood and expressed through my body, rather than merely being a series of witnessed insertions of phenomena in my mental life. In other words, I am an autonomous agent who engages with the experiences to which my body is responsive.

4. Real selves are unified: they are patterns of endorsements and rejections, valenced by hodological spaces, the latter provided by the manner in which emotions tie together experience, regulatory preference, and agency.

Where Am I? Subjective Space, Objective Space, and the Conceptual Problem

Have these ideas given us a good sense of real selves? I contend that such a conception of selfhood is still attenuated and thus still susceptible to the conceptual problem of other minds. Ganeri has claimed that "a certain conception of self" bridges the divide between a first-person stance and a third-person stance. It is unclear just how his ownership view bridges the divide, but the suggestion seems to be something like this: since we can answer the question "What?" independently of "Which one?" we can say something about how mentalistic predicates—those that are dominated by ownership, or "whathood"—are related to embodiment, or "whichhood." This is, namely, through the relation between exemplary and nonexemplary causes. Yet such an account still seems quite attenuated: it says nothing about the more robust question "Who am I?" and the related slew of place-based questions: "Where am I, how did I get here, and where am I going?" There can hardly be adequate answers to Ganeri's questions without knowing the *place* of such a dualistic—or, perhaps better, pluralistic—human being in his or her experience of his or her singular life. I may be the owner of my experiences in the sense of being a metaphysical location for mental properties, while also being individuated by inhabiting a body.

But none of this is of any consequence so long as this individuating inhabitation is not articulated in regard to a life—that is, a living, breathing person with a particular biological and sociocultural background through and in which his or her patterns of endorsements, aversions, preferences, intentions, and so on are gathered. Navigating the conceptual problem of other minds might thus require recourse to our dynamic proximity with others, for to understand how you can be the same sort of thing as me despite my inability to inhabit your sphere of ownness (to use a Husserlian turn of phrase) requires that I understand the manner in which an embodied subject can traverse spaces that I don't occupy. Moreover, negotiating attenuation requires a robust account of the manner in which my I-ness—my ownership of myself—is forged through a history of engagements with those who are in variable ways proximal. Thus, we don't simply stand close to each other—both evolutionarily as a matter of being the same species and physically in the manner of being in the same room. We actually churn out each other's experiences by bringing with us unique backgrounds that influence the ways in which we interact. To flesh out these ideas, I will first make reference to Jeff Malpas' attempt to solve the conceptual problem of other minds using the distinction between subjective and objective spaces. This may give us a decent sense of "where I am" while rendering the conceptual problem rather impotent, but it doesn't say much about "how I got here," "where I am going," and "who I am." To handle these latter issues of attenuation, I will turn later to the notions of intersectionality and decentered subjectivity.

It seems that if we are going to approach questions like "Who am I?" or "Where am I?" or "How did I get here?" through some embodied framework, including a dualistic one like Ganeri's, we need to understand embodiment as regulating the self's relationship to its environment. For my embodiment, with all the habitual tendencies established evolutionarily and historically through which I live out my existence—this historicality being part of what it means to be a "who" that has a "whither" and a "whence"—always places me *here*. Edward Casey suggests as much when he points out, "The self has to do with the agency and identity of the geographical subject; body is what links this self to lived place in its sensible perceptible features; and landscape is the presented layout of a set of places, not their mere accumulation but their sensuous self-presentation as a whole."[12] We can see, under such a construal, a careful (if not exactly ontological) distinction, not just between oneself and the body one engages the world with, as Ganeri has it, but also between these two factors and the world that one engages in the mode, minimally, of an array of places that can be occupied and traversed. And such places are not mere vacuous and static space. As we will see, places are highly articulated and dynamic, involving all the axiological significance of politics and culture.

For now, let us dwell on how our general emplacement might help advance us regarding the conceptual problem of other minds and the question I have juxtaposed with it—namely, "Where am I?" We can begin with Casey's notion of "here-being."[13] Being "here in part," I find myself "within" my body—often "in the head." That is, I can have a sense of focus on some aspect of my embodiment—it becomes salient—to such an extent that what we might call a region or, more dynamically, regions of such awareness are "brought to light," emphasized in and by experience. Such hereness is related to the "here of my body proper" in the sense that I am my body and find myself wherever it is. We should be careful with such a declaration, though. It seems that Casey doesn't exactly wish to make strict ontological distinctions between one's body, one's self, and one's place. Ganeri, on the other hand, identifies the self as that which exemplifies mental predicates, whereas the body is merely featured in those exemplifications by way of regulating hodological spaces through which to travel. Still, Casey's point here holds: we can distinguish between my sense of being in a certain part of my body (generally the head but perhaps, as he points out, in my torso when I dance) and being my body in the sense of living it—or, to keep

Ganeri's terminology, owning it. In other words, we need not abandon Ganeri's more ontological dualism to acknowledge Casey's phenomenological point. As Casey puts it, "We stand only with our full body, not with part of it."[14]

Another form of here-being identified by Casey is the "here of my by-body," which is my embodied mobility. Such hereness is, in Malpas' terminology, "subjective space" that "'gives space' for action."[15] Such mobility requires the "regional here," the totality of places that an embodied subject can traverse. Finally, and more pertinent for our present discussion, is what Casey calls the "interpersonal here." It is this sense of hereness that Malpas targets with his distinction between objective space—what Casey would consider a static and inarticulate, container-like vacuum—and subjective space, that space through which an embodied subject grasps its own locality and orients itself. For in being *here* through my embodied locality and mobility, I make it impossible for you to be *just here* with me. My here-being, in the manner of a self that owns a body that occupies a place through which a world is engaged, ineluctably forces you to be *there*. By saying "here" in answer to the question "Where am I?" I necessarily raise the conceptual problem of other minds. For what sense can be made of a *there* that I cannot make a *here*, even in all my "by-body" activity? As Casey puts it, "What is at stake is not just *my* own body but also the other's body as it relates to, and differs from, mine (and vice versa). My own here remains mine, yet I am aware of another here precisely as *another's here*: a here that is conveyed to me only indirectly by the other's body as *there* in my perception."[16]

Utilizing concepts similar to those in Casey's discussions of here-being, Malpas begins his inquiry into the difficulty of the interpersonal here by noting what it means to have a *grasp* of space: "For a creature to have a grasp of space, then, is for it to exhibit behavior the explanation of which necessarily requires reference to a spatial framework."[17] In other words, a grasp of space is merely a creature's ability to utilize a spatial framework, one that can be—and, by us, has been—conceptualized. More particularly, if a creature has some grasp of subjective space—something like Casey's first three "here-beings"—it must have some grasp of objective space. A grasp of subjective space is the mere ability of some organism to orient and locate itself and to utilize the spatiality of its own embodiment to move around the world. In more Caseyesque terms, subjective space is a creature's ability to find a place for itself. But in having such a grasp, an organism has a grasp—though not necessarily a *concept*—of objective space, since, in its awareness of its own embodied capabilities, it must also be aware of a larger space through which its capabilities are able to be enacted. Indeed, it is this quasi-Dharmakīrtian dual-aspectuality of our grasp of space that gives us the impression, according to Malpas, that we can merely derive a *concept* of objective space by assembling together a concatenation of subjective spaces.[18] But, Malpas contends, a concept of objective space is not simply derived from a grasp of subjective space, since there is no necessary connection—as we have seen in the arguments against Dharmakīrti's inference to others—between my subjectivity and yours. Thus, as Malpas puts it, "The capacity to conceptually 'detach' ourselves from the subjective space of our experience is thus indicative, not of the derivation of objective from subjective space, but of the prior grasp of objective space that enables such conceptual detachment."[19]

It is this conception of objective space, indicative of a prior grasp of objective space irreducible to but inseparable from a grasp of subjective space that Malpas finds pertinent to sociality. For it is through such a conception of space that we can think of this perspective—this grasp of subjective space—as being one of many. Objective space is, so to speak, decentered. Or, rather, the very notion of centrality is incoherent in the concept of objective space. For the concept of objective space is the concept of a space devoid of place—that is, devoid of a spot from which one can view the world, devoid of perspective. The concept of subjective space, on the other hand, is precisely the concept of a place from which we not only view the world but also engage with it. Malpas argues that the concept of a subjective space is dependent on the concept of objective space. In other words, the *concept* of subjectivity, of an agent who has a grasp of his or her ability to move around and do things, requires the *concept* of a space through which more than one agent can move. Thus, I can conceive of myself as merely one subject among many because, through my grasp of the spatial framework that my embodiment affords, I can conceive of a larger space that has no center, no perspective. And in being able to do that, I can coherently think of the concept of others who grasp their own embodied ability to move and act through a neutral space in which no single perspective holds sway. Thus, as Malpas puts it:

> To have a grasp of the concept of sociality is to have a grasp of the possibility of there being other perspectives on the world than that which one possesses oneself—this is indeed the essence of a grasp of the *concept* of otherness—and so to have a grasp of one's own perspective on the world as one perspective amidst a multiplicity of other possible perspectives. To have a grasp of the concept of sociality is thus to have a grasp of objective space and vice versa.[20]

Does this solution to the conceptual problem give us a robust, nonattenuated sense of what Casey calls the "interpersonal here"? Perhaps it does, at least to the extent that it gives us a way of understanding how it is possible for there to be a multiplicity of "heres," all but one of which must be "there." In this sense, we have something of a philosophical answer to the question "Where am I?"—and so we have a less attenuated, more conceptually robust notion of selfhood. Yet this is a very static notion of selfhood, one that conceives of the subject as the pure center of its world. To be sure, there is some sense to this notion: I can never escape my here, and my here is always correlated with my body. Yet my here has moved through time and space, from place to place, and this movement has not been simply ineffective. I have gathered much of my selfhood from being, in a sense, displaced across time and space and, in being so displaced, from having encountered others who have influenced my manner of being myself—that is, having grasped sociality, having found (often enough, having been given) a place. Some you was always *there*, wherever I went. This dynamic tension between the impossibility of your sameness—your never being *just here*—and the familiar presence of your difference is the very structure of society. Where I am, and my having arrived here, are a result of the ways in which my background is enactively embodied as the expression of my presence in response to the absent yet responsive presence of a life who's *here* is perpetually over *there*. Our sociality thus consists in the emplacement of myself by another who is a *removed here*, resistant to the subjective space I enact through my presence. It is to these ideas that we now turn, in order to flesh out a more robust sense of self.

Whither, Whence, Who?

Our interpersonal here is not merely our ability to conceive of an objective space through which embodied subjects—conceivable only insofar as objective space is—comport themselves, precisely because the grasp of space is, for animals whose embodied dexterity includes socially complex and skillful interactions, already a sort of social grasp. We are born keen, so to speak, to the human form and its mobility—especially facially. Newborns are capable of distinguishing between faces and inanimate objects.[21] In addition, they are capable of mimicking facial expressions,[22] implying a primitive semiotic distinction between oneself and another through a responsive form of proprioceptive awareness. Such a capacity is not exactly a passive affair. According to Colwyn Trevarthen, "it is more a remodelling and integration of components already in spontaneous expression."[23] Even when they don't imitate, infants by as early as three to four weeks of age are interactive with other persons, smiling, waving, and frowning, as the case may be, in response to the activity of a second person, usually the mother.[24] Infants thus generally vocalize and gesture in a way that is attuned to the vocalizations and gestures of other people.[25] These abilities are foundational in our grasping of sociality at the same time as exhibiting a certain grasp of spatiality—namely, proprioceptive and kinesthetic possibilities of human bodies. Eventually we engage in collaborative efforts. Infants begin to track the eyes of others,[26] ostensibly understanding through the perception-proprioception bodily schematic discussed above, and thus at least at a prepersonal embodied level, that others are *looking* at the world around them. Around ten to eleven months of age, infants begin to show evidence of an ability to parse action by intentional boundaries.[27] By eighteen months, they show evidence of understanding the unfulfilled goals of others by reenacting to completion the other's unfinished goal-directed behavior.[28] In doing so, they become capable of engaging with others in ways they haven't yet. They begin to participate in interactive pragmatic contexts where others can be jointly involved with them in goal-directed activities.

These spatially and socially significant capacities are where our notions of others begin. It is in our ability to feel the presence of others as both different from and the same as me—to imitate, detect, and interact with them—that we experience our world and, through it, our place. Through this setting we address each other. Abhinavagupta paints a picture of the manner in which such address constitutes reality. The power of this vocative dimension of sociality should not be underestimated. It is not just that your presence signals to me possibilities beyond my repertoire, possibilities that I might appropriate. It brings about a whole new world, one that is a challenge to, an uncanny upsurge within, my totalized world that feels centered on myself, my concerns and my needs. The *Paratrīśikā*, a Kaśmīr Śaiva text commented on by Abhinavagupta, describes the very generation of the world through an interaction between Śiva and Śakti. It begins by Śakti asking Śiva a question:

> God, how does the ultimate spontaneously confer beauteous union of this individual subject on the universal subject [*kaulikasiddhidam*] by the very moment of awareness on account of which there is a sameness of consciousness-power (*khecarīsamatām*) achieved?[29] My Lord, tell this same-self [*kathayasva*] about that which, in its abundant clarity, is concealed.[30]

The answer is in the question itself. As Abhinavagupta pointed out in his *vivaraṇa*, Śiva is being *addressed*. Both "God" (*deva*) and "My Lord" (*mama prabho*) are in the vocative case. As such, "God" and "Lord" are not mere nouns, designating an object in the world. As Abhinavagupta puts it, they "have a greater connotation than an ordinary noun."[31] This connotation is the seconding of the other, thus opening up an interactive space for our continuing spontaneous solicitations of each other. And indeed it is in the embodied language, in our embodied semiotic and reflective semantic understandings used to coordinate this conversation, that the world itself is generated. Your very presence is thus a sort of decentering of my world. Indeed, for at least the Pratyabhijñā school of Kaśmīr Śaivism, the ultimate reality itself appears to be a decentered subjectivity.

Now, this space between us is already filled with and is always being filled with images, meanings, significances, and so on, all of which, as suggested, are shot through with a grasp of sociality (at least for beings such as we are). And part of this sociality is just that our proximity to each other generates both a gap and a bridge, a sense of our having come from somewhere and going to somewhere different, even if proximal. As Levinas suggests, your presence exceeds every idea I can have of you: "The face of the Other at each moment destroys and overflows the plastic image it leaves me."[32] Indeed, he notes that such general conceptions of others as terms related to us through society is inimical: "When taken to be like a genus that unites like individuals the essence of society is lost sight of."[33] In other words, when we try to universalize that particularity that is irreducibly its own, we do that owner a disservice and an injustice. The strict, formal sense in which we can be understood as the *same*, as being *of a kind*, is an aspect of our mutual finitude as well as our respective autonomy; for this just is our being here, despite never being, both of us, *just here*. This is our informal awareness of our mutually opposed, yet ontologically similar, whence and whither. And such an awareness need not be immediately a formal or semantic understanding of our mutual sameness. Our concept of sociality is thus dependent, not merely on our concept of objective space, but also on our grasp of an interpersonal here that exhibits a sense of universality in the midst of particularized differences—a grasp from which is derived our concept of the objective, or perspectiveless. Our sociality is thus essential to our individuality. For as stated, some you was always *there* everywhere I went. So just as, for Malpas, the concept of subjective space requires the concept of objective space, the latter requires a grasp of subjective space—a space irrevocably tied to a grasp of objective space. In the same way, the concept of sociality relies on a concept of the interpersonal here, which, for certain organisms, depends on a grasp of interpersonal space. There is thus a sort of universality in our individuality, a grasp of otherness in our grasp of ourselves.

Still, such a conception of self is attenuated, for the axiological impact of such an exposition of the interpersonal here must be incorporated into any adequately robust account of selfhood. And the axiological impact, while expressing a kind of universality, is always expressed by a particular individual. Though, as Levinas puts it, alterity "is prior to every initiative, to all imperialism of the same,"[34] still we never merely encounter a face. Because we can't help but reify, because the essence of expression, of our communicative sociality, is generalization, our encounter of each other's faces is always an encounter with a friend, a foe, a sibling or parent, a stranger. And even strangers aren't mere strangers. You are always engendering a specific gender, a specific race, a specific sexual orientation, ethnicity, age, nationality, and so forth. Thus, we emplace each other as unique and enlivened regions of an otherwise apparently inert world, and we often do so at social intersections, even in the midst of strangers, for first impressions always make the stranger somehow known. But no one is ever just one or the other of the social categories mentioned above. Everyone is shot through with multiple identities, even in their ability to keep these identities unified, integrated.

As feminist authors have emphasized, the effects of such intersectionality is of paramount importance to our understanding of the subordination of social groups as well as our understanding of our own selves as autonomous agents, as individuals emplaced by sociocultural factors that differentiate us along social categories. In such a case, our autonomy is thus—perhaps paradoxically— dependent on the way our societal emplacement decenters our apparent unity as the unique owner of this mental life. In other words, where I come from is integral to my being *here*, no matter who or what is proximal to me. And it will similarly help drive where I am going. But as one's whither and whence expands, separating itself out, decentering itself amidst the "heres" one encounters, a "who" is born. And this robust who is much more than mere heres or theres, for its being here, in a dynamic and multifaceted way, emplaces others—not just *over there*, but *in their there*.

Thus, the real "problem of other minds" (and an appropriate detour for a question like "Who am I?") is a set of axiological issues related to ethics, politics, and aesthetics: it is a problem of making sense of difference, not sameness. To this end, let's take a brief look at the two aforementioned effects of intersectionality on selfhood: that of the potentiality for subordination and that of the autonomous ownership of multiple senses of identity. It will be suggested that I must always already acknowledge the manner in which I am emplaced in and by society. Only then can I own up to who I am—that is, live autonomously as a member of society.

Because of the manner in which your presence, as Sartre phrased it, "steals my world from me"[35]—that is, insofar as you are for me an absent yet responsive presence that can decenter my sense of my own presence—you make me responsible for and owner of attributes the interpretations of which I didn't necessarily choose to be responsible for. In this respect, you are the oppression of my freedom. But the specific forms such subjugation takes are tied to the litany of sociocultural categories noted earlier. Alleviation of such subjugation, as Kimberle Crenshaw points out, requires that we take critical notice of the manner in which our intersectional, socially constructed identities affect our life-experiences. Thus, intersections are places at which my embodiment— my biosociohistorical experience—crisscrosses over itself as I traverse the value-laden field of possible emplacements society may present me. For some of us, such intersections are more or less invisible, since these are places that are rarely the site of subjection. For others, however, these places of intersection are sites of struggle and oppression.

Crenshaw, for example, notes the struggles unique to individuals whose identities prominently intersect at such crossroads as gender and race. She identifies three ways in which such intersectional identities are adversely affected by societal considerations. First, she notes that women of color's experience of violence and remediation is quite different from white women's experience— there is a difference in *structural* experience. Citing the example of the emendation of the marriage fraud provisions in the Immigration and Nationality Act, which made it so that people who immigrated to the United States to get married needed to stay married for two years, she observes that women, particularly those of color, are singled out in a multiphrenic way. By not taking into account the possibility of women being subjected to spousal abuse, this amendment, designed to make immigration and permanent residence difficult to attain, put many immigrant women in a tight spot: leave an abusive husband and get deported, or absorb the battering and stay in the United States. As Crenshaw puts it, "Congress positioned these women to absorb the simultaneous impact of its anti-immigration policy and their spouse's abuse."[36]

Furthermore, Crenshaw points out the manner in which black women are positioned *politically* so as to have to "split their political energies between two sometimes opposing groups."[37] Because antiracist strategies are often taken up from the perspective of black men and feminist strategies are often taken up from the perspective of white women, the political strategies of antiracism and feminism are limited for women of color. Emplaced at the intersection of two subjugated groups, they must sometimes choose antiracist politics at the expense of feminism and feminist politics at the expense of antiracism. Indeed, the example of anti-rape politics is quite eye-opening. Crenshaw notes that racial solidarity in the black community is more likely to form behind a black man charged with rape than a black woman who has been raped: "As a result of this continual emphasis on Black male sexuality as the core issue in antiracist critiques of rape, Black women who raise claims of rape against Black men are not only disregarded but also sometimes vilified within the African-American community."[38]

Finally, Crenshaw describes *representational* intersectional oppression from the point of view of the effects of rap music on women of color, who are often demeaned in the lyrics. Citing the charge of obscenity brought against the rap group 2 Live Crew, she states that a focus on their misogynistic lyrics could blind us to the racial discrimination inherent in charging black men with producing obscene cultural products while white performers who produce similarly explicit material are not prosecuted for their expression. In this case, apparently antisexist concerns provided an occasion for racism. On the other hand, an antiracist focus on such a case may provide "occasion for defending the misogyny of 2 Live Crew."[39] Thus placed at the intersection of gender and race, women of color must struggle to make manifest to others the manner in which their identity can suffer compound oppressive effects.

But such emplacement along potentially contradictory or ambiguous lines as race and gender does not merely provide for a space of subjugation and marginalization. Though your presence pulls my world out from under me, making me responsible for aspects of myself the interpretations of which I don't choose, it also enlivens and enriches my potentiality. Insofar as I struggle with what you make of me, you become the condition for my autonomy, for my ownership over myself. As Levinas suggests, you invest and promote my freedom by making me responsible—by making me "own it," making me own up to who I am. The intersectional context gives us further tools to articulate such autonomy at the extremes of multiphrenic and marginalized identities. One's emplacement by society potentially opens up ambiguous and contradictory "endorsements," to return to a term used by Ganeri in describing the ownership a self has over mental life. Through "owning up to" such endorsements—and not merely feeling angst or remorse or shame at such ambiguity—we realize ourselves as capable of overcoming the struggles society imposes on us.

This is what Gloria Anzaldúa is trying to get at in her articulation of mestiza consciousness (an ownership of coming from mixed, sometimes contradictory ancestry—for her, being Chicana, of mixed Spanish and Nahua ancestry). With such explicit awareness of one's identity as, in her words, as one of "crossing borders," mestiza consciousness is always in motion, never static, always a *travesía* (crossing), unable to stay in the same place.[40] Owning oneself as owning up to one's multiplicitous background—even if that multiplicitous background does not consist in commonly subjugated identities and is thus somewhat invisible—requires a continuous, dynamic integration of forces that place me at the crossroads of multiple responsibilities at once, many of those responsibilities having to do with a sociocultural background that is represented by society in ways over which I have no control. As Edwina Barvosa suggests, the ambiguity of multiple identities gives a person both an understanding of various, sometimes opposed lifeworlds while at the same time affording the tools to own up to one's own oppositional identities in creative and critical ways.[41] Indeed, she suggests that too much homogeneity in one's self-understanding results in a certain critical blindness and thus a certain lack of autonomy. Those of us whose sense of self becomes ossified, immobile, totally centralized, might be unable to see or understand the struggles of others and the way we might contribute to or help alleviate those struggles. Thus, such a centralized sense of self might itself lack the autonomy of an individual who struggles against the place foisted on them by the sociocultural world through which they live. As Linda Barclay points out, autonomy, and thus the sense in which one owns oneself, is a matter of how we fashion our responses to social forces.[42]

Thus, who I am is in part a matter of the dynamics of my response to the way society emplaces me—that is, to the way society situates me. I own this who, I am autonomous, when I can creatively and critically engage with the various emplacements society imposes on me, when I can to this extent, reenact society and my place in it anew. I am my ownness to the extent that I bring myself *just here*, from a historical facticity that feeds my decentered identity, to the possibilities that I can enact given the many "heres" through which I find myself.

First-person realism requires much more than mere ontologically oriented answers to questions of kind and individuation. Though such questions must indeed be broached for us to make sense of real subjects (including a subject's sense of agency, autonomy, and ownership), failing to go beyond answering only these questions would, in and of itself, leave us with an attenuated, merely conceptual understanding of selfhood. A more robust sense of self must take into account where one finds oneself. Yet without understanding *how* one finds oneself where one does, we are still left with a merely conceptually extensive understanding of real first-persons. A more robust, less attenuated concept of first-persons requires recourse, not just to how it makes sense that multiple selves can be, in some sense, the same, of a kind; it requires that we investigate how such individuals find themselves placed among differences—differences that influence the manner in which one understands who one is, including where one is going and where one has come from. This, in turn, requires the investigation of axiological concerns—concerns that were highlighted here under the rubric of the dynamic between the compound subjugation of individuals whose decentered sense of multiple identities is made salient through sociocultural forces, and the manner in which these individuals own up to these identities, crafting their own places in the world in such a way as to push back against such compound offenses. Even in those of us who do not experience such compound oppression, our ownness requires that we navigate, of our own accord, the multiple identities through which society places us. Ownness, autonomy, agency—these are just the self-regulated manner in which a decentered subject is responsive to his or her social environment.

NOTES

1. Jonardon Ganeri, *The Self: Naturalism, Consciousness, and the First-Person Stance* (Oxford: Oxford University Press, 2012), 238.
2. Dharmakīrti, *Santānāntarasiddhi*, trans. Theodore Stcherbatsky in *Papers of Theodore Stcherbatsky* (Calcutta: Indian Studies Past and Present, 1969), 83.
3. Jeremy E. Henkel, "How to Avoid Solipsism While Remaining an Idealist: Lessons from Berkeley and Dharmakīrti," *Comparative Philosophy* 3, no. 1 (2013): 70–71.
4. R. K. Sharma, "Dharmakīrti on the Existence of Other Minds," *Journal of Indian Philosophy* 13, no. 1 (1985): 58.
5. Dharmakīrti, *Santānāntarasiddhi*, 89.
6. Abhinavagupta, *Īśvarapratyabhijñāvimarśinī*, trans. Kanti Chandra Pandey (Varanasi: Sampurnanand Sanskrit University, 1998), 62.
7. Ibid.
8. Isabelle Ratié, "Otherness in the Pratyabhijñā Philosophy," *Journal of Indian Philosophy* 35, no. 4 (2007): 330.
9. Ganeri, *The Self*, 257.
10. Ibid., 15.
11. Śaṅkara Miśra, *The Vaiśeṣika Sūtras of Kaṇāda, with the Commentary of Śaṅkara Miśra*, trans. Nandalal Sinha (Allahabad: Panini Office, Bhuvaneswari Asrama, 1911), 257.

12. Edward S. Casey, "Between Geography and Philosophy: What Does It Mean to Be in the Place-World?," *Annals of the Association of American Geographers* 91, no. 4 (2001): 686.

13. Edward S. Casey, *Getting Back into Place*, 2nd ed. (Bloomington: Indiana University Press, 2009), 52–54.

14. Ibid., 53.

15. Jeff Malpas, "Space and Sociality," *International Journal of Philosophical Studies* 5, no. 1 (1997): 56.

16. Casey, *Getting Back into Place*, 54.

17. Malpas, "Space and Sociality," 55.

18. Ibid., 63.

19. Ibid.

20. Ibid., 70.

21. Maria Legerstee, "The Role of Person and Object in Eliciting Early Imitation," *Journal of Experimental Child Psychology* 51, 3 (1991): 423–433.

22. Andrew N. Meltzoff and M. Keith Moore, "Imitation of Facial and Manual Gestures by Human Neonates." *Science* 198 (1977): 75–78.

23. Colwyn Trevarthen, "Communication and Cooperation in Early Infancy: A Description of Primary Intersubjectivity," in *Before Speech*, ed. Margaret Bullowa (Cambridge: Cambridge University Press, 1979), 332.

24. Ibid.

25. Alison Gopnik and Andrew N. Meltzoff, *Words, Thoughts, and Theories* (Cambridge, MA: MIT Press, 1998), 131.

26. Atsushi Senju, Mark H. Johnson, and Gergely Csibra, "The Development and Neural Basis of Referential Gaze Perception," *Social Neuroscience* 1, no. 3–4 (2006): 220–234.

27. Dare A. Baldwin, Jodie A. Baird, Megan M. Saylor, and M. Angela Clark, "Infants Parse Dynamic Action," *Child Development* 72, no. 3 (2001): 708–717.

28. Andrew N. Meltzoff, "Understanding the Intentions of Others: Re-enactment of Intended Acts by 18-Month-Old Children," *Developmental Psychology* 31, no. 5 (1995): 838–850.

29. Abhinavagupta, *Parātrīśikavivaraṇa* (Delhi: Motilal Banarsidass, 1985), 4. (*anuttaraṃ katham deva sadyaḥ kaulikasiddhidam tena vijñātamātreṇa khecarīsamatāṃ* / [my translation].)

30. Ibid., 84. (*etad guhyam mahāguhyam kathayasva mama prabho//* [my translation].)

31. Abhinavagupta, *Parātrīśikavivaraṇa*, trans. Jaideva Singh (Delhi: Motilal Banarsidass, 1988), 55–56.

32. Emmanuel Levinas, *Totality and Infinity*, trans. Alphonso Lingis (Pittsburgh: Duquesne University Press, 1969), 50–51.

33. Ibid., 213.

34. Ibid., 38–39.

35. Jean-Paul Sartre, *Being and Nothingness* (New York: Washington Square Press, 1984), 475.

36. Kimberle Crenshaw, "Mapping the Margins: Intersectionality, Identity Politics, and Violence against Women of Color," *Stanford Law Review* 43, no. 6 (1991): 1250.

37. Ibid., 1252.

38. Ibid., 1273.

39. Ibid., 1292.

40. Gloria Anzaldúa, *Borderlands/La Frontera: The New Mestiza* (San Francisco: Aunt Lute Books, 1987), 70.

41. Edwina Barvosa, *Wealth of Selves: Multiple Identities, Mestiza Consciousness, and the Subject of Politics* (College Station: Texas A&M University Press, 2008).

42. Linda Barclay, "Autonomy and the Social Self," in *Relational Autonomy: Feminist Perspectives on Autonomy, Agency, and the Social Self,* ed. Catriona Mackenzie and Natalie Stoljar (New York: Oxford University Press, 2000), 54.

Accommodation, Location, and Context   7

CONCEPTUALIZATION OF PLACE IN INDIAN TRADITIONS OF THOUGHT

Meera Baindur

According to Edward Casey, a geographical self is constituted by a human being who incorporates the ideas of location and place into her or his lived experiences. In this chapter, I explore several other concepts, equivalent to that of place, that might be used to further understand the geographical self,[1] doing so with specific reference to the complex relation between place and identity in Indian traditions of thought.

Sundar Sarukkai claims that translating concepts across cultures is fraught with problems of finding equivalences[2] and suggests using translation as a method for cross-cultural studies of specific concepts.[3] Recognizing that the translation of concepts involves much more than an interlinguistic act since the words used for concept translation must have "meaning-bearing capacity," he argues that "when we evaluate concepts across cultures, we cannot be looking for equivalences but only for the potential to bear possible meanings."[4]

Taking up his suggestion of using translation as a comparative method to analyze concepts, through which new meanings can be generated for concepts,[5] I will translate the concept of "place" using Sanskrit words that are still employed in many Indian languages. In addition to exploring how the conceptualization of "place" can be given new meanings and nuances through these Sanskrit words, I will also examine whether these meaning-bearing Sanskrit words better capture the complexities of the concept of place in relation to issues of identity and displacement. Admitting at the outset that it can be argued that these Sanskrit words are premodern and may have undergone many changes intraculturally, I offer my reflections here as preliminary to further comparative work on the concept of place in Indian traditions of thought.

Although there are many words that are related to the idea of place and also to the idea of shelter and inhabitation, I confine myself in this discussion to the vantage points afforded by four place-associated terms. The first of these is a perspective of place as cosmological. This is given by the term *loka* (world-place). As a metaphysical location, the world is mythic-geographical and has its origins in many religious belief systems and the accounts embedded therein of

127

such nonearthly places as various heavens. The second perspective on place is developed through looking at the related terms *sthala* (accommodative location/place) and *sthāna* (designated location/place).[6] The term *sthala* refers to an accommodative place or a surface and is close in meaning to the simple concept of "place" in English. In contrast, the term *sthāna* refers to a designated or appropriated location. There is a subtle difference in the embodied placement of a being *on* an accommodative location (*sthala*) and a being placed *in* a designated location among an order of many entities (*sthāna*). Identity, as given by these two locations, extends into the third perspective of place that is related to one's land (*deśa*) and one's home (*gṛha*). Particularly constitutive of one's identity, the land and the household form a sociopolitical-scape of identity and give expression and particularity to location. As cultural conceptualizations, the land and the household also form a context against which exile and displacement are understood. They also represent the outer and inner places of inhabitation, creating the binaries of the social and the personal. Finally, a more phenomenological account of the idea of place can be found in the use of the term *kṣetra* (field), which is connected to the embodied experience of a human being and is often closest to the notion of emplacement. The inhabiting of locations makes them fields of experiences—*karma-kṣetra* (action-field/arena). Philosophically, this term captures both the subjective and objective aspects of place and contextualizes the other three perspectives to be considered here.

Worlds as Place: Surfaces and Beings

The first cosmological understanding of location comes to us from a collective locus we are said to share with other beings. We are denizens of a *loka* (world-place), which can be loosely translated as a "realm." Many surfaces make up these world-places. We can say there are geo-surfaces, meso-surfaces, and aqua-surfaces, each located within a container-like world referred to as *loka*. Each world-place is inclusive of phenomena, beings, and their experiences. It is, of course, to be understood that the cosmic-*loka* is not to be found in the ordinary sense of a geographical location on this earth, but the imagination of such a place-term is nevertheless geographical. One can find descriptions of perceptive elements that are place markers, much like travelers' descriptions of a strange new continent. If we find ourselves suddenly in a different world-place, we can assume that these landmarks can be recognized and that we can orient ourselves in that realm. Thus, *loka* may represent what Yi-Fu Tuan calls a mythical space:

> The second kind of mythical space functions as a component in a world-view or cosmology. It is better articulated and more consciously held than mythical space of the first kind. Worldview is a people's more or less systematic attempt to make

sense of environment. To be livable, nature and society must show order and display a harmonious relationship.[7]

Each world-place is inhabited by different classes of beings—gods, humans, and mythical beings like *yakśas*, divinities, ghouls or divine sages. *Loka*, from the perspective of a place-based category, describes a world of spatiotemporal experiences. It is important to note that the passage of time in each of these *loka*s is different. Many eons (*yuga*s) of the earthly world-place are equivalent to one day in Brahma's (the creator's) world. These worlds are said to be situated in an ordered manner along a central axis, or the mountain called the Sumeru (Mount Meru), arranged vertically and thus creating a hierarchy from subtle to gross, from highly moral to the immoral—a hierarchy of so-called higher and lower worlds.[8]

As a category, *loka* influences the way we categorize the differences between humans and other-than-human beings. The cause for a particular being inhabiting this or that world-place is understood in a framing discourse regarding a naturalized order of beings, with each soul-being having acquired eligibility to inhabit one or another of these various world-places during the event of creation. However, after this primary location in the hierarchy of world-places, the soul-beings can lose their current eligibility and acquire a new one, based on karma and a value hierarchy through which the soul-beings' location within any given world-place takes on moral valence. The eligibility to migrate to the so-called heavenly world-place (Swargaloka) or to fall down into the netherworld (Pāthālaloka) is explained through a discourse of merits and demerits acquired by action (*karman*). For instance, a position in the heavenly world-place is acquired by performing fire-sacrifices in the earthly world-place (Bhūloka). The concept of karma thus makes possible the discourses of movement and dislocations that I undertake in the last section of this chapter.

Thus, when seen from the perspective of the world-place, the concept of an accommodative location becomes different from the concept of a designated location, particularly within a systematic moral hierarchy that is connected to place and origin.

Place and Being Placed: Location and Access

Accommodative location (*sthala*) is a concept that is deeply related to the idea of a surface. As an illustration, I will use a cultural experience of place. Just a few hours ago, as I performed my yoga exercises, I was intensely aware of the ground against which I could push myself, lie on, or feel through the flat surfaces of my body. The idea of place as it occurs to me in the everyday experiences of life is dependent on my being connected to the ground. I had to place different parts of my body at different spots and balance myself spatially. The locus I occupy is intimately felt through the floor. I may think of myself as being contained in a room that allows me to be extended out into space, but all the while my body is connected to a surface, a "flat" on which I locate my bodily self. The Indian concept of this surface against which or on which I can move relatively is *sthala*, or accommodative location. *Tala* means spread or a section of a land. The word *tala* in many Sanskrit texts is used in conjunction with different materials— for example, *rasa* (liquid/water) in *rasātala*, the sea surface. The word *stha* is linked to the root verb that means "to stand." Situatedness becomes bound to an earth-ground in the concept of *sthala* (accommodative location) and, as such, a material surface is intimately bound to contact with a corporeal body. *Sthala* prevents penetration; as a surface, it is made of material that resists that non-subtle corporeal body called *sthūla śarīra*. We are not within these surfaces, not related to locations as being contained in them. Rather our habitation *of* them occurs *on* them. These materials may be water, clouds, air, or land. All these surfaces are spreads, platforms on which the body rests and marks its position relative to other objects. The earth's surface and the surface of bodies of water are the most easily discernible places on which embodied beings are found. On the other hand, the designated positions that different beings are allotted in these narratives within the naturalized order creates the *sthāna*, a concept for place/ position that I translate as "designated place":[9]

> Accommodative places are named and demarcated to distinguish them from the general surfaces. . . . One may use cardinal and ordinal points to describe precisely the location of different entities. On the other hand, place referred to by the term *stana* [is deeply culture specific]. . . . It is a created place, a "designated place" often connected to ethics and rights of occupancy. When one asks about one's designated place, it has a meaning closer to its use in the metaphor "to put someone in their place" or "to know one's place." This idea of "designated place" is specifically used to create boundaries and exclusions[, so one may call it a kind of hierarchical ordering].[10]

As I have argued elsewhere, the logic of value hierarchy plays itself out at the level of situated physical bodies.[11] Each physical body is place-bound in this order and cannot transcend the social boundaries or the *loka* (world-place) barriers. The higher worlds are not accessible to beings of lower worlds. The reverse may not always be true. A few exceptions are recounted in myths, but the general belief prevails that where we are born in our next life is given by our action in this lifetime. The corporeal body of each individual, through the act of karma fruition, is placed in its designated location within the caste system (the *varna-jāti* system) and also engendered. The caste system stipulates duties to be performed by each individual according to a preordained order. Dharma (duties), as caste- or gender-related dharma, becomes the concept-bearer of this place-ordained duty. The type of body one acquires is supposed to be a moral result of acts performed in previous lifetimes, resulting in what are called merits (*punya*) and demerits (*pāpa*). This body is accordingly placed in a *loka* among a class of beings—animal, human, or divine.

All humans are placed in Bhūloka, the earthly plane. The immortal soul is equal for all living beings, but the bodies are differentiated. This placement of bodies along a hierarchy of beings located in their spheres or *loka*s, and further differentiated within a socio-naturalized hierarchy within the *loka* itself, creates a complex, systemic order of beings. Moreover, each position carries with it a set of essential characters and duties that have to be fulfilled based on that position. This is why the word *sthāna* captures one's particular position on the surface of the earth, which at the same time becomes one's political and moral locus. The *sthāna* supports dwelling in what Casey calls "somewhere in particular."[12] The particularities of a given *sthāna* restrict movement in a cosmological sense. They are accommodating places (*sthala*) that one must occupy and that bound one's "reachability."[13] Stability and the inhabitancy are thus given both by the cosmic place and by the moral-social locus of one's designated place (*sthāna*).

Within the social register of human communities, *sthāna* as place is therefore socially given by the body that is created from *karman* (a consequence of past actions), thus becoming a rigid designator of people's abilities. According to this belief, the designation of one's identity is given by one's position in the caste system, which determines both what one *can* do and what one *should* do. The injunction of caste duties and duties related to gender implies that "you must do what is ordained because of who you are." Or, in other words, "you are the person you are because of where you have come from." For instance, a woman "must" bear children because she is a woman.

The Home-Place and the Shelter

The place-centric concept of home as a place connected with a private sphere of comfort and security has many references in premodern texts such as the Vedas. The home-place is described by terms such as *ālayā* (house), *grha* (household/home), and *āyathanam* (shelter/abode), the oldest of the terms found in the Vedas. Dwelling takes place inside a house. The house is built, constructed through an act of place making that separates the inside from the outside. Types of houses are described in poetry and literature: huts, mansions, palaces, and caves. The house achieves its complexity as a location through the prescriptive texts of the Vāsthuśāstra, the traditional system of architecture that is based on the correspondence between function and the cardinal and ordinal directions. Through this, inside is linked to outside, and the orientations and locations of

various created elements—such as doors, the altar, the well, or the kitchen fire—
are appropriately aligned.

The word *āyathanam* can be translated as "home-shelter" or in contemporary philosophical terms as "dwelling." This *āyathanam* describes a way that the human being is placed in relationship with an environment. In turn, the person who has an abode (*āyathanavān*) becomes a shelter and support for other beings. The term for the act of sheltering, also sometimes called *āśraya*, is used in a generic fashion to indicate "shelter." The act of sheltering in a sociohierarchical matrix of locations approximates the idea of a primary or foundational support. The mantra from the Yajurveda (popularly called Mantrapūṣpam) suggests that "the person who knows the abode of the waters shall become one possessing of abode."[14] The implied meaning in many similar textual passages is that the person who possesses such secret knowledge as "where the abode/shelter of the waters is" would himself or herself lack no foundation and would be firmly situated or rooted. The question "What shelters?" is similar to the question "What is the foundation of . . . ?" That is, taking shelter and sheltering other beings and entities are mutually entailing:

> In Sanskrit, this relationship is called *āśritabhāva* when the being is dependent or being sheltered and *āśrayabhāva* when the being supports other[s] or gives shelter. There is a very important conceptualisation that could be understood from these two ways of looking at creation. Every created being that is a part of the phenomenal world exists in a way that it supports the existence of other beings. From the typical notion of an embodied being occupying a world that is a mere empty field of experience or life for it, this notion of dependency and support posits the idea of a series of beings that are embodied in *prakṛti* [primal material energy] and themselves as *prakṛti* en-world other beings.[15]

One who has a dwelling becomes in turn the dwelling for others—those who depend on him or her. Dwelling as *āyathanam* involves shelter from the larger environment, but at the same time, the dwelling itself opens a place for others to dwell, as well as possibilities for certain ways of dwelling within relationship. How one dwells with others, and others dwell in us, is mediated by a kinship-based, sociorelational concept of a household. Such a constructed discourse finds its full expression in the concept of a home, a *gṛha*. Casey posits that one should think of places we live in—for example, an apartment—as much more than a mere spot: "The power a place such as a mere room possesses determines not only *where* I am in the limited sense of cartographic location but *how* I am together with others (i.e., how I comingle and communicate with them) and even *who* we shall become together."[16] The *gṛha* is not only the place of dwelling but also the center of kinship relations that bind people together. The basis for dwelling in this case is a sphere of kinship within a sphere of socioreligious place-locations. This concept is very fundamental to texts known as the

Gṛhyasūtra that deal with the sphere of the domestic. In her extensive study of the *Gṛhyasūtra*, Jaya Tyagi points out that within these texts the *gṛha* can be translated as "household," but only if it is kept in mind that the word has wider connotations: "The *gṛha* in the *Gṛhyasūtra*s is construed as a spatial setting in which members who are bound to each other through rituals live together, performing activities related to production, reproduction and social linkaging."[17]

Gṛha as a home-place[18] must have been a simple enclosure of rooms around a courtyard in the fifth or sixth century BC when these texts of rituals and conduct were composed.[19] The meaning of the word *gṛha*, derived from its proto-indological root, is "an enclosed space."[20] We must also remember that, conceptually, the home-shelter (*āyathanam*) discussed earlier makes possible the existence of a *gṛha*.

The home-place (*gṛha*) is not given to a person at all phases of his or her life; one has to mature to be associated with the act of maintaining a household. The person (particularly a male)[21] enters into the relations and responsibilities around the home-place (*gṛha*) after his student life (*brahmacharya*) or after his apprenticeship/training. The person in adulthood is emplaced in a household and is called a *gṛhstha* (literally, one situated in a household). A person sets himself up in a household, becoming a productive independent unit of dharma, and along with his wife carries out appropriate traditional duties.[22]

This is not only a place-bound duty but also a phase-bound duty called *āśrama-dharma*. The home-place as the household becomes the primary social unit that interacts with the social world. Households are economically and socially the target of political and social control. The idea of family derives from the idea of the household.[23] Drawing on scholarship around kinship and households, Tyagi suggests that the households also affect the society through transmissions of tradition: "Thus, households actually link space with traditions—on the one hand, its physical presence roots it in the society that it exists in, and on the other, it carries with it age-old traditions that continue through it and get reformulated in different chronological spaces."[24] The social and spatial unit of a person's interaction with community and the environment he or she inhabits is *gṛha*. A *gṛha* is contained, not only within its place-designators such as a town or a forest or a valley, but also within the social status of the patriarchal head—the *gṛhapati*. The *gṛhapati* (lord of the household) is ritually and socially placed, much like the central axis of Mount Meru, and he holds in place all the activities of the household. He is often referred to as the "one" shelter of all beings in a household. The identity of the household headed by a patriarch becomes firmly established in other social structures such as lineages or traditional status hierarchies. A famous person of social status can take on or be allotted duties such as being the chief sponsor of a temple, or he can assume the position of a landlord because of the household he belongs to or inherits from his father.[25] Having seen how identities are constructed through multiple levels—cosmically in *loka*, socioculturally through the caste system, and at the household level through *grha*—we already can see how place establishes "the who" and the "how" of a person and her or his actions.

Region: The Land and the Located People

Two place-centric concepts that address location with reference to a context are *deśa* and *kṣetra*. The word *deśa* is loosely translated as "country" or "region,"[26] and the word *kṣetra* is equivalent to "field." Both of these words occur in many Indian languages and currently are used in a different interpretative sense from what they meant in the older Sanskrit texts.[27] "Region" (*deśa*), in its significant usages in many texts, takes on the meaning of a particular place—marked by boundaries—that may be geopolitical, bioclimatic, or sociocultural. Both of these terms address meaningful relations to land and are associated with a set of concepts and terms that lend themselves to a discourse of place-based identity.

Mostly, geographical classifications of land are referred to by the term *deśa*, and smaller geographical parts therein may be called *pradeśa*. People thus refer to *parvata-pradeśa* (mountainous land) or *vana-pradeśa* (forestland). On the other hand, we find references to Kuru-deśa and Pānchala-deśa in the *Mahābhārata*—designations that refer to geopolitical regions being ruled by the Kuru dynasty or the Pānchalas. It is from these references, perhaps, that we find the origins of the idea of a country or nation—for example, Bhāratadeśa (the region/country of Bhārat).[28] While the word *deśa* seems to denote a whole unitary entity, the word *pradeśa* represents "the part of the whole." (In the Nyāya philosophy, the word has a very technical and accurate meaning, but in common usage, parts of a kingdom were sometimes called *pradeśa*.) Region (*deśa*) is always connected to direction, or *dik*—the cardinal and ordinal directions—and thus there are both northern and southern regions (*deśa*s). Regions as *sthala*s are accommodative places that share some common properties. These may be climatic zones (e.g., the wetness or dryness of a region), or they may be sociocultural.

What insights does the idea of a region as place afford us? Region (*deśa*) is co-constituted conceptually by time (*kala*) and land (*bhūmi*). The word *deśa* does not seem to occur in descriptions of other worlds (*loka*). In a way, one can say that region is a real and tangible place of experience that is deeply connected to cultural and social phenomena; it gives the "where and when" context of place. The concept of place as region requires a particular complementary concept when it is used in literature. This is *kala*, or time. In its conceptualization, region forms a background of time, landscapes, and events. Region thus relates to the spatialization and directionality of entities. The deep connection between time and place is well documented in place studies. For instance, Tuan claims that "objects anchor time."[29] Do placements of certain objects thus serve to mark time in various ways? Traditional architectures in India and elsewhere seemingly attend to landscape and placement as well as to seasons and other time cycles.

When it comes to human beings, region constitutes an essential part of their identities within a discourse of nativity and origin. A region is where you hail from, where your community hails from. Due to its close connection with the concept of nativity, a region (*deśa*) becomes *svadeśa*, or one's own region. A sense of pride and cultural unity gets attached to the idea of the region to which one belongs. The relationship of belonging is reinforced by registers of culture, language, customs, and regional pride. The body, in some cases the woman's body, becomes the site of the belongingness. Clothes, headgear, and other body markers such as jewelry or tattoos indicate regions of origin (*svadeśa*).

I suggest that in Indian traditions of thought, the collective idea of place is given by the concept of region (*deśa*). Earlier, I had suggested that *sthala* could be like landscape.[30] Casey points out the difficulty of distinguishing between *place* and *landscape*: "A landscape seems to exceed the usual parameters of place by continuing without apparent end; nothing contains it, while it contains everything, including discreet places, in its environing embrace."[31] I now find that the concept of region includes elements of both place and landscape. Landscape is an integral part of the region. Recent cases of state formation in India seem to be based on this collective identification with a region as different from other regions.[32] The very acts of place-making and place-naming occurring in connection with this idea of region are parts of a process that Casey refers to as one of being "designated"—an act of naming that is intended "to institutionalize this name in a geographic and historical setting." The act of naming a region is political.

We can say, then, that landscape is a vital factor in the acts of habitation occurring in specific places by their distinct peoples. That a region gets essentialized and identified with the body of a person is due to the actual matter of the land being infused into the bodies of the people who live on it and who eat food gained from it. Through a process of material transfer, the land becomes food and food becomes body. The land as region embodies the person. This understanding is not found very often in textual traditions but is commonly found in cultural adages. Famous people are children of the soil, with the soil here representing the region.

The notion of cultural identification with the land is common across many areas of the globe. I posit that in Indian tradition, however, the land is not just abstractly represented in the imagination of a people. It manifests as qualities of the material that is ingested to become the people's bodies. Recognizing this leads to the necessity of considering the ways the qualities of soil are said to be absorbed into the body, which will be undertaken here by drawing from the medicinal traditions of India.

Andrew Brennan suggests that the Ayurvedic medicinal texts contribute to a place-based understanding of habitation that describes the interrelationship between people and places:[33]

> The quality of a place that emerges seems to be predominantly anthropocentric: an ecology of agriculture, cooking and pharmacy, not an ecology of interacting systems defined without a reference to human meanings and practices. It is a profoundly human ecology, in other words, yet one which sees the world in terms of processes linking different individuals in populations (within and across species)— for example, the processes of concentrating essences through feeding.[34]

Francis Zimmermann describes the classification of land in Ayurvedic texts into the categories of *ānupa*, *jāngala*, and *sādharaṇa*. *Ānupa-deśa* refers to wetland regions that are marshy and wet, and *jāngala* to wilder and drier lands. In-between regions of intermediate wetness are called *sādharaṇa*.[35] Landscape features are constructed as place-scapes in order to describe their suitability for human habitation. By themselves, these geographical features are sufficient to describe the landscape—rivers, mountains, hillocks, and flatlands. The Ayurvedic classification of landscapes into the above categories specifically converts natural geography into human geography, creating a context for the intimate interactions of one's own type of body with the specific climate, soils, and waters in various landscapes. It is in such interactions that human habitation is necessarily contextualized.

Much as landscapes are classified into three types, the human body is constituted of three types of bodily "agitables" called *doṣas*—*vāta* (wind), *pitta* (bile), and *kapha* (phlegm). These are found in different proportions in each individual's body, causing ill health when agitated. Among various factors that agitate the *doṣas*, inhabiting the corresponding landscape can accentuate a particular *doṣa*.[36] The soil, peculiarities of geographical categories (mountains, deserts, or marshes), water, and climate are seen to enter the body through food and habitation on a land that is called *cāra*. Zimmermann places importance on the human interaction with the environment through the concept of *cara* (literally, foraging behavior/subsistence): "*Cara* is a perfect example of a word with a double reference: to nature and to man. The objective or spatial reference—the environment—is incorporated within the subjective or practical reference—the environment regarded as a source of the means of subsistence."[37] Thus, through *cara* (subsistence), a *kapha* (phlegm-dominant) person would imbibe more *kapha* (phlegm) by living in a wetland region (*ānupa-deśa*), not only through the climate and air but also through the food that is available there, which has the same qualities as the land. The saying "You are what you eat" is represented again and again in local sayings and idioms. Wanderers with no land or unknown lands are seen as fickle and unstable in their morals. The word *deśa* (region) therefore points to a conception of place as a context that is at once natural and sociocultural.

The Field: The Place as Embodied

When the actual landscape is referred to as located on the surface of the earth, the territory acquires a more tangible form that is limited by the reach of the human experience, through the corporeal body. This is called the *kṣetra* (field). In this section, we endeavor to understand the idea of *kṣetra* as a "field," both directly and metaphorically. The earliest instance of the term *kṣetra* occurs in the Ṛgveda, where the cultivated earth is called *kṣetra* and where the lord of the field is addressed as *kṣetrapati*, which, in this case, refers to a plow. The cultivated field is inclusive of the power and agency of the cultivator. The human ability to create food from the land is an ability to "milk" the land of produce through agriculture. *Kṣetra* (cultivated field) includes the phenomena and experiences that are given by such notions of agency and action.

It is easy to see how the act of creation by using a plow invests power and control over place and land in the agent who makes land into a field, an area into an arena. There are actions appropriate to the field, and power over the field is vested in the plow wielder. The idea of such an agent of action imagined in connection with metaphorically imagined fields of interaction is not a mere doer but also a knower. The epistemic turn of such an agent was first articulated in Sāṃkhya philosophy and later in much more detail in the *Bhagvadgīta*. The word *kṣetra* is used in such texts to refer to *prakṛti* (nature) as the known world. It is open to the experience of knowing by an aware subject, *kṣetrajña*.[38] *Kṣetra* includes within it a potential, not only to be known and to be acted upon by agents, but also to be able to act in turn upon them.

Kṣetra thus is place in its immediacy. It is the perceptible and lived world that presents itself to the knower who is aware and active. Every action of this agent produces consequences, just as seeds produce harvest in agriculture. There are two contextual imaginations of *kṣetra* that are interpreted metaphorically. The first is given by the context of dharma, the ethics of position, and the ethics of time. Dharma as duty is based on a person's position in the *loka* (worldplace) and in a social structure. It is also dependent on the period of one's life (*āśrama*), the time of day, one's gender, the season, and one's knowledge of the field. Every action is determined by the context of dharma. Therefore, every action becomes a moral act. Not to perform the ordained actions enjoined by one's position is to break an ethical code. In the *kṣetra*, simple passivity or not doing one's dharma becomes an immoral act. This position-based code of dharma ethics creates a discourse of social morality that often ends up privileging one section of society over another.

The second type of *kṣetra* relates to free will and intentional action. The field of action (*karma-kṣetra*) is open to the agent to willfully exercise his or her control to produce beneficial consequences. Sacred places are known as *kṣetra* because in these spots the possibility of karma and dharma is multiplied. *Kṣetra* is a place-word that captures action and free will at the same time referring to a contextual, geographical location that at once opens and restricts possibilities for action. *Kṣetra* is where the "how" of emplacement is played out dynamically.

Displacements, Dislocations, Movements, and Restrictions

The relation between the various place-centric concepts becomes clearer when viewed in the context of displacement or dislocation. How do the ideas of exile and of transgressing boundaries create discourses of sociopolitical restriction? Here I argue that the conceptualizations of place to be found within the Indian tradition are not merely descriptive and interesting but can, when extended in considering and understanding displacement, afford new and nuanced ways of engaging in a number of contemporary sociopolitical discourses.

Dislocations and movement across realms are imagined as noncorporeal events. The movement of denizens of the earth realm to the so-called higher worlds is restricted, particularly for those with an unsuitable corporeal body. The denizens of the heavenly plane have a relatively immortal life (not eternal, because of final dissolution, or *pralaya*), and their bodies are said to be made of light. So access to these worlds is denied to those with ordinary bodies. Myths often have contrary claims, but, generally speaking, movement across realms occurs when the soul is reborn into a divine body or into a body that is restricted to the nether realms. One has to leave one's mortal body and travel upward in one's divine body, or soul-body (*sūkṣma śarīra*).[39] The divisive nature of these worlds is based on a concept of progressive movement from dense worlds to the lighter worlds or a "fall from" (*pathanam*) the heavier and the grosser. Tuan suggests that even the hierarchy is spatially coded:

> "High" and "low," the two poles of the vertical axis, are strongly charged words in most languages. Whatever is superior or excellent is elevated, associated with a sense of physical height. Indeed "superior" is derived from a Latin word meaning "higher." "Excel" (*celsus*) is another Latin word for "high." The Sanskrit *brahman* is derived from a term meaning "height." "Degree," in its literal sense, is a step by which one moves up and down in space. Social status is designated "high" or "low" rather than "great" or "small."[40]

The terms "lower" and "higher" in connection with worlds reinforces the hierarchy of beings. The idea of pleasures obtained in each of these worlds is also progressive, with the highest worlds yielding the highest pleasure. Narratives of divine beings' "fall from heaven" because of transgressions are not unusual in myths. Often sages curse the denizens of heaven by wishing them to be "born as a human." The case of an *avatār* in the Hindu religious belief system is interesting as an act of deliberate descent from the heavens to the earth by a deity. The god or deity (in most cases Viṣṇu), who occupies his or her own transcendent world (Vaikuṇṭa), leaves that world in an act of compassionate sacrifice and descends to the earth, taking birth in a corporeal body in the earthly realm to help his or her devotees. On earth, the deity then occupies a normal *sthāna* (position), just as does any other living being or any particular human in a sociocultural milieu. The interesting impact of the *avatār* on the earth is that all the places that the divinity has supposedly moved within become construed as sacred landscapes.

Embodied Dislocations

There are two possible types of dislocation from designated places. As discussed earlier, the topocentric view of Ayurveda suggests that people with particular propensities of *doṣa* (body humor) tend to have illnesses if they live in contrary landscapes. Not living in the right place affects one's health and longevity. To actually see "dislocation" as a cause in one's state of illness is one of the most intriguing ideas of place-centric thought. A person with *vāta* (wind) troubles is likely to have bone problems (induced by *vāta* agitation) if he or she occupies a place that is also of a wind-inducing type, bioclimatically.

Although this health effect of bodily displacement may be seen as somewhat accidental, that is arguably not true for the displacements caused by social transgression. Displacement from a designated place is social when a particular person, within an existing hierarchical framework, aspires to transition to another position that is valued as higher or to change his or her social roles and functions, particularly within the caste (*varna-jāti*) system.

Here, place as *sthāna* becomes connected to the idea of identity in the order of beings, qualified by moral eligibility within social structures. The *sthāna* then transposes itself onto the *sthala* (accommodative location) and becomes the designator of positioning and identity. These are places to which we can aspire or from which we can be rejected. In the Indian context, rejections of eligibility are based on the already prevalent caste system. Restrictions of access based on caste positions (*varna/jāti*) sometimes play a role even in the way the dwellings of different communities are distributed across village-scapes and town-scapes. The dominating castes occupy positions upstream or closer to the center, while the "outcastes" are relegated downstream or to the periphery.

While those in the so-called lower orders of the hierarchy can aspire to climb higher, those in more highly valued positions can be displaced from their exalted positions for dharma transgressions. Such major transgressions are rare, but displacements within one's own caste also occur through social ostracism and punishment. Social ostracization is a kind of social displacement; people are not politically excluded (as in the case of exile), but in cases of social and cultural boycott, those who are ostracized are denied resources and participation in social relations. Even communication of any sort may be forbidden. "Outcaste" is the word commonly used for an ostracized person.[41] The outcastes are displaced, their place denied. Although they may continue to live in their habitation in the same *sthala* (accommodative location), they have lost their *sthāna* (designated position), or become "outcaste." Given the layered social relations that are constitutive of many communities in Asia, particularly in India, an "outcaste" is displaced much more if he or she continues to occupy the same place. To move away to a new place or to exile oneself by moving away to a distant land is actually more painful than to be displaced in one's own place. In both these ways the person who is socially punished bears the burden of being displaced, from the familiar *region* or from the designated position. If one chooses the region and nativity (*deśa*) and does not move away from the home-place, one's designated position (*sthāna*) is lost; one is cast out from all social relations. If one chooses to establish oneself in a different society and keep one's designated position by not revealing the transgression, one's familiar region is lost.

It is to be noted that while caste divides the community socially along a value hierarchy, the discourse of region (*deśa*) tends to unite people at the level of place. The collective place orientation of region thus becomes a strong marker of identity. Displacement from one's region as a political act or as an act of forced migration is seen as being exiled—displaced in such a way that the soul laments for its home-place and is continuously faced with a sense of loss of self. Exile and loss of one's homeland are two powerful psychological affects driven by the concept of region. The most famous exile stories are those of Rāma and Sītā in the *Rāmāyana* and of the Pāndavas in the *Mahābhārata*. Literature abounds with such narratives of exile from the homeland.

The act of deliberate migration or dislocation without coercion is not viewed as exile. Within the right contexts, migration is seen as progressive and pioneering. Region captures the idea of a homeland in the sense that even communities belonging to a region living as migrants in different places are seen as belonging to and being of their original region. Such people are from *svadeśa*, one's own land, not because of place markers or landscapes, but because the land persists in the bodies of its people. For instance, after living for a time as a householder, one may move away from the settlement in a deliberate act of displacement and detachment, departing for a life in the *vana*, or forest. The household is the basic productive unit, economically and reproductively, and to leave the household is an act of sacrifice. But in the *vānaprasta* (literally, departure to forest) phase, although the socioeconomic productivity of an individual is declared complete, his or her sacred or spiritual duties continue. The male householder must continue to entertain guests, perform rituals, and be with his spouse even in the forest. However, a final rejection of these socioreligious duties can also be undertaken during the phase of *sanyās* (renunciation). This can be seen as a final act of displacement in preparation for departure to other worlds and lifetimes. One is exempt from one's place-bound and phase-bound duties only in this final phase of one's lifetime. Leaving home and the loss of a dwelling can, in other words, also be seen as soteriological acts and thus as different from being sent to the forest because one has been abandoned or banished by one's kinspeople.

We have seen how at every level of place—as conceptualized in Indian traditions—the idea of displacement also seems to follow a twofold logic of accommodation and designation. One kind of dislocation occurs through the deterministic values of place-making that assign and require positions to be held rigidly. On the other hand, the very same place concepts allow for accommodation and free will, where beings of the cosmos can create and aspire for positions and eligibilities across lifetimes through their own effort.

NOTES

1. Edward. S. Casey, "Between Geography and Philosophy: What Does It Mean to Be in the Place-World?," *Annals of the Association of American Geographers* 91, no. 4 (2001): 683–693.

2. Sundar Sarukkai, "Translation as Method: Implications for History of Science," in *The Circulation of Knowledge between Britain, India and China: The Early-Modern World to the Twentieth Century*, ed. Bernard Lightman, Gordon McOuat, and Larry Stewart (Leiden: Brill, 2013), 309–329.

3. Ibid., 313.

4. Ibid., 314.

5. Ibid., 322.

6. I use the term "location" instead of "place" to culturally separate the Western philosophical reference to "place" from the term used in Indian thought.

7. Yi-Fu Tuan, *Space and Place: The Perspective of Experience* (Minneapolis: University of Minnesota Press, 1977), 88.

8. Mention must be made of the Jaina geography, which has a rich and detailed description of these types of worlds and their measurements and arrangements in mathematical terms.

9. In this naturalized order, which is very much like the seating arrangement of a formal dinner, each person is put in his or her place, or *sthāna*.

10. Meera Baindur, "A Place in Space: Marking Emptiness," in *Commercial Space Exploration: Ethics, Policy and Governance*, ed. Jai Galliott (Surrey, UK: Ashgate, 2015), 287–288.

11. Meera Baindur, "Nature, Body and Woman: An Indian Perspective on Value Dualisms," in *Science and Narratives of Nature*, ed. Jobin M. Kanjirakkat, Gordon McOuat, and Sundar Sarukkai (New Delhi: Routledge, 2015), 33–54.

12. Edward S. Casey, *Getting Back into Place: Toward a Renewed Understanding of the Place-World* (Bloomington: Indiana University Press, 1993), 109.

13. Ibid., 110.

14. Taittirīya Āraṇyaka, verse 1.22. A note on the use of the suffix *vān*: In one of the peculiarities of Sanskrit grammar, this suffix is usually used to create an abstract noun out of the possessions that a person has. So a person with *dhana* (wealth) becomes *dhavānaḥ*, "wealth-ful."

15. Meera Baindur, *Nature in Indian Philosophy and Cultural Traditions* (New Delhi: Springer, 2015), 193.

16. Casey, *Getting Back into Place*, 23.

17. Jaya Tyagi, *Engendering the Early Household: Brahmanical Precepts in the Early Grihyasūtras* (Hyderabad: Orient Longman, 2008).

18. Tyagi, in *Engendering the Early Household*, translates *gṛha* as "household," but I prefer the word "home-place."

19. Thapar (141) and other historians claim that the homes built in these early periods were simple, walled rooms with very little complexity of place divisions. See Romila Thapar, *The Penguin History of Early India*, vol. 1 (New Delhi: Penguin Books, 2002).

20. Bruce Lincoln, *Death, War, and Sacrifice: Studies in Ideology and Practice* (Chicago: University of Chicago, 1991), 107.

21. It is also clear that a woman, as a *gṛhinī* (one in a spousal bond), is not independent but through the social act of marriage enters into a household as the partner to the male in that household. Her duties are enjoined according to her gender and age, progeny, and seniority among the women already present in the household.

22. It is important to note that there was a similar set of duties enjoined for the women, but most of these references fall within a patriarchal framework.

23. In a very modern usage of this categorization in India, a card to purchase rations at subsidized rates is given to households at one address. Individuals cannot apply for this benefit if they are living away from their family. My father-in-law continues to be the head of my household, though my husband and I stay elsewhere.

24. Tyagi, *Engendering the Early Household*, 29–30.

25. Even now in parts of Karnataka and Kerala the person is hailed as coming from the "house of so-and-so"—for instance, "Ilayaveetil," with *veetil* meaning "from the house of."

26. The word "region" is also derived from two meanings, "rule" and "tract of land," or "spread," very similar to the two uses of *deśa*.

27. Rather than focus on a history of meanings, I shall instead speculate on the concept itself as related to place studies. I choose to ignore for the time being any meaning that is too far away from the place-centric discussion at hand.

28. This idea contests the prevalent argument that the word *deśa* refers to the nation-state. Though the word is used in contemporary times in place of a country or nation, the meaning is slightly different. This argument is outside the purview of this chapter, however.

29. Tuan, *Space and Place*, 187.

30. Baindur, *Nature in Indian Philosophy*.

31. Casey, *Getting Back into Place*, 25.

32. Telangana and Uttarakhand are two states that were formed because of people seeing themselves as belonging to a different region/place.

33. Andrew Brennan, "Asian Traditions of Knowledge: The Disputed Questions of Science, Nature and Ecology," *Studies in History and Philosophy of Biological and Biomedical Sciences* 33 (2002): 567–581.

34. Ibid., 574.

35. Francis Zimmermann, *The Jungle and the Aroma of Meats: An Ecological Theme in Hindu Medicine* (New Delhi: Motilal Banarsidass, 1999), 37–55.

36. The factors that affect *doṣa* include primarily food, seasonal weather, time of day, age of the person, and daily habits.

37. Zimmermann, *Jungle*, 21.

38. Baindur, *Nature in Indian Philosophy*, 93.

39. The story of Triśanku in the *Mahābhārata* is a direct example of the protagonist being cast out of heaven because of his unfit body.

40. Tuan, *Space and Place*, 37.

41. The common idiomatic phrase used in many places in North India, in Hindi, is *Hookah Pani Bandh* (smoke and water denied), and in South India, in Karnataka, an ostracized person is called *BahiskAra* (one made an outsider). The use of these terms is different from the use of the derogatory term "outcaste" to refer to Dalits and other people who are oppressed in the caste system as belonging outside of the legitimized castes (*varna*).

PART III

PERSONHOOD AND ENVIRONMENTAL EMPLACEMENT

Public Reason and Ecological Truth

8

Michael Hemmingsen

In this chapter, I consider the kinds of validity claims used in moral discourse—that is, what kinds of reasons we can offer when we are discussing what we ought to do in situations of disagreement and conflict. I suggest that the ones that are typically used in Western society, or that match our common sense in terms of the kinds of activities we undertake in discourse—claims about facts in the world, claims about what is normatively appropriate, and claims about the honesty of self-expressions—do not encompass the full range of possible validity claims available to us in principle or, in fact, those claims used in practice in societies other than Western ones. In particular, I suggest that some indigenous societies utilize at least one kind of validity claim that is not captured in this set, a claim that I call "ecological truth."[1]

In order to make this argument, first I identify instances of this claim in discussions about animal subjectivity. I suggest that these statements do not fit within the framework established above. Then I look at some possible alternatives to my own explanation of how we should make sense of these statements, and I try to show why these alternatives are mistaken. Having provided reasons why we should consider these claims as unlike facts, norms, or self-expressions, I finally sketch, very briefly, the contours of "ecological truth" as a validity claim. Due to space limitations I cannot offer a full defense of ecological truth here, and in fact it is not my intention to do so; I put forward ecological truth, not as a kind validity that I have settled on as a final interpretation, but more in the nature of a suggested possibility, given the inadequacy of the other ways of interpreting the apparently problematic statements by indigenous peoples that I discuss in this chapter.

The Subjectivity and Abilities of Nonhuman Animals

In many indigenous societies, nonhuman animals are conceptualized very differently from how they are conceptualized in Western societies. According to the typical Western understanding, "animals are 'resources' more akin to objects than to persons" and "knowledge about them must be objective and empirical."[2] In contrast, many indigenous peoples view nonhuman animals as "active individuals [that are] capable of intentional social interaction that can be understood via the same basic relational concepts used to conceptualize human social interaction . . . such as reciprocal exchange . . . and are in this sense different from (or more technically, members of a different ontological category from) passive objects that react mechanistically to physical forces."[3]

Many indigenous Canadians hold the view that nonhuman animals are persons in the same way that people are (though, of course, with different abilities and responsibilities). This worldview holds that nonhuman animals are in the same ontological category as humans and that they are "conscious, sentient beings who possess volition, plan and deliberate, interact socially and communicate with each other and with humans."[4] For instance, in the case of the James Bay Cree, their word for "person"—*iiyiyuu*—does not distinguish between humans and nonhuman animals.[5] Similarly, the Gitxaala of British Columbia do not consider there to be any fundamental distinction between humans and animals, as both are social beings,[6] and the Mistissini think of relations between humans and nonhuman animals as "exchange[s] between 'persons' at a reciprocal or equivalent level."[7] For the Rock Cree, nonhuman animals have *ahcak*, "the seat of identity, perception, and intelligence," in the same way that humans do.[8]

It is not the case, however, that this is a symbolic sense of being a person. It is not that animals are *like* people; they *are* people.[9] Conversely, I am not suggesting that Westerners consider nonhuman animals to be nothing but inanimate matter or that Westerners do not interact with animals in many different ways, including as friends and companions. Furthermore, it is clear to Westerners that many animals *do* communicate and plan and interact with each other socially; I am not claiming anything to the contrary or suggesting that Westerners are somehow ignorant of this reality. But indigenous beliefs about the intelligence and power of nonhuman animals often go far beyond those attributed to nonhuman animals by Westerners, and for many indigenous peoples the idea of animals as a resource rather than as fellow persons is well-nigh inconceivable. For example, according to the Waswanipi, nonhuman animals "act intelligently, and have wills and idiosyncrasies, and understand and are understood by men."[10] In the view of the Makah, Inuit, and Inupiat, whales are volitional beings that exceed human beings in power and intelligence.[11] For the Chipewyan, nonhuman animals possess *inkonze*—"power and knowledge"—and teach this power and knowledge to humans.[12] In all of these cases, the intelligence of nonhuman animals exceeds the typical Western view, as well as the powers attributed to them by Western science.

So why is this interesting, from the perspective of validity claims? This claim, that animals are people—that they have the same or greater mental capacities, similar subjective inner lives as human beings, and greater power—does not seem to me to be obviously a factual claim, a normative claim, or a self-expression. This may seem like an odd thing to say, at first. After all, on the face of it these claims are apparently empirical; what else could they be but either facts or perhaps philosophical claims about the definition of "person," able to be settled (or at least debated) without raising the specter of any new, strange, and unintuitive kind of validity claim?

Nevertheless, I argue that statements regarding nonhuman animal subjectivity, intelligence, and power are, in many cases, not simply a matter of philosophical disagreement, nor are they discussions about empirical, factual matters. The way claims about the nature of nonhuman animals are mobilized in real-world discourse by indigenous peoples suggests to me that facts—in the sense of empirical observations and the theorizing about such observations—do not really trouble indigenous views on this matter. Thus, it does not seem to be obviously considered as a fact in practice. Similarly, while claims about the *personhood* of nonhuman animals do seem to have *some* normative content—the definition of "person" seems to me to be, quite obviously, a normative discussion—it is *not* entirely evident that the claims about nonhuman subjectivity, power, and intelligence rest solely on the definition of this concept. Finally, as there *does* seem to be some kind of assertion being made about states of affairs in the world (for instance, that "whales are more intelligent than humans"), it is difficult to see these claims as merely self-expressions of the feelings and experiences of those who make such declarations—that is, of purely personal, subjective states.

Given the above, I argue that statements about the subjectivity, power, and intelligence of nonhuman animals on the part of many indigenous peoples are made not as factual, normative, or self-expressive claims: rather, they are a different kind of claim, with different criteria of validity. I refer to such claims as "ecological truth claims." However, I can certainly concede that postulating an entirely new[13] kind of validity claim to explain these statements is not the most obvious possibility, especially if there are alternative ways of explaining and understanding these statements. Thus, if I want to assert the existence of ecological truth as a validity claim and to suggest that statements about the subjectivity, power, and intelligence of nonhuman animals are instances of this kind of claim, I need to show why alternative explanations for these statements are implausible.

Alternative Explanations

There seem to me to be four ways we could explain indigenous claims regarding nonhuman animals, other than as a new kind of validity claim: (1) such claims are simply nonsensical; (2) such claims actually fit within the standard categories, but those using these claims in practice are just wrong; (3) such claims are fundamentally strategic—they are aimed at manipulating others to achieve a particular end and are not honest statements of genuine belief; and (4) such claims are actually metaphors—they are not intended literally, and we should not take them as such.

I submit that all of these alternative explanations for indigenous statements regarding nonhuman animals are misguided. Of course, none of my arguments against these alternatives are likely to prove conclusive, but nevertheless I maintain that they show these alternatives as much less likely, and therefore my contention that such indigenous statements are best explained by the postulation of ecological truth as a new, different kind of validity claim becomes far more plausible by comparison.

The Claims Are Meaningless

The first possible interpretation, and by far the least plausible in my view, is that indigenous statements regarding nonhuman animals are mere nonsense; they are empty noise, and nothing about them is worth bothering to understand to begin with. As statements, they are simply not well-formed: they are not facts, norms, or self-expressions, but neither are they anything else.

It should be immediately obvious, however, that this view rests on an understanding of indigenous peoples that is incredibly condescending, as well as on a mode of interaction that holds that if one is not able to make sense of something someone else is saying immediately, then one ought to conclude that the reason for this is that no sense can be made. Now, certainly for *me* the idea that nonhuman animals have humanlike subjectivity and greater-than-human intelligence and power is difficult to wrap my head around. Ostensibly, it is hard to credit, and I was not raised in such a way as to be able to easily make sense of these kinds of statements. But this difficulty should not be, on its own, reason to think that these beliefs are mere nonsense.

Of course, conversely, the fact that I struggle with the meaning of these statements about nonhuman animals should not be taken as reason to accept these claims as true or even as well-formed. Recent studies have demonstrated quite nicely the propensity of many people to treat nonsensical statements as profound merely on the grounds that they are nonsensical,[14] and I undoubtedly do not want to advocate for that kind of attitude. Nevertheless, *many* indigenous people speak about nonhuman animals in this way, and they treat their own and each other's statements as if they were meaningful. So while there is no case here for automatic acceptance of such statements as *true*, it also does not seem warranted to dismiss these statements out of hand as nonsensical. After all, if people appear as perfectly rational agents in other respects—as indigenous people undoubtedly do—why would we conclude that they are somehow uniquely irrational when it comes to this one topic?

The Claims Are Mistaken

The second alternative explanation is that the statements made about animal subjectivity make sense—there is no trouble understanding *what* is being said—but what is being said happens to be mistaken. So, for instance, it might be that indigenous statements of this sort about nonhuman animals are intended as factual claims, but *as* factual claims they are untrue. In other words, indigenous peoples who make claims of this sort are perfectly coherent but are just wrong.

This explanation seems to be at least somewhat more respectful than the first. After all, each of us is sometimes wrong about things. In fact, whole groups of people often believe things that are manifestly false, given the available evidence. Many people deny the existence of climate change, are fully persuaded by the theory of intelligent design, hold that the moon landings were faked, consider 9/11 a false flag operation, and are absolutely convinced that Barack Obama is a secret Muslim socialist. So it is not out of the realm of possibility that indigenous talk about animal subjectivity, powers, and intelligence is explicable as assertions of fact, but that those assertions are just incorrect, in the same way as the above beliefs are.

But when it comes to people who hold the above kinds of views, we typically find that they do not take countervailing seriously. This does not mean, of course, that countervailing evidence is given its due or that such people reason well when presented with the evidence. But they nevertheless attempt to explain it away. So, in the case of climate change deniers, for instance, data must be accepted selectively, and the information not fitting with desired conclusion is put down to the pernicious practices of greedy climate scientists or is otherwise explained away as not valid. Similarly, creation scientists typically attempt, however unsuccessfully, to poke holes in evolutionary theory, and they see the battleground of their dispute as being the realm of truth; to them, evolutionary theory and intelligent design are two competing theories that attempt to explain the same phenomena. In their view, so long as evolutionary theory is true, intelligent design must be false, and vice versa.

However, I am not certain that indigenous claims about the abilities of nonhuman animals is necessarily subject to refutation by countervailing facts. I am not even sure that indigenous peoples, when making these kinds of statements, consider countervailing facts *relevant*. Unlike climate change deniers, they do not need to explain these facts away; to them, these facts are simply beside the point.

We can take the cutting of salmon among the Puyallup, a Coast Salish tribe, as an example to illustrate this. Among the Puyallup, it is very important to cut salmon lengthwise, and never crosswise. If salmon are cut the wrong way, other salmon "would get insulted and not come any more."[15] Now, we can certainly ask here whether the salmon will be insulted, factually speaking, if cut crosswise. To be somewhat facetious, we could put a salmon in an fMRI machine, cut another salmon crosswise, and see whether we can record the first salmon having brain activity that would indicate insult. But I do not imagine that the Puyallup would take this to be anything other than an act of unnecessary cruelty to the salmon. They do not need to explain away whatever data would come out of this experiment, as creation scientists would need to explain away data that suggested problems with their own theory, because the issue of salmon brain activity is really beside the point. There seems to be something else going on here—countervailing facts do not play the same role as they do in the other examples—and I suggest that this is because claims of fact are not being made in the first place.

The Claims Are Strategic

Perhaps when indigenous people speak about animal subjectivity, they are not asserting beliefs but are merely making strategic statements with the intention of influencing others. For instance, according to Frances Widdowson and Albert Howard, when indigenous Canadians make the kinds of statements we have been discussing, they do so purely to gain advantage against settler governments—in the authors' words, to justify "demands for more funding and programs for the [so-called] Aboriginal Industry."[16]

Widdowson and Howard's work has been dissected by a number of talented scholars,[17] and there is little purpose in my adding to the heap. But if we put aside the well-documented problems with the scholarship behind their research, it is still worth engaging with the suggestion that certain kinds of claims are made strategically. However, it is easy enough to assess such a claim, because what this allegation amounts to is that indigenous people, when speaking about the powers and intelligence of nonhuman animals, are not honestly self-presenting. We can therefore match behavior to speech to see whether the two are consistent, and when we do so, I think we can fairly comprehensively reject the idea that indigenous people are dishonestly self-presenting.

There are a number of considerations we might want to keep in mind when assessing the honesty of these kinds of claims:

1. Indigenous people actually *practice* what they claim to believe. Why engage in ceremonies that are premised on the salmon's having a certain kind of subjectivity unless you honestly believe that the salmon does have it? Of course, these kinds of activities might be part of some complex plot to defraud settler governments and taxpayers, but if so, it is really rather

elaborate. There does not seem to be any good reason to have such an unusually high level of suspicion toward indigenous peoples.

2. Given that there are discourses that are much more likely to be effective in prosecuting indigenous political aims—the discourse of human rights comes to mind—why would indigenous peoples utilize much less reliable discourses, unless they did so because they are actually expressing their own genuine reasons? There are plenty of quite legitimate moral claims that indigenous peoples can make on settler governments and that can be made in terms much more politically palatable to the bulk of settlers. Thus, there does not seem to be any good reason to use language that is almost guaranteed to aggravate large sections of the settler electorate, aside from that the claims are sincerely held beliefs.

3. Discourses involving claims about the powers of nonhuman animals (as well as other claims related to mystical beings, creation myths, and traditional ecological knowledge), to the extent that they *are* effective—and it is certainly debatable whether they in fact are, with only a few places and instances excepted—have only become so recently. If we are to think of these kinds of claims as being part of a cunning plot to trick settlers and settler governments, indigenous peoples have been playing an extremely long game.

These are only some of the considerations we might want to keep in mind, but already we can see that the idea that indigenous peoples are speaking strategically when they talk about nonhuman animals in this way involves an unwarrantedly high level of skepticism and paranoia. There is very little real evidence that indigenous people speak disingenuously and strategically when they talk about nonhuman animal subjectivity, yet there are a good many reasons why we might think they do not.

The Claims Are Metaphors

The fourth possibility, that these kinds of statements are really metaphors, is a bit more promising. When we find that we cannot understand the claims of indigenous peoples, perhaps this is because we take a "literal interpretation . . . based upon the methods of a literate mind."[18] We take the statements at face value, but they are not straightforward claims, factual or otherwise. Rather, they are metaphors.

There is something to be said for this way of understanding statements about nonhuman animals. After all, in discussions of evolution, it is common for natural selection to be spoken of in metaphorical terms, as evolution "selecting" an adaptation: it is all there in the expression "natural selection." But evolution does not choose; it is not conscious, so strictly speaking this notion is mistaken.

We nonetheless understand this kind of statement, and so long as we do not accidentally slip into the view that evolution *is* some kind of conscious being that makes choices, there seems very little to take issue with. Why then could we not understand indigenous talk about the power and intelligence of nonhuman animals as this same kind of figurative, heuristic anthropomorphization?

Although I deny that indigenous statements about nonhuman animals are *only* metaphors, I do not deny that they can be *metaphorical*. I am quite certain that indigenous statements about all manner of things are, like almost all instances of human expression, absolutely riddled with metaphor.[19] But this hardly exhausts the content of such statements. Some indigenous scholars, such as Vanessa Watts, push back against this tendency to subsume all talk that is difficult or problematic (for Westerners) under the heading of "metaphor." Though speaking about Haundenosaunee and Anishinaabe stories generally rather than about nonhuman animals specifically, Watts' point remains the same: "These . . . events took place. They were not imagined or fantasized. This is not lore, myth or legend. These histories are not longer versions of 'and the moral of the story is . . .' This is what happened."[20]

Similarly, in support of the view that indigenous people mean what they say in a relatively straightforward way are the actual practices of indigenous peoples. For instance, returning to the practices surrounding the killing of nonhuman animals, if we do not assume that indigenous peoples really believe that the animal has the same kind of consciousness as human beings, then it is difficult to make sense of many such rituals. The rituals have no purpose outside of this understanding. After all, as Andrew Brighten puts it, "Aboriginal cultures do not typically kill animals *for the purpose* of undertaking a ritual; rather, the ritual is an *inherent part* of killing the animal, necessitated by obligations owed to the animal (or to its species as a whole)."[21] In other words, why engage in a ritual that shows respect for the slain nonhuman animal as a person, if you do not actually think that it *is* a person or that it truly deserves respect? Something that is only *metaphorically* an intelligent, conscious partner with whom we can communicate requires only *metaphorical* respect. But these rituals are part and parcel of showing the nonhuman animals *real* respect, and this is difficult to reconcile if we interpret statements about nonhuman animals as metaphorical.

Ecological Truth

We have looked at what I take to be the most plausible alternatives to the view that indigenous statements about the subjectivity, power, and intelligence of nonhuman animals are expressions of a kind of validity claim entirely different from facts, norms, and self-expressions. None of them, however, provides a particularly persuasive way of understanding these claims. Therefore, it is now worth considering the idea of "ecological truth," and I now briefly outline its basic contours.

Nature and Culture

If these kinds of indigenous statements about nonhuman animals are not facts, then of course we cannot consider them to be factually true. But if we take Watts' statements seriously, then these kinds of statements are *literally* true: they are not metaphors. Hence, if we are to make sense of these claims as ecological truth claims, we need to understand ecological truth as somehow literally, but not factually, true. But is there a difference?

One of the keys to getting at the space between literal truth and factual truth is appreciating that, for many indigenous peoples, the distinction between "nature" and "culture," which seems obvious to Westerners, is not necessarily a part of their common sense. Since we typically conceptualize the world around us as a resource available for our use, "nature" is something *over there* that we can draw on or not, depending on our needs, while culture is something that exists purely in the interactions between human beings.

But seeing all space and nature as interchangeable sets of resources (the commodification of place, we might call it) is not the view of many indigenous peoples. If "nature" is a collection of quite distinct, unique—that is, not interchangeable—entities and phenomena, then it makes much less sense to speak of nature as something separate from culture; any particular society's culture is going to be completely intertwined with the specific features of the place in which it is located. As Watts puts it, indigenous thinking of this sort involves theories that "are not distinct from place."[22]

If culture and nature are not distinct, then the ability to exist within the particular space, and the particular ecosystem, in which a society is located is a deeply cultural matter. It is not about a set of techniques that can be alienated from the place of their original application and used indiscriminately, as is the case with Western science. Rather, since "many Native traditions are about putting oneself in accord with the natural world in which the goal is harmony with nature and ethical reciprocity,"[23] the cultural is completely inalienable from the means of existing in a particular place.

Ecological Knowledge

Statements about nonhuman animal subjectivity, powers, and intelligence are based in a sense of sacredness involving "radical kinship and interdependence, an ongoing 'cosmic give-and-take' among beings large and small, creative and destructive, visible, invisible, or dimly perceived, beneficent and danger-ous, all interacting on a spectral scale of mutuality rather than in a dualistic opposition."[24] This system of thought "[limits] individual and group action toward the animals and the ecosystems in which they were embedded within an ecologically acceptable set of choices."[25] That is, these beliefs, along with their concomitant rituals and practices, help condition the right attitudes toward the world and the beings in it, giving rise to the ethical constraints that maintain the long-term sustainability of indigenous communities. Returning to the case of the Puyallup, the salmon's concern with how it is cut is not a factual claim but is part of a system of knowledge and practice that encourages participants to *respect* the salmon; this system "establishes values and rules"[26] and leads participants to have the right *ethical stance* toward them.

One might say, in this case, that such claims are *not* really true. Efficacy and truth are two separate issues. But I am not so sure. Certainly, efficacy and *factual* truth are probably not the same thing. But I agree with Barry Allen when he suggests that we overemphasize propositional truth in Western thought and give it a status that is perhaps unwarranted. He argues that we are mistaken to think that "knowledge—or the philosophically most important knowledge—has to be [propositionally] true."[27] I suggest that the belief in animal subjectivity is not a propositional statement amenable, in isolation, to being proved true or false but is part of a set of *practices* that exist for the purpose of continuing a society in a particular space and in response to particular conditions. Taking a part of the practice out of context, expressing it as a propositional statement, and then assessing its truth is to mistake the fundamental nature of these kinds of practices.

By breaking down the distinction between nature and culture and by seeing statements of animal subjectivity as representations of a deeper, more sophisticated, and complete body of practice that is tied to a particular location and a particular environment and ecology, we can see such statements as being instances of a distinct kind of claim: ecological truth. Ecological truth, therefore, is a matter of what is efficacious in allowing a community to persist over time in a specific place, in contrast with factual truth, which is "context free." Hence, ecological truth is *literally*, though not *factually*, true.

Many statements about the subjectivity, intelligence, and powers of nonhuman animals seem hard to understand as factual, normative, or self-expressive statements. They are certainly treated as meaningful statements in discourse among indigenous peoples, and there does not seem to be any good reason to presume them to be nonsensical. There is a significant amount of evidence that the statements are honest expressions of the sincerely held views of the speakers. The fact that countervailing evidence seems beside the point—it is not relevant enough even to require dismissal—suggests that they are not beliefs in a factual sense. Yet, judging both by the actual practices of those who make such statements and by the explicit declarations of indigenous scholars such as Watts, such statements are nevertheless held to be literally true.

Given the failure of the alternative explanations for statements of this sort about nonhuman animals, I have proposed that we understand them instead as statements of ecological truth—expressions of high-context practice tied to a particular environment and ecology that situates participants in ethically appropriate ways, given the need to sustainably maintain communities in that environment and ecology over hundreds or even thousands of years. Since the nature/culture distinction is not made in such communities, it is not meaningful in many cases to distinguish practices that have some kind of normative content from views about how the world *is*. Thus, ecological truth claims are distinct from both norms and facts, and their being fundamentally tied to practice and efficacy rather than being primarily linguistic and propositional in nature means that they have their own criteria of validity and can be considered as a distinct kind of validity claim.

NOTES

1. I use the word "indigenous" here as shorthand for the native peoples of a number of societies—primarily those subject to Western colonialism—who have continued, in some way, traditional practices. However, nothing in my argument rests on the definition of "indigenous": I am perfectly willing to accept that urban natives, for instance, are indigenous or that there are plenty of indigenous peoples who see nothing of what I describe in their own societies. In short, I am using the term heuristically and am not trying to define who does or does not count as indigenous.

2. Andrew Brighten, "Aboriginal Peoples and the Welfare of Animal Persons: Dissolving the Bill C-10B Conflict," *Indigenous Law Journal* 10, no. 1 (2011): 53.

3. Ibid., 60.

4. Ibid., 61.

5. Colin Scott, "Science for the West, Myth for the Rest? The Case of James Bay Cree Knowledge Construction," in *Naked Science: Anthropological Inquiry into Boundaries, Power, and Knowledge*, ed. Laura Nader (New York: Routledge, 1996), 72.

6. Charles R. Menzies and Caroline F. Butler, "Returning to Selective Fishing through Indigenous Knowledge," *American Indian Quarterly* 31, no. 3 (2007): 461.

7. Adrian Tanner, *Bringing Home Animals: Religious Ideology and the Mode of Production of the Mistassini Cree Hunters* (London: Hurst, 1979), 153.

8. Robert Brightman, *Grateful Prey: Rock Cree Human-Animal Relationships* (Berkeley: University of California Press, 1993), 118.

9. Paul Nadasdy, "The Gift in the Animal: The Ontology of Hunting and Human-Animal Sociality," *American Ethnologist* 34, no.1 (2007): 31.

10. Harvey A. Feit, "The Ethno-Ecology of the Waswanipi Cree," in *Cultural Ecology*, ed. Bruce Cox (Toronto: McClelland and Stewart, 1973), 115.

11. Robert J. Miller, "Exercising Cultural Self-Determination: The Makah Indian Tribe Goes Whaling," *American Indian Law Review* 25, no. 2 (2001): 237–238.

12. Henry S. Sharp, *Loon: Memory, Meaning, and Reality in a Northern Dene Community* (Lincoln: University of Nebraska Press, 2001), 73.

13. New, that is, from the perspective of Westerners. It is hardly new to indigenous peoples, if it is a kind of claim embedded in their everyday, real-world practice of discourse.

14. Gordon Pennycook, James Allan Cheyne, Nathaniel Barr, Derek J. Koehler, and Jonathan A. Fugelsang, "On the Reception and Detection of Pseudo-Profound Bullshit," *Judgment and Decision Making* 10, no. 6 (November 2015): 549–563.

15. Marian W. Smith, *The Puyallup-Nisqually* (New York: Columbia University Press, 1940), 101.

16. Frances Widdowson and Albert Howard, *Disrobing the Aboriginal Industry: The Deception behind Indigenous Cultural Preservation* (Montreal: McGill-Queen's University Press, 2008), 9.

17. F. C. Decoste and Hadley Friedland, "Not So Naked After All," review of *Disrobing the Aboriginal Industry: The Deception Behind Indigenous Cultural Preservation*, by Frances Widdowson and Albert Howard, *Ottawa Law Review* 41, no. 2 (2009): 377–395; Leanne Simpson, review of *Disrobing the Aboriginal Industry*, by Widdowson and Howard, *Wicazo Sa Review* 25, no. 1 (2010): 104–107; Raynald Harvey Lemelin, review of *Disrobing the Aboriginal Industry*, by Widdowson and Albert Howard, *Arctic* 62, no. 3 (2009): 356–357.

18. Jay Hansford C. Vest, "Myth, Metaphor, and Meaning in 'The Boy Who Could Not Understand': A Study of Seneca Auto-Criticism," *American Indian Culture and Research Journal* 30, no. 4 (2006): 42.

19. George Lakoff and Mark Johnson, *Metaphors We Live By* (Chicago: University of Chicago Press, 1980), 4.

20. Vanessa Watts, "Indigenous Place-Thought and Agency amongst Humans and Non-Humans (First Woman and Sky Woman Go on a European World Tour!)," *Decolonization: Indigeneity, Education and Society* 2, no. 1 (2013): 21. See also Kenneth Maddock, "Myth, History, and a Sense of Oneself," in *Past and Present: The Construction of Aboriginality*, ed. Jeremy Beckett (Canberra: Aboriginal Studies Press, 1988).

21. Brighten, "Aboriginal Peoples," 59.

22. Watts, "Indigenous Place-Thought," 22.

23. Vest, "Myth, Metaphor, and Meaning," 53.

24. Leo Schelbert, "Pathways of Human Understanding: An Inquiry into Western and North American Indian Worldview Structures," *American Indian Culture and Research Journal* 27, no. 1 (2003): 67–68.

25. George M. Guilmet and David Lloyd Whited, "American Indian and Non-Indian Philosophies of Technology and Their Differential Impact on the Environment of the Southern Puget Sound," *American Indian Culture and Research Journal* 26, no. 1 (2002): 39.

26. Lucia Earl Mitchell, "First Salmon Ceremony Marked Start of Season," *Puyallup Tribal News* 12, no. 8 (2001): 3.

27. Barry Allen, *Knowledge and Civilization* (Boulder, CO: Westview Press, 2004), 3.

The Wisdom of Place

9

LITHUANIAN PHILOSOPHICAL PHILOTOPY OF ARVYDAS ŠLIOGERIS
AND ITS RELEVANCE TO GLOBAL ENVIRONMENTAL CHALLENGES

Justas Kučinskas and Naglis Kardelis

In the philosophical history of place titled *The Fate of Place*, Edward S. Casey notes that, throughout the history of philosophy, the "rich tradition of place-talk has been bypassed or forgotten for the most part, mainly because place has been subordinated to other terms taken as putative absolutes: most notably, Space and Time":[1]

> In the era that stretches from Aristotle to Newton, then, place lost out to space. . . . By the end of the era, place had become the faceless minion of space. Having lost its uniqueness (i.e., as *this* particular place) as well as its boundedness (i.e., as precisely this place and *not another*), it merged with space in the generation of infinity of the universe from an unlimited set of simple locations.[2]

Lithuanian philosopher Arvydas Šliogeris, echoing Casey's quest, puts the thinking and seeing of place at the center of his own philosophy, which may be understood as one of the instances where philosophical thinking about and from place is truly being reinvigorated. Šliogeris' thinking of and from place positions *seeing of particular things in particular places*, rather than abstract thinking, at the forefront of his philosophy. In addition, his philosophy of language identifies possibilities for human beings to meet "things-in-themselves" in the moments of "languageless-ness."[3] These notions, taken together, are foundational for his concept of philotopy, a neologism he has coined to refer both to a specific mode of being and a way of philosophizing endowed with the wisdom that is granted by truly being in and thinking from particular places.

A conception of place apparently close to Šliogeris' notion of philotopy is developed by Yi-Fu Tuan in his *Topophilia*.[4] However, the term "philotopy," which literally means "love of place," differs somewhat from Tuan's topophilia, which serves as "a general framework for discussing all the different ways that human beings can develop a love of place,"[5] a neologism that Tuan sees as usefully encompassing the entirety of human affective ties with the material environment.[6] In short, topophilia is identified as one of the generally describable

159

human "emotions" emanating from a variety of culturally-linguistically bound human experiences.[7] In Šliogeris' case, the love of place is not an emotion born out of attachment to some specific cultural, historical, or even instrumentally or pragmatically conceived features of place. Rather, it is love and attachment directed to the particularity of place as the ultimate source of reality, the core of our existence as human beings. Moreover, with its echoing of "philosophy," the term "philotopy" refers not only to love but also to wisdom born out of such love. That is, love of place is, in itself, a form of wisdom. Thus, "topophilia" refers to culturally determined and semantically meaningful experiences that happen to be related to particular places, whereas "philotopy" refers to love that, although it is a human experience, actually originates from "silence," or the noncultural, nonlinguistic core of the place that discloses itself in its particularity, irreplaceability, and noncultural "roughness" and "otherness." In other words, philotopy is not a love of particular place *for various reasons* but a love of the *particularity itself*—a love that occurs *because of the particularity*, and thus the true placeness, of every possible place. As a sort of ontology of place, philotopy can be seen as more fundamental than topophilia, which actually describes the phenomenon of love of place. But on the other hand, philotopy may be seen as falling under the more general and abstract term "topophilia" and denoting a very specific case of topophilia—the philosophical one.

Philotopy, for Šliogeris, extends from being merely a deep thinking about or from place as a sort of descriptive ontology to an imperative *to be in place* as a sort of existential choice, which is also for him the ultimate stance of a human being that results in moderation in terms of relating to the living environment. Thus, philotopy may also be understood as a sort of ethics found in the ontology of place. Such a normative imperative to act with moderation, originating from grounding human existence in the particularity of place, can be of special interest to environmental philosophers. Here we want to build on the interpretation of Šliogeris and the concept of philotopy, doing so as a way of exploring a very specific aspect of philotopy—namely, its relevance amidst the global environmental challenges. However, rather than complementing current environmental ethicists' discussions or locating philotopy among them, the approach taken here will be that of a more general deliberation on how Šliogeris' philotopy can contribute to discussions of human beings' appropriate relationships with their living environments. The enormity, universality, and relative recency of global environmental crises, and especially the persistent lack of understanding and agreement regarding how to address these crises, makes such an exploration not only interesting philosophically but relevant practically.

At present, environmental philosophers' discussions of the kinds of approaches that would be appropriate in addressing such global crises seem to be incomplete. One of the more general problems is the "one-many problem," as J. Baird Callicott puts it.[8] The world and the environmental problem are one, yet the cultures and their offered approaches are many. Any single doctrine chosen for universal practical application would dominate over the rest and thus would be coercive and ineffective. Yet, relying on a multiplicity of approaches that are only local would never be sufficient to address problems of truly global scope—problems that in some sense require universally applicable solutions. Callicott offers a synthesis of two distant possibilities. On the one hand, the solution cannot be only a Western enterprise—we should look at the way different cultures may understand, express, or apply their worldviews and try to reconstruct each of their environmental ethics. On the other hand, Callicott argues, "A unity and harmony in multiplicity must be achieved, if our common environmental crisis is to be cooperatively—and successfully—addressed. What is needed is a Rosetta stone of environmental philosophy to translate one indigenous environmental ethic into another, if we are to avoid balkanizing environmental philosophy."[9] The Rosetta stone for him, or the way to unite the world's many cultures into a systemic whole, is to join them to the "postmodern scientific worldview" as part of an "evolutionary-ecological environmental ethic." And, Callicott argues, since "there are interesting similarities between the ideas of the new science and non-Western traditions of thought[,] . . . [i]ndigenous worldviews around the globe can contribute a fund of symbols, images, metaphors, similes, analogies, stories, and myths to advance the process of articulating the new postmodern scientific worldview."[10]

On the one hand, philotopy can be understood and discussed as a very local or locally born (indigenous) expression of human relations to place. And, as such, it could also be translated into an environmental ethic that could be measured against the findings of universal modern science and the "evolutionary-ecological environmental ethic" based upon it. On the other hand, philotopy itself has a universal dimension and may be understood as a challenge and an alternative to Callicott's proposed universal framework. Philotopy could itself be understood as a locally born yet universal approach that lacks, however, any imperialistic flavor. Philotopy stresses the importance of the particularity of any and every particular place—the thinking, attachment, and wisdom originating from it—and is thus truly local in terms of its own origins and the constitutive importance it accords locality. Yet philotopy also remains within the realm of the nonlinguistic experience of the particularity of place (and of every particular place) and, as such, has a dimension of universal applicability. But this is a universality independent of culture and any particular cultural content, and thus one that is never overdomineering. Some critics may emphasize the impossibility of such a noncultural, nonlinguistic human relation to reality (or things), but this is exactly the point of Šliogeris' philotopy—only by truly getting into particularity and the placeness of place does one also find oneself at the precultural and prelinguistic meeting point, where love of things and thus true wisdom are possible.[11]

In sum, our aim in what follows is to explain how philotopy, as a specific way of being in and relating to the world and, most of all, getting back to place, could be understood as a sort of universal principle, inviting a solution to global environmental challenges, which would be based locally but in ways that are noncultural and nonlinguistic. Philotopy, although seemingly passive in ways similar to the Chinese concept of *wuwei* (nonaction), may—in contrast to many voluntarist imperatives of moral philosophies or the complex theorizing and far-reaching insights of the "connectivity of everything" prevalent in modern science—ultimately be the most productive stance to take amidst the current realities of global environmental crises.

Place as a Place of Reality

"Be the change you want to see in the world" is a much overused and rarely implemented quote attributed to Mahatma Gandhi. It calls us to focus on what is near and relevant (most of all ourselves), at the same time suggesting that the world is really out of reach of any particular individual. Therefore, we should not change ourselves *for the sake* of changing the world (which is often the misleading interpretation of this saying) but should focus on changing ourselves or our closest environment because it is the only (and the only relevant) domain of interaction to which we have direct access. And indeed, by looking upon our daily lives, we can observe that we can truly care for only that which we can see, experience, or influence.

Our attention is most often drawn to events that can really influence us and in that sense feel "near," rather than events that feel "distant" in the sense that they do not "touch" us. We also care about that which we can comprehend and understand, and thus drawing something into the sphere of our interest is to make it "near" in the intellectual sense. This concern for what is near also affects the way we tend to treat events in time. Events to come in the immediate future or that occurred in the near past influence our thinking and actions much more than the events that are more distant, even if at the outset they may appear more important, grand, or noble. At the level of instinct, we, as human beings, tend to be beings of nearness—at least in our everyday matters of life and, therefore, we may say, life itself.

Dwelling on the principle of nearness as we do now, we may also turn to a more abstract way of thinking and say that the sense of nearness in its essence is related to clearly defined and therefore observable limits of things or events that appear in front of our minds' eyes as concrete, and therefore limited, entities. Only such limited entities or things (even when interconnected by less tangible relations of interdependence and meaning) actually define our reality, which manifests itself as a field of immediate importance and also a field of our reach.

Thus, whatever is real is also *near*, to the extent that we can observe or comprehend its limits. Furthermore, the appearance of particular and defined entities—substantial individuals—happens in particular and defined (or contoured) places. The particular place is therefore the only territory where reality appears. And, in that sense, only a particular and defined place, consisting of particular and defined substantial individuals, is a place of reality.

Only the objects within a sphere of immediate reality (or a field of reach) can become a true sphere of attention and, therefore, of care. It is only the reality of being in a real place that is expressed in the empathic recognition of an "other" as a living being endowed with its particular nature (*natura*, or *physis*). Being truly rooted in the reality of a particular place allows a very natural sense of caring for the coming into being and passing away of things, which disclose themselves as particular finite entities of that particular place. Such a recognition invites recognition of the need to uphold their being or to preserve them, as we might put it, not only because the substantial individuals reveal themselves as living beings within the sphere of reality, but also because, in their own turn, they define the place by making it unique through their own particularity. Thus, they define our own reality. Furthermore, our rootedness in and love of places populated by transient substantial individuals endows us with a sense of finitude—both of things and of ourselves. And this is followed by an instinctively felt sense of appropriate measure and moderation in action, as well as an understanding and recognition of one's natural field of influence. This is then followed in turn by a natural sense of responsibility to place and its substantial individuals. Thus, the totality of substantial individuals, which appear in the defined field of sensual experience, naturally calls for respectful and caring engagement, albeit a caring that is undertaken moderately.

In contrast, whatever does not appear as part of the defined place of sensual experience to some extent becomes distant and irrelevant—and in that sense is no longer perceived as real. The world understood as an immensely large sphere or globe is instinctively felt as endless, limitless, and borderless. No individual is capable of directly experiencing (in a phenomenological sense) the world's limits and its finiteness—nor is anyone able to directly comprehend it as a whole. Thus, the world is not perceived as a particular and defined place and therefore fails to be viewed and felt as a place of reality. The instinctively felt placelessness (*atopia*) of the world makes it difficult to truly sense the needs of the world in the same way that an individual can sense the needs of particular substantial individuals (things) belonging to a particular place. This could maybe explain why humans, in the course of history, have found it so difficult to either preserve the world's ecological equilibrium or to focus on solving global problems.

However, in the context of global environmental crises like climate change, water and soil contamination, species extinction, and so on, the world necessarily reveals its precariousness and natural limits. That is, it starts to reveal itself as if it were a place (which, in some sense, it is). The world reveals itself as a living organism endowed with its particular nature and defined by its natural limits, a living organism that is finite and capable of suffering—a being "other" than human and yet worthy of being perceived by humans as an object of empathy. The world's perceived finitude allows it to be felt empathetically in human terms and deemed worthy of preservation. It is, in other words, the world's finiteness and suffering that call us humans to serve as upholders (or preservers) of this finite, limited, and suffering being. The finiteness of the world as a place and its perceived finitude in time remind us of our own finitude, thus inviting us to embrace a more moderate way of being in and relating to the world. As we humans start to recognize ourselves as the cause of these crises, we for the first time start to perceive the world as our true sphere of influence. Therefore, the crisis itself is not only causing grief but also imparts a strengthened sense of responsibility. The world becomes perceived as a place of reality—and thus a place in its true sense.

World as Place

It is interesting to note that the Lithuanian word for the world, *pasaulis* (literally, the under-sun), conveys the notion of a place illuminated by the sun—a place both of moderate dimensions and situated within the radius of a particular person's immediate visual apprehension. That is, the word *pasaulis* already implies an inherently philotopical perspective on the world. We might even imagine *pasaulis* as a cozy earthen pit or a glen of circular shape that perfectly fits under the sun and is covered with the sky as a lid, just as is described in Čiurlionis' *Tales of the Kings*. It is a limited space made visible and defined by sunlight—a kind of place that arguably was anticipated by the ancient Greeks, since the Greek word *theōria* implies a view or looking that, like the bright light of the sun, enables us to accurately discern concrete substantial individuals. Identified as such, these individuals become the objects of care and preservation. From a Lithuanian perspective, the world is first of all a particular place, often envisaged as a village. And even the wider—that is, global—world is sensually perceived and mentally comprehended through the features of a particular place and from the mental and ethical perspective of that particular place. Such perspective may be called truly philotopical.

Philotopy in this sense is not new. It began with the ancient Greeks who lived in defined places, *poleis*, and who always emphasized human finiteness and called for moderation. Defining the macrocosm in terms of the human being as microcosm—and also, for that matter, in terms of the human place of sensual experience—the ancient Greeks were disposed toward caring for beauty and appreciating the finitude of all substantial individuals. Although it is not new, recalling both the "felt sense" of ancient Greek living and an inherent attitude toward the world within traditional Lithuanian culture, philotopy neverthe-less may attain new relevance in our contemporary world, given the precari-ousness of the global environmental crisis and the imperative resulting from it to perceive the world as if it were a place in its true sense.[12] However, while ancient Greeks and premodern cultural and some modern philosophical trends of Lithuanian thought (first made explicit in the philosophy of Šliogeris) have taken our living places to be the world (*pasaulis*)—thus projecting the larger world to be a sort of extension of a particular place—in our contemporary situ-ation we find ourselves as if starting from the other end and asking whether the actual globe, as a starting point, can be perceived, lived in, and treated philo-topically (as though it were a place in its true sense). That is, we are being made to ask whether we are able to be in the world as *place* today as, for example, the ancient Greek or traditional Lithuanians did, dwelling in our places and both calling and feeling them as though they really were the whole world (to us).

Although the world in our current situation does appear to be a place (and this is positive, because it draws our attention and makes us more responsible), it actually cannot be the ultimate starting point, because such comprehension, although positive, does not hold the same sense of reality that the comprehen-sion of a particular place holds. The world, therefore, cannot be an object of philotopy in its true sense. Such a conclusion expresses the fact that we can speak of philotopy only in relation to a particular place, which the whole world can never be. But, that said, philotopy is not necessarily limited in terms of its application in acting on or bringing about change within the world as a globe. Later, we elaborate on why focusing on the world and its problems is not a phi-lotopical approach in its true sense, and yet how philotopy can still become a stance from which we human beings can alter our orientation to the world and affect the world as a whole.

Although the sharpening perception of the world as a place is a positive step toward some change amidst the crisis, it may not be sufficient and could even become a distraction from working out actual solutions. Even in the face of starting to recognize the world as a place, we humans persist in perceiving and treating our particular places as once we had perceived and treated the world as a whole. By transcending the horizon of sensual experience and turning to vir-tuality of *the world* (instead of the particular singularity of the *under-sun*), we forfeit moderation and transgress the limits and all possible modes of finiteness set by particular places. We also breach the principle of *nearness* in the sense that when we call for global action to solve global issues (which are always out of our immediate field of reach), it results in a global reality (the *far*) becoming the *near*, while the real *near* (which is my particular place) and the care that I myself could provide, although remaining physically close, becomes mentally the *far*. Just as in the misinterpretation of Gandhi's quote, the *near* becomes merely the means to the *far* (which is the world), and thus it loses its true sense of actuality as the only possible reality worthy of attention. In that sense, our actual particular places do not become objects of philotopy and the true caring it invites. Ultimately, the lack of care for a particular place makes it impossible to truly and effectively care for anything that is beyond it.

Yet the urgency of the *far* is made *near* through various channels of media, which affect us by locking our attention on the need for global action and on the perceived inability to make a difference alone. Our minds become focused on virtuality rather than actuality, which is always particular, defined, and sensual. Thus, we are distracted from the possibility of love and care that we could generate, if only we were able to turn to our places as truly the places of ultimate reality. Our attention to global crises and the need for action is only one of the many instances in which we are locking ourselves in the virtuality of language and imagination. Although effective and useful in many ways (also defining us as human beings), however, this does not bring us closer to a philotopical way of being in place and therefore cuts us short of generating true care and love as the basis of any significant change. Essentially we are beings of nearness, but we somehow tend to forfeit the objective nearness of place in exchange for the nearness of virtuality (which is the *far*). Too often, by not finding the same qualities of reality that only the philotopically approached nearness could bring, we tend to lose a sense of reality altogether.

In order to remedy this situation, the global mind-set has to give way to a radically new "thinking from place" endowed with the *wisdom of place*. Not only does the world have to become a place, but particular places should also be approached and appreciated as such, in a radically philotopical sense. It is therefore worth drawing attention to the fact that an understanding of global environmental problems should be sought, not in the debate of global action versus local action, but rather in the essential difference between two mind-sets—the global and the truly local or philotopical. Only by embracing the latter will we be able to find the reality of place, and only through doing so, the world as a place. By becoming truly near to what is important and actual, we shall be able not only to become loving and caring beings. By becoming more attentive and observing, we would argue, it is possible to sense intuitively the real needs of particular places and things (as well as ourselves)—and therefore to choose courses of wise actions.

The Philotopical (Truly Local) and the Global Mind-sets

The philotopical approach (or the truly local mind-set) is essentially the approach from nearness—the existential stance that both values and naturally cares for the things within one's reality, which itself is somewhat defined and supported by them. Furthermore, this approach generates a nonintrusive "moderate care" as a result of perceiving how substantial individuals are living beings endowed with their own inner nature and needs, which are to be respected in their own right. Philotopy thus enables us to enter into intimate contact with things that nevertheless remain respectfully distant, nonintrusive, midwife-like, allowing these cared-for things to be self-generating rather than being forcefully created entities. Such an approach is possible only when the reality of substantial individuals within a defined place becomes noticed as it appears for its own sake: that is, as the only ultimate reality, which shall not be exchanged either for the sake of different experiences or for practical purposes. This way of engaging things is close to what ancient Greeks called *wonder*. (As we know, for the Greeks, a state of wonder was understood as a source of philosophy. Through discovering the state of wonder as an essential experiential moment, which happens while being in place with a truly local mind-set, we also emphasize the inherent relation of philotopy to philosophy. That is, we may also consider philotopy in some sense to be at the roots of philosophy.)

The philotopical stance can be described as a way of being that dwells equally within subject and object participation. This way of being, as a meeting and an equilibrium point between the look and the view, an eye and the image, a subject and the object—an equal proportion of subject and object participation within *being*—means that neither of them disappears into the other. The object remains radically "other" and not the extension or another version of the subject, and yet at the same time the subject does not contract into a merely passive (irresponsible) observer of an overwhelming reality of sensory impressions of objects. Contrary to the common view that subject-object dualism (often mentioned as the "Cartesian paradigm") is the cause of human alienation and the dominant and imperialistic attitude of the subject toward the objective natural world, philotopy opens prospects for realizing how granting equal reality to subject and object can be a way of ensuring the respect commanded by embracing the distance-based, observable limits and intuitively felt radical "otherness" of an object.

A balanced meeting point makes possible representations of things as they appear, without adopting a stance either too close or too distant—stances from which the object would be prohibited from revealing the reality it would otherwise manifest in a place framed by observable and comprehensible limits. Yet it is also a point of maximum engagement and attention from the subject side. Such a "meeting" is therefore a state of balance between the observer and the observed, which is not merely a state of care in the sense of preservation but, rather, a state of care in which *seeing* involves a constant striving to see things as they are, in their particularity, and a commitment to stating their reality as it appears in the place of vicinity.

The philotopical stance is partly a human decision to dwell on the reality of substantial individuals within the defined place and to commit to their being-ness. But it is also an effect that a place, with its whole multitude of substan-tial individuals, has on a human being. Even the sense of love and care, which is mostly perceived as human choice, is partly a gift, or an invitation "from the other shore." Love and care are invited by their object in the same way as a look is invited by an image and therefore are not something that one can impose on oneself. The philotopical stance, as staging a meeting point, or a point of bal-ance, is therefore the attentiveness to the call of substantial individuals, a sort of midwifery to that which wants to be seen and acknowledged.

Šliogeris avers that most of our meetings with things are mediated by lan-guage and, thereby, through culture. We are unable to meet things in their true beingness in our everyday situations in part because we treat them instru-mentally (as Heidegger describes). But, according to Šliogeris, such a meet-ing is also nearly impossible because of the general human tendency to dwell in the virtuality of language, to read or understand the reality rather than to see it as it appears. The tendency to dwell within a sphere of linguistically con-strained world perception amounts to the domination of subjectivity (and thus anthropocentrism)—a domination that does not allow for the appearance of the true nature of an object. The philotopical approach is to counterbalance this linguistic overreach with the silence that comes from the side of objects. This is what Šliogeris calls "the silent phenomena of being" or "the substantial individuals."[13]

Such a move toward a silent reality is not a straightforward act. If imposed, it only creates false ideals, thus contributing to even more reality-hiding lan-guage. Perhaps the wisest step is at least a minimal suspension of language and the adoption of a sort of *anticipating openness* to the appearing of things as they reveal themselves in places of close vicinity. Engaging things in their particu-larity while one is infused with wonder enables an optimal balancing of one's own humanness (which is subjectivity) and the silence and reality of things that reveal themselves (in their objectivity) as worthy of love and preservation.

This approach not only preserves things, allowing them to appear and remain in their own true nature and thus preserving the world as a whole, but also invites us as human beings to develop a capacity for appreciation, care, and contentment, which are the basis of compassion and true interhuman dia-logue. Paradoxically, "thinking from place," "being truly rooted in and caring for the place," recognizing the "otherness" even in nonhuman substantial indi-viduals, is also the basis of true social connection, where the sense of connect-edness (granted by true being in place) spills over, thus becoming a source of connectedness among human beings. (We can observe instances where love of place bonds people into communities, which, in their turn, become the preserv-ers of places.) And, on the more personal level, being in a place in its true sense may also be said to be a certain existential stance, where the particular relation to things around oneself is also considered to be a sort of wisdom granted by place—a mode of being that not only preserves and does good to the environment but also brings peace and contentment to the human being. Overall, then, the philotopical way of being allows true care for and preservation of particular places, sincere and compassionate interhuman relations, and personal contentment. Philotopy thus brings recognition that meaningful change starts with love and the wisdom granted by (being in) the particularity of place.

In contrast to the philotopical stance, a global stance is one of distancing—a virtual approaching (of the *far*) that fails to engage the particularity of things and places and thus fails to make evident the real order, contingency, and requirements of things themselves. Such an approach is often intrusively creative or place-changing, but it can also foster indifference to the reality of place and the field of what is within reach. This sort of approach, by disconnecting human beings from the experience of the richness and fullness of particular places, not only does no justice to particular things or the world as a whole, but also leaves them empty of the love and care that could otherwise be invoked in them by other things and beings. This emptiness easily results in seeking superficial qualities of produced things that promise to fulfil the need for a true experience of reality, but that actually inevitably fail to bring the contentment—a contentment that can be granted only by other substantial individuals in particular places within a living cosmos. This emptiness also generates a felt need for a constant change, a felt lack of rootedness within a proliferation of possible fields of reference. This nomadism, however, works against building true interhuman relations or attaining personal contentment in life.

The global mind-set represents the loss of a balanced meeting point between a human being and a substantial individual in a particular place (the loss of subject-object equilibrium). In such a case, reality gets drawn either too much inwardly (subject contraction) or too much outwardly (subject domination). Either way, the point of true meeting is missed and, along with it, reality as it is. The loss of this reality of the middle coincides with the loss of moderation in relation, and in this instance any love and care that might be generated by a human being becomes either not enough or too much and is thus either destructive or intrusive. The global mind-set can manifest itself as a constant reaching toward the extremity of projecting oneself into ever new (literal and/or experiential) territories, almost as if conquering the world, even in attempts of care. Or it can manifest as a fall into experiential self-enclosure through which the outer world becomes at once overwhelming and irrelevant. Either way, the global mind-set embroils us in a constant transcending of the reality of place, a departure from any particular places by going too far either extensively or intensively. Yet this virtual departure from the reality of place is also ultimately a loss of reality that takes the form of global environmental destruction.

Both mind-sets—the philotopical and the global—in some sense are ways of identifying reality. While the philotopical mind-set finds its reality in actual things as they appear in particular and defined places, revealing their minimally mediated nature, the global mind-set is that which transcends this reality in various ways as a function of choosing to focus on something other than what appears in the scope of sensual experiences and to immerse oneself in the virtuality of language that can refer only to generalities and never to substantial individuals found only in particular places.

Philotopy as an Optimal "Stance in Between" and Its Relevance to East-West Dialogue on Environmental Issues

It should not be thought that the philotopical perspective stands in direct opposition to the global mind-set in a dual structure of perceptual possibility. Rather, to take a philotopical stance in the world is to dwell in an optimal place between two different modes of what we called the "global" perspective of the world. These perspectives are what Šliogeris refers to as the Caligula and Nirvana syndromes.

It is worth drawing attention to quite symbolic meanings of the names of the two extreme syndromes (found in Šliogeris' *Niekis ir Esmas*), between which, as a point of balance, an "Ithaca" syndrome is also located. For Šliogeris, Nirvana is a state of consciousness, Ithaca is a place, and Caligula is a person. Place, here, stands for the ultimate place of reality, while the state of consciousness and the person stand for two different, yet related, ways of losing that reality. Nirvana and Caligula are similar in the sense that both entail dwelling in the realm of a subjectivity and the loss of balance between subject and object—a sort of solipsistic anthropocentric approach. Yet they are different in the sense that while the former is a transcending of reality by passively merging with (and under) it, the latter is a transcending of reality by actively extending oneself over it. The case of Caligula represents the extended ego, the domination of the subject over the object, imperialistic self-extension, and object annihilation. The Nirvana syndrome represents a contracted ego that gets overwhelmed by the object and its impressions thereof, merging with it—not by self-extension (as in the case of the Caligula syndrome) but by self-submersion.

Thus, our choice as human beings is not an either-or selection of one of two different mind-sets—the global and the philotopical. Rather, our choice is framed as one of opening possibilities for discovering a fine line of balance between two opposing yet structurally similar ways of being, each of which involves transcending the placeness of place and the mode of philotopical being. Thus, the philotopical perspective may be likened to a camera focal setting that is the exact point of balance between a focal setting that produces a blurred image of the desired photographic object and a focal setting that produces a clear image, but one in which the actual shape of the desired photographic object is either obscured or only partially revealed. The ideal focal setting is one that represents the balance point of reality as a crossroads between two distinct possibilities for both transcending and losing it.

The focal point of the camera is similar to the philotopical stance in the sense that it most clearly, and in that sense respectfully, allows representing an object. It thus enables us to be called to care for the object as it appears, without changing its nature. But also it allows us to maintain a sense of the reality of things appearing in the representational field of image, thus allowing us to really know our place of reality and, through this, to discover the contentment of being in a particularly defined place. The focal point is reflected in a language that actually refers to the substantial individuals found in the particularity of place—a language that itself emerges on the fine line of inner balance between the silence of a thing and the "language-ness" of a human being.

To continue with the camera metaphor, zooming the objective of the camera inwardly makes the image blurred, and no particular shapes can be identified. Just as in the Nirvana syndrome, the blurred shapeless picture, in which the colors of an object merge into each other, represents a sort of impressionistic dream—a "picture" of reality in which reality merges into the immanent states of one's consciousness and is absorbed by it. Thus, the world (or the sphere of ultimate reality, as we may say) becomes one's own consciousness, which in a way reflects the deeper or more subtle patterns of objective reality that impinge on it as a stream of undifferentiated impressions—a stream that might be thought of as energy flows like those associated with yogic *prana* or Chinese *qi* or as the waves and particle beams identified by contemporary physics. Or these impressions might be encountered as "Nothingness," *purusha*, atman, Brahman, and the like. In any case, one's attention thereafter could be directed, on one hand, toward either filling one's consciousness with various contents of experiences or practices meant to capture, control, or release these hidden energies, waves, or particle beams or, on the other hand (though not necessarily in opposition), toward purifying consciousness through meditational and devotional practices aimed at spiritual enlightenment. This syndrome consists in a deep (as it were, vertical) connection to nature whereby one, through inward concentration, also gets connected to the deeper aspects of both oneself and nature in ways that enable one to control both to the point of achieving their complete cessation. This may offer a way toward spiritual enlightenment and ultimate happiness, as expressed in many Indian and other Asian traditions—a way beyond the sufferings that are seemingly unavoidable at the level of everyday life.

Unsurprisingly, this approach is not very much concerned with the shapes, forms, and limits of the actual substantial individuals as they appear in particular places. But even less so is it inclined toward engaging things for their own sake. Rather, it is an approach predominantly focused on becoming able to effectively control oneself (and one's experience) through mastering one's inner nature and, through doing so, to be able to merge with deeper patterns within the natural world. In classical Ashtanga yoga, for example, one has to master one's body through *asana* and one's vital energies through *pranayama* before one can effectively purify one's consciousness in the stages of *pratyahara, dharana,* and *dhyana.* Contrastingly, in some shamanic traditions, one performs rituals that include the use of psychedelic or mind-altering substances as a way to bring "deep," unconscious layers of oneself up to the "surface" of conscious experience as a means, ultimately, of cleansing one's consciousness in preparation for spiritual inspiration.

One manifestation of the global mind-set, what Šliogeris terms the Nirvana syndrome, also finds expression in some of the proffered solutions to global environmental crises. In this context of framing ecological strategies, the syndrome is parsed, for example, into appeals to animism, deep ecology, or a land ethics, all of which seek to ground the intrinsic value of things on the (generally expressed) idea of deep interconnecting patterns. Accordingly, individual natural things are seen either as participating in some transcendent Self or in deeply and essentially interconnected communities. The world around us is considered to be identical with my deeper Self as "I once more," in the Nietzschean sense that the world is actually my Self. Any intrusion into the external world also means an intrusion into the subjective identity of every conscious individual. According to this syndrome, the human relation to the external world should be moderate, even retracted, and any real change or action (such as building strong mental/theoretical foundations for ecologically addressing current environmental crises) must depend on transformation from within. In a nutshell, advocacy of external measures are subordinated decisively in favor of internal or perceptual change. However, the called-for change of perception may, in some cases, amount simply to a reversal away from Caligula-type approaches on the pendulum of two globally oriented mind-sets—a reversal that, if strong enough, would seemingly be bound to bypass the optimal middle of being able to focus on the particularity of place.

Coming back to the camera metaphor, in contrast to inward focus, zooming the focal point outward beyond the desired photographic object brings clearly into view an environment or objects that are farther away, rendering nearby objects indistinct or invisible and those farther away more real. This distancing transcendence of the place of vicinity expresses the nature of the Caligula syndrome, in which the actual outward reality of a particular place is deemed insufficient as it is and is always "looked through" in an effort to see the objects or realities that are farther away, above, or beneath it. Attention, here, is constantly projecting the self into territories that are always new and ever more distant. This attitude of "never enough" represents a sort of horizontal approach to the world, where the whole surface of nature (and the world) can be claimed to be known and thus controlled. In this sense, the Caligula syndrome is liable to foster an imperialistic expansion of power and control. But it also undergirds modern science, which always goes further and deeper into the essences of its objects—projecting the epistemic urge either into the unlimited vastness of space or into the unlimited inner depths of any given entity, always looking for ever smaller particles.

According to Šliogeris, either way, whether outward or inward, this act of projection always evidences an egoistic, solipsistic, and anthropocentric stance from which, although looking far into the essences of entities, it is ultimately possible only to encounter representations of oneself. The actual shapes, forms, and limits of substantial individuals, although seemingly constituting the sphere of knowledgeability, are in actuality sought out, not for their own sake (as transient and particular living beings), but in search of power (e.g., when science searches for particular materials to heal cancer or create an H-bomb) or in search of control and safety (e.g., when science seeks life-forms under ice caps to envisage a possible human life on Mars).

In terms of ecological strategies, the Caligula syndrome takes an active stance, advocating all types of creative solutions involving manipulating, and therefore intruding into, the natural world and finding clever ways to address environmental crises (e.g., by genetically modifying organisms, cooling the climate by geoengineering, using nanotechnology to improve health, or at least setting clearly achievable carbon emission reductions through some carbon-trading scheme). In short, this way of addressing environmental crises focuses more on human interests and begins paying attention to "nature" only when a given crisis starts threatening human lives and interests. Yet this utilitarian approach does not exhaust the possibilities for a Caligula-syndrome extension or projection of self. This can also be done in compliance with a deontological argument premised either on some divine will or on human nature and dignity. An example of such an approach is the doctrine of "stewardship," according to which human beings are not the owners of land but, rather, caretakers who have been granted this duty by God. In either case, however, the human being remains in a position over and above the environmental situation, presumed capable of comprehending it and executing his or her immediate duties through outwardly projected measures.

It is interesting to note that the activity of this Caligula-type approach, which in some sense is historically more responsible for enormous environmental crises facing us today, seems to take a more proactive and therefore seemingly more positive stance at the solution-generating level, calling for the global implementation of concrete measures to deal with these crises in the same spirit and vigor with which the crises were created in the first place. The Nirvana-type approach, although seemingly positive in the sense that it calls for no external interference with nature whatsoever, becomes sort of a negative (or foot-dragging) perspective once a crisis is full-blown and quick fixes are needed. This alternation of roles is evident today in the disagreements between so-called developed and developing nations about how best to tackle climate change.

Our own position is that any debate on which point of view is more moral, effective, or right is actually meaningless. The real problem lies in both of these perspectives breaching the contours of place-based reality and thus failing to embrace a philotopical approach with respect to both particular places and the world as a whole. However, although these perspectives are two sides of a single global mind-set that breaches the contours of being truly local, or philotopical, they breach the boundaries of the local in two opposing directions. This suggests the possibility that if those from so-called developed and developing nations were each to take a half a step toward each other, this might create a situation where dialogue directed toward philotopical ends might be possible, and thus an alternative understanding of the way we think about and dwell in the world might be realized. Callicott's attempt to reconstruct and unite the multiplicity of the environmental approaches that exist in the world today (many of them of the Nirvana type) with scientific views could be regarded as one such attempt. However, in our view, such an attempt will be successful only if the meeting of the developed and developing worlds is understood as a meeting of two distant and yet deeply connected approaches, as described above. The goal, then, would not be an extension and mixing of the ways in which they similarly engage our contemporary environmental crises—resulting in further entrenchment in a global, universality-oriented, and linguistically bound type of mind-set—but, rather, would be for each to seek in the other what it is lacking: the philotopical or the truly local mind-set attached to the particularity of place.

Šliogeris identifies this truly local mind-set with the Ithaca syndrome, which he describes as the most optimal and least nihilistic mode of being in the world. As mentioned earlier, the philotopical stance is a possible point of balance between the two orientational extremes (Nirvana and Caligula)—a point of balance that can be attained only by the willful act of overcoming temptations to forfeit one's place of particularity for the sake of beguiling ways of transcending it. Just as Homer's Odysseus resisted tempting proposals for the sake of being able to return to a very dear place of his own—a place of particular things that truly can be called home—so we human beings today are in a position to resist succumbing to the "otherworldly" realities that are manifestly possible if we indulge in a retreat either into the immanence of consciousness or into the transcendence afforded by the myriad objects beyond our present, particular place, a transcendence that finally only extends our human needs rather than affording access to the actuality of things themselves. Šliogeris invites us to dwell on the reality manifesting itself immediately before us, clearly defined and dear. Odysseus' home (the place in its true sense), as a metaphor, also happens to be an island—a limited and defined piece of land that can neither be extended nor reduced by one's own will. Through the image of Odysseus, Šliogeris invites us always to see the limits of our place and therefore remain within our own limits. Staying within our limits means, here, to dwell in moderation as an expression of our ability to live fully within the boundaries of our own "home island" or particular place, responding to its real needs and, through this, becoming truly responsible.

In a word, the difference between the two mind-sets (the global and the local) explains why, as long as particular places continue to be perceived from the perspective of an as yet unreformed mind-set—one that is nonphilotopical in a radical sense—the (seemingly) philotopically perceived world as a whole cannot undergo sufficient change. Yet, as our discussion has aimed to make clear, committing to the philotopical perspective is not a matter of choosing sides; it is to abide in the middle between the opposing directions of transcendence that just happen to point both toward current developmental extremes and the opposing ecological strategies being generated in accord with them.

Although it is positive and productive to talk about global environmental crises—it is certainly a step toward a more philotopical approach to the world—doing so may appear unproductive and even harmful in the sense that it may result in calls for *global* action of a type that undermine our newfound sense of place. In light of this possibility, it is even more important to stress the need to relearn how to recognize the placeness, or locality, of particular places, to approach them philotopically, and not globally, since only this kind of approach can become the basis of sustaining the view of and being in the world as a place.

NOTES

1. Edward S. Casey, *The Fate of Place: A Philosophical History* (Berkeley: University of California Press, 1997), x.

2. Ibid., 334.

3. Arvydas Šliogeris, *Names of Nihil* (Amsterdam: Rodopi/Brill, 2008).

4. Yi-Fu Tuan, *Topophilia: A Study of Environmental Perception, Attitudes, and Values* (New York: Columbia University Press, 1990).

5. Ibid., xii.

6. Ibid., 93.

7. According to Tuan, "Topophilia takes many forms and varies greatly in emotional range and intensity." He refers to his effort to capture the variety of human experiences or emotions that would usually and generally fall under the categories of love or attachment to place: "It is a start to describe what they are: fleeting visual pleasure; the sensual delight of physical contact; the fondness for place because it is familiar, because it is home

and incarnates the past, because it evokes pride of ownership or of creation; joy in things because of animal health and vitality" (ibid., 247). See also Yi-Fu Tuan, *Space and Place: The Perspective of Experience* (Minneapolis: University of Minnesota Press, 1977).

8. J. B. Callicot, *Earth's Insights, A Survey of Ecological Ethics from the Mediterranean Basin to the Australian Outback* (Berkeley: University of California Press, 1997), 187.

9. Ibid., 186.

10. Ibid., 192.

11. The conception of the human ability to face the transcendence, which for Šliogeris is always the languageless reality of substantial individuals—things opening up for their visual apprehension and disclosing themselves as they are in the moments of silence— is developed in his most prominent philosophical work, *Nothing and Isness* (Arvydas Šliogeris, *Niekis ir Esmas*, 2 vols. [Vilnius, Lithuania: Apostrofa, 2005]).

12. Indeed, the love of place, and the love of particular place is not new; it is evident in various expressions of the love of homelands from people across the globe. As Yi-Fu Tuan puts it: "This profound attachment to the homeland appears to be a worldwide phenomenon. It is not limited to any particular culture and economy. It is known to literate and nonliterate peoples, hunter-gatherers, and sedentary farmers, as well as city dwellers. The city or land is viewed as mother, and it nourishes; place is an archive of fond memories and splendid achievements that inspire the present; place is permanent and hence reassuring to man, who sees frailty in himself and chance and flux everywhere" (*Space and Place*, 154). However (as noted at the beginning of this chapter), although philotopy is similar to every love of place, including instances of patriotism, it is also different in the sense that is based on the actual seeing of what is appearing and evident about the place, especially its surface and contours as well as the substantial individuality of things—all that reveal it as irreplaceable particularity. Such a philotopical approach is more similar to ancient Greek *theōria* and a sense of wonder inspired by the reality and actuality of visual appearances than it is to generally perceived love and attachment, which are more related to culturally and linguistically bound experiences.

13. Šliogeris, *Niekis ir Esmas*.

Landscape as Scripture   **10**

Rein Raud

Any sufficiently thorough reading of Dōgen's *Core Transmission* inevitably leads to a point where the division of his texts into "philosophical" and, for example, "poetic" or "metaphoric," will gradually lose significance.[1] To place fascicles such as *Genjōkōan* and *Uji* in opposition to *Sansuikyō* or *Gattō* would in this sense be similar to saying that Heidegger's readings of Trakl and Hölderlin or Deleuze's engagement with Proust are just literary criticism and should not be seen as part of their philosophical work. If we exclude Dōgen's practical instructions for meditation and notes on the organization of monastic life (and even these occasionally reach toward metaphysical issues), then what remains is a relatively holistic body of text that expresses a philosophical point of view with a variety of available means and linguistic techniques. Of course, some of these texts concentrate on topics that are less pertinent to the debates we are accustomed to label philosophical in our own practice. Nonetheless, they all exhibit the same systematic worldview, and the vocabulary that Dōgen uses in his allegedly less philosophical fascicles is quite often just as loaded with philosophical connotations as that in his more explicitly conceptual pieces. In fact, the beginning of the *Mountains and Waters Sutra* (*Sansuikyō*) fascicle can be seen as a very condensed summary of several key positions of his:

> The mountains and waters of the absolute present are how the way/words of ancient buddhas become apparent. Together they abide in their respective dharma-configurations and exhaust their potential in their becoming. As a message from before the aeon of emptiness, they are the livingness of the absolute present. As selfhoods from before any first-person-designation, they are the unrestraining of the becoming-apparent. The entire potential of the mountains is so high and wide that the power to ride the clouds is necessarily derived from them, the subtle ability to float in the wind is definitely unrestrained by them.[2]

Some translation choices here probably need justification. I am using "absolute present" for the term *shikin* in order to underscore Dōgen's view that all (material) existence is momentary and that the past and future are contained in it as causal histories and potential futures.[3] The expression "how the way/words of ancient buddhas become apparent" (道現成 *dōgenjō*) makes use of the ambivalence, current since Wang Bi's third-century commentary on the *Daodejing*, of the word *dō* 道, which can be read both as "way" and as "saying." Dōgen indeed often uses the word just to refer to something he has quoted from an ancient Zen master. But his idiosyncratic view of language conflates the two: there is no "way" apart from "language," the two are synonymous, actions are also expressions. As Hee-jin Kim has argued, "The range of the functions of language (in its broadest sense as Dōgen understood it) became coextensive with that of human activities . . . ; language and activity were inseparably one in his thought."[4] Ralf Müller adds that this concept entailed not only the verbal, aesthetic, or moral expressions of human beings but also, crucially, the manifestations of the nonhuman and nonliving world.[5] However, as Morimoto Kazuo warns us, it would be incorrect to assume that Dōgen is speaking about "reality as language," because there is no difference—reality *is* language, and there is no ground to make a distinction between things/processes, actions, and words.[6]

Moreover, as most translators of the fascicle agree, its title, *Mountains and Waters Sutra*, refers to the mountains and waters themselves, which *are* interpretable, textual, signifying phenomena. This position has a long tradition in East Asian thought. For example, the Chinese "dark learning" (*xuanxue*) of the Six Dynasties period, which exerted by way of poetry a strong influence on the forming cultural thesaurus of Japan, perceived nature as a text that should be read for mystical significance. Similarly, the semiotics of the Japanese esotericist Kūkai (774–835) treat nature as a text that can be approached with the help of esoteric methods of interpretation in order to gain access to the constant preaching of Buddha Mahāvairocana. Unlike Kūkai, however, Dōgen does not credit the signifying character of nature with any subjectivity that stands behind it and delivers the message through it. Mountains and waters are indeed a message—to those capable of receiving it—but the message is from these very mountains and waters and about these mountains and waters, or, more precisely, about their way of being. This is also why I have chosen to translate the word *shōsoku* 消息 in its more colloquial meaning of "letter, message" and not the "changes in circumstances" (that messages are usually about), which most other translators have opted for.

The term "livingness" (活計 *kakke*) is used by Dōgen in other contexts[7] as an explanatory attribute to his concept of Buddha nature, as the basic mode of being of all existents, sentient or not.[8] In fact, that concept in itself nullifies that difference, as Dōgen's idea of Buddha nature is not a derivate of biological life or consciousness but, rather, akin to the idea of panpsychism,[9] an undercurrent of Western thought recently revived by speculative realists such as Graham Harman and their fellow travellers.[10] Dōgen's "livingness" thus indicates not biological life but, rather, the capacity to interact with other existents, to be a part of causal chains, perhaps something akin to Deleuzian intensity, except that Dōgen's "livingness" is a general rather than particular characteristic of what is. "The livingness of the absolute present" thus indicates a dynamism within the dimensionless, the vectorial character of existence as movement and not of what moves or is being moved. "Selfhoods from before any first-person-designation" brings to mind another of Deleuze's concepts, preindividual singularities:

> Far from being individual or personal, singularities preside over the genesis of individuals and persons; they are distributed in a "potential" which admits neither Self nor I, but which produces them by actualizing or realizing itself, although the figures of this actualization do not at all resemble the realized potential. . . . We cannot accept the alternative which thoroughly compromises psychology, cosmology and theology: either singularities already comprised in individuals and persons, or the undifferentiated abyss.[11]

What Deleuze rejects here, just like Dōgen before him, is the classical (Platonic-Parmenidean) formulation of the "one versus many" problem: either there is homogeneous oneness that pervades all being, or there is a multiplicity of distinct particulars. Different developments allow these two to coexist in conceptual constructions as different levels, or visions from particular angles. For Dōgen (and Deleuze), however, the mistake has already occurred with the posing of this problem. As it is well known, Greek philosophy has been based, from its very beginnings (Thales, Anaximenes, Anaximandros), on the presupposition of a unitary source from which all being has emanated. But precisely this presupposition is, from Dōgen's point of view, a step in the wrong direction. Even substituting "nothingness" or "emptiness" for that first principle would not correct the mistake, because these, too, might easily develop into conceptual reifications. On the other hand, viewing reality as the interaction of autonomous, self-identical, and temporally continuous entities is even more problematic. For Buddhist thought in general, such entities are the product of mental activity rather than real things "out there," and Dōgen is no exception— on the contrary, his view of Buddha nature as the ultimate nonreferentiality of designations of things is a consistent development of this position. Quite evidently, neither of the traditional ways to conceptualize being is satisfactory from the point of view that Dōgen and Deleuze share.

It is interesting that in the phrase "selfhoods from before any first-person-designation" (朕兆未萌の自己 *chinchōmibō no jiko*), Dōgen uses a rather rare word, 朕 *chin*, to denote the first person—originally a word to designate an imperial prince that later evolved into a personal pronoun, an "imperial we," the use of which conveyed the superiority of the speaker in respect to the addressee. It has been used for similar purposes also by Chinese Zen masters, and the sense of "first-person-designation" clearly implies the raising of the self above its world, to the position of looking at it instead of being an integral part of it. This is not necessarily the case with the word *jiko* 自己, or selfhood (which refers to the idea of spontaneity, something happening by and of itself, yet reduced to particularity), and that is why I have resorted to the clumsy equivalent in this translation.

What exactly does this term refer to? Morimoto argues that reality "before any first-person-designation" is just things "as they are," and "unrestraining" does not at all mean leaving them behind but, rather, means a disentanglement, a release from our twisted view of them.[12] Therefore, he proceeds to argue that this anteriority to signification is comparable to the Heideggerian notion of *Sein*, or being, as opposed to *Dasein*, or being-in-the-world.[13] While I whole-heartedly agree with the former argument, I find it difficult to accept the latter one, as I do not believe that Dōgen opposes an underlying "being" to particular existents. Rather, he resolves this question, treated at length in the *Busshō* fascicle, as an outright denial of a last point of reference for any existent, which is, in fact, a prerequisite of being as dynamism and activity.[14] The more appropriate way to approach these things from within Western philosophical language is consequently as nonreferential singularities, unavoidably particular perspectives on reality as a total and constant dynamism.

The "becoming-apparent" is *genjō*, one of Dōgen's key terms, most widely known from his argument in the *Genjōkōan* fascicle, a highly condensed text from seven years earlier. Another seminal notion, "abiding in a dharma-configuration" (法位に住す *hō'i ni jū-su*, or, shortly, 住法位 *jūhō'i*), which was also introduced in the same text. Together, these terms present a metaphysical basis for Dōgen's view of reality as momentary existence that acquires continuity in the perceiving mind: ontologically, "things" are not self-identical existents that have temporal continuity, but result from designations that are given to ways in which minimal carriers of existence are "configured," situated in relation to each other. Thus, famously, there is a way in which these particulars are arranged that we call "firewood" and another way that is called "ashes"—and therefore it is as mistaken to say that "firewood" turns into "ashes" as it would be to claim that "spring" turns into "summer."[15] Just as the words we use for seasons refer not to "things" that are self-identical and continuous parts of reality but to sets of ways how different circumstances relate to each other, the same is true of the words for "firewood" and "ashes," which we, because of the deficiency of our own perspective, consider to be different. *Genjō*, or becoming-apparent, can be seen in this context as the site of interaction between the continuity-bestowing mind (not to be confused with human consciousness) and the momentary existence of such configurations. It is a challenge (*kōan*), but any conscious effort to willfully overcome it will only produce more of it. The alternative is unrestraining, letting loose, destructuring, unclinging—joining everything that exists, in its dynamic being, to ride the clouds and to float in the wind. This is praxis.

Insentient Expounding

What is noteworthy about Dōgen's position is that, unlike many before him, he sees his praxis not as an overcoming of our immediate reality but as an engagement with it. The aim is not to access a hidden and more authentic reality behind what is available to us but to develop an unmediated relation to what surrounds us. This is what, in the *Genjōkōan*, he calls "to be testified to by the myriad things,"[16] a state of mind that is aware of its being conditioned by everything it is in contact with. Nature has a big part to play in this, and Dōgen is well aware of the history of nature-related ascetic practices, the kind of wisdom Allan Grapard has called geosophia, or "particular forms of knowledge of the spatial environment" as well as "specific relations of society to the natural world," and geognosis, or "soteriological knowledge (i.e., leading to salvation) that is gained through specific spatial practices of a predominantly ritual or mystical character."[17] Indeed, there are many stories of enlightenment's having been achieved as a reaction of the mind to a natural event. Dōgen refers in particular to the story of the Chinese poet Su Shi, or Su Dongpo (1037–1101), who claimed to have realized the ultimate nature of things when hearing the sound of a brook in the mountains and who presented a poem as a support for his claim:

> The sound of the valley is the broad, long tongue.
> The colors of the mountains are nothing but the pure body.
> When night comes, there are the eighty-four thousand verses,
> On the next day—how can I bring them to people?

"The broad, long tongue" refers to the voice of the Buddha, as this is listed in *Dighanikāya* 30.1.2. as one of the Buddha's attributes.[18] Su Shi's experience of nature as the manifestation of the Buddha speaking to him, its equivalence to the verses of scripture, produced a momentary understanding he immediately realized could not be properly reified in order to be transmitted to people later in a self-identical form. (In the *Keisei sanshoku* fascicle, Dōgen tells us that Su Shi had listened to a discourse on the insentient expounding of the Dharma on the day just before having this experience,[19] and thus he was, not surprisingly, more open to such an experience than he perhaps usually was.) There are many more such stories from before the times of Dōgen and after; thus, enlightenment attained in interaction with the natural environment is not at all exceptional. "Insentient expounding of the Dharma" is, again, a notion Dōgen strongly subscribes to, and he has dedicated a whole fascicle to its analysis, in which he discusses the situation where signification appears without any consciously signifying party behind it. There is, he writes, a fundamental quasi-linguistic activity at work in all being. Expression—expressing itself—is a part of the dynamism that keeps reality up and running:

> Expounding the Dharma by expounding the Dharma is the manifest chal-
> lenge that is conferred to buddhas and ancestors by buddhas and ancestors. This
> expounding of the Dharma is what the Dharma itself expounds. It is not sen-
> tient; it is not insentient. It is not with purpose; it is not without purpose. It does
> not rely on a causal chain linking with-purpose and without-purpose; it has not
> emerged because of causal chains from the past. This being so, it is not directed
> toward the roads of the birds; it is given to the followers of the Buddha. When
> the great road is complete, expounding the Dharma is also complete. When the
> Dharma is conferred, expounding the Dharma is also conferred. When a flower
> is raised, expounding the Dharma is also raised. When the robe is transmitted,
> expounding the Dharma is also transmitted. This is why all buddhas and all ances-
> tors since before the times of the King of Majestic Sound (Bhīsmagarjitasvararāja)
> have continued to uphold this expounding of the Dharma. Since before the time
> of all buddhas, expounding of the Dharma has continued as the primary activity.
> You should not think that expounding of the Dharma continues as established by
> the buddhas and the ancestors. It is the buddhas and the ancestors that have been
> established by this expounding of the Dharma.[20]

Dōgen immediately underscores that it is the Dharma itself that does the
expounding, and thus the expounding is not the object of some other agent's
discourse. It is something always present when the transmission from mind to
mind occurs, and even though the founding myth of Chan/Zen opposes the
silent message of the Buddha upholding the flower to verbal explanations of the
doctrine, Dōgen insists that expounding the Dharma is similarly present in that
very act as well. It couldn't be otherwise: this fundamental activity of the universe is itself what has produced the mind that can have an authentic relationship to it. It stands outside causal chains and is independent of dichotomies. We
could perhaps say that it is the becoming-available of the conditions of meaningful experience that has been designated by this term.

To say that reality carries signification may seem to be a mystical thesis par
excellence, but on closer investigation it should appear no more so than the
belief, shared by many Western thinkers of various persuasions, that reality has
a logical structure that natural languages reflect. Some, such as Charles Sanders
Peirce, go even further and believe much more strongly than Dōgen that semiosis, or the production of signs, is a primary characteristic of how the world-
process works[21]—more strongly because they see such signs as carriers of an
unequivocal meaning—and the work of influential biosemioticians has ensured
that sign production is now seen as an essential part of how the natural world
functions. Indeed, all forms of life can be seen to rely on certain kinds of codes
such as that of DNA, as semiotically inclined thinkers have been quick to notice.
For example, Roman Jakobson states that "among all the information-carrying
systems, the genetic code and the verbal code are the only ones based upon the
use of discrete components which, by themselves, are devoid of inherent meaning but serve to constitute the minimal senseful units, i.e., entities endowed

with their own, intrinsic meaning in the given code," and he goes on to point out that both these languages function similarly, as systems of binary oppositions.[22] With just a little effort, we can construe a view according to which the world is in fact speech that uses the vocabulary of elementary particles combined according to the grammar of the laws of physics. The only thing missing from this picture is a speaker. But neither is one to be found in Dōgen's world, where the "expounding of the Dharma is what the Dharma itself expounds." Eight centuries later, this very same view is reiterated by Martin Heidegger:

> We would reflect on language itself, and on language only. Language itself is—language and nothing else besides. Language itself is language. The understanding that is schooled in logic, thinking of everything in terms of calculation and hence usually overbearing, calls this proposition an empty tautology. Merely to say the identical thing twice—language is language—how is that supposed to get us anywhere? But we do not want to get anywhere. We would like only, for once, to get to just where we are already.
>
> This is why we ponder the question "What about language itself?" This is why we ask, "In what way does language occur as language?" We answer: *Language speaks*. Is this, seriously, an answer? Presumably—that is, when it becomes clear what speaking is.[23]

Moreover, while the aforementioned theories see the semiosis of the world as workings of an unequivocal code producing self-identical meanings, then Dōgen does not: "Because buddhas and ancestors transcend both sages and foolish people, there can be no unity in what all these sages hear."[24] Each attainment-expression is by definition unique in its own unrepeatable present, and even if the words might be the same, they mean something different each time they are uttered: "Do not think that the expounding of the Dharma of the buddhas of before is the expounding of the Dharma of the buddhas of after. Just as the buddhas of before do not become the buddhas of after, so also in the case of expounding the Dharma the expounding of before does not transform into the expounding of after."[25]

And yet there is a quality, a formational principle that an utterance has to have in order to be an instance of expounding. Dōgen uses the words "ground" (literally, "bottom," *tei* 底) and "proper form" (*gi* 儀) to designate these: "ground" is used for a particular utterance that can be judged as adequate or inadequate, while "proper form" is the abstract quality that unites adequate expressions. As an example, Dōgen brings up the story of Bodhidharma's transmission, in which four monks are examined. Three of these summarize their understanding of Chan/Zen in competing sentences, but Huike, to whom Bodhidharma entrusts the leadership of his school, just bows three times and goes back to his place. While the first three are told they have attained the teacher's skin, flesh, and bones, Huike is the one who has attained the marrow. In the *Attainment-Expression* (*Dōte*) fascicle, Dōgen writes:

When such an attainment-expression expresses attainment, the not-expression remains unuttered. Even if we do recognize that attainment is being expressed, but the utter ground of the not-expressed is not yet reached, it still is not the face of buddhas and ancestors; it is not the bones and marrow of buddhas and ancestors. Therefore, how could the expression-ground of the "three bows and returning to one's place" be the same as the expression-ground of the "skin-flesh-bones-marrow"-fellows? The expression-ground of the "skin-flesh-bones-marrow"-fellows has no way to touch the attainment-expression of "three bows and returning to one's place"; it has no way to provide the conditions for it.[26]

The first sentence of this passage brings to mind Wittgenstein's famous finishing sentence of the *Tractatus Logico-Philosophicus* (7): "What we cannot speak about we must pass over in silence."[27] For the early Wittgenstein, this silence must encompass the domain of all that cannot be analyzed with the tools of logic. For Dōgen, the ground of the not-expressed necessarily has to be reached by understanding in order for the latter to be adequate. However, it is also not correct to read this passage as a claim that mystical (or mystifying) silence is superior to verbal communication. Elsewhere in his work, notably in the fascicle *The Vines Entwined* (*Kattō*) of *The Core Transmission*, Dōgen unambiguously explains that the silent answer of Huike was no better than all the others and that therefore the "skin-flesh-bones-marrow"-fellows, or those who make distinctions of quality between the four answers, are wrong.[28] The "proper form," however, refers to a more fundamental quality that all adequate expressions possess and that cannot be reduced to its perceptible form:

Do not think that the proper form of insentient expounding is necessarily unlike the one of the sentient one. Because it is similar to the voice of the sentients as well as the proper form of sentient expounding, it is not the case that when we remove the voices of the sentient world, we get to the voices of the insentient world. The insentient expounding of the Dharma is not necessarily a part of the voice-domain at all. By analogy, it seems that the sentient expounding of the Dharma is not a part of the voice-domain either.[29]

What Dōgen is saying here means that the quality by which an utterance (or a phenomenon) can be counted as an instance of expounding the Dharma is not at all connected to the channel through which signification is being transmitted. Even though later in the fascicle Dōgen says that the expounding voice should be heard not by the ears but by the eyes, this does not mean that seeing has any precedence over hearing; it is just that the recipient apparatus of voice (or any other domain of sensory perception) is not the proper one to apply. Not unexpectedly, the key to comprehension in fact consists in letting go of all our own signifying facilities:

On the whole, listening to the Dharma is not limited to the voice-perceptions and voice-consciousness. From before your father and mother were born, from before the time of the King of Majestic Sound, up until the exhaustible future and the inexhaustible future, gathering your forces and your mind, gathering your body and your words, you listen to the Dharma. You listen to the Dharma with your body first and your mind second. These ways of hearing the Dharma are equally beneficial. Don't say that there is no use in listening to the Dharma if it does not connect to your mind-consciousness. It is those who extinguish their minds and get rid of their bodies who are able to extract any use from listening to the Dharma. Those with no mind and no body are able to extract any use from listening to the Dharma. All buddhas and all ancestors, shifting through their moments like this, made themselves buddhas and became ancestors.[30]

To recapitulate: The availability of a meaningful experience of reality is, for Dōgen, in itself a linguistic phenomenon. Verbal language is therefore not a form of expression inferior to profound and allegedly banality-transcending silence: both of these need to be grounded in a more primordial authenticity of understanding that is unique at every single moment and yet both recognizable and transmissible. Therefore, not-speech (the silence of a speaker), nonspeech (nonverbal ways of communication), and un-speech (a situation perceived to be significant but not produced by a signifying entity) are all fundamentally linguistic as expressions and are not essentially different from those produced through code-based signifying systems—at least as far as the communication of essentials is concerned. Such communication, however, emanates not from a transcendental subject, a divine Other we would have to look up to, but from the arrangement of being itself. All names we can give to the entities through which such communication reaches us are therefore just heuristic. This is because these entities are not the points of origin of the expressions in question but the results of their activity. Language is thus not to be disdained, but also not to be taken at face value. Whenever it works as a vehicle for the communication of essentials, what it carries is not immediately visible for the idle eye but is accessible only as a result of an effort that totally engages the recipient person's resources, physical and mental. (That, we must presume, is also the way Dōgen intended his own text to be read.)

Dōgen's Idea of Landscape

Let us now look, from these premises, at Dōgen's ideas on landscape as scripture. First, we should note that "mountains and waters" is not just a juxtaposition of two kinds of natural phenomena but a system that is based on their opposition to each other. This phrase had established itself as a technical term in art theory at least since the influential writings of Zong Bing (375–443), who was among the first to forcefully articulate that a successful painting should reflect, not a superficial similitude to the outer form of things, but a deeply experienced inner dynamic of the depicted. Thus, even though Dōgen dedicates approximately one-half of the fascicle to discussing mountains and the other half to waters, the idea that they are significant is still reliant on the culturally meaningful system they form together. What sets them apart—and thus makes this system possible—is the different kinds of dynamism both of them possess and exhibit. As to the mountains, Dōgen has chosen to discuss a dictum by Furong Daokai (1043–1118), who once said that "green mountains are always walking."[31] Dōgen writes:

> It is not the case that mountains do not have their own inherent qualities. This is why they are constantly stable and constantly walk. This capacity for walking should be examined with special attention. Given that the walking of the mountains is similar to the walking of people, it should not be doubted, even though one might say we cannot see that it is the same as how people move. . . . Because of walking, there is constancy. The green mountains might be walking at a greater speed than the wind, and yet the people in the mountains would not notice or know this. Being in the mountains is the opening of blossoms on the inner side of the world. People who are outside of the mountains do not notice or know this. People who do not have the eyes for seeing the mountains do not notice or know, do not see or hear that this is how it works. If you had any doubt about the mountains' walking, this would mean you do not yet understand your own walking either—not that you do not walk, but that you do not understand this walking, not clearly enough. Just as you understand your own walking, you should definitely understand the walking of the green mountains. It is not that the mountains are already sentient or insentient. Neither are you yourself sentient or insentient. Now, doubt in the walking of the mountains is something you should not have. You do not even know to what extent you use your world as a source of measures for making sense of the green mountains.[32]

According to Gudo Nishijima and Chodo Cross, the expression "opening of blossoms on the inner side of the world" refers to the Indian sage Prajñatara, Bodhidharma's teacher, who is supposed to have likened the phenomenal world to blossoming flowers.[33] Dōgen has connected this to the idea that our life-world can be seen as if contained by an enclosure, within which our habitual rules operate and things appear to us as we believe them to be. This yields a self-contained world, which looks quite different from the outside. The geological shifts that actually characterize mountains everywhere may not take place "at a greater speed than the wind," but they are just as invisible to the human eye as is the much greater velocity of the rotation of the earth at 465 meters per second (at the equator) when observed with the sun as the center. But "[to] use your world as a source of measures for making sense" of reality is a blind alley. From the perspective of an organized particular world, one is unable to conceive of the dynamism that fundamentally animates both the whole of reality and the particulars in it as well. This is why Dōgen says there is no difference between the "walking" of the mountains and the walking of human bodies: the relation between them is similar to the one, discussed above, between verbal communication in natural language and the insentient expounding of the Dharma.

Yorizumi Mitsuko suggests that "walking" here is a stand-in for "praxis," or acting out of an authentic relationship with the totality of existence.[34] Indeed, if we define "walking"—from the particular perspective of the human body—as moving feet in a particular way, we obviously cannot understand how this activity could pertain to mountains. However, if we see our own walking as a particular, perspective-bound variety of dynamic activity, this is no longer so.

Thus, what has to be let go of is not our perspective as such but our tendency to universalize and naturalize the conceptual apparatus it engenders. In a sense, this echoes the famous position formulated in the *Genjōkōan* fascicle: "To study the buddha-way is to study the self. To study the self is to forget the self. To forget the self is to be testified to by myriad things."[35] In the present context, the testimony of myriad things amounts to nothing else than the dynamism of the mountains "walking," or the shifting of reality from one momentary configuration into another at a level where dichotomies such as "sentient/insentient" make no sense.

Dōgen returns to the topic of perspective-bound views of nature later on in the fascicle, when he discusses various approaches to water. He describes how different kinds of beings see water differently and how they are unable to abandon their own perspectives, and then he concludes:

> However the landscape is viewed, the result is different according to who the viewer is. . . . So even though we say that there are many kinds of [perceived] water, it seems there is no "original" water and no "many kinds of" water. Though that is so, the many kind-specific waters are not dependent on mind or body, not engendered by karma, not reliant on self or other—they are reliant only on the unrestraining of water itself.[36]

This view resounds quite closely with discussions of the idea of "landscape" in recent Western theory. Beginning with Erwin Panofsky and Nelson Goodman, art historians and philosophers of art have argued that what has been taken for a "scientifically" correct code of representation is not necessarily more than just a culturally correct view of seeing things.[37] Geometrical perspective is not "correct" and, indeed, in some cases—such as East Asian scroll paintings, for which the position of the observer has to move constantly along the scroll (because their content is represented from the position of a moving observer of nature)—is not even physically impossible. That point has been developed even further to demonstrate that "landscape" is itself a constructed system subjected to certain rules of viewing, and not something that would, independently of the observer, exist "out there." For example, Anne Cauquelin has problematized the concept as follows:

> Through the window painted on the illusionist canvas, one sees what one is supposed to see: the nature of the shown things in their conjunction. What one sees are not the things in isolation but the link that unites them—in other words, a

landscape. The objects that reason recognizes separately do not count anymore, other than in the ensemble proposed to our view.[38]

As a result, "nature" independent of the authorizing gaze ceases to exist:

> What is then legitimized is the transferal of the image onto the original, the substitution of the former for the latter. Even more, it is the emergence of a sole image-reality that corresponds perfectly to the concept of nature, neglecting nothing. The landscape is not a metaphor for nature, a manner of evoking it—it is nature itself in reality.[39]

Precisely this is the position that Dōgen seeks to abandon. Perspective-bound, or culturally correct, ways of seeing necessarily obscure what is seen. Groups of tourists moving from one designated "sight" to another and carefully shielded from the life of the society they visit have a very different impression of where they are than the people who inhabit that particular country do. But neither are the latter in a wholly privileged position:

> When dragons and fish regard water as a palace, it is just like when people see a palace and they do not recognize it as flowing at all. If there were someone looking at it from the side and saying to them: "Your palace is nothing but flowing water," then just like us now hearing someone's claim that mountains are flowing, the dragons and fish would be startled and doubtful.[40]

In the end, there is no point of reference than that of nature itself, in its immediate being:

> Water is not to be found in strong-versus-weak, in wet-versus-dry, in movement-versus-quiet, in cold-versus-hot, in is-versus-isn't, in deluded-versus-enlightened. When it freezes, it is harder than a diamond. Who can destroy it? When it melts, it is softer than milk. Who can destroy it? As this is so, one should not doubt all the qualities it has in its various manifestations. You should think a little about how the water of ten directions has to be seen at a particular moment as the water of ten directions. It is not a consideration for when humans and celestials see water, because it is a consideration for when water sees water, when water practices water and realizes water. It is a consideration for when water expresses water, because this is what makes apparent the path on which self encounters self. This is the living path on which the Other gets to the bottom of the Other—you should walk it forward and backward; you should leap over and out of it.[41]

I believe that the row of opposition pairs, typically for Dōgen, refers, not to the possible qualities water might or might not have, but to the impossibility of defining it with the help of such oppositions. Indeed, at one point water might be frozen and hard, and at another liquid and soft. To read "water is neither strong nor weak . . . existent nor nonexistent"[42] leaves open the possibility of a more mystical reading. But if we take *u-mu ni arazu* (有無にあらず) to mean "is not definable according to the system of existence and nonexistence," the phrase makes much more sense: the opposition of existence to nonexistence requires an ontology, a definition of what exactly we mean by these terms—for example, whether we can establish the necessary conditions of "existence," by which we can then judge water. But this would move us one step away from the direct experience of water. "Destroy" here means to annihilate water-as-water, taking its "waterness" away, which is impossible even though water has no essential qualities that would have to be present at any given moment. In that sense, "ten directions" can be taken as a pun, because it can also be read as "ten ways of being"—each of these is present as a past and potential future in every momentary configuration in which water appears. This shifting-without-ground is the practice of water.

Read in this way, Dōgen's position is both absolutely clear and completely rational: there exists a particular that is called "water," but this designation does not refer to a cluster of essential properties that water necessarily has; on the contrary, what is correctly denoted by this designation cannot be adequately defined by stable and preexisting conceptual structures. Whenever we think about water as something that has temporal continuity, we should be able to think of it as containing, as traces or potentials, all the other sets of qualities that might characterize it at a different moment in time. There is no other essence to water besides the dynamism behind the shifts from any one of such sets to another, and that dynamism is of the same kind that makes up our own continuity. Water as something normally liquid and unstable is the perfect example for illustrating this view, but the same applies just as well to any other continuous particulars, including mountains (which also "flow," as we just saw) and our own selves.

Within the larger system of "nature," or "mountains-and-waters," in the framework of which such particulars relate to each other, such dynamism is even more immediately visible. Steven Shaviro has used the concept of "metastability," defined by Gilbert Simondon, as a characteristic of nature at large: "All-encompassing Nature is traversed by potentials and powers, or by energy gradients and inherent tendencies. At any moment, these may be activated and actualized. The most minute imbalance or the most fleeting encounter can be enough to set things into motion, and there is generally more to the effect than there is to the cause."[43] Similarly to the trajectories contained by a particular (which include incompatible courses as potential futures), these gradients and tendencies, in interaction, make it impossible for the underlying dynamism to cease, however serene a view from the mountains may seem. This is how and why the mountains "are constantly stable and constantly walk"—just as we are and do while observing them.

Dōgen's views on nature are a continuation and development of a long tradition in East Asian thought and aesthetics in particular. Just as the theorists of

Chinese landscape painting, thinkers of "dark learning," and esoteric Buddhists such as Kūkai were, Dōgen was convinced that nature is meaningful in itself, as reality. Unlike most of his predecessors, however, he did not suppose that this meaning was structurally similar to the code-based nature of natural language. Signs of nature could not be "read" in the same way that characters can be read on a page. On the other hand, neither was Dōgen skeptical of language as a means of expression for the experience of authenticity, or enlightenment. In his view, dynamic being—being-itself, not in spite of, but in the form of constant change and shifting from one momentary configuration to another—was as such an activity of assertion, structurally not unlike linguistic communication. This is how he understood the doctrine of "insentient expounding of the Dharma" that had been developed by Chinese Chan masters and served as the context for enlightenment stories such as the one about the poet Su Shi.

This view of nature is immensely positive. It embraces the reality of the here and now instead of dismissing it in favor of a mystical, ultimate truth hidden behind its veil. Dōgen's uncompromising rejection of essences and self-identical continuities serves for him as the base of valorizing nature in its constant flux. Similarly, Dōgen's critique of the limited nature of any particular perspective does not mean that individuals who have these perspectives would be irrevocably condemned to a flawed perception of reality. Transcending such perspectives does not mean abandoning them—it only means we should refrain from absolutizing or naturalizing any particular perspective as the only correct angle for looking at the world.

NOTES

1. I translate the title *Shōbōgenzō* as *The Core Transmission*, and not as *The Storehouse of the Eye of the True Dharma*, because the term originates in the founding myth of Chan, where the Buddha promises to transmit to Mahākāśyapa this "storehouse" after the latter has spontaneously reacted to his silent demonstration of the flower—thus Dōgen, too, obviously uses the term as a metaphor for the collection of teachings he himself wants to transmit.
2. Dōgen, *Dōgen*, ed. Tōru Terada and Yaeko Mizuno, vols. 12–13, *Nihon shisō taikei* (Tokyo: Iwanami, 1972), I 331.
3. See Rein Raud, "The Existential Moment: Rereading Dōgen's Theory of Time," *Philosophy East and West* 62, no. 2 (2012): 153–173.
4. Hee-jin Kim, *Eihei Dōgen: Mystical Realist* (Boston: Wisdom Publications, 2004), 82.
5. Ralf Müller, *Dōgens Sprachdenken: Historische und symboltheoretische Perspektiven* (Munich: Karl Alber, 2013), 189.
6. Morimoto Kazuo, *Derida kara Dōgen e* (Tokyo: Chikuma Shobō, 1999), 92–93.
7. Dōgen, *Dōgen*, I 72.
8. See Rein Raud, "Dōgen's Idea of Buddha-Nature: Dynamism and Non-Referentiality," *Asian Philosophy* 25, no. 1 (February 2015): 1–14.

9. David Skrbina, *Panpsychism in the West*, Bradford Books (Cambridge, MA: MIT Press, 2005).

10. Graham Harman, *The Quadruple Object* (Alresford, UK: Zero Books, 2011), 118ff; Steven Shaviro, *The Universe of Things: On Speculative Realism* (Minneapolis: University of Minnesota Press, 2014), 62ff.

11. Gilles Deleuze, *The Logic of Sense* (London: Continuum, 2004), 118.

12. Morimoto, *Derida kara Dōgen e*, 92.

13. Ibid., 93.

14. Raud, "Dōgen's Idea of Buddha-Nature."

15. Dōgen, *Dōgen*, I 36.

16. Ibid.

17. Allan G. Grapard, "Geosophia, Geognosis, and Geopiety: Orders of Significance in Japanese Representations of Space," in *NowHere: Space, Time and Modernity*, ed. Roger Friedland and Deirdre Boden (Berkeley: University of California Press, 1994), 374.

18. Maurice Walshe, trans., *The Long Discourses of the Buddha: A Translation of the Dīgha Nikāya* (Boston: Wisdom Publications, 1995), 442.

19. Dōgen, *Dōgen*, I 290.

20. Ibid., II 61.

21. Peirce writes, "It seems a strange thing, when one comes to ponder over it, that a sign should leave its interpreter to supply a part of its meaning; but the explanation of the phenomenon lies in the fact that the entire universe—not merely the universe of existents, but all that wider universe, embracing the universe of existents as a part, the universe which we are all accustomed to refer to as "the truth"—that all this universe is perfused with signs, if it is not composed exclusively of signs" (*Collected Papers*, ed. Charles Hartshorne and Paul Weiss [Cambridge, MA: Belknap Press of Harvard University Press, 1960], 5:448).

22. Roman Jakobson, *Selected Writings*, vol. 2, *Word and Language* (The Hague: de Gruyter Mouton, 1971), 679.

23. Martin Heidegger, *Poetry, Language, Thought*, trans. Albert Hofstadter (New York: HarperCollins, 2001), 188.

24. Dōgen, *Dōgen*, II 64.

25. Ibid., II 61.

26. Ibid., I 385.

27. Ludwig Wittgenstein, *Tractatus Logico-Philosophicus*, trans. D. F. Pears and B. F. McGuinness (London: Routledge, 2001), 89.

28. Dōgen, *Dōgen*, I 427.

29. Ibid., II 63.

30. Ibid., II 67.

31. Andy Ferguson, *Zen's Chinese Heritage: The Masters and Their Teachings* (Boston: Wisdom Publications, 2011), 418.

32. Dōgen, *Dōgen*, I 331–332.

33. Dōgen, *Master Dogen's "Shobogenzo,"* trans. Gudo Nishijima and Chodo Cross (Woking, UK: Windbell, 1994), I 229.

34. Yorizumi Mitsuko, *Shōbōgenzō nyūmon* (Tokyo: Kadokawa, 2014), 96.

35. Dōgen, *Dōgen*, I 36.

36. Ibid., I 335.

37. Erwin Panofsky, *Perspective as Symbolic Form* (New York: Zone Books, 1991); Nelson Goodman, *Languages of Art: An Approach to a Theory of Symbols* (Indianapolis: Bobbs-Merrill, 1968).

38. Anne Cauquelin, *L'invention du paysage* (Paris: Presses Universitaires de France, 2000), 74.

39. Ibid., 30.

40. Dōgen, *Dōgen*, I 338.

41. Ibid., I 335.

42. Dōgen, *Treasury of the True Dharma Eye: Zen Master Dogen's "Shobo Genzo,"* ed. Kazuaki Tanahashi (Boston: Shambhala, 2010), 158; Dōgen, *Master Dogen's "Shobogenzo,"* I 221.

43. Steven Shaviro, "Twenty-Two Theses on Nature," *Yearbook of Comparative Literature* 58 (2012): 207.

PART IV

SHARED PLACES OF POLITICS AND RELIGION

Public Places and Privileged Spaces

11

PERSPECTIVES ON THE PUBLIC SPHERE AND THE
SPHERE OF PRIVILEGE IN CHINA AND THE WEST

Albert Welter

Public places—that is, Habermas' "public sphere"—have privileged status in modern democracies as arenas for the free exchange of ideas and commodities. Likewise, private interests enjoy a privileged status beyond state control, authorized as free expressions of the autonomous individual. In this chapter, I compare the notions of public place and private space against common assumptions in the Chinese tradition, where public and private realms were never thought of as distinct but were considered part of a continuum of harmonious, if sometimes contested, terrain. In place of a public sphere where the principles of an engaged democracy are manifest, Confucian models in China provided for a "sphere of privilege" that allowed access to the mechanisms of power and arenas of cultural privilege through control mandated by central authority. This authority designated and privileged an inside sphere, a "sphere of privilege," where sanctioned activities deemed to foster government aims operated as legitimate organs of government policy.

Problematizing the "Public Sphere"
vis-à-vis Religion

"Religion" is a word born in the West and exported around the globe with the advance of Western institutions and the frames through which knowledge is referenced. As Western institutions and frames of reference were transplanted in lands and cultures far removed from their origins, they were adapted and assumed a normative quality, variously understood. These newly acquired knowledge structures competed with latent cultural practices and norms that strove to find places within the new systems of modernity. One of the concepts in which this is abundantly clear is "religion."

The fact that "religion" is a problematic notion is hardly new. That it is a term embedded in particular Western linguistic and cultural frameworks is often pointed out.[1] Richard King, for example, asserts:

The modern concept of "religion" carries with it certain key assumptions about the world that are . . . ultimately grounded in a hegemonic Euro-American myth about the origins of "modernity" and the birth of the secular nation-state. These assumptions are not ideologically neutral but rather are encoded according to a specifically European history of the world.[2]

The long association of religion in the West with Christianity and other mono-theistic traditions likewise influenced the ways in which the category of "religion" has normally been understood.[3] Moreover, the use of the concept "religion" as presently understood is of quite late vintage, emerging in Western thought during the Enlightenment.[4] Lest we fall victim to blindly mapping our cultural concepts onto other, indigenous contexts, we must be mindful that we are imposing alien importations, along with the map of the world that we use to manage and control them.

The Metaphor of Proximity: The Confucian Rejection of Universalism

Russell McCutcheon argues that modern European rhetorical innovations delimited religion as a private concept "in a way that was designed to seques-ter it from the state," creating the "public sphere" and the "private sphere" and establishing the "separation of church and state." However externalized, objec-tified, or reified as natural or eternal this order was suggested to be, there was nothing natural about it. Instead, it is a fabrication that segregates (or "strait-jackets") the world, and although it might be a fabrication that benefited mod-ern Europe, it is an ordering of the world that is hardly self-evident.[5] Habermas expressed it in this way:

> The bourgeois public sphere may be conceived above all as the sphere of private people come together as a public; they soon claimed the public sphere regulated from above against the public authorities themselves, to engage them in a debate over the general rules governing relations in the basically privatized but publicly relevant sphere of commodity exchange and social labor. *The medium of this politi-cal confrontation was peculiar and without precedent*: people's public use of their reason (*öffentliches Räsonnement*).[6]

Others, following Habermas' lead, have helped refine our understanding of the concept of the public sphere. It has been described as "a discursive space in which individuals and groups congregate to discuss matters of mutual inter-est and, where possible, to reach a common judgment,"[7] as "a theater in mod-ern societies in which political participation is enacted through the medium of talk,"[8] and as "a realm of social life in which public opinion can be formed."[9] These elaborations draw on well-known notions put forth by Habermas of a public sphere that mediates between a "private sphere" and the "sphere of public authority."[10] According to Habermas, whereas "the private sphere comprised civil society in the narrower sense, that is to say, the realm of commodity exchange and of social labor,"[11] and the "sphere of public authority" dealt with the state (the realm of the police) and the ruling class,[12] the public sphere crossed over both these realms and "through the vehicle of public opinion it put the state in touch with the needs of society."[13] In this sense, according to Nancy Fraser, the public sphere is an arena "conceptually distinct from the state"; rather, it is "a site for the production and circulation of discourses that can in principle be critical of the state."[14] Fraser argues that the public sphere "is also distinct from the official-economy" and "is not an arena of market relations but rather one of discursive relations, a theater for debating and deliberating rather than for buying and selling."[15] She adds that these distinctions between "state apparatuses, economic markets, and democratic associations . . . are essential to democratic theory."[16] The people themselves came to see the public sphere as a regulatory institution against the authority of the state.[17] The study of the public sphere centers on the idea of participatory democracy and how public opinion becomes political action. A basic premise of public sphere theory is a belief in the efficacy of enlightened debate. Political action is instigated by public sphere debate; the only legitimate governments are those that listen to the public sphere.[18] As Gerard Hauser puts it, "Democratic governance rests on the capacity of and opportunity for citizens to engage in enlightened debate."[19]

These characterizations invite comment in several respects. The discussion is framed essentially around Habermas' characterization of a "public sphere" drawn from eighteenth-century European bourgeois society and is a category that presupposes a number of unique features pertaining to that society: participatory democracy, the role of public opinion, and attitudes toward citizen activism, not to mention the lack of regard for status among participants, the domains of common ground over which private citizens could exercise authority, and ever-expanding notions of inclusivity that in principle could exclude no one, to name but a few. As a realm that mediates between the "private sphere" and the "sphere of public authority," the "public sphere" can hardly be said to exist outside modern democracies, so the first question that must be addressed is the applicability of a notion of the "public sphere" to a premodern or non-Western context. Clearly, the term does not apply. Yet, to the extent that democratic forms of government provide a normative model against which modern governments are judged, one can hardly dismiss discussions of the "public sphere" out of hand, even in the Chinese context.[20] As with the case of democracy, even when it is not subscribed to, countries like China are frequently forced in international forums to explain their actions against the norms that democratic systems presuppose, so that even when China does not sanction a "public sphere" where democratic presumptions prevail, large portions of the rest of the world and even some of its own citizens presume that this is a model that China should aspire to. There are fewer arenas in China where this is more self-evident than that of religion and the limits of China's tolerance toward its public display. The question thus turns to why there is such resistance to a "public sphere" in the Chinese context. How does Chinese thinking about things like a "private sphere" and the "sphere of public authority" work to inhibit the growth of a "public sphere"? To answer this question requires a shift away from the Western discourse surrounding a "public sphere" initiated by Habermas, and an entry into the Chinese discourse that delineates how arenas of influence are apportioned and managed through bureaucratic apparatuses in the Chinese context.

As Oskar Negt and Alexander Kluge point out, the German term for "public sphere" in Habermas' title, *Öffentlichkeit*, includes a variety of meanings but implies a spatial concept, social sites or arenas where meanings are articulated, distributed, and negotiated, as well as the collective body constituted by "the public."[21] The public sphere as spatial concept provides a good entry point for understanding how the Chinese rationalize and manage the flow of public discourse according to criteria different from those in the model assumed by Habermas. While Habermas' model of the public sphere is predicated on the creation of free and open public spaces—sites or arenas where meanings are articulated, distributed, and negotiated—the Chinese model is built upon notions of symbolic spatial proximity, where distance from the center is viewed as a means to manage and control access and privilege. Chinese notions of "space" are thus managed on the basis of proximity that positions participants around a centrifugal force creating a symbolic social universe that arranges and manages articulated, distributed, and negotiated spaces in relation to each other. Access to power and privilege is managed through proximity to the center. This includes the power to express oneself publicly—that is, to engage in public debate.

Chinese notions of proximity that govern access and privilege are firmly rooted in the Confucian tradition. These notions dominated the Chinese imperial state and continue to resonate down to the present under different guises. It is not that the Chinese were unaware of alternatives. The Confucian consensus emerged out of the protracted intellectual turmoil among the "hundred schools of thought" (*zhuzi baijia* 諸子百家) of the Spring and Autumn and the Warring States periods of Chinese history (770–221 BCE). Among the schools of thought that challenged for supremacy was one instituted by the philosopher Mozi 墨子 (or Mo Di 墨翟; 470–ca. 391 BCE) and his disciples, who became known as Mohists (*mojia* 墨家). Mozi argued for a form of universalism whereby everyone is equal before heaven, as well as for standards to be followed: "There is nothing better than following Heaven."[22] He advocated that no distinctions based on kinship proximity were warranted, that freedom from partiality through "universal love" (*boai* 博愛) would rid the world of chaos and friction. The universal standard provided by heaven created norms applicable to all alike, and all became equal before heaven.

The Confucian consensus actively disputed the model endorsed by Mozi and his followers. Whereas Mohists saw in their universal standard the seeds of social harmony, Confucians viewed it as a pretext for chaos. It was unnatural, the Confucians argued, to love another's parents as much as one's own or to regard the members of other's families as the equal to one's own. Human relationships naturally followed a spatial proximity determined by kinship ties: those closer to one on the kinship scale were more deserving of affection and regard than strangers at a distance. The hypothetical standard that rendered everyone equal violated the law of natural human instincts, where love or affection was apportioned on a sliding scale based on relative proximity. In the Confucian constellation, filial piety was transformed from a bland respect for one's parents to an ultimate mandate by which one's virtue was measured. Filial piety was thus not a voluntary choice but a mandate written into the order of the universe, the violation of which threatened the natural law of Heaven. In this constellation, human relations became a finely tuned balancing act dictated by symbolic notions of proximity. Confucian texts provided the code books through which proximate human relations were understood and managed.

The influence of the Confucian kinship model did not stop with the family but was superimposed on the framework of society as a whole, whereby the entire population was regarded as the "Chinese family." The emperor, as patriarch of the nation, presided over the Chinese family, just as patriarchs presided over individual Chinese clans. Ministers of state proffered their obedience and respect to the emperor in a manner modeled on the filial respect learned as children toward one's parents. The deference ministers showed to the emperor was mitigated by the Confucian tradition of remonstration, whereby the minister also had a duty to respectfully guide imperial decision making to the point of actively disagreeing with the emperor if the situation warranted it. This was a privilege accorded only to Confucian-educated advisers, who "earned" the right to remonstrate (i.e., express their "public" opinion, though the public in this case was restricted to the emperor and his court) through their command over the Confucian curriculum and the moral virtues it allegedly instilled in them. The hierarchy of the Chinese bureaucracy thus imitated the kinship proximity model that the Confucian tradition enshrined. Entrance into the bureaucratic constellation marked one as a privileged member of the ministerial family, where rank and position determined a relative scale for access and privilege. Gaining entrance to this world of access and privilege was an overwhelming preoccupation of the aspiring elite.[23]

How do these notions affect the way religion has been managed in the Chinese context? In the following sections, I look at how Buddhism was managed through Chinese bureaucratic structures in traditional China, based on the notion of allowing and denying privileges according to the model of spatial proximity. Because Buddhism was often consigned to outside status, removed from the arenas of state power and privilege, a look at how it engaged the state to win access and legitimation reveals much about how the process worked in the Chinese context.

Gernet's Description of Buddhist Monastic Institutions in China

Some years ago the French sinologist Jacques Gernet outlined a model, based on material and economic criteria, for how Buddhism functioned in Chinese society, the relevance of which is still evident.[24] While noting the great diversity that characterizes the Buddhist institutional presence in China, from great monasteries housing dozens of monks to village chapels and mountain hermitages with one or two inhabitants,[25] Gernet also calls attention to a similar diversity in terms of status:

> Some monasteries are official places of worship and are recognized as such. They have received their name (*e* 額) by imperial bestowal as well as gifts of land, funds, servants, allotments of local families, and certain privileges. They are entitled to annual subventions from the court. Their monks have been selected and ordained by the emperor and are supervised by officially appointed clergy who are held accountable for their conduct. The other kind[s] of establishments are merely tolerated and are always the first to fall victim to repressions. These are private places of worship, serving the great families as well as the people.[26]

Following the distinction in status accorded Buddhist institutions, Gernet stipulates that there were three kinds of Chinese monks: "the official monk, maintained at state expense and responsible for the performance of ceremonies of the imperial cult"; "the private monk, fed and clothed by the great families"; and "the common monk who lived in the country side, either in isolation or as a member of a small group."[27] What Gernet indicates, in effect, is that there was great distinction between official and private monasteries and that private monasteries were also divisible into two types: those constructed by officials and members of prominent families, and those erected to serve the interests of the common people. Great divides of privilege and power separated these three types of institutions and the monks who inhabited them. It is important to recognize that a diversity of types of institutions and monks constituted the Buddhist world, rather than there being a single Buddhist institution. The recognition of these distinctions weighed heavily on the fate of Buddhism in China. An imperial court that tolerated Buddhism and even one that identified with Buddhism was obliged to resist uncontrolled expansion of clergy and monastic constructions: expansion and construction perpetrated by imperial relatives and high officials, although highly visible, were difficult to control, owing to the influence and privilege of the perpetrators; developments at the popular level occurred in response to diffuse forces and relatively anonymous patrons.[28]

Just as elite families coveted entrance into the privileged world of ministerial position in the government bureaucracy (ostensibly through the examination system but also through backdoor-type connections), so did great families seek to convert their private monasteries into official establishments and exercise all their influence in order to do so. Similarly, clergy members whose ordinations had not been officially accredited benefited from imperial decrees sanctioning their ordained status. As Gernet notes, "This amounted to a steady and highly effective pressure exerted upon the religious policy of the court, tending to favor a development of Buddhism in China well beyond the bounds that governments might have reasonably wished to impose on it."[29]

In short, while religions like Buddhism faced serious challenges to gain acceptance in China, there did exist legitimate avenues whereby Buddhist institutions and clergy were allowed access to privilege. Official monasteries and clergy served at the behest of the emperor and were recognized as legitimate members of the bureaucratic establishment. Clergy residing in monasteries sponsored by the great families, and protected by the prestige of their patrons, also enjoyed a kind of privileged status and held out the hope of conversion to official status. In times of suppression, however, these monasteries were vulnerable to the vagaries of imperial policy, and the protections afforded them by their patrons could easily evaporate. The "common" monasteries and the clergy who inhabited them were the most vulnerable and least tolerated, but any of the private, nonofficial monasteries and clergy could be subject to closure at government whim. The elite Buddhism practiced at official monasteries, the reserve of a privileged few, was the "official" face of Buddhism and, as such, immune from persecution.

The Administration of Buddhist Monasteries and Clergy in China

According to binary oppositions that divide reality into competing hierarchical spheres, monastics and their institutions can hardly fit anywhere but on the religious/sacred/church side, juxtaposed against the secular/profane/state, with which they share little in common. What do we make of the Buddhist monastery as government institution, or of members of the Buddhist clergy as officials in the government bureaucracy? Such arrangements strike the modern reader as medieval, at best, and relegated to a dark age of confusion where the natural lines of demarcation separating (i.e., protecting) religion (the irrational) from the state (the rational) are not in force.

What the following suggests is that the conceptual categories of modernity separating the sacred and the secular are not the only "natural" means available to adjudicate between the rational and irrational forces that the state manages. This is not to suggest that binaries do not also apply to the Chinese context, as even passing familiarity with yin/yang ideology attests. But borrowing the metaphor of proximity based on kinship, the Chinese paired their binaries to a model of spatial proximity. This produced, not strict oppositions per se, but graded distinctions of acceptance/tolerance based on symbolic proximity to a central authority. It was this model that was used to adjudicate between the various Buddhisms that existed in the Chinese context as described by Gernet, to determine and legislate between acceptable Buddhist "rational" behavior and unacceptable "irrational" behaviors. This does not mean that China was exempted from the "violent hierarchy" that, according to Derrida, such binaries suggest,[30] but the model of spatial proximity did serve to soften the violence, for binaries were regarded as less absolute and more pliable. This is evident in the different bureaucratic arrangements employed for dealing with Buddhist clergy and institutions in the Chinese context.

As Buddhist monks officially entered China in the first century CE, existing bureaucratic mechanisms determined how they would be administered.[31] When the first "delegation" of Buddhists arrived in China, Emperor Ming (r. 58–75 CE) greeted them with delight and held official receptions in their honor.[32] In doing so, Emperor Ming followed established protocols at the Chinese court for receiving foreign guests and dignitaries. Initially, he extended courtesy to them at the Court for Dependencies (*honglu si* 鴻臚寺), or Chamberlain of Dependencies (*dahong lu* 大鴻臚), which functioned as the residence for extending courtesy to non-Han peoples from the four border regions of China (*siyi* 四夷) or from distant countries (*yuanguo* 遠國).[33] Later on, the emperor selected a separate location for the newly arrived foreign monks—outside the Xiyong Gate (西雍門; Gate of Western Harmony) in Luoyang—and ordered that a "purified dwelling" (*jingshe* 精舍) be built for them to reside in.[34] Because a white horse (*baima* 白馬) transported Buddhist scriptures and images to the new location, it became known as the White Horse Temple (or Monastery), the Baima Si 白馬寺.[35]

The use of the character *si* 寺 to designate both "court" in the name *honglu si* (Court for Dependencies) and "temple" in the name *baima si* (White Horse Temple) makes it apparent that the commonly used term for a Buddhist temple or monastery in China derives from its usage as an office for government administration. Among terms used for government agencies, *si* is one of several terms used to designate minor or less prestigious government agencies.[36] Although numerous other terms are available in Chinese to refer to Buddhist dwellings—such as *ārāma* (*qielan* 伽藍, a transliterated Sanskrit term for a monastic dwelling), *jingzhu* 淨住 (pure dwelling), *yuan* 院 (cloister), *lin* 林 (grove), *aranya* (*lanruo* 蘭若, "forest retreats"), and *daochang* 道場 (chapel; literally, place for practice)—*si* served as the common designation. Thus, the term *si* carries with it the prospect of a government-sanctioned institution, and this perhaps accounts for its popularity.

While the origins of Buddhist temples and monasteries in China as *si* authorize them as legitimate bureaucratic structures—that is, as institutions designed to handle foreign envoys and guests (e.g., the Court for Dependencies)—they clearly occupy space on the outskirts of the symbolic proximity referred to above. They are legitimate but are on the periphery and well demarcated from loci of power. Chinese tradition invokes a well used dyad, *nei* 內 and *wai* 外 (literally, inside and outside), to indicate proximity to power, authority, legitimacy, and so on and to separate, in a sense, what we might refer to as what is orthodox/accepted from what is unorthodox/unaccepted. Yet *nei* and *wai* are not indicators of any hard-and-fast division but are markers for a scale of relative inclusion/exclusion. It does not mean, however, that the model could not be invoked for exclusionary purposes. The model allows for either exclusion (categorical nonacceptance) or peripheral inclusion (conditional acceptance or tolerance). The manner in which Buddhism was first received and administered in China suggests peripheral inclusion, but at a distance far removed from the center. Under the jurisdiction of the Bureau of Guests or other similarly designated bureaucratic offices, the status of Buddhism was legitimized, but only so far as it was recognized as a foreign entity—it had no viable status as a permanent fixture in the Chinese bureaucratic constellation. The challenge that Buddhism faced, following this analogy, was to work its way up the scale, to advance from the periphery as an outlier, toward the center and full recognition as a legitimate tradition in China (i.e., as *nei* rather than *wai*).

Through the centuries that followed its official reception in China, Buddhism weathered the vicissitudes of changing imperial attitudes and preferences and the ensuing bureaucratic policies that accompanied them.[37] As the numbers of Buddhist clergy increased, special branches within the Chamberlain of Dependencies or the Court for Dependencies were created to administer them. In the Northern (or Latter) Wei dynasty (386–534), a Superintendency of Buddhist Blessings (*jianfu cao* 監福曹) was instituted to supervise the groups of monks, but jurisdiction for this was subsequently changed to the Office for the Clarification of Buddhist Profundities (*zhaoxuan si* 昭玄寺).[38] The former was "a unit subordinate to the Chamberlain for Dependencies that catered to the needs of foreign Buddhist priests during their visits to China."[39] The latter was "an agency of the Court for Dependencies . . . responsible for monitoring the teaching of Buddhism throughout the state; headed by a Controller-in-Chief (*datong* 大統) with the assistance of a Controller (*tong* 統) and a Chief Buddhist

Deacon (*du weina* 都維那)."[40] Essentially, these were special bureaucratic units created to supervise Buddhist monks, resulting from their increased numbers and activities.

The *Book of Sui* (隋書), the official dynastic history of the Sui dynasty (589–618), also stipulates the growing role of Buddhist officials in the Office for the Clarification of Buddhist Profundities in the administration of the clergy.[41] It indicates that Buddhism was winning greater official acceptance and continued to be administered through offices of the government (*si* 司). The increasing numbers of Buddhist clergy and their activities necessitated more specific and nuanced bureaucratic arrangements to deal with them. This included the institution of specific Buddhists as officials (*guan* 官), down to the territorial level, who were recognized members of the bureaucratic structure. That these arrangements were acknowledged in an official dynastic history indicates their legitimacy and acceptance.

As intricate and embedded as the administration of Buddhism was becoming in China, entailing the institution of specific Buddhist officers in the Chinese bureaucracy, administrative arrangements still kept Buddhism at arm's length, away from the bureaucratic centers of power. While the names of agencies administering Buddhism changed, from the Bureau of Receptions (*chongxuan si* 崇玄寺) and the Court of Diplomatic Relations (*tongwen si* 同文寺) to the Bureau of Guests (*sibin* 司賓), they all acknowledged Buddhism as an essentially foreign entity. When Empress Wu Zetian 武則天 (r. 690–705) decreed that Buddhist monks and nuns be administered through the Bureau of National Sacrifices (*cibu* 祠部),[42] an important bureau in the Ministry of Rites (*libu* 禮部),[43] it marked a significant change in the way Buddhism was regarded in the Chinese bureaucracy.[44] The Bureau of National Sacrifices was the central agency for conducting imperial sacrifices and services; it administered major sacrifices to heaven and earth (*tiandi* 天地) and to ancestors at imperial shrines (*zongmiao* 宗廟). That members of the Buddhist clergy were charged in the execution of these rites is especially noteworthy and marks a significant change for the fortunes of Buddhism in China. With Empress Wu's decree, members of the Buddhist clergy were authorized by the Bureau of National Sacrifices to carry out intrinsically Chinese (or *nei*) rituals, rather than be supervised by the Bureau of Receptions and the Court of State Ceremonial, branches of the government charged with handling foreign (or *wai*) matters. The pretext for the acceptance of Buddhism derived from the claim that "their good deeds [*shan* 善] warded off evils, and their blessings [*fu* 福] alleviated disasters,"[45] a sentiment in keeping with the common pretext for that "Buddhism possesses blessings for protecting the nation and saving others, and virtues for alleviating disasters."[46]

The "insider" status enjoyed by Buddhism and members of the Buddhist clergy did not go unchallenged. During the major suppression of Buddhism during the Huichang era (ca. 845), when the government destroyed Buddhist monasteries and images,[47] it was decreed that Buddhist monks and nuns must not be attached to the Bureau of National Sacrifices but instead be placed under the jurisdiction of the Bureau of Receptions, one of four top-echelon units in the Ministry of Rites that, in conjunction with the Court of State Ceremonial, was responsible for managing the reception of foreign dignitaries at court. The decree was based on a petition by the Secretariat-Chancellery (*zhongshumenxia* 中書門下), stipulating that since the Bureau of National Sacrifices administered the major sacrifices to heaven and earth and at imperial shrines, it was *particularly inappropriate* that Buddhist services (*foshi* 佛事) be conducted (emphasis mine). The chancellery made special note that the origins of Buddhism were foreign and that, consequently, it should be administered through the Bureau of Receptions.[48] At issue here was whether Buddhism should be regarded as a "domestic" (i.e., Chinese) religion or, as the decree and petition suggest, a foreign (i.e., non-Chinese) one.

Buddhists countered the charge that Buddhism was a foreign, non-Chinese teaching that should either be excluded or kept on the periphery. The Buddhist scholar-monk Zanning 贊寧 (919–1001) suggested a domestication process through which Buddhism became accepted in China as a *Chinese* tradition:

> The duty of the Court for Dependencies was protocol in dealing [*li*] with foreign peoples from the four directions and people who have come from afar. When [those who] taught the Dharma first came [to China], they were obliged to attach themselves to this court. . . .
>
> It so happened that as the taste of pepper was claimed to be exquisite and wearing leather boots was [thought] to be elegant, [there was] the saying: "[All within] the four seas are one family; to the Emperor there is nothing foreign."[49] . . . As a result, the Latter Wei [dynasty] instituted the Superintendency of Buddhist Blessings, the Office for the Clarification of Buddhist Profundities, and the Bureau of Receptions [*chongxuan si*], and set up administrative offices [*guan*] and spread agency bureaus [*zhu*] [throughout the land] in order to supervise Buddhist monks and nuns.
>
> Pepper was subsequently produced in our own land [i.e., China], and leather boots were subsequently acknowledged as Chinese attire. As a result, the Tang court ordered [Buddhist monks and nuns] to be placed under the jurisdiction of the Bureau of National Sacrifices.[50]

While the orders proscribing Buddhism were subsequently rescinded, the sentiments prompting them remained. Subsequent administrations vacillated between restoring Buddhist clergy to oversight by the Bureau of National Sacrifices and creating a new position, Commissioner of Merit and Virtue (*gongde shi* 功德使), what might be termed a kind of "commissioner of religion or religious affairs," subordinate to the State Councilor (*zaizhi* 宰執).[51] The State Councilor was closely associated with the Grand Councilor (*zaixiang* 宰相), the chief head of state (or prime minister), who served as principal adviser to the emperor. Commissioners of Merit and Virtue were established in the late Tang to supervise Buddhist establishments in the two capitals, Chang'an and Luoyang, but evolved to oversee the activities of other religions as well. By the beginning of the Song dynasty (960–1278), the Buddhist clergy was administered by both government agencies: the Commissioner of Merit and Virtue supervised ordination requests and examinations on the scriptures; the Bureau of National Sacrifices issued ordination certificates. This is in keeping with the Song preference for creating a system of checks and balances under a centralized administration, where two agencies have combined oversight for one jurisdictional matter.

One consequence of the successful embedding of Buddhism within Chinese bureaucratic structures was tighter control by the government. As Buddhist institutions and the Buddhist clergy became arms of the administrative system, they were compelled to abide by the bureaucratic rules and structures determined by that system. And as membership in the Buddhist clergy acquired prestige, procuring ordination certificates that legitimized one's status as an officially sanctioned monk (or nun) became increasingly desirable. Because clergy bore the responsibilities and privileges of civil servants, they were administered in similar ways. In the Song dynasty, the examination system became firmly entrenched as the primary means to admission into the ranks of official-dom, and the means to entrance into the Buddhist clergy mimicked this system. The Buddhist system entailed moving through five ranks (*wupin* 五品):[52] "Clergy Appointment" (*sengxuan* 僧選),[53] when one met the required standards for scripture recitation (*songjing* 誦經) and obtained a passing grade in the administered test; "Removing Ordinary Clothing [to assume official duties]" (*shihe* 釋褐),[54] when one received tonsure and donned the *kāsāya*;[55] "Official Rank" (*guanwei* 官位), when one was granted the formal and formless precepts by official decree;[56] "Tathāgata Representative" (*rulai shi* 如來使), when one lectured on the teachings of the *Tripiṭaka*;[57] and "Instructor of the People" (*limin* 理民), when one instructed people at both Buddhist and non-Buddhist assemblies. Not every monk who entered the clergy would aspire to the last two ranks, which were clearly elite positions within the Buddhist clergy, restricted to the most successful monks (and nuns). Normally, aspiring clergy would aim to acquire Official Rank, the bureaucratic equivalent of full acceptance into the cleric ranks, symbolized by tonsure and the donning of monastic robes. Elite Buddhists formed a special category of Buddhist nobility, whose designation in Chinese as Buddhist *junzi* (*famen junzi* 法門君子) reveals their association with the Confucian model of gentlemanly nobility, the *junzi* (君子), and moral exemplar par excellence. As in the case of Confucian officials and nobility, Buddhists were unwavering in their support for "king and country" and were resolved in carrying out the imperial will. The imperatives of the Buddhist clergy were to practice the Way for the sake of the country, to protect the people and alleviate disasters,[58] and, in these ways, to contribute to the execution of the imperial mandate. Officially ordained monks, as Buddhist "bureaucrats" at officially designated monasteries (i.e., government institutions), were charged with fulfilling these tasks, and government monasteries carried out routines that were determined by the imperial agenda.

As Buddhism endured a period of crises in the early Song dynasty, Zanning's proposals epitomized the strategy for survival in the face of mounting criticisms from a confident, resurgent Confucianism. While some Buddhists were wary of the degree to which official Buddhist monks and institutions were co-opted into the Confucian system of imperial protocols, Zanning vindicated secular (i.e., imperial) control over Buddhist affairs, believing that increased imperial oversight was beneficial to the Buddhist clergy as well.[59] Zanning's strategy involved a unique perspective on the role that China's "three teachings"—Confucianism, Daoism, and Buddhism—played in fulfilling the imperial mandate. Prior to Zanning, Buddhists acknowledged the positive aspects of Confucian and Daoist teachings but uniformly relegated them to an inferior, preparatory status in anticipation of a higher Buddhist truth. Amid increasing multi-ideological tensions and mounting antagonistic pressures, Zanning conceded Buddhist superiority in return for a legitimate role for Buddhism in the Chinese milieu. Zanning put forth four propositions:[60]

1. The emperor, as undisputed head of the Chinese state and leader of Chinese society, is the legitimate supervisor of the Buddhist religion.
2. Buddhism is useful to the emperor for conducting affairs of state.
3. Each of China's three traditions—Buddhism, Confucianism, and Daoism—has a legitimate position in the function of the state.
4. It is the duty of the emperor to supervise the activities of the three traditions and to direct them in accordance with the aims of the state.

The first proposition was an admission of the reality that Buddhism faced. Through imperial sanction, Buddhism could be guaranteed a legitimate role in China and protected against anti-Buddhist interference. The second proposition recognized the reality of widespread support for Buddhism. Properly guided, Buddhism provided an important governing tool in the imperial arsenal. The third proposition acknowledged a legitimate role for all three of China's traditions, each of which represented an aspect of a unified imperial ideology. Zanning's propositions acknowledged the unfettered authority of the emperor, supported by the three traditions in a tripodlike harmony beneath. Were any of the three to be denied, the metaphor suggests, support for the entire system would topple. As a result, the fourth proposition conceded that it was the duty of the emperor to determine the proper role and function of each tradition, for the welfare of the emperor and the country as a whole.

In this manner, Zanning provided a functional model for determining the legitimate roles of China's competing ideologies. In doing so, Zanning likened the three traditions to the possessions of a single family, the Chinese nation, with the emperor as its head. Buddhism, as a member of this family, had a legitimate place in Chinese society (i.e., deserved *nei* institutional status).

Along with Zanning's acknowledgment of Buddhism as a domesticated Chinese tradition, the model of Zanning as a scholarly monk also reflected the blurring boundaries between elite monks and the secular literati. In education, temperament, and persuasion, there was little to suggest how elite monks differed from their secular counterparts. In fact, the history of Buddhism in China, when seen from the level of human interactions, is less about the Buddhist monk as reclusive hermit and more about the Buddhist monk as urbane literatus. Elite literati-monks shared much in common with their secular counterparts: they came from similarly privileged backgrounds, had similar educations, spoke the same language of the privileged and educated elite, held common interests in poetry and other literary pursuits, believed in the sanctity of ritualized protocols in the conduct of everyday life, and so on. On a personal level, elite literati-monks shared a common worldview and a common sense of purpose with their secular counterparts, no matter what ideology they aspired to.

The Implications of the "Sphere of Privilege" Model: Chinese Secularism and Religion

The experience of Buddhism in the Chinese context provides a clear glimpse into the principles guiding Chinese secularism and its managing of religious affairs. While the case I considered here pertains to the Chinese state's management of Buddhism, the principles espoused are easily transferable to the management of other religious traditions and other religious activities in China. Even the officially atheist modern Chinese Communist Party's (CCP) policies on religion are heir to these principles. According to current policy, religious activities are officially permitted for five religions: Buddhism, Daoism, Islam, Catholic Christianity, and Protestant Christianity.[61] The activities of these groups are subject to CCP oversight, on the one hand, but they are also supported institutionally and financially. Members of officially acknowledged groups must abide by rules mandated by the CCP, including provisions regarding patriotism, and a key aspect of these groups is that they are regarded as patriotic associations.[62] Accounting for religious adherents who are not included as members of CCP-authorized groups is difficult, with estimates varying widely, but the majority of religious practitioners (and, by most estimates, the vast majority) operate in autonomous communities outside of state sanction and authority. Toleration of these groups varies according to the public-versus-private nature of their activities (reprimands are less likely in the case of private, behind-closed-doors, or "house" activities) and the vagaries of state tolerance. Beyond this are groups whose practices are labeled as "superstitious" (Falun Gong being the most famous example) and deemed to be intrinsically disruptive to the socialist aims and policies of the state for its citizens. Any activity so labeled is liable to be prohibited, at times forcefully, especially activities with public dimensions.

It is easy to correlate modern CCP policy toward religion with traditional dynastic government policies toward Buddhism. Recall Gernet's tripartite division introduced above—"the official monk, maintained at state expense and responsible for the performance of ceremonies of the imperial cult"; "the private monk, fed and clothed by the great families"; and "the common monk who lived in the country side, either in isolation or as a member of a small group"—and we see a semblance of CCP policy toward religion: officially authorized religious groups, autonomous private groups, and groups branded as active in "superstition."[63] Sedition is a common concern in the regulation of nonofficial groups, in both traditional and modern China.

On a more theoretical level, the discussion of Chinese secularism and its relation to the administration of religion raises important questions regarding the nature of religion in connection with modernity, as commonly understood. The discussion of "modern" or "modernity" invokes the spirit of Max Weber and his formulation of modernity, its relation to tradition (especially religion), and the West's alleged uniqueness over the non-West, including China (the very essence of Weber's formulation of modernity).[64] While contemporary theorists have moved beyond Weber, his formulation in this regard casts a long shadow over our understanding. Weber's formulation of modernity derives from European Enlightenment notions of rationality and subjective freedom that grew out of Protestant Christianity and the rejection of "traditional" Christianity, or Catholicism, that preceded it. Weber's formulation essentially negates everything that is nonmodern: the past (medieval Europe) and the other (Asia). By necessity, Asia and medieval Europe are lumped together as lacking rationality and subjective freedom—the essential components of Weber's modernity (actually, "rationality" is the Weberian term; "subjective freedom" is the functionally equivalent term used by Habermas). In the Weberian project the key concepts of modernity were products of Christian civilization, universalized as truths applicable to all times, all societies, and all civilizations.

Weber's notion of modernity was predicated on a notion of secularism that isolated and marginalized religion under the rubric of "separation of church and state," assigning religion a primarily private function and curtailing religious participation in the public sphere. By historicizing the Weberian project as a product of a particular time and a particular civilization (thus depriving it of its universalizing mission), we are forced to reconsider the fallacious underpinnings of Weber's "modernity" and how the conceptual framework deriving from it has tainted our understanding of the non-West, including China. In this regard, it is necessary (citing Habermas) to "[disassociate] 'modernity' from its modern European origins . . . and [break] the internal connections between modernity and the historical context of Western rationalism, so that processes of modernization can no longer be conceived of as rationalization, [or] as the historical objectification of rational structures."[65]

What does this have to do with our understanding of religion and secularism, of private and public spheres? Quite a lot, I would contend, for the separation or noninvolvement of religion in the operation of the secular state is a normative principle of modern nation-states formed on the Western model, as is the subsequent privatization of religion. The Chinese model of Confucian secularism, or "secularism with Chinese characteristics," seriously challenges the presuppositions of Western normative principles, allowing for, even encouraging, judicious participation of religious institutions and their representatives in the public sphere. Confucian secularist encouragement of religious participation does not tolerate the unbridled reign of subjective freedom, but it sanctions responsible religious expression that openly subscribes to government aims and sees religious participation as a fulfilment of such aims. Access to the public sphere is privileged, and entrance to it is determined by specific markers and conditions of acceptance. To the extent that Chinese governments incorporate traditional policies toward the administration of religious groups (and current CCP policies toward religion suggest that they do), we will see a new understanding of religion vis-à-vis the secular that challenges and supplants the hitherto normative pattern imposed by Western secularism.

By questioning the applicability of the Weberian project to cultures like China, we are questioning Weberian notions of modernity itself, based as it is on concepts of allegedly universal applicability that privilege uniquely Western developments. In this regard, we must understand our new mission: to explain how the concept of rationalization has been employed for all societies and historical periods as a conceptual and theoretical principle, how it has organized and regulated our view of social and cultural history, and how it has managed to align all historical data into a seamless historical discourse—one that marginalized most human experience, especially Asian. Wang Hui's point is that the trope of Western modernization (following Weber) has been validated by a negation of the past and the non-West.[66] The rise of the non-West necessarily questions this premise, and confronting and challenging Weber is a step in this process. Beyond this, we must recognize a challenge to the entire European Enlightenment project based on Hegel's "principle of subjectivity," the notion that individual autonomy constitutes the essence of what it means to be human and entails freedom from all forms of external authority.[67] Religion, in the Chinese context, does not represent a notion of subjective freedom from all forms of external authority, a privileged private sphere. To the contrary, it represents the potential for privileged access to the levels of public participation, for full and inclusive membership in the execution of state policy.

With my own contribution here, I hope in some small way to engage this process by analyzing linguistic and conceptual concepts that are important to notions of religion and secularism, private and public—key components of the modernization project—as linguistic and conceptual concepts in their natural Chinese logographic habitat. Rather than invoking the normative frames of reference applied to "religion" and "secularism" as Western concepts based on Western modernization theory, I have tried to look at Chinese equivalent frames of understanding. Finally, I suggest that the Chinese frames of understanding not be simply relegated to a "past" or "other" (Weberian markers of the absence of true "modernity") but be viewed as indicators of an alternate modernity not indebted to Western frames of reference, with an accompanying alternate understanding of how relations between religion and secularism are adjudicated.

NOTES

This chapter also appears as "The Sphere of Privilege: Confucian Culture and the Administration of Buddhism (and Religion) in China," in *Religion, Culture, and the Public Sphere in China and Japan*, ed. Albert Welter and Jeffrey Newmark (London: Palgrave Macmillan, 2017) and is reprinted by permission.

1. See, e.g., Russell T. McCutcheon, *The Discipline of Religion: Structure, Meaning, Rhetoric* (London: Routledge, 2003); and Craig Martin, "Delimiting Religion," *Method and Theory in the Study of Religion* 21 (2009): 157–176.

2. Richard King, "The Association of 'Religion' with Violence: Reflections on a Modern Trope," in *Religion and Violence in South Asia: Theory and Practice*, ed. John R. Hinnells and Richard King (London: Routledge, 2006), 235.

3. Within the discipline of religious studies, "religion" is understood as a collection of cultural systems, belief systems, and worldviews that relate humanity to spirituality, often based on the supernatural. The word itself is from Old French *religion*, meaning "religious community," and derives from Latin *religionem* (nom. *religio*), meaning "respect for what is sacred, reverence for the gods," and "obligation, the bond between man and the gods." Through Christianity and other Abrahamic traditions, religion became exclusively associated with monotheistic faith in the "one true God." Note also this observation by Malory Nye: "The concept of religion is a trope, or a typology, . . . it is untranslatable into many of the languages that religion scholars work in, and . . . it bears little relation to any 'emic' discourses" ("Religion, Post-Religionism, and Religioning: Religious Studies and Contemporary Cultural Debates," *Method and Theory in the Study of Religion* 12, no. 1/4 [2000]: 451, cited in McCutcheon, *Discipline of Religion*, 236). See also McCutcheon's discussion (252–253), in which he observes that "*for languages unaffected by Latin, there is no equivalent term to 'religion'*—unless, of course, we pompously assert that our local word captures something essential to the entire human species, thereby distinguishing local *word* from universal *concept* (i.e., although they do not call 'it' religion, they still have It; . . .)" (italics in the original). McCutcheon goes on to note how this assertion is made easier through the long history of European influence on other languages and cultures through trade and conquest.

4. Peter Harrison, *"Religion" and the Religions in the English Enlightenment* (Cambridge: Cambridge University Press, 1990), 1.

5. McCutcheon, *Discipline of Religion*, 230–290, as described in Martin, "Delimiting Religion," 173–174.

6. Jürgen Habermas, *The Structural Transformation of the Public Sphere: An Inquiry into a Category of Bourgeois Society*, trans. Thomas Burger (Cambridge, MA: MIT Press, 1989; German edition, 1962), 27 (emphasis added).

7. Gerard A. Hauser, "Vernacular Dialogue and the Rhetoricality of Public Opinion," *Communication Monographs* 65, no. 2 (June 1988): 86.

8. Nancy Fraser, "Rethinking the Public Sphere: A Contribution to the Critique of Actually Existing Democracy," *Social Text*, no. 25/26 (1990): 56–80.

9. Robert Asen, "Toward a Normative Conception of Difference in Public Deliberation," *Argumentation and Advocacy* 35, no. 3 (Winter 1999): 115–129.

10. Habermas, *Structural Transformation of the Public Sphere*, 30.

11. Ibid.

12. Ibid.

13. Ibid., 31.

14. Fraser, "Rethinking the Public Sphere," 57.

15. Ibid.

16. Ibid.

17. Habermas, *Structural Transformation of the Public Sphere*, 27.

18. Seyla Benhabib, "Models of Public Space," in *Habermas and the Public Sphere*, ed. Craig Calhoun (Cambridge, MA: MIT press, 1992), 87.

19. Hauser, "Vernacular Dialogue," 83.

20. The impact of Habermas is described by Weidong Cao in "The Historical Effect of Habermas in the Chinese Context: A Case Study of the Structural Transformation of the Public Sphere," *Frontiers of Philosophy in China* 1, no. 1 (January 2006): 41–50.

21. Oskar Negt and Alexander Kluge, *Public Sphere and Experience: Toward an Analysis of the Bourgeois and Proletarian Public Sphere* (Minneapolis: University of Minnesota Press, 1993). According to Cao ("Historical Effect of Habermas," 44), Chinese scholars also disagreed on how to translate *Öffentlichkeit* into Chinese. Some thought it should be translated as *gonggong lingyu* 公共領域 (public domain/sphere/field/territory/ area), some thought that it should be translated as *gonggong lunyu* 公共论域 (domain/ sphere/field of [critical] public discussion), while others thought it should be translated as *gonggong kongjian* 公共空间 (public space). The first alternative became the commonly accepted one. The second one preserves the polemical nuances that Habermas associated with the "people's use of reason" (*öffentliches Räsonnement*) (*Structural Transformation of the Public Sphere*, 27).

22. *Mozi* 墨子, book 1, "On the Necessity of Standards" (*fayi* 法儀), sec. 3: 莫若法天. Chinese Text Project, consulted June 28, 2012, http://ctext.org/mozi/on-the-necessity -of-standards.

23. The Confucian bureaucracy in premodern China approximates Habermas' description of the world of letters of courtly-noble society, whose influence extended to the public sphere in the world of letters (*literarische Öffentlichkeit*) (*Structural Transformation of the Public Sphere*, 29–30).

24. Jacques Gernet, *Buddhism in Chinese Society: An Economic History from the Fifth to the Tenth Centuries*, trans. Franciscus Verellen (New York: Columbia University Press, 1995); originally published as *Les aspects économiques du bouddhisme dans la société chinoise du Ve au Xe siècle* (Saigon: École Française d'Extrême-Orient, 1956).

25. Ibid., 3.

26. Ibid., 4. I have added the Chinese character for the temple name tablet conferred by the emperor (額) and changed the pronunciation from Wade-Giles *o* to pinyin *e*.

27. Ibid. To give an idea of the relative numbers of institutions housing each of these three types, Gernet refers to the *Bianzheng lun* 辯正論 (*Taishō Shinshū Daizōkyō* [hereafter cited as T] 52, no. 2110), by Falin 法琳 (572–640), which enumerates the following for the Northern Wei dynasty (386–534): 47 great state monasteries; 839 monasteries of princes, dukes, eminent families, etc.; and 30,000 or more monasteries built by commoners.

28. Gernet, *Buddhism in Chinese Society*, 5.

29. Ibid.

30. Jacques Derrida describes meaning in the West as defined in terms of binary oppositions, "a violent hierarchy" where "one of the two terms governs the other" (*Positions*, trans. Alan Bass [Chicago: University of Chicago Press, 1981], 28–30).

31. The explanation that follows is largely taken from Zanning's *Da Song Seng shilue* (hereafter cited as SSL) I, sec. 4 (T 54.236c13–237a25).

32. This information is recorded in various places, such as the biographies of the principal Buddhist delegates Jiashe Moteng 迦葉摩騰 (Kasyapa Matanga) and Zhu Falan 竺法蘭 (Dharmaraksha) contained in the *Gaoseng zhuan* (hereafter cited as GSZ) 1 (T 50.322c–323a). According to GSZ 1 (T 52.322c), Emperor Ming frequently sponsored receptions in their honor.

33. Here I am following the way Charles Hucker translates the meaning of the term *honglu si* for periods prior to the Tang dynasty (Hucker, *A Dictionary of Official Titles in Imperial China* [hereafter cited as "Hucker"], no. 2906). According to Hucker, the Court for Dependencies was instituted in the Northern Qi as "a central government agency responsible for managing the reception at court of tributary envoys, continuing the Han-era tradition of Chamberlain of Dependencies" (*dahong lu* 大鴻臚; Hucker no. 5947). Note, however, that for later periods the meaning is translated as "Court of State Ceremonial."

34. The Xiyong Gate is sometimes referred to as the Xiyang Gate (西陽門; Gate of the Western Sun). The term *jingshe* is frequently used to translate the Sanskrit *vihara* (temple or monastery).

35. On the background to this story, see Erik Zürcher, *The Buddhist Conquest of China* (Leiden: Brill, 2007; first published in 1959), 22. See also Kamata Shigeo, *Chūgoku bukkyō shi* (Tokyo: Tōkyō daigaku shuppankai, 1994), 15–16, in which Shigeo concludes that since the name of the White Horse Temple fails to appear in the traditions about Emperor Ming's search for Buddhist teaching recorded in early Buddhist sources and dynastic histories, it is clearly the fabrication of later Buddhists. The existence of an alternate explanation for how the White Horse Temple received its name, differing substantially from the generally accepted one, supports this conclusion. According to the biography of Jiashe Moteng (Kasyapa Matanga) in GSZ 1 (see T 50.323a), a foreign king destroyed Buddhist temples, until only the Zhaoti Temple remained. Before he could destroy this temple, the king was made aware of his evildoing by the mournful neighing of a white horse circling the pagoda of the temple. Hence, the temple was spared, and its name changed to the White Horse Temple.

36. See Hucker no. 5534, entry on *si* 寺.

37. For a review of Chinese imperial policies regarding the administration of Buddhist monks and nuns, see Zanning's discussion in SSL II, sec. 37 (T 54.245b23–246a24). I am highly indebted to this discussion in the presentation that follows.

38. On this, see the *Shilao zhi* 釋老志 (*Wei shu* 魏書 114.3040).

39. Hucker no. 823, entry on *Jianfu cao* 監福曹.

40. Hucker no. 285, entry on *Zhaoxuan si* 昭玄寺.

41. *Sui shu* 隋書 27.765 states: "The Office for the Clarification of Buddhist Profundities administers Buddhism. It employs one Controller-in-Chief (*datong* 大統), one Controller (*tong* 統), and three Chief Buddhist Deacons (*du weina* 都維那). It has members placed in Personnel Evaluation Sections (*gongcao* 功曹), and as Assistant Magistrates

(*zhubu* 主簿), in order to administer the *śramaṇa* in various regions, commanderies, and districts."

42. Regarding the Bureau of National Sacrifices, see Hucker no. 7566; regarding its importance for Buddhism, see Kenneth Ch'en, *Buddhism in China: A Historical Survey* (Princeton, NJ: Princeton University Press, 1964), 255.

43. The Ministry of Rites (Hucker no. 3631) was one of the six ministries that formed the administrative core of the central government. In addition to supervising the Bureau of National Sacrifices, it also took on duties activities previously performed by the Foreign Relations Section (*kecao* 客曹; or Bureau of Guests, Hucker no. 3204), the Section of Ministry Affairs (*yicao* 儀曹) in the Bureau of National Sacrifices, and various subordinate agencies in the Court of Imperial Sacrifices (*taichang si* 太常寺) and the Court of State Ceremonial (*hunglu si* 鴻臚寺; formerly the Court for Dependencies). The Ministry of Rites was generally responsible for overseeing all imperial and court rituals, codifying rituals, managing visits by foreign dignitaries, supervising state-sponsored education, monitoring Daoist and Buddhist communities, and managing the civil service examination recruitment system.

44. See *Tang huiyao* 49 (*Sengni suoli* 僧尼所隸 section) and 59 (*Cibu yuan wailang* 祠部員外郎 section). The same information is recorded in *Tong dian* 23 (*Libu shangshu* entry; *sibu langzhong*). As the only woman to officially rule in Chinese history, Empress Wu understood well the strictures of Confucian patriarchal orthodoxy and the outsider status it consigned her to. Throughout her career, she identified with various forms of Buddhism and ultimately drew from Buddhist ideology to justify her reign. This was no accident. Female gender, like foreign status, was a powerful inhibitor to certain kinds of access, privilege, and power.

45. T 54.245c8.

46. *Fozu tongji* 39 (T 49.370a).

47. Regarding the Huichang suppression of Buddhism, see *Tang huiyao* 49 (*Sengni suoli* 僧尼所隸 entry) and the *Chaisi zhao* 拆寺詔 in *Tang da zhaoling ji* 唐大詔令集 113. For a general description of the Huichang suppression, see Ch'en, *Buddhism in China*, 226–233.

48. The petition is recorded in *Tang huiyao* 49. It reads, in part: "According to the [*Compendium of Administrative Law of the*] *Six Divisions of the Tang Bureaucracy*, the Bureau of Receptions administers the foreigners from over seventy countries who have presented gifts to the court. Five Indian countries are also included in this number. The Sakya clan emerged from India. His majesty, on account of this, currently does not count [the members of this clan] as Chinese. The registry of names of Buddhist monks and nuns has been altered [to reflect this]. Accordingly, it is ordered that they be connected to the Bureau of Receptions, and not attached to the Bureau of National Sacrifices or the Court of State Ceremonial."

49. This is cited by Zanning as a proverbial saying, which might be taken loosely as equivalent to "The whole world is one family; the Chinese emperor is the master of the family." A similar sentiment is expressed in the *Hou Han shu* 後漢書 biography of Wang Fu 王符 (ca. 78–163 CE).

50. T 54.246a12–18.

51. According to Hucker (no. 6810), the term for State Councilor (*zaizhi* 宰執) was used only after the Song, but the evidence here suggests that it was in use at the end of the Tang.

52. My description here follows Zanning's comments in SSL II, section 37A (T 54.246a25–b4). Officials in the Chinese bureaucracy were categorized into nine ranks that determined prestige, compensation, priority in court audience, and so on. Each rank was commonly divided into two classes (first and second) or grades (upper and lower). The lower five ranks (5 through 9) were eligible to Buddhist officials. However, judging by Zanning's comments, the reference here is to an alternate, quasi, or unofficial ranking

system specifically for Buddhist monks that was not part of the normal official ranking system. After Zanning describes the Buddhist ranks, he calls on the emperor to "confer clear dictates authorizing an array of specific offices [*guan* 官] and specific ranks [*pin* 品] [for the Buddhist clergy]."

53. The term *xuan* 選 (Hucker no. 2653) indicates the process used by the Ministry of Personnel (*libu* 吏部) to choose men for appointment in the bureaucracy.

54. The term *shihe* 釋褐 (Morohashi 40129-10) normally refers to the act of putting aside one's ordinary clothing and donning the robes of an official on the occasion of first assuming duties. Here the meaning is adapted to a Buddhist context. Morohashi Tetsuji, ed., *Dai kanwa jiten* (Tokyo: Tasishūkan shoten, 1955–1960), 11:409c.

55. The monk's robe donned here—the *kāsāya* (*jiasha* 袈裟), or Buddhist surplice— indicates official entry into the clergy.

56. Receiving the formal and formless precepts indicated full admission into the Buddhist order. The first three ranks indicated here may be taken as admission into the Buddhist order, acceptance as a novice in training, and status as a fully ordained monk.

57. The word *tripitaka*, or "three baskets," refers to the three divisions of the Buddhist canon into sutra (teachings of the Buddha), abhidharma (commentary or doctrinal analysis), and vinaya (monastic rules).

58. T 54.246b2.

59. T 54.246a24.

60. These propositions are taken from Zanning's concluding discussion in SSL III, sec. 59 (T 54.254c13–255b12). These have been discussed elsewhere, especially in Albert Welter, "A Buddhist Response to the Confucian Revival: Tsan-ning and the Debate over *Wen* in the Early Sung," in *Buddhism in the Sung*, ed. Peter N. Gregory and Daniel Getz (Honolulu: University of Hawai'i Press, Kuroda Institute Studies on Buddhism, 1999), 21–61.

61. There are far too many sources to mention here that discuss the current state of religious practice in China and the government policies surrounding it. For a comprehensive, if slightly dated overview, see the articles contained in Daniel L. Overmyer, ed., *Religion in China Today* (Cambridge: Cambridge University Press, 2003).

62. See, e.g., Pitman B. Potter, "Belief in Control: Regulation of Religion in China," in Overmyer, *Religion in China Today*, 11–31. Potter characterizes CCP policy as an attempt to manage a balance between socioeconomic autonomy and political loyalty (12–13, 27), noting the inherent tension: "To the extent that policies on regulation of religion require a degree of subservience that is inconsistent with religious conviction, compliance will be elusive" (29).

63. The sociologist Fenggang Yang uses a similar tripartite division to describe the administration of religion in contemporary China. See Yang, "The Red, Black, and Gray Markets of Religion in China," *Sociological Quarterly* 47 (2006): 93–122.

64. My thoughts on this topic have been informed by Wang Hui, "Weber and the Question of Chinese Modernity," in *The Politics of Imagining Asia* (Cambridge, MA: Harvard University Press, 2011), 264–306.

65. Jürgen Habermas, *The Philosophical Discourse of Modernity*, trans. Frederick Lawrence (Cambridge, MA: MIT Press, 1987), 2; originally published as *Der philosophische Diskurs der Moderne: Zwölf Vorlesungen* (Frankfurt: Suhrkamp Verlag, 1985).

66. Hui, *Politics of Imagining Asia*.

67. As characterized by Habermas in *Philosophical Discourse of Modernity*, 7, 18.

Seeking a Place for Earthly Universality in Modern Japan

12

Suzuki Daisetz, Chikazumi Jōkan, and Miyazawa Kenji

Takahiro Nakajima

Suzuki Daisetz 鈴木大拙 (1870–1966) and Chikazumi Jōkan 近角常観 (1870–1941) were contemporaries. In modern Japan, both of them explored the religiosity and social characteristics of Buddhism and had a major influence during the period. They were both born in 1870, and their birthplaces were not far apart: Daisetz was born in Ishikawa Prefecture, and Jōkan in Shiga Prefecture. Their education followed a similar path as well. Daisetz studied in the Philosophy Department of the Faculty of Literature (elective course) at Imperial University between 1892 and 1895, while Jōkan studied in the same department between 1895 and 1898.

The redefinition of Buddhism in modern Japan may be characterized as having two aspects—religionization and philosophization—which were closely interrelated. In that context, Daisetz and Jōkan both tried to grasp Buddhism as a religion rather than a philosophy. In other words, they emphasized belief or experience rather than knowledge or theory. However, this did not mean they sought to preserve the conventionally established system of Buddhism. The place that Buddhism articulates as ideal salvation is not exclusively for the preserve of professionals such as monks but is equally for ordinary secular people. We can say that Daisetz and Jōkan both exited the established Buddhist system to practice Buddhism in secular society. If we embrace the proposition that one of the major characteristics of modern Japanese Buddhism is a connection between the religionization of an individual's interiority and religious practice in society, it can be argued that Daisetz and Jōkan sought to realize this direction in distinct ways.

However, this idea might easily turn into an understanding of the individual as being directly joined with the nation-state. For example, in the last years of his life, Nishida Kitarō 西田幾多郎 (1870–1945), who was close friends with Daisetz, came to advocate seeing the state as a "reflection" of the Pure Land. This idea finds expression in his essay "The Logic of *Topos* and the Religious Worldview" (written in 1945 and published in 1946), as follows:

216

> The real state must be religious at its roots. As a corollary, who has undergone real religious conversion must naturally be a member of the state in his history-forming praxis. The standpoint of religion and that of the state must also be clearly distinguished. The alternative is a medieval view that would hinder the genuine development of both religion and the state. This is why modern states have recognized freedom of belief.
>
> While the affinity between Christianity, the religion of a sovereign God, and the state is easy to see, Buddhism has sometimes been thought to have nothing to do with the state. . . . It helps us to imagine the state in the spirit of True Pure Land Buddhism: the reflection of the Pure Land in this land.[1]

Here, Nishida argues that the nation-state must be religious and religion must be national. He did not reaffirm the conventionally established religious system as it existed. He thought that through the experience of a modern process of secularization, a new religion would join with the nation-state:

> I wonder whether Buddhism, standing on the horizon of global history today, could contribute something to the new era. Certainly, the old conventional Buddhism is only an antique. Even if a religion is a universal religion, so long as it is formed in history, it bears certain particularities according to the time and the place of the people who give shape to it. Even though the essentials of religion may be preserved, it is inevitable that any religion exhibits demerits along with its merits. I merely propose that for the religion of the future, the direction of immanent transcendence is more promising than one of transcendent immanence.[2]

The "religion of the future" would be based on "immanent transcendence": a religion that seeks transcendence via immanence. In this coming moment, Nishida would try to articulate it as a new "universal religion," "standing on the horizon of global history." In this moment of creation, Buddhism, as well as Christianity, were assumed to be major contributors. Moreover, Nishida stated that a nation supported by such a "universal religion" would also contribute to establishment of a world order, surpassing its place as a mere nation-state.

The connection between individuals and nation-state is much more complicated in Miyazawa Kenji 宮沢賢治 (1896–1933). Kenji had a twisted relationship with Jōkan and could not take sides with him. Thereafter, Kenji approached Tanaka Chigaku 田中智学 (1861–1939) and his Pillar of the Nation Society (Kokuchūkai 国柱会), which Kenji understood as a secular religious movement trying to directly join individuals with the nation-state. However, after Kenji returned to Iwate Prefecture, he developed an original movement, which did not seek to directly join with the nation-state but, rather, tried to associate with farmers and the earth.

The "earthly universality" that I consider here is not like Nishida's idea, which joins individuals with the nation-state by referring to a new religion that possesses "heavenly universality" and a unique ethnic condition. By indicating the religiosity of individuals that can neither be reduced to the nation-state nor be defined as mere particularity but may instead be connected horizontally, I hope to designate the "earthly universality" as an alternative universality. In this context, I reconsider the significance of Daisetz' *Japanese Spirituality*.

Chikazumi Jōkan: Kyūdō Gakusha and Kyūdō Kaikan as a "Place" to Share Individuals' Internal Religious Experiences

A short walk from the main gate of the Hongō campus of the University of Tokyo brings one to Kyūdō Kaikan 求道会館 (Kyūdō Hall). Once a month it is open to the public. On one such occasion, Chikazumi Shinichi 近角真一, an architect and a grandson of Jōkan, gave a speech. Kyūdō Kaikan was built in 1915 by Takeda Goichi 武田五一 (1872–1938), one of the representatives of modern Japanese architecture. In its design, the hall harmonizes the architecture of Christian churches and Buddhist temples. This style expresses well the spirit of Jōkan's interest in reviving Buddhism as a religion after its confrontation with modern Christianity. Accordingly, the name "Kyūdō" is read as *kyūdō* rather than as *gudō*, as one would expect from the Buddhist tradition.

Kyūdō Kaikan was quite an important place for Jōkan to share religious experiences with young people. In a public talk he gave in 1903 about the purpose of establishing Kyūdō Kaikan, Jōkan explained that he had inherited the place where his mentor, Kiyozawa Manshi 清沢満之 (1863–1903), had conducted a spiritual lecture (*seishin kōwa* 精神講話) and lived with young people under the same roof.[3] This was called Kōkōdō 浩々洞, which Kiyozawa had opened in 1900. There, following a Christian service, Kiyozawa presented his spiritual lecture every Sunday. A journal entitled *Spiritual World* (Seishinkai 精神界) was published there as well. In 1902, after Jōkan returned from an inspection of Europe, he opened Kyūdō Gakusha 求道学舎 (Kyūdō School) at the same place and conducted a "Sunday Lecture" as well. Later he started to build Kyūdō Kaikan, which was formally established in 1915. For the creation of both Kyūdō Gakusha and Kyūdō Kaikan, what Jōkan had in his mind was the YMCA. He confessed that he was deeply moved when he met George Williams, the YMCA's founder, in London.[4]

What did Jōkan do at this place? It was a place where participants confessed their experiences of suffering to others and received sympathy from them.

> I cannot bear to appropriate the [Buddhist] way only by myself. I would like to express my experience [*jikken* 実験] and appeal to sympathy from the heart, to express my thinking and make a confession. That is why I opened the Sunday Lecture, in which we have Buddhist words, to extinguish the fire of suffering in our interiority and to enjoy living in a perfectly clear world with other participants seeking the way.[5]

Jōkan's invocation of the concept of "experience" is worth noting. It does not mean a scientific experiment; rather, it refers to a person's actual experience. This notion was often used among Kiyozawa's group of Modern Shinshu [Pure Land], as well as in the nonchurch movement of Uchimura Kanzō 内村鑑三 (1861–1930).[6] For Jōkan, too, this notion led to a criticism against the understanding of Buddhism as philosophy and opened the way to understand it as religion:

> What I propose as the essence of religion is neither a religion of philosophy nor that of ecclesiasticism. It is a so-called religion of experience. What I mean by experience is the fact one personally has in one's mind. In other words, it is surely a living and experienced belief in one's mind that is always suffering and changing.[7]

In Meiji Japan the move to interpret Buddhism philosophically was quite important for its establishment as an academic discipline. However, this included by consequence a weakening of Buddhism as a religion. In this respect, Jōkan criticized philosophical Buddhism in 1902:

> In the past twenty years, philosophy has praised Buddhist values. However, it was also philosophy that darkened the religious value of Buddhism.[8]
>
> The reason why belief in contemporary Buddhism cannot appear is that people are occupied by this ontology, and they just spend their days with philosophical theory. Religious life is becoming fainter with each day. Those who advocate a new Buddhism [*shinbukkyō* 新仏教] do not have a firm belief, because they set pantheistic theory as their fundamental value. Dr. Murakami repeatedly tries to worship Buddha as the ideal. Dr. Inoue Tetsujirō tries to listen to the voice of the great ego [*taiga* 大我], by negating one's personality. People of spiritualism [*seishinshugi* 精神主義] often fall into pantheistic *tathāgata* worship [*nyorai* 如来] by calling on Amida restlessly. In sum, all of them regard this philosophical ontology as the core of religion.[9]

"New Buddhism" is a movement that insisted on abolishing the conventional Buddhist system, its rituals, and the social participation of Buddhism. Starting in 1900, the movement was centered on the publication of a journal, *New Buddhism* (Shinshūkyō 新宗教), to which Daisetz often contributed.[10] Dr. Murakami is Murakami Senshō 村上専精 (1851–1929), whose *Outline of Unification of Buddhism* (Bukkyō tōitsuron taikōron 仏教統一論大綱論; 1901) theorized that the Mahayana teachings did not directly stem from the historical Buddha (*daijō hibutsu setsu* 大乗非仏説). For this theory, Murakami was forced out of the Ōtani sect of Shinshū. Inoue Tetsujirō (1856–1944) was one of the professors who taught Jōkan at the University of Tokyo. He stated that all religions share the value of overcoming the "small ego" (*shōga* 小我) by listening to the "great ego" (*taiga* 大我). The more important point is spiritualism understood as chanting *tathāgata*. This is nothing other than Kiyozawa Manshi's idea of relying on the salvation of *tathāgata*. Jōkan studied under Kiyozawa and was supposed to succeed his position and practice of spiritual activities. However, Jōkan tried to decline even his idea of salvation as philosophy.[11]

If that is the case, what was the Buddhism that Jōkan considered as religion? He concluded that it was a "Buddhism of salvation" by referring to Luther and Calvin.[12] This understanding of Buddhism should be connected with the values of the "reformation of the human mind" (*jinshin kaikaku* 人心改革) and "social reform" (*shakai kaizō* 社会改造).[13] In sum, by removing the mediation of philosophy, Jōkan tried to combine the religionization of the interiority based on individual experience with salvation and social reform as religious practices in society.

Miyazawa Kenji: "Genius Loci" and Earthly Men

Miyazawa Masajirō 宮沢政次郎 (1874–1957), the father of Miyazawa Kenji, was among those strongly influenced by Jōkan. According to Iwata Fumiaki 岩田文昭, Masajirō first met Jōkan in 1904, when intellectuals in Hanamaki invited Jōkan to their summer seminar.[14] After that, Masajirō followed Jōkan as a mentor and contributed to the "confession" column in Jōkan's journal *Kyūdō* 求道, writing: "I feel deeply ashamed of the depth of my worldly passions and admire Amida Buddha's compassion (*jihi* 慈悲) to save me."[15] In April 1906, Masajirō visited Kyūdō Gakusha with his family. Henceforth, his friendship with Jōkan continued.

However, unlike Masajirō, his son Kenji and his sister Toshi were dissatisfied with Jōkan. Right after entering Japan Women's University in April 1915, Toshi visited Jōkan. Although she listened to his lecture and read his books, Toshi could not find belief in his teachings.[16] It has been said that Kenji also visited Jōkan, in January 1919.[17] However, Kenji left Shinshū 真宗 and took up a belief in the *Lotus Sutra* (法華), especially the Nichiren sect (Nichirenshū 日蓮宗). Before that, when Kenji entered Morioka Agriculture High School in August 1915, he heard a lecture by Shimaji Daitō 島地大等 (1875–1927) at Gankyō Temple (願教寺) of Shinshū. At that time, Shimaji talked about the *Lotus Sutra*,[18] and Kenji gradually became fascinated by it. Over time, a serious conflict around beliefs arose between Kenji and Masajirō. Kenji tried unsuccessfully to convert Masajirō to a belief in the *Lotus Sutra*. In January 1921, Kenji left Hanamaki and began working for the Pillar of the Nation Society in Tokyo.

Founded by Tanaka Chigaku, the Pillar of the Nation Society (Kokuchūkai) was a lay-Buddhist organization based on Nichirenism (日蓮主義). When it was originally established in 1884, the organization had been called the Risshō-Ankoku Society (立正安国会), but Chigaku changed its name to Kokuchūkai in November 1914. It came to support *kokutai* (national polity 国体), or *hakkō ichiu* (universal brotherhood 八紘一宇). By criticizing the modern principle of the separation of church and state, Kokuchūkai aimed for the reunification of politics and religion. Practically speaking, it tried to join individuals to the nation-state based on Nichirenshū, to which the emperor had converted. In comparison with Jōkan's emphasis on individuals' interiority and social practice, Chigaku's idea was rather rapidly inclined toward nationalism.

Kenji came to admire Chigaku and joined the Pillar of the Nation Society in October 1920, and he started to work for the organization in January 1921. However, following an illness that confined his sister Toshi to bed, Kenji returned to his hometown in August 1921 and started teaching at Hienuki Agriculture School (later Hanamaki Agriculture School). Scholarly opinion is divided on whether Kenji abandoned his belief in the Pillar of the Nation Society or kept it for the remainder of his life. It is at least certain that once he came to understand its purpose, Kenji did not return to the society.[19]

In which direction did Kenji's belief in the *Lotus Sutra* next lead him? That direction was neither finding a "place" to share religious experience as Jōkan had sought to do, nor was it imagining a "place" in a religious nation as Chigaku had espoused. As Amazawa Taijirō 天沢退二郎 indicates, Kenji could be said to have headed to a "place" in which one could conduct "spiritual communication" with "genius loci": "Kenji's works and texts derived from the deep spiritual communication with genius loci. That communication shows the core place of religion in Miyazawa Kenji."[20] As an example of "genius loci," Amazawa refers to "An Earthly God and a Fox" (Doshin to kitsune 土神と狐; 1934), in which Kenji described a story of a fox as a poet who is tragically killed by an earthly god.

We can find another example of "spiritual communication" with "genius loci" in the Rasu Earthly Men Association (Rasu Chijin Kyōkai 羅須地人協会), which was active between August 1926 and March 1927. "Earthly men" [*chijin* 地人] literally means 'farmers,' but it was used more broadly to connote men living on the earth. Although this association did not last long, Kenji tried to discuss natural science and art with earthly men. As one of the textbooks in this association, Kenji wrote *Outline of the Introduction to Farmers' Art* (Nōmin geijutsu gairon kōyō 農民芸術概論綱要; 1926), in which he observed:

> All of us are farmers. We are pretty busy and work hard.
> We would like to find a way of living that is much brighter and livelier.
> Because among our old teachers and fathers, there were some who lived in such a way.
> We would like to discuss the coincidence between the proof of modern science, the experience [*jikken* 実験] of those who seek the way [*kyūdōsha* 求道者], and our intuition.
> Unless the whole world becomes happy, there is no happiness for an individual.
> The consciousness of ego gradually evolves from an individual to a group, [to] a society, and to the universe.

This direction is the way that ancient sages walked along and taught, isn't it?

The new era has a direction in which the world becomes a single consciousness and organism.

To live right and strong is to be conscious of the galaxy in one's interiority and to go in response to it.

We shall seek for the true happiness of this world. Seeking the way [*kyūdō* 求道] is already the way.[21]

Iwata hints that "we can find the trace of Jōkan" in Kenji within his expression "the experience of those who seek the way,"[22] but this is not certain. In *Development of Farmers' Art* (Nōmin geijutu no kōryū 農民芸術の興隆), Kenji wrote: "Religion becomes tired and is replaced by science, and science is cold and dark." He also added a note to this phrase: "Religious people being threatened by invisible shadow. Shinshū."[23] We might say that, at that moment, Kenji had not yet received Shinshū as religion.

In contrast to religion, Kenji called forth a "farmers' art" as a *place*, in which one could have "spiritual communication" and "socialization of affections":

A farmers' art is a concrete expression of cosmic affections communicating with earthly men and their personalities.

It is a conscious or unconscious creation using internal experiences of intuition and affection as materials.

It always affirms real life and goes to deepen and heighten it.

It teaches us to contemplate and enjoy our life and the natural world as constant artistic photos, inexhaustible poems, and huge theatrical dances.

It tries to make people's spirits communicate, socialize their affections, and lead everything to the ultimate place.

Thus our art is a foundation of new culture.[24]

For Kenji, spiritual communication with "earthly men" and their artistic expression was none other than social engagement. Only this activity was able to show an alternative universality, surpassing both religion and natural science.

Suzuki Daisetz: Earthly Universality

Just as for Jōkan, so too Buddhism as religion was a crucially important problem for Suzuki Daisetz. However, unlike Jōkan, Daisetz did not seek the strong experience of belief in the interiority of individuals. Rather, the religiosity he sought was a mysterious dimension that was not different from ordinariness but was concealed in it. In 1964, Daisetz wrote a short essay entitled "Myō" (妙; "The mysterious" or "The mystery"), which begins:

In recent days, I came to have an interest in *myō*. The *Daodejing* says that "the mystery of mysteries is the door of all mysteries" [玄之又玄、衆妙之門]. For a long while, I have tried to translate this *myō* into European languages, especially English, but there is no suitable translation. This may be due to my lack of skill with languages. Anyhow, I am satisfied with *myō* in Chinese. When I refer to English terms such as "wonderful," "mysterious," "magical," "beyond thinking," and so on, they don't positively fit *myō*. I happened to read the Bible the other day, when I was struck by the following phrase:

And God saw everything that he had made, and, behold, it was very good. (Genesis 1)

This very ordinary notion of "very good" is nothing but *myō*. This "good" is neither wrong in right and wrong, nor beautiful in beautiful and ugly. It is the absolutely incomparable that passes out of any dichotomy. It is the form itself, being in itself. *Myō* is nothing but that. It is equal to the "good" in the phrase "Every day is a good day," by Yunmen [雲門; a Tang-dynasty Zen/Chan master]. It is also equal to the "good" in the phrase "Every morning is a good morning," by Meister Eckhart. We can call it "The ordinary mind is the way" [平常心是道]. I am wondering if the most mysterious *myō* could be found in the most ordinary place.[25]

The *myō* that Daisetz was thinking of is the mystery found in ordinary life in a differential manner. The thing before one's eyes has duplicity involving the mystery of creation behind what it is in itself.

Daisetz tried to find such a mystery in a duplicated structure of ordinary life in the Chinese and Japanese traditions of Buddhism. However, this structure of religiosity must be universal, beyond the dichotomy between the West and the East. He did not seek the universality particular to Japan.

Daisetz published *Japanese Spirituality* in 1944. In this book, he aimed to find the dimension of spirituality or religiosity, which was distinct from the "Japanese spirit" that had in that period become a highly politicized concept and also distinct from the spirituality of established religions. In my understanding, by imagining "earthly universality," he hoped to constitute a society based on the earth but open to universality, in order to resist Japanese totalitarianism.[26]

In *Japanese Spirituality*, Daisetz described the earth and spirituality as follows:

Religious consciousness with regard to heaven, quite simply, will not be brought forth by heaven alone. When heaven descends to earth, man can feel it in his hands; he has knowledge of heaven's warmth because he can actually touch it. The potential in cultivated land derives from heaven's light falling to earth. For this reason religion bears its greatest authenticity when it appears among peasants and farmers who live and work on the soil.[27]

Spirituality may appear to be a faint and shadowy concept, but there is nothing more deeply rooted in the earth, for spirituality is life itself. The depth of the earth is bottomless. Things that soar in the firmament and things that descend from the sky are wonderful but are nonetheless external and do not come from within one's own life. The earth and the self are one. The roots of the earth are the roots of one's own existence. The earth is oneself.[28]

"Religious consciousness with regard to heaven" can be realized by farmers through "the potential in cultivated land." Spirituality is embodied in the farmers who till the soil. *Myōkōnin* 妙好人 (local saints) are farmers possessing such spirituality.

Daisetz vividly describes Asahara Saichi 浅原才一, a *myōkōnin* living in Shimane Prefecture. The important point of his sacredness lies in that although he is an ordinary person, or because he is an ordinary person, he is Amida Buddha 阿弥陀仏 at the same time. Daisetz introduces Saichi's phrase:

> I do not become Amida,
> Amida becomes me—
> "Namu-Amida-Butsu."[29]

This phrase is a piece of poetry. Even though the mystery is ineffable, it sometimes becomes crystallized in poetry through a person. Daisetz interpreted this phrase as follows:

> The Name comes from Amida and "strikes" Saichi. Although Saichi remains Saichi, he is no longer the former Saichi; he is "Namu-Amida-Butsu." Viewed from "Namu-Amida-Butsu," one side is Amida and the other side is Saichi, and moreover each side is retained.[30]

As Saichi remains Saichi, he is Amida Buddha at the same time. This is not a simple self-identity; rather, "Saichi and the Buddha are contradictory yet have a nature of self-identity."[31] In other words, "the self-identity of Saichi and the Buddha must be seen through a viewpoint in which spatial is temporal" and in which "Saichi operates within Amida, and Amida moves within Saichi."[32]

Daisetz describes the spirituality found in *myōkōnin* as "Japanese spirituality." It is not *Japanized* spirituality but a universal spirituality produced *through Japan*:

> One can understand that because of this, spirituality has universality and is not limited to any particular people or nation. To the extent that the Chinese, Europeans, Americans, or Japanese possess spirituality, they are similar. Following the awakening of spirituality, however, each have their respective differences in the patterns or forms in which the phenomena of *seishin*'s [spirit's; mind's] activity manifest themselves.[33]

According to Daisetz, this spirituality has universality, but it appears in a unique form for each people. We might say that the universality of spirituality is not a heavenly overarching form but, rather, an earthly one springing up from below.

Daisetz conceived of a society embedded in the spirituality of earthly universality, not as one for the aristocracy of the Heian period, but as one for the warriors (*bushi* 武士) of the Kamakura period. Those who supported a new society in Kamakura were the farmers living on the land. The axis of society was aligned, not with aristocrats occupying the higher position in a vertical social hierarchy, but with farmers who formed horizontal associations with others. Daisetz thought that in the coming society in Japan, this form of spirituality, having earthly universality, should be realized.[34]

Each of our protagonists—Jōkan, Kenji, and Daisetz—sought the possibilities of Buddhism as religion in modern Japan. Jōkan left Buddhism as philosophy and emphasized the importance of the experience of belief within one's interiority. Kyūdō Gakusha and Kyūdō Kaikan were the places in which participants shared their experiences of belief. Kenji followed the direction of social relief after converting to belief in the *Lotus Sutra*. Instead of affirming the nation-state as the Pillar of the Nation Society had, he finally established the Rasu Earthly Men Association, as a place in which farmers living on the land gathered together and had spiritual communication. This was not so different from Jōkan's direction. Daisetz, who had contributed to a new Buddhist movement, left the established Buddhism and sought a spirituality with earthly universality in traditional Japanese thought. This was, at the same time, a criticism of Japanese ultranationalism.

The "places" that all three of these thinkers opened up with their critique were not heavenly ones. They were rooted in the earth and open to the universal. In such places people could bond themselves horizontally and participate in religiosity beyond modern interiority.

NOTES

1. Kitarō Nishida, "The Logic of *Topos* and the Religious Worldview" [Basho teki ronri to shūkyō teki sekaikan 場所的論理と宗教的世界観; 1946], trans. Michiko Yusa, *Eastern Buddhist* 20, no. 1 (1987): 119.

2. Ibid., 118.

3. Jōkan Chikazumi, *Problems of Belief* [Shinkō mondai 信仰問題] (Tokyo: Bunmeidō, 1904), 190.

4. Ibid., 197.

5. Ibid., 193.

6. Cf. Thoshihiro Omi 碧海寿広, "From Philosophy to Experience: Chikazumi Jōkan's Religious Thought" [Tetsugaku kara taiken he: Chikazumi Jōkan no shūkyō shisō 哲学から体験へ——近角常観の宗教思想], *Shūkyō kenkyū* 宗教研究 84, no. 1 (2010): 7–8; Thoshihiro Omi, "Modern Shin-Buddhism and Christianity" [Kindai shinshū to kirisutokyō: Chikazumi Jōkan no fukyō senryaku 近代真宗とキリスト教——近角常観の布教戦略], *Shūkyō to shakai* 宗教と社会 17] (2011): 55; Ryūta Sasaki 佐々木竜太, "On the Notion of 'Jikken' in Japanese Understanding of Christianity: The Difference of the Notion of

'Jikken' in Honda Yōichi and Uchimura Kanzō" [Nihonjin no kirisutokyō rikai niokeru "jikken" gainen no kenkyū: Honda Yōichi to Uchimura Kanzō no sai 日本人のキリスト教理解 における「実験」概念の研究: 本多庸一と内村鑑三の「実験」概念の差異], *Kyōiku kenkyū* 教育研究 48 (2004): 1–11.

7. Jōkan, *Problems of Belief*, 1.

8. Ibid., 10.

9. Ibid., 18.

10. Shinichi Yoshinaga, "Discursive Space of Religious Movement by the Intellectuals in Modern Japan: Study of Intellectual History and Cultural History on *New Buddhism*" [Kindai Nihon ni okeru chishikijin shūkyō undo no gensetsu kūkan: *Shin Bukkyō* no shisōshi·bunkashi teki kenkyū 近代日本における知識人宗教運動の言説空間—『新佛教』の思想史·文 化史的研究], *Report of Grants-in-Aid for Scientific Research* (2012): 36–37, 50–51, 56, 60, 67.

11. According to Shuntarō Nakano 中野駿太郎, Jōkan said that his belief was differ-ent from Kiyozawa's. See Shuntarō Nakano, "Kiyozawa Manshi and Chikazumi Jōkan" [Kiyozawa Manshi to Chikazumi Jōkan 清沢満之と近角常観], *Daihōrin* 大法輪 22 (1955): 72.

12. Ibid., 19–20.

13. Ibid., 22.

14. Fumiaki Iwata, *Modern Buddhism and the Youth* [Kindai bukkyō to seinen: Chikazumi Jōkan to sono jidai 近代仏教と青年——近角常観とその時代] (Tokyo: Iwanami shoten, 2014), 185.

15. Jōkan Chikazumi, *Kyūdō* 求道 3, no. 2 (1906): 187.

16. Ibid., 288–293.

17. Ibid.

18. In the following year, 1916, Shimaji published *Myōhōrenge kyō* 妙法蓮華経.

19. See Pullattu Abraham George and Kazuhiko Komatsu, *The Deep Structure of Miyazawa Kenji: Irradiation from Religion* [Miyazawa Kenji no shinsō: Shūkyō karano shōsha 宮沢賢治の深層——宗教からの照射] (Kyoto: Hozōkan, 2012), 6.

20. Taijirō Amazawa, "The Core Place of Religion in Miyazawa Kenji" [Miyazawa Kenji no shūkyō no kakushin 宮澤賢治の〈宗教〉の核心], in George and Komatsu, *Deep Structure*, 22.

21. Kenji Miyazawa, *Complete Works of Miyazawa Kenji* [Kōhon Miyazawakenji Zenshū 校本宮沢賢治全集] 13, no. 1 (1997): 9.

22. Iwata, *Modern Buddhism and the Youth*, 216.

23. Miyazawa, *Complete Works*, 18.

24. Ibid., 11.

25. Daisetz Suzuki, *Oriental Point of View* [Tōyō tekina mikata 東洋的な見方], ed. Shizuteru Ueda (Tokyo: Iwanami shoten, 1997), 105–106.

26. Fumihiko Sueki 末木文美士 points out that there are simultaneous positive and negative aspects in Daisetz' attitude toward the nation-state. See Fumihiko Sueki, *Modernity for the Others and the Dead* [Tasha·Shisha tachi no kindai 他者·死者たちの近代] (Tokyo: Transview, 2010), 98–119.

27. Daisetz Suzuki, *Japanese Spirituality* [Nihonteki Reisei 日本的霊性], trans. Norman Waddell (Tokyo: Yūshodo, 1972), 42.

28. Ibid., 43.

29. Ibid., 185.

30. Ibid.

31. Ibid., 186.

32. Ibid.

33. Ibid., 17.

34. In "The Constitution of Spiritual Japan" [Reisei teki Nihon no sōken 霊性的日本 の創建] (1946), Daisetz writes: "Spiritual Japan is not out of economy, industry, natural

science or morality, but it could be realized in parallel with them. No, we should make efforts to realize it at the same moment with them. That is why spiritual Japan is not out of ordinary life, but it resides in the latter. All we have to do is to be aware of it. The problem consists in how to make this self-awareness possible." See Daisetz Suzuki, *Living in Zen* [Zen ni ikiru 禅に生きる], ed. Tomoe Moriya (Tokyo: Chikuma shobō, 2012), 328. In this citation, the non-separable relationship between spirituality and ordinary life is repeated.

Transforming Sacred Space into Shared Place   13

REINTERPRETING GANDHI ON TEMPLE ENTRY

Bindu Puri

This chapter philosophically explores the efforts of Mohandas Karamchand Gandhi (1869–1947) to transform sacred spaces into shared places in the context of the depressed classes' movement in India.[1] It also brings out the relationships between Gandhi's efforts and reinterpretations of his role in that movement in the work of contemporary Dalit writers. Gandhi's reasons for giving importance to temple entry in the movement for the eradication of untouchability, and contemporary responses to these reasons, can afford some insights into the need to overcome memories of oppression in personal and theoretical space. By examining the argumentative transition from Gandhi's raising issues of temple entry to Gopal Guru's raising the issue of the ownership of humiliating experiences and the right to theorize about such experiences, it is possible to disclose significant connections among the reconfigurings of oppressive spaces and contemporary conceptions of the self, trust, and justice.

In this chapter, I first bring out the philosophical implications of Gandhi's reasons for giving importance to having equal access to sacred space in the movement for the eradication of untouchability. Next, I discuss the transition from sacred to conceptual spaces in Gopal Guru's arguments about restricting the right to theorize in the social sciences about Dalit or tribal experiences to "owners" of those experiences.[2] The transition from Gandhi to Guru is unsurprising, given the history of the *avarna*/outcaste Hindus/Dalits[3] having been denied the right to enter sacred and conceptual spaces by the *savarna* Hindus (those within the caste system for generations). Finally, before presenting my conclusions, I speak briefly about the importance of sacred and theoretical space in terms of developing trust, which seems as necessary for a redefinition of the oppressed self as it is for breaking free from circles of suspicion.

Equal Access to Sacred Space: Philosophical Implications

Whether the issue be racial, gender, caste, or religious discrimination, physical and conceptual spaces have played a critical role in establishing asymmetrical relations that make it possible for the targeted group to be oppressed. This chapter examines a specific case, that of the depressed classes in India.

Space and the History of Dalit Exclusion and Oppression

For centuries the *avarna*s (literally, outside *varna*, or those who were outcastes placed outside the fourfold hierarchical caste system of the Hindu society) were denied access to temples, wells, public roads, and schools. They were made to live in designated areas outside the village, "within the confines of their dark hole: *hulgari* or *cheri*, *Mahar* or *Mangwada* or *Chamar Tola*," Gopal Guru observes. He adds that "village India entailed the division of two mutually connected and yet culturally exclusive social spaces: agrahara (the puritan inner) and the cheri, the untouchables' ghetto (the impure exterior)."[4] The *avarna*s were also denied the right to enter intellectual and conceptual space, because the hereditary caste system refused them access to literacy.

While history records many other kinds of oppression, such as slavery and racial discrimination, there were perhaps three features that characterized and distinguished the caste system in India, making it more oppressive than other systems of domination. The first feature was an ideological justification within Hinduism for the caste system and untouchability. This justification took the form of the theory of predetermination, or karma. The theory recommended resignation, for the present life was seen as the result of one's own actions in the past and was part of a moral order in the universe. The second feature of the oppression associated with untouchability was that it made the individual outcaste invisible/unseeable. Confined to living space outside the village, the outcaste was considered a part of Hindu society only for the purpose of doing the dirty menial work for the higher castes in that same society. Associated with this was the idea of pollution by touch, which made the individual *avarna* a "sociological danger" to the higher caste, the members of which were held to be polluted even by the shadow of a Dalit. Invisible, unseeable, denied the training to theorize or to speak, Dalits were to live a life where happiness was to be found in the acceptance of their condition as the result of their own past actions in previous lives. A third feature that distinguished untouchability from other kinds of oppression was that it was the Hindu religion itself that declared that the *avarna*s were Hindus by faith but outcastes from Hindu society. Consequently, the *savarna* Hindus practiced untouchability not because they were irreligious but because they were religious. B. R. Ambedkar understood this, and in his essay titled "Annihilation of Caste," he made this point: "Religion compels the Hindus to treat isolation and segregation of castes as a virtue."[5]

Gandhi and Ambedkar: Changing Positions on Temple Entry

Gandhi was the first person to make untouchability an important concern of Indian politics. However, he insisted on treating it as a religious issue related to the internal reform of Hindu religion and society. It was in this context that Gandhi put emphasis on the importance of temple entry to the movement for the eradication of untouchability. The Vaikom Satyagraha (Vaikom movement) of 1924–1925 offered Gandhi his first opportunity to act publicly on behalf of the untouchables and their rights to temple space. Over time, Gandhi and Ambedkar took changing positions toward the temple entry movements as part of the larger movement for the eradication of untouchability in colonial India.

In the early years, Ambedkar had supported some of the temple entry movements (*satyagrahas*). He had taken an interest in the Vaikom movement in 1924, the Mahar temple entry movement into the temple at Amraoti in 1927, the movement at the Parvati Temple at Pune in 1929, and the movement at Nasik in 1930. However, by 1932 Ambedkar had lost interest in such movements. By 1934 he had finally dissociated himself from the temple entry issue and Hinduism, and in 1935 he announced his decision to convert at Yeola. In 1935 and 1936 Ambedkar considered conversion to Christianity, Islam, or Sikhism. In 1948 he published *The Untouchables*, in which he argued that the untouchables were former Buddhists. In 1956 he formally converted to Buddhism.

Different Approaches to Eradicating Untouchability: Gandhi and Ambedkar

Whereas Ambedkar had dissociated himself from the temple entry issue by the 1930s, Gandhi had taken it up more strongly. Before I reinterpret Gandhi's arguments in support of the position that temple entry was a critical part of the movement to eradicate untouchability, it is important to look at the context of the Gandhian arguments. An essential part of the context was that Gandhi and Ambedkar differed in their views of the role of temple entry in the larger movement. The differences between them heightened after a conflict about political rights for the untouchables and Gandhi's opposition to the communal award that granted separate electorates to the *avarna* Hindus.[6] There were two chief differences between Gandhi and Ambedkar on the nature of the movement for the eradication of untouchability.

The first difference emerged from Ambedkar's consistently arguing that untouchability was not a religious matter internal to Hinduism but was primarily a civil, political, economic, and social issue. Gandhi, on the other hand, while accepting the urgent need for securing rights, emphasized that untouchability required the internal reform of Hinduism and was primarily a religious issue. However, Gandhi did not think of temple entry as a substitute for other parts of the movement related to securing economic, social, and civil rights for the *avarnas*: "The fact is temple-entry is not a substitute for any other uplift."[7]

Related to this was a second line of divergence. Gandhi saw the movement for the eradication of untouchability as a movement for the self-purification of the *savarna* Hindus. On the other hand, Ambedkar wanted the depressed classes to take the lead in the eradication of untouchability and to speak on their own behalf. Educated in the liberal tradition and influenced by thinkers like Dewey, Ambedkar spoke the language of rights and entitlement. He was clear that the agency for reform should rest with the untouchables themselves.

In this context, it is interesting to see how this argument transforms itself and gets reflected in contemporary readings of the conflict when Guru makes the point that "Dalits are expected to take the initiative in giving moral lead to doing theory in the country."[8] While Ambedkar had raised questions about the right to lead the movement for the eradication of untouchability, Guru and his coauthor Sunder Sarukkai ask who really has the right to theorize about Dalit experiences in the social sciences.[9]

Gandhi, Temple Entry, and the Eradication of Untouchability

Gandhi addressed the members of the depressed classes as Harijans. This signified his rejection of the earlier derogatory names and the idea of inequality that had been associated with the hierarchical caste order of Hindu society. It seems natural to ask why Gandhi (who had fought against all kinds of discrimination for the rights of the poor and the dispossessed) felt convinced that the problem of untouchability was a matter for the internal reform of Hindu society and religion.

Gandhi's Reasons

Several reasons for Gandhi's position that untouchability was a religious matter can be identified. First, Gandhi was not a modernist and had a deep appreciation of the importance of tradition in the life of individuals and communities. His critique of modern civilization in *Hind Swaraj* is so well known that it needs no recounting.[10] Gandhi also had an understanding of individual identity as being embedded in the community of one's birth, language, and upbringing, as well as abiding in a sense of continuity with one's past, however unbearable its memories might be. In that sense, Gandhi's conception of the self was what the philosopher Michael Sandel would describe as "encumbered" by the present and the past.

Gandhi rejected a certain tradition of thinking about the individual self that has been influential in post-Enlightenment Western philosophy. This way of thinking is perhaps best represented by the Kantian/Rawlsian idea of the rational self who can make purely disinterested choices uninfluenced by religious and cultural encumbrances. A different but related way of thinking about the unencumbered self is to emphasize the radical freedom of making choices that characterizes the human being. This idea finds expression in philosophies like existentialism that are concerned with individual freedom as freedom of choice. For Gandhi, the idea of an individual or a group making choices from a completely disinterested position (what Thomas Nagel has characterized as "the view from nowhere") would be incoherent and self-deceptive. He would also have found it difficult to accept the position that an individual is radically free to make choices unencumbered by the past or by his or her constitutive attachments. This also brings home the point that Gandhi's opposition to modernity was much deeper than the rejection of the outward signs of modernity. Gandhi would not have been able to accept the essentially modern experience of radical freedom of choice to reject one's past and choose a new self.

Although Gandhi would not accept unencumbered freedom of choice, he believed that it was a duty to make moral choices in response to oppressive religious practices. He thought that both the tormented and the tormentor have to recognize the relationship between the overcoming of oppressive memory and the well-being of the self and society. The most appropriate way to deal with oppressive memories in a Gandhian framework was neither to make the choice to forget the past nor to choose to deny it. It was, rather, to face such memories and choose to take a moral position toward them. In the case of the tormentors, this moral position would mean to accept moral responsibility. In the case of the tormented, it would be to use ahimsa (nonviolence) to arrive at the truth and make the oppressor face the enormity of his or her crime. In either case, for Gandhi, the individual or group had to have the courage to overcome or work out the bad memories, whether these were of a racial, colonial, or religious nature or were a function of caste oppression. Working out the past was essential for the well-being of the individual and society.

Gandhi rejected another idea fairly important to liberal modernity. This was the idea that an essential precondition of securing justice is impartiality, which could be secured only by creating a distance (theoretical and physical) between the crime and the allocation of responsibility for it. As early as 1909, Gandhi declared his opposition to this idea of third-party justice administered through law courts.

Gandhi accorded an important space to the sacred in individual life. He thought of religion in terms of the relationship between humankind and God. Such a relationship involved all kinds of cultural-religious symbols and ethical belief systems, and these became part of an individual's sense of self as much as they became part of a community's self-understanding. However, religious symbols were important because they were made for the presence of the sacred in human life. This is why Gandhi understood the place of the temple in the life of both *savarna* and *avarna* Hindus. For the believing Hindu, the inner sanctum of the temple is the place where God is present, and being there means getting a *darshana* (vision) of the divinity. For Gandhi, the sacred also had an important role in a religious person's ordinary way of life. Perhaps it made such persons comfortable with the moral and material disasters that are an inevitable part of individual human life. In this context, one may recall Gandhi's references to hearing the inner voice at many difficult times in his life.[11] Interestingly, Ambedkar had thought of religion almost entirely in terms of the social value it provided to a community. He spoke of the value of religion largely in terms of promoting fraternity in a social or religious group. His conversion to Buddhism should not be taken to mean that Ambedkar had accorded space to the sacred in individual or community life. He radically reinterpreted Buddhism. Ambedkar's text *The Buddha and His Dhamma* is devoid of any reference to the metaphysical or to the sacred. It is as if the experience of humiliation and exclusion from sacred space by *savarna* Hindus had banished the sacred from Ambedkar's life and thought. In a 1938 essay in support of conversion, he was quick to admit this: "The force of the argument, of course, rests on a view of religion which is somewhat different from the ordinary view according to which religion is concerned with man's relation to God and all that it means. According to this view, religion exists not for the saving of souls but for the preservation of society and the welfare of the individual."[12]

Another reason for Gandhi's position that untouchability was a religious matter is that he thought of history, what he called *itihas*, not as a record of momentous events and empires but more in terms of "it so happened"—that is, in terms of a narration of the continuity in ordinary life. Gandhi thought that history should be understood in a narrative form, as putting together simple little things that kept people together in their homes and communities. Consequently, he thought that there was so much in the past that it could not be summarily wiped out as a record merely of wars, empires, domination, humiliation, and oppression.

Gandhi: The Encumbered Self and Individual Identity

Gandhi's conception of the individual self was the theoretical source of his position on the importance of sacred temple space and the somewhat critical need for the self-purification of the oppressors in the context of the eradication of untouchability. One can best understand the conflict between Ambedkar and Gandhi on the eradication of untouchability if we see the conflict not only as one between tradition and modernity but, more importantly, in terms of Gandhi's rejection of a certain conception of the self. This was a conception that almost defined the work of Enlightenment philosophers like Kant. Perhaps the best place to philosophically unpack this conception is by looking at Michael Sandel's critique of the dominant conception of the self in post-Enlightenment Western philosophy.

Kant perhaps contributed the most to modern philosophical thinking about the self as a somewhat solitary autonomous rational will. For Kant, an individual would act authentically when his or her will was free from all encumbrances—religion, culture, desire, emotion, and inclination. Such a will was free when it acted in accordance with pure practical reason and in obedience to the dictates of the law of pure reason that it gave itself. Sandel argues that, for Kant, insofar as we think of ourselves as free, we cannot think of ourselves as merely empirical beings tied up to the laws of nature and the irregularities of cause and effect. Sandel moves on to speak about another Kantian idea that finds expression in John Rawls' thought, the idea that the self must be prior to its ends:

> But what exactly is the sense in which the self, as an agent of choice, "must" be prior to the ends it chooses? One sense of the priority is a moral "must" which reflects the imperative to respect above all the autonomy of the individual, to regard the human person as the bearer of a dignity beyond the roles that he inhabits and the ends he may pursue. But there is another sense in which the self "must" be prior to the ends it affirms—prior in the sense of independently identifiable—and this is an epistemological requirement.[13]

What this means is that the self has an "antecedent unity"—that is, "the subject, however heavily conditioned by his surroundings, is always, irreducibly, prior to his values and ends."[14]

Sandel argues that Rawls' account rests on a certain view of the self, as unencumbered by any constitutive attachments or by any loyalties or commitments "whose moral force consists partly in the fact that living by them is inseparable from understanding ourselves as the particular persons we are."[15] Sandel notes that this creates problems for both agency and self-knowledge: "Where the self is unencumbered and essentially dispossessed, no person is left for *self*-reflection to reflect upon."[16]

The reason I have looked at Sandel's critique is that it offers some insights into Gandhi's conception of the individual self. It would be fair to say that Gandhi's critique of modernity was philosophically subtler than has so far been understood. In 1909, when Gandhi wrote *Hind Swaraj*, he criticized the outward signs of modernity—the institutions of modernity like the British Parliament, the instruments of modernity like railways, and modern professions such as those in the medical and legal fields. However, in the same text, he also made it clear that the malaise of modernity was that the civilization it offered "takes note neither of morality nor of religion."[17] Further, he saw that modernity was concerned with individual freedom only in terms of political rights.

In sharp contrast, Gandhi made a distinction between home rule/political freedom and self-rule/moral self-control. This has been explained as "one's rule over one's own mind."[18] Gandhi equated true freedom with "self-rule"— that is, rule of the self by the self. This meant two things. First, the self needed to overcome ego-driven intentions, which are based in the individual's mind as the seat of the sense of an "I." Second, Gandhian self-control translated into an overcoming of selfish interests to develop into a concern for others and a capacity to suffer for their sake and to arrive at truth. It also involved the idea that *swaraj*, as home rule or collective political self-determination, could be arrived at only by overcoming the "me's" and the "I's" that limited individual concerns. It is here that Gandhi's opposition to modernity and to the predominant tradition of thinking about the self in modern Western philosophy becomes most apparent. Gandhi's self has a textured interiority. Such a self is capable of sacrifice (*tapasya*), acknowledges the claims of duty to "others," and reflects on the untruth within.

What this implies is that the Gandhian conception of the self is opposed to two of the strands of tradition regarding how to think about the self that I have been discussing. The Gandhian self was not only happily encumbered but also powerfully situated. First, one should note that Gandhi thought of the self as powerfully situated in a tradition, history, religion, and culture and with a certain orientation toward living a good human life, which he denoted as "civilization." Second, for Gandhi, a human being was essentially encumbered and constituted by his or her tradition and also by attachments and obligations/duties. In fact, Gandhi spoke of the *khaas lakshana*, or special virtue, of humanity as being nonviolence and went on to argue that such nonviolence involved duties toward all "others" with whom a person shared the world. The *khaas lakshana* of humanity was that "*ahimsa* (love), not *himsa* (hate), rules man."[19] In Gandhi's writings, *ahimsa* was a very broad term. It did not solely mean physical, mental, and verbal nonviolence; it also meant an expansive disinterested love of all others. Gandhi argued that being *ahimsanat*, or nonviolent and full of love, implied that the human being had constitutive and one-sided obligations (*ekpakshi farj*) to think of the rest of creation as an extension of his or her family. Gandhi had emphasized the point that a person had a duty to own such "kinship with not merely the ape but the horse and the sheep, the lion and the leopard, the snake and the scorpion." He continued: "The difficult dharma which rule my life, and [which] I hold ought to rule that of every man and woman, impose this unilateral obligation [*ekpakshi farj*] on us. And it is so imposed because only the human is the image of God."[20]

It would be wrong to say that Gandhi thought of these one-sided obligations as encumbrances as much as he believed them to be constitutive of an individual's sense of self. One place that this becomes evident is when Gandhi speaks about the relationship between rights and duties. While it has been commonplace in modern Western rights discourse to link a right for oneself with a corresponding duty to another, Gandhi said that there can be no authentic claim to a right unless one has earned it by the due performance of the corresponding duty. Gandhi thought that an individual's sense of self was constituted by attachments and allegiances in such a way that there could be no thought of what was due to him or her without first attending to the claims that arose from such attachments and, in the whole, from claims that arose from one's situation in life.

Gandhi's self would be secured from the objections raised by Sandel, who points out that, without constitutive attachments, there would be no "self" in *self*-reflection. In a sense, this brings out the fact that the predominant tradition in thinking about the self in modern Western philosophy has left the self without what Charles Taylor describes as "an orientation to the good" and to the "narrative" sense of individual life.[21] Gandhi's conception of the self was that of a being situated in a certain tradition with a history and a way of looking at the world and with constitutive attachments to persons and beliefs.

Gandhi: Individual Self-understanding, Tradition, and Memory

Tradition-based beliefs could be very important to an individual's sense of himself or herself as a being in the world. Gandhi often stressed the importance that tradition and heredity played in an individual's self-understanding. The Gandhian self was self-conscious about the fact that his or her sense of self and relationships to the world were powerfully influenced by the tradition in which he or she happened to be situated. This is why—for Gandhi—tradition, religion, language, and culture became important to both individual and collective well-being. The self who was aware of being situated in a tradition and of having a relationship with the tradition was encumbered and situated. His or her authentic engagement with himself or herself in self-understanding involved some sort of owning up to that tradition. For Gandhi, such owning up meant that the individual had to have a critical discourse with the tradition—using its resources for self-understanding and taking moral responsibility for its defects. This would explain Gandhi's difficulties with conversion as posing a challenge to one's truthful engagement with oneself and one's past.

Since Gandhi was looking at the Hindu self, he argued that both the *savarna* and the *avarna* self had to confront the defects in their tradition because there could be no truthful self-understanding without the act of confrontation and reform. For the individual outcaste self, the tradition became important in a negative sense, inasmuch as it was both that from which he or she was being excluded and something in which he or she was being kept or confined in the sense of being held in an enclosure. This had all kinds of implications, for any radical redefinition was to mean a reform of that tradition, a complete denial of the past, or a rejection of the tradition as unjust. In all these cases, a considered response to the cruel tradition remained central to a sense of comfort and to closure of conflict. The reason Gandhi seemed uncomfortable with an act of denial was that he did not think that it was possible for the self to unmake itself by denying its situatedness in tradition. Recall that Ambedkar had argued that the untouchables were former Buddhists and therefore not really ever part of the Hindu tradition.[22] Rejecting, rather than denying, the authenticity of such situatedness was always possible. However, rejecting the tradition would involve an act of conversion, which, in a precise and almost surgical maneuver, would sever the continuity between a community's past tradition and the present. This act would disconnect, not merely the oppressive memories from an individual's sense of himself or herself in the present, but also all other continuities of culture, ritual, myth, traditional skill sets (weaving, tanning), festivals, and so on. Carving these out from the religious superstructure would require psychological ingenuity of a kind that might seem difficult, given the many intricate connections among all these elements and individual well-being.

The contemporary Dalit scholar D. R. Nagaraj describes the pain in the process of denial: "The birth of the modern individual in the humiliated communities is not only accompanied by a painful severing of ties with the community, but also a conscious effort to alter one's past is an integral part of it."[23] Nagaraj speaks of two difficulties that such "wilful amnesia regarding one's past on the part of an influential group" gave rise to. To begin with, it meant "a firm riveting of the Dalit movement to the present." The second difficulty was a theme that emerged in Ambedkar's work: "the problem of defining alternative cultural values not only for an individual Dalit but also for the entire movement." Nagaraj points out that Ambedkar could not accept that "the state of amnesia induced a state of stupor," even though this landed him in many difficulties while "defining the relationship between a movement and the structure of its memories."[24]

Since Gandhi thought that one's sense of the self was constituted by elements coming not only from one's traditional attachments but also from one's civilizational orientation toward the world, he had a deep belief in the importance of the past in the constitution of a sense of comfort with one's own self. Gandhi argued that the *avarna* Hindu could not forget or forgive the past, but that he or she could develop a relationship with the memory of the past as that of having lived a lie. However, this could happen only if the *savarna* Hindus

admitted and took responsibility for the moral mistake committed for generations. The entire Hindu community needed to confront the ideological justification offered for untouchability by recognizing that it was untruth.

One way in which the untruth could be admitted by all Hindus was to
open the temples, admitting the religious equality of all and thus symbolically
denying the authenticity of all religious texts that had denied religious equality
to *avarna* Hindus. The entrance into the temple would constitute a symbolic
admission by the upper caste that the Hindu tradition had been untruthful and
inauthentic in placing the *avarna* Hindus outside the temple and on the fringes
of Hindu society. The act of owning up would help transform the memories of
oppression because the oppressor would admit that this memory was real but
was based on a lie:

> The fact is that temple-entry is not a substitute for any other uplift. It is an indis-
> pensable test that religious untouchability has been abolished and the Harijan
> is no longer the pariah of Hindu society. . . . Temple-entry prohibition and the
> consequent segregation that it carries with it constitute the distinguishing bar of
> perpetual degradation. When that is lifted, and only then, will religious untouch-
> ability be said to have been abolished.[25]

Gandhi: An Alternative Understanding of Justice

The previous discussion brings me to points made by contemporary Dalit writers
on Gandhi's preoccupations with atonement and self-purification of the upper-
caste Hindu self as the means to eradicate untouchability. Nagaraj, for instance,
speaks about this preoccupation: "Gandhiji's take-off point was that the problem
of untouchability was a problem of the self, which in this case was the collective
Hindu self. . . . The untouchable is a part of the self. He saw the movement to
eradicate untouchability as a sacred ritual of self-purification."[26] As Gandhi said,
"The movement for the removal of untouchability is one of self-purification."[27]
What this meant was that Gandhi placed the agency of the movement primarily
with the upper-caste Hindu reformer. Nagaraj has brought this out:

> Even philosophically, the Gandhian model provided the caste Hindu self with
> much needed textured interiority, and what generated tensions was the way it
> initiated the self-conscious Hindu reformer into the sacred ritual of confronta-
> tion against the orthodoxy. There was very little scope for a Congress Harijan
> leader to develop interesting and useful models of praxis from within. This was
> the basic limitation of the Gandhian mode: Sugreeva, Hanumantha, and Guha
> could never aspire to act the major part displacing the hero in the Ramayana. Only
> Rama is the hero and Ambedkar could never settle for the roles of Hanumantha
> and Sugreeva.[28]

I argue that Gandhi's emphasis on atonement and the self-purification of the
upper-caste self as a mode of securing justice for the Dalits was not connected

with an inauthentic attempt to keep the upper-caste Hindu at the center of the movement to eradicate untouchability. It had to do with Gandhi's thoughts about a proper conception of justice. As is well known, Gandhi had rejected the modern Western notion of third-party justice. As early as 1909, in *Hind Swaraj*, Gandhi made it clear that he was opposed to law courts and the arbitration by third parties completely disconnected from the context of the crime: "Surely, the decision of a third party is not always right. The parties alone know who is right. We, in our simplicity and ignorance, imagine that a stranger, by taking our money, gives us justice."[29]

For Gandhi, the mode of doing justice to a victim had to involve some access to the truth of the conflict between parties. Gandhi thought that there were two elements involved in justice: giving victims their due, and remaining impartial while finding out the truth so that victims could be identified and given their due. The best way to ensure this was to make sure that justice was secured as close as possible to the context of the act of injustice. This, however, does not mean that Gandhi failed to appreciate the difficulties that this might cause in terms of the close conceptual connection between justice and impartiality. Gandhi understood the need for impartiality. However, where he differed from Western liberal modernity was in not believing that a system of administering justice through law courts situated at a physical and conceptual distance from acts of injustice could keep together the two aspects of doing justice—giving victims their due and remaining impartial.

Gandhi believed that these two elements could be brought together if the individuals and communities involved assumed the moral responsibility of giving conflicting "others" their due. *Satyagraha*, which literally meant firmness (*agraha*) in the interest of truth (*satya*), was Gandhi's method of securing justice. It involved the practice of nonviolence by the oppressed in the face of the wrongdoers so that they could both come to the truth that lay somewhere in between their conflicting situations. The important question is how impartiality would be built into this Gandhian method of securing justice. Gandhi believed that *satyagraha* was a method by which the oppressed sought justice only by arriving at the truth and not by denying the truth that might lie in the possession of the oppressive "other." The very process of nonviolent firmness in the interest of truth required the *satyagrahi*s (practitioners of *satyagraha*) to suffer nonviolently and remain impartial between opposing viewpoints in the interest of arriving at the truth.

Given that this was how Gandhi thought about justice, temple entry *satyagraha*s played a critical role in securing justice for the oppressed. By participating in direct nonviolent resistance to such injustice, both the *avarna* and *savarna* Hindus were seeking to confront the false ideological justifications that higher-caste Hindus had offered as religious arguments to perpetuate such social oppression. If the upper-caste self saw this as a movement of atonement and self-purification, it meant that the upper-caste self had assumed responsibility for the injustice that had been done. This was the first step toward giving the oppressed their due recognition and due respect. It was the oppressor who was uniquely situated to do this, according to Gandhi:

> Untouchability will not be removed by the force even of law. It can only be removed when the majority of Hindus realize that it is a crime against God and man and are ashamed of it. In other words, it is a process of conversion, i.e., purification of the Hindu heart.[30]

Gandhi: The Sacred and the Well-being of Humankind

For Gandhi, the sacred played an important role in individual and collective well-being. It is true that Gandhi himself did not attach importance to temples as essential for experiencing a sense of the sacred. Yet he understood that denying access to temples symbolized the fact that *savarna* Hindus did not recognize the presence of the sacred in the life of the outcaste. That life was seen as a kind of perpetual exercise in atonement for the sins of the past. This was taken to justify the banishment of the sacred from the present life of the *avarna* Hindus. Since Hindus regarded temples as sacred spaces where one could enter the presence of God, opening temples meant revoking the banishment of *avarna*s from sacred space and sacred presence.

> Attempt is being made only to have public temples opened to Harijans on the same terms on which they are open to the other Hindus. . . . [S]*avarna* Hindus have to lift the bar against Harijans. For those millions who regard temples as treasure-chests of spiritual wealth, they are living realities which they hold dear as life itself. If they are truly repentant towards Harijans, they must share these treasures with the latter.[31]

Gandhi argued that equality before God was important for the upper-caste Hindu to recognize the religious equality of all the Hindus. In 1933 he said, "The throwing open of temples will be an admission of the religious equality of Harijans. It will be the surest sign of their ceasing to be outcastes of Hinduism, which they are today."[32] The reason Gandhi thought that religious equality was important to the well-being of the *avarna* self can perhaps be better understood if one recalls the importance of the sacred in Gandhi's conception of the good human life. Gandhi himself had an intimate relationship to the Hindu religious tradition and acknowledged this at several places in his writings. He saw it as a cultural, social, and spiritual resource for millions of Hindus.

Gandhi believed that people of faith felt a living presence of God in their lives through their participation in the religion that they had been born into. There are systematic references to the "inner voice" in Gandhi from 1916 onward. He called it the "still small voice" and "the voice of God."[33] He took comfort and guidance from this voice. Gandhi also argued that the religion of one's ancestors placed both persons and communities in continuity with their own pasts. This could provide a sense of comfort to those conscious of temporality and death. Witness this sense of continuity in the term *sanatan* (eternal), used to describe the Hindu religion.

Gandhi: History and Itihas

The idea of continuity brings me to Gandhi's conception of history as *itihas*.[34] In *Hind Swaraj*, Gandhi spoke of the need to have a proper conception of history. I have often wondered why he thought it appropriate to draw the distinction between the modern Western understanding of history and the conception signified by the Sanskrit term *itihas*. One can get a clue from the context in which he draws the distinction. In *Hind Swaraj*, Gandhi introduces this distinction while replying to the reader's objection that history gives no evidence of the success of *satyagraha*, what Gandhi describes as "soul force or truth force."[35] He argues:

> It is . . . necessary to know what history means. The Gujarati equivalent means: "It so happened."[36] If that is the meaning of history, it is possible to give copious evidence. But, if it means the doings of kings and emperors, there can be no evidence of soul-force or passive resistance in such history. . . . History, as we know it, is a record of the wars of the world, and so there is a proverb among Englishmen that a nation which has no history, that is, no wars, is a happy nation. . . . The fact that there are so many men still alive in the world shows that it is based not on the force of arms but on the force of truth or love.[37]

The significance of the distinction between history and *itihas* was that Gandhi realized that the way that individuals saw their relationships to the past through memory depended on what they understood by history. Gandhi knew that the modern Western conception of history was dictated by the dominant modern Western conception of the unencumbered self, about whose history it was an account. This meant that "history" primarily referred to the political history that characterized the public political life of a people. Any account of the cultural and the religious was included only so far as that account affected the political events that defined the public life of the community. If one understood history in the sense of *itihas*, it would have to contain much more than the record of conflicts. It would also encompass the happenings in "families and communities,"[38] thus bringing the present into continuity with the past through parallels in people's cultural and emotional lives. If a community denied its history by a complete and willful amnesia about the past, it would leave behind much more than the memory of oppression. Such a denial would also mean leaving out the past in the sense of denying a narrative unity to their present life. That is, people in such a community would have to forget the religious practices they had followed, the cultural life they had lived, and their connections with the rest of Hindu beliefs, myths, stories, songs, and dances that had "so happened" in the past. This would also create an emotional and cultural void that in turn would create a need to find alternative values and construct an alternative past.

Here my reinterpretation of Gandhi's arguments about temple entry has attempted to demonstrate that Gandhi offered reasons of a philosophical kind for emphasizing temple entry as an essential part of the movement to eradicate untouchability.

Sacred and Theoretical Space and the Development of Trust

Having explored Gandhi's understanding of the importance of transforming sacred spaces into places that could be shared by all members of the same faith, I now turn to another significant space that *avarnas* had been excluded from: conceptual space. It was this exclusion that led Ambedkar to stress the need for the depressed classes to reclaim theoretical space as thinkers and leaders of their own movement. Almost ten decades later, in *The Cracked Mirror*, Gopal Guru and Sunder Sarukkai presented a significant set of essays about the rights to conceptual space.[39]

From Sacred Spaces to Conceptual Space: Gopal Guru on Owners and Authors

Gopal Guru has brought forth moral arguments to build an ethics of doing theory that reconstructs itself by responding to the need to articulate experiences in the mind of a group whose experiences are being written about. Guru has argued that the individual self is an encumbered self with a historical memory that can be of an oppressive past. Such a self is situated in a set of cultural and social practices and has experiences about which he or she needs to theorize—indeed, about which *he or she ought to* theorize. It should be part of the ethics of doing theory to build theory around this need and the moral duty of the subject who has to speak.

Sunder Sarukkai examines the term "experience" to argue that what we call experience comes powerfully mediated by and through concepts we already have. There is little or no experience that comes to an individual completely innocent of concepts. Social science theory, which reflects on experience, is also dependent on concepts that are, for the most part, derived from the Western knowledge traditions. This then leads Sarukkai to raise ethical concerns about the need to choose the right concepts:

> To do theory is to choose certain kinds of concepts and structures, and this choice cannot be legitimized on an epistemological basis alone but should also be ethically answerable to what is right or wrong in talking about certain experiences. Thus, the chosen concepts are not only judged on whether they are "correct" or not but whether they are also "right" or not.[40]

Regarding this view, it becomes imperative for the social scientist to ask normative questions about doing theory. One can ask, for instance, "Who really has the right to theorize in the social sciences?"[41] This question can be asked about social sciences in general, about the practice of social sciences in India, and about social sciences seeking to say something about Dalit/*avarna* experience in particular. Much of the book is about normative concerns relating to theoretical "outsiders" who seek to reflect upon tribal or Dalit experience. Guru has argued: "Speaking for the Dalits (or anybody) constitutes a *jajmani* [caste-derived] relationship, structurally involving a patron and a client. In the present case, the *muknayak* [voiceless] becomes the patron, and the 'dumb' becomes the client to define the patron."[42]

According to this view, the Dalits have an inner need to have a say about their experience. There is a social necessity for the Dalit to become "the subject" of his or her own thinking, and, moreover, there is a moral necessity for the Dalit to theorize about his or her experience. The correlative to this is that non-Dalits ought not to "appropriate" Dalit experience by attempting to theorize about it. This raises a question about theorizing about another's experience—namely, is it ethically correct to "parachute into" someone else's experience?[43]

Owners and Authors

The first point in Sarukkai's response to Guru's argument raises the notion of "lived experience" and related notions of ownership, authorship, and authenticity.[44] Sarukkai supports Guru's argument that "that non-Dalits have no moral right to theorize about Dalits," by arguing that experience cannot be materialized/commodified and transferred without taking the subject of the experience into account.[45] Sarukkai argues that what makes lived experience authentic and different from what he calls "vicarious experience" is that "lived experience" refers only to "those experiences that are seen as necessary, experiences over which the subject has no choice whether to experience or not."[46] This qualification of having no choice in the matter of what constitutes one's lived experience is important. What is meant is that the term "lived experience" cannot be used, for instance, to describe an outsider's attempt to live with Dalits or tribal members. Lived experience is about being them, about being insiders "in the sense that you *cannot* be anything else."[47] A related way to assess the nature of experience and theoretical reflection about experience is by bringing in the notion of ownership of experience and authority. Guru says that "only an owner can be an author."[48] Sarukkai introduces a binary of emotion and reason to support Guru's position. He states that theory should relate the epistemological with the emotional. Theory cannot be legitimated by establishing a distance from experience. If it is at a distance, it will be doubly "vicarious"—first, by vicariously appropriating the other's experience; and second, by trying to do theory vicariously as a site on which to distribute one's own guilt to the "other" who has been one's victim.

This position may be mistaken at several levels. First, one should ask if it makes sense to speak about a theory being right or wrong according to whether the author is or is not the owner of the lived experience he or she seeks to understand. To my mind, this question can be answered by reflecting on the different ways in which individuals may be related to their experiences. If we think that lived experience is the experience that belongs necessarily to the experiencer—as when a person has no choice about having it—then lived experience is, by definition, private to the individual who has it. In that sense, only one person can own an experience. There cannot be a joint ownership of the same experience even though two or more people experience the same situation. This is important. It makes clear that no Dalit can really be the owner of another Dalit's experience. Thus, the relationship a Dalit has to the experience that he or she owns is different from the relationship he or she has to another Dalit's experience. A Dalit can empathize with or understand that other Dalit's experiences, but they are not his or her own experiences.

One may argue that this is a difficult position because the Dalit can theorize and reflect only in plural terms, by understanding the experiences of "others" in his or her community through an act of sympathetic imagination—putting himself or herself in that place. In that sense, a Dalit must imagine the experience of another Dalit before being able to theorize about it. However, one can ask what justifies the strict limitation of this principle of sympathetic imagination only to members of the same community. Can one not sympathetically imagine the experience of others when one has similar, though not *the same*, experiences? In this case, people sympathetically imagine experiences, not because they have had similar experiences on account of coming from the same community, but because they have had experiences of the same type. For example, a person of color may not have experienced oppression on account of being a Dalit, but having experienced oppression on account of race can help him or her understand what it means to have a lived experience of oppression. A person of color can understand the humiliation, anxiety, and indignation involved in the Dalit's experience of oppression *as if* he or she had lived it. This makes it possible to understand that people can reflect on and say something about experiences similar to those that they have experienced.

In this context, I would like to consider the points made by both Guru and Sarukkai about Gandhi's relationship to Dalit experience. Ambedkar was thrown out of a lodge in Baroda, Jyotirao Phule out of an upper-caste marriage procession in nineteenth-century Pune, and Gandhi out of a first-class compartment of a train in Pietermaritzburg. The first two were cases of caste discrimination, the last a case of racial discrimination. However, if Ambedkar could understand Phule's experience, why should Gandhi not be able to understand Ambedkar's experience? Gandhi had experienced not being allowed to be in the same space with whites in South Africa and might therefore be able to extend that understanding to the oppression suffered by Dalits in India.

Guru maintains that when Gandhi spoke about the Dalits, he was reflecting on the experience of the "other." He was making categorizations to help understand something of which he could never have had a lived experience. Guru argues that since Gandhi's effort to simulate the experience of the Dalit was voluntary and Gandhi could exit it at any time, it was by definition *not* a lived experience. This leads to the fairly important conclusion that since Gandhi could not have a lived experience as a Dalit, Gandhi's categorizations were not only inadequate for understanding Dalit reality but inauthentic as well. For Guru, this inadequacy and inauthenticity can be brought to light if we take note of the differences between Gandhi's categories and those employed by Ambedkar—for instance, the differences among self-respect, social justice, and egalitarianism in Ambedkar's thought and care, trusteeship, and *seva* (service) in Gandhi's. Guru argues that "it is the *achar* (practice) and *anubhava* (experience), mostly of others, in Gandhi, and the authentic anubhava, in Ambedkar, that have formative impact on their respective thought."[49] The absence of having had the lived experience thereby becomes a serious lacuna. The inauthenticity leads Gandhi, in Guru's view, to representations that are theoretically inadequate to throw light on the Dalit experience.

I would like to make a few points here. First, Gandhi tried to identify himself in sympathetic imagination with the Dalit experience by attempting to live the experience of the Dalit. Guru argues that Gandhi had a choice, which made his experience different from lived experience, and that Gandhi's experiences could not authenticate his pretensions to theorize about Dalit experience. One can argue that Gandhi's experience of living the life of the Dalits by adopting voluntary poverty, weaving his own clothes, and cleaning spaces was not such that it was *necessarily* his experience. However, it cannot for that reason become an experience reducible to one from which he could choose to exit. Gandhi chose to have certain experiences. But once he made the initial choices, he could no longer exit those experiences if and when they became painful. This was because he chose complete transparency by writing to the public at large about such experiences. He also took vows to have experiences so that he could no longer exit from them. This was the reason he took vows to perform bread labor and to practice nonstealing and nonpossession.

One thus can call into question Guru's conclusion that the experiences of poverty, hunger, and bread labor were unable to authenticate Gandhi's efforts to speak about Dalit experience. It is possible that the authenticity came from Gandhi's choice to immerse himself in experiences over which he had no control, as an act of taking responsibility for the oppressive experiences of the Dalits over which the Dalits themselves had no control. Taking responsibility for the experiences of the oppressed "other" by choosing to impose both the experience and its necessity on oneself can play a role if one is to justify speaking about the experience of the other.

The Hermeneutics of Suspicion: "Creating the Space to Communicate"

The importance of space to experience and theory is explored by Guru in his essay "Experience, Space, and Justice," whose title, the author explains, "involves an epistemological claim in as much as it suggests a concept of space embedded in experience as the source for both the formation for thought and its articulation."[50] Guru argues that "the tormentor reconfigures spaces . . . so as to seek the ultimate regulation of the victim into hegemony."[51] This makes it urgent for the victim to reconfigure these spaces of confinement by discovering himself or herself as an active or reflective agency by cultural and intellectual mobilization.

It is in the context of the relationships among space, experience, and the theoretical representation of experience that Guru brings in the debate between Gandhi and Ambedkar. Though both shared the belief that experience provides a vantage point for making epistemological moves and for ideological and political mobilization of the masses, Guru locates an important difference between them in that Gandhi experimented with the experience of "others" and that "the experience of Ambedkar and his community becomes an object of Gandhi's experiment."[52] The contrast between the two relationships to experience—representing one's own lived experience and representing experience of the other—comes out, for instance, in the manner in which Gandhi and Ambedkar handled sacred space.

Guru emphasizes the significance of the difference between Gandhi and Ambedkar on temple entry. While Ambedkar spoke of temple entry in terms of entitlement and rights, Gandhi placed "emphasis on the moral duty of the high-caste Hindus to allow the untouchables to enter the Hindu temples."[53] Ambedkar used the principle of recognition of the labor of untouchables in constructing the temple to generate an argument for rights to enter the temple.

Gandhi, however, spoke of temple entry in the language of morals, using words like "purification," "penance," "sin," and so on.[54]

Perhaps it would be hasty to conclude, from Guru's arguments, that Gandhi viewed temple entry as a site for making experiments that would work as opportunities for the atonement of upper-caste guilt, with the whole movement being conducted as an experiment in upper-caste penance. On such an interpretation, it would appear that Gandhi's temple entry movements responded only to the needs to the upper castes to become more comfortable with the consequences of what they had done to the untouchables.

However, before settling down to such distrust, one might need to pay attention to Gandhi's reasons for pursuing the removal of prohibitions on temple entry. Those reasons make clear that Gandhi spoke about the symbolic character of the movement for temple entry. He had argued that removing the prohibition on temple entry should not be done because the untouchables wanted to enter temples, and he recognized that "it may be that they are as disgusted with caste Hindus and Hindu religion itself as to want nothing from them."[55] Gandhi was unequivocal that "whether . . . Harijans desire the consolation of temple-entry or not, . . . caste Hindus . . . have to open their temples to Harijans to offer worship in, precisely on, the same terms as for themselves."[56] Gandhi recognized the right to religious equality.

Certainly, while speaking to upper-caste Hindus, Gandhi used the language of self-purification, penance, chastisement, and so on. But as theoreticians, we should be wary of taking this to be sufficient justification for being completely suspicious of Gandhi, regarding him as having parachuted into Dalit experience. That kind of justification might lead to a dismissal of Gandhi's religious motives as either purely ritualistic or as directed toward the displacement of upper-caste guilt. There is theoretical room, instead, to differently engage the moral arguments made by Gandhi. One needs to think carefully about whether Gandhi was involved in vicariously taking on guilt as a hero acting in a high-caste drama or whether he was assuming and locating moral responsibility for historical wrongs.

My point is that there is some room for looking at Gandhi at face value. There may at least be room for some doubt about whether he was subconsciously playing out upper-caste guilt. We may, on reflection, think that in Gandhi's attempts to reflect on the experience of the Dalits, there was no conscious deception. And this is part of a more general point I wish to make about the hermeneutics of suspicion in oppressed groups. While there is much reason for distrust in practices of upper-caste domination, orientalism in theory, and racism, that should not mean that one can no longer make distinctions between sincere and self-motivated gestures and theory. By the nature of the case, one can break out of the circle of suspicion only by locating something to trust.

One can, of course, ask why the oppressed should break out of the circle of distrust. In politics, in practice, and in theory, one can settle down to a suspicion that prevents engagement with what the other does and says at face value. Here I have traced the transition from distrust deriving from memories of oppression to conceptual distrust about the legitimacy of theorizing about Dalit experience and memory. The purpose of doing so is to create a platform for investigating the respective roles of experience and reflection in constructing theory. This discussion must by definition involve communication among social scientists. Such communication cannot proceed without theoretical trust. At the very least, it is important to listen to what the other is saying and to take it at face value. The political space involves struggles for the goods of power, and therefore it is not the first place to look for space to communicate and understand divergent perspectives. The theoretical space becomes important to breaking out of a circle of suspicion, because theorizing involves taking what the other says seriously and engaging with it, even if eventually only to disagree. What might be needed is a theoretical space that creates opportunities for debate between Dalit and non-Dalit perspectives on Dalit experience. Consequently, it might be self-contradictory for an ethics of theorizing to restrict the right to theorize so that debate between perspectives no longer remains theoretically possible.

I have made the case that Gandhi's arguments in support of temple entry in the movement to eradicate untouchability are an indication that he recognized the moral and epistemic mistake at the heart of the Hindu religion. He had a significantly different understanding of the self and of history than modern Western conceptions of the same. His understanding led him to believe that trust was important, not only to reconfigure conceptual and sacred spaces, but also to give the oppressed their due. Gandhi recognized that the problem of overcoming the past is a difficult one. Ashis Nandy notes what happens even after one has located the oppressor: "One cannot forget or overcome the past and move on, because one has in the meanwhile redefined oneself and given a central place in one's self to the repeated attempts to reinvoke and undo the past through violence; these attempts become the means of holding together one's fragile self-definition."[57]

Finally, the authenticity of Gandhi's arguments rests on the fact that Gandhi had also dealt with a humiliating oppressive past. His arguments about temple entry and his emphasis on overcoming the memory of hatred associated with it should be located against his own manner of dealing with his experiences of racial humiliation. As Nandy observes, Gandhi drew out "creative possibilities" from his own humiliating experiences: "That humiliating encounter in a lonely South African railway station turned out to be a boon not only to the world but also to Gandhi himself."[58] Making such creative self-transformations available to the oppressed was perhaps the point of all Gandhi's arguments about untouchability.

NOTES

1. M. K. Gandhi was the leader of India's struggle for freedom from colonial rule. More recently there has been an increasing philosophical interest in his writings.

2. Sunder Sarukkai, "Experience and Theory from Habermas to Gopal Guru," in *The Cracked Mirror: An Indian Debate on Experience and Theory*, by Gopal Guru and Sunder Sarukkai (New Delhi: Oxford University Press, 2012), 38.

3. In this chapter, I use these terms interchangeably, depending on the context.

4. Gopal Guru, "Experience, Space, and Justice," in Guru and Sarukkai, *Cracked Mirror*, 86.

5. Valerian Rodrigues, ed., *The Essential Writings of B. R. Ambedkar* (New Delhi: Oxford University Press, 2009), 286. B. R. Ambedkar was born in 1891 into an untouchable Mahar family at Mhow in Madhya Pradesh. His father was a Subehdar major in the British Indian army. After graduating from Elphinstone College, Mumbai Ambedkar received financial support from the Maharajas of Baroda and Kolhapur to study abroad. He earned an MA and a PhD from Columbia University in economics and wrote an important paper around this time, titled "Castes in India: Their Mechanism, Genesis and Development." Ambedkar went on to complete an MSc degree at the London School of Economics and also qualified as a lawyer and was called to the bar from Gray's Inn, London. Ambedkar returned to India in 1923 and started working for the upliftment of the depressed classes soon after that.

6. British prime minister James Ramsay MacDonald granted separate electorates to the depressed classes by the communal award of 1932.

7. M. K. Gandhi, *Collected Works of Mahatma Gandhi Online* (hereafter cited as *eCWMG*) 95, http://gandhiserve.org/cwmg/cwmg.html, 60:302 (site subsection "cwmg" discontinued). Note that there are disputed differences in content and in volume and page numbers between *Collected Works of Mahatma Gandhi CWMG*, 100 vols. (Ahmedabad: Navajivan Publishing, 1955) and the electronic edition, *eCWMG*.

8. Gopal Guru, "Egalitarianism and the Social Sciences in India," in Guru and Sarukkai, *Cracked Mirror*, 28.

9. Sarukkai, "Experience and Theory," 30.

10. See Anthony J. Parel, ed., *Gandhi: "Hind Swaraj" and Other Writings* (New Delhi: Cambridge University Press, 2009).

11. See Bindu Puri, "Gandhi's Translation of the *Apologia*: An Unexplored Dialogical Space," *Journal of Indian Council of Philosophical Research* 26, no. 2 (April–June 2009): 47–72.

12. Rodrigues, *Essential Writings*, 238.

13. Michael J. Sandel, *Liberalism and the Limits of Justice* (New York: Cambridge University Press, 1998), 20.

14. Ibid., 22.

15. Ibid., 179.

16. Ibid.

17. Gandhi, in Parel, *"Hind Swaraj,"* 36.

18. Ibid., 36n116.

19. *eCWMG* 36:6.

20. *eCWMG* 36:5.

21. Charles Taylor, *Sources of the Self: The Making of the Modern Identity* (Cambridge, MA: Harvard University Press, 1989), 47.

22. See B. R. Ambedkar, *The Untouchables: Who Were They? And Why They Became Untouchables* (New Delhi: Amrit Book Co., 1948).

23. D. R. Nagaraj, *The Flaming Feet and Other Essays*, ed. Prithvi Datta Chandra Shobhi (Ranikhet: Permanent Black, 2010), 32.

24. Ibid., 33.

25. *eCWMG* 60:302–303.

26. Nagaraj, *Flaming Feet*, 35.

27. Gandhi, quoted in ibid., 35.

28. Nagaraj, *Flaming Feet*, 47.

29. Gandhi, in Parel, *"Hind Swaraj,"* 59.

30. *eCWMG* 76:335.

31. *eCWMG* 63:287.

32. *eCWMG* 61:353.

33. Gandhi, in R. K. Prabhu and U. R. Rao, comps. and eds., *The Mind of Mahatma Gandhi* (Ahmedabad: Navajivan Publishing, 2007), 33.

34. *Itihas* is a Sanskrit word sharing the sense of the English word "history." It is common to all languages originating from Sanskrit.

35. Gandhi, in Parel, *"Hind Swaraj,"* 86.

36. The Gujarati equivalent is the term *itihas*.

37. Gandhi in Parel, *"Hind Swaraj,"* 87.

38. Parel, *"Hind Swaraj,"* 88.

39. Guru and Sarukkai, *Cracked Mirror*; V. V. Ramana Murti, ed., *Gandhi: Essential Writings* (New Delhi: Gandhi Peace Foundation, 1970).

40. Sunder Sarukkai, "Ethics of Theorizing," in Guru and Sarukkai, *Cracked Mirror*, 153.

41. Sarukkai, "Experience and Theory," 30.

42. Guru, "Egalitarianism," 25.

43. Gopal Guru, "Experience and the Ethics of Theory," in Guru and Sarukkai, *Cracked Mirror*, 126.

44. Sarukkai, "Experience and Theory," 33.

45. Ibid.

46. Ibid., 35.

47. Ibid., 36.

48. Ibid., 39.

49. Guru, "Experience, Space, and Justice," 88.

50. Ibid., 71.

51. Ibid., 73.

52. Ibid., 75.

53. Ibid., 97.

54. *eCWMG* 61:354; *eCWMG* 54:359; Murti, *Gandhi*, 357.

55. Murti, *Gandhi*, 357.

56. *eCWMG* 61:354.

57. Ashis Nandy, "Humiliation: Politics and the Cultural Psychology of the Limits of Human Degradation," in *Humiliation: Claims and Context*, ed. Gopal Guru (New Delhi: Oxford University Press, 2013), 54.

58. Ibid., 52.

Israel and Palestine $\qquad$ 14

A Two-Place, One-Space Solution

Michael Warren Myers

Contested real estate plays an important part in the Israeli-Palestinian conflict, but there is more to it than merely a dispute over finite space. Sayyid Qutb, an early leader of the Muslim Brotherhood, writes, "The idea of homeland [Ar. *watan*] [is] an idea of the consciousness [*fikrah fi al-shu'ur*], not a piece of land."[1] Qutb's definition involves a concept of place that transcends the more conventional understanding of land as merely that which occupies space. This chapter argues that it is possible to construct an Israeli and Palestinian *place* that is plural, peaceful, and conceptually without limit even while acknowledging that Israeli-Palestinian *space* is confined, contested, and finite. Drawing on the work of Yi-Fu Tuan, I argue that the concept of "space" implies location and the possibility of different kinds of presence, while "place" incorporates the experiences and aspirations of a people.[2] The Jewish people, within and outside Israel, see the land of Israel as their ancestral home, the land promised in the Hebrew Bible. Palestinians experience the same space as their continuous, historical homeland. A humane solution to the conflict acknowledges that both peoples share the same space but as different places. Recognition of the deeply rooted aspirations of both peoples in religion, culture, and history is a necessary condition for establishing and maintaining a peaceful path forward.

The distinction between place and space may serve as a hermeneutical tool for interpreting some of the salient ways people have conceptualized the conflict. Palestinians, for example, have maintained that Jewish Israelis mythologize the places mentioned in the Bible and assume those places as their own, to the exclusion of Palestinian aspirations and legal right to the land.[3] Jewish Israelis have argued that Palestinians do not recognize that Israel constitutes the best place in the world that can provide a safe haven for Jews, a haven necessary to protect the Jewish people in the wake of the Holocaust.[4] These diverse perspectives are acknowledged as real, contending points of view. Present solutions conflate concepts of space and place and thus tend not to look deeply enough into religion, culture, and the history of the region. Two-state solutions, for example, have merit but too often take only spatial forms. They draw and redraw boundaries in an attempt to provide space for both peoples. Meanwhile, the spaces where Palestinians live become more dangerous, isolated, and squeezed smaller and smaller, while the spaces in which Jewish Israelis live become increasingly militarized, unsafe, and threatened by attack from hostile neighbors. Neither Palestinians nor Jewish Israelis feel the joy of repose in their own respective places.

Yi-Fu Tuan's *Space and Place: The Perspective of Experience* is an interdisciplinary exploration into the interrelated concepts of place and space. The "perspective of experience" implies that Tuan's work is not purely theoretical; rather, it suggests that clarification of space and place might help sort out pragmatic difficulties in particular situations in which we human beings find ourselves. *Space and Place* was published in 1977. At that time, the Israeli-Palestinian conflict was nearing its thirtieth year. Israel and Palestine (with its Arab allies) had fought major wars in 1948, 1956, 1967, and 1973. More than forty years later the conflict has still not been resolved. The building of a separation wall or barrier in the West Bank, begun in 1994, serves as vivid confirmation that this is a dispute where space—or, rather, the lack of it—is a central concern. Tuan defines space as given by the ability to move: "Hence space can be variously experienced as the relative location of objects or places, as the distances and expanses that separate or link places, and—more abstractly—as the area defined by a network of places."[5] Given our human powers to move about, space ideally signifies openness and possibility. It shares meaning with general words like "land," "sea," and "air." Space specifies a necessary condition for human flourishing. One can see that, under Tuan's definition, the construction of the separation barrier implies that humans can also experience space in its finitude and constriction. The separation barrier, built to impede the movement of Palestinian suicide bombers into areas where Jewish Israelis live and work, affects people's sense of place on both sides of the barrier. It has the correlative effect of constricting peaceful movement between places that are important to people's everyday lives. Tuan's distinction between space and place helps one to see the effects of the separation barrier on the inhabitants' ability to move and flourish.

Raja Shehadeh, a Palestinian attorney and writer, speaks of the inhabitants' acute sense of finite space when he writes of Palestine, "Such a small land with an outstanding variety of topographies: one snow-capped mountain, which belongs to Syria, one desert, one freshwater lake and another very salty one, and one proper river. One of everything."[6] Shehadeh's remarks imply that whatever kind of statist solution Israelis and Palestinians determine, they will need to share a space that is finite. Elsewhere Shehadeh describes Palestinian space as "beautiful," thereby conferring on this particular finite space an aesthetic and cultural sense of place. He writes, "The persistent pain at the failure of that struggle [to save this land] would in time be shared by Arabs, Jews and lovers of nature anywhere in the world. All would grieve, as I have, at the continuing destruction of an exquisitely beautiful place."[7] The concept of place involves value; it is less abstract than that of space. Tuan views place as a type of object: "We define place broadly as a focus of value, of nurture and support."[8] Shehadeh thus describes Palestine as a place rich with cultural meaning and aesthetic value. He provides, from the Palestinian perspective, a beginning to the mutual acknowledgment of the diverse meanings involved in appreciating this valued and valuable space.

When one links Shehadeh's remark that Palestine contains just "one of everything" with a quotation from Franz Oppenheimer, one of the delegates to the Sixth Zionist Congress in 1903, it becomes apparent that Palestinians and Israelis share a deep sense of place in this same finite space. The Sixth Zionist Congress is also known as the Uganda Congress, because it was there that Theodor Herzl suggested that a Jewish homeland might be established in Uganda or somewhere other than Palestine. Herzl's suggestion was not taken seriously. Oppenheimer responded, "Allocating [the Jews] the most magnificent expanses of farm land in Canada or Argentina will not enhance the strength of the wandering Jew as much as settling on the lowly Plain through which the Jordan flows and upon which the Lebanon looks out."[9] The Jordan is the "one river" that Shehadeh mentions, while "the Lebanon" refers to the single snow-capped mountain in the north. Clearly, both Jewish Israelis and Palestinians within and beyond the borders of the State of Israel are deeply attached to this land as place. Shehadeh offers a defining value judgment when he speaks of the natural beauty of Palestine in its wholeness as part of a natural ecosystem. He appeals to broad values shared by all human beings who picture themselves as part of a larger, natural whole. Oppenheimer and Shehadeh's remarks show that Jewish Israelis and Palestinians share deep values of place in this single geographical space. A good way to begin to connect these mutual values is to explore the aesthetic concepts of natural beauty and wholeness that are held in common by Palestinians and Jewish Israelis.

The separation barrier serves as a constant reminder that the finite space of Israel-Palestine is contested. This particular constriction of space has implications for people's sense of place. One way to see this is to point out that the modern highways and roads that *link* Israeli towns and settlements are in the Palestinian view seen as *separating* places. Shehadeh's book, *Palestinian Walks*, is an appeal to readers to step into the shoes of residents of the West Bank and see for themselves how Israeli settlements have made it increasingly difficult to take a simple walk along the natural paths defined by Palestinian space and place. Shehadeh characterizes the Palestinian sense of place in terms of both natural beauty and culture. He shares memories of his aunt wearing a turban in the Palestinian style, festooned with holed coins saved from the time when Palestine was a province of the Ottoman Empire. He gives details of the family summerhouse, or *qasr* (Arabic; cf. "castle"), where his uncle, a stonemason, built a comfortable, rock-hewn "throne" called an *a'rsh* in which to sit, relax, and while away the hours. The *a'rsh* was built with a full view of the fields where olive trees had been planted and grew side by side with grapevines that crept along the ground over ancient stone walls. Shehadeh's lifelong avocation has been to walk along the paths where his ancestors enjoyed their lives. As a hiker, he is an explorer of his extended family's past.

Shehadeh contrasts the muted colors of thistle, grass, and bush, as appreciated by his family, with the ugliness associated with Palestine, as characterized by Westerners who visited the place and overlooked its subtle beauty. Mark Twain, for example, called Palestine "desolate and unlovely." William Thackeray described it as parched, savage, and "a landscape unspeakably ghastly and desolate."[10] Thackeray's account mixes in a good bit of cultural and religious stereotyping when he writes, "The place seems quite adapted to the events which are recorded in the Hebrew histories. . . . There is not a spot at which you look, but some violent deed has been done there: some massacre has been committed, some victim has been murdered, some idol has been worshipped with bloody and dreadful rites."[11] Western visitors to Palestine saw what they expected to see, their vision colored by their own preconceptions of history and religion. This preconception was formed in light of Christian attempts to supersede Judaism with a vision of Galilee and surrounding regions as places of new meaning. Surprisingly, the criticism of Palestinian geography that found its way into such accounts as Thackeray's has an analogue in some official Israeli characterizations of the land. When officials declare that the establishment of the State of Israel "made the desert bloom," one might point out that it is a confusion of place and space to associate desert with emptiness. Shehadeh's robust characterization of a preexisting Palestinian place makes this exceedingly clear. In fact, Jewish Israeli accounts of the natural beauty of the land would corroborate Palestinian appreciation of the land as place. When the spatial concept of emptiness is disentangled from the variegated places that were historical Palestine, it becomes possible to see the plural values that both Palestinian and Jewish Israeli stakeholders share in their particular aesthetic, cultural, and religious appreciations of the land.

Shehadeh spent much of his life as an attorney working on land cases in the West Bank. He amassed a great body of documentation pertaining to the loss of land by Palestinians. One of the major contributions of his book *Occupier's Law: Israel and the West Bank* is that it highlights that the Israeli government has applied its own laws to the West Bank, which before occupation in 1967 came under Jordanian law.[12] Israel has circumvented Jordanian law, and its common law traditions, in a number of ways. For example, the Israeli government established the principle that if a landowner physically leaves her property for any length of time, the land is considered empty and "reverts" to public land. Shehadeh argues that this unusual principle goes against both Jordanian and

Ottoman legal practice. He has produced documents in court clearly showing prior ownership by Palestinian people, yet Israel has continued to allow increasing amounts of such "public land" to be occupied by Jewish Israeli settlers. Land that was formerly occupied by the Jordanian army is another example. It has been taken over by the Israeli army and then deemed open to further settlement by Jewish Israelis. Israel has thus applied an "occupier's law" to a region where it lacks sovereignty or where sovereignty is contested.

Shehadeh's careful attention to the legal struggles of ordinary Palestinians came to a head in 1993, when Palestinian diaspora leaders signed the Oslo Accords. This agreement gave certain rights and recognition to Palestine, but at the cost of casting in stone the status quo in the West Bank. Shehadeh lost the accumulation of twenty years of painstaking legal work at a single stroke, through the actions of Palestinian leaders who failed to represent the interests of common West Bank landowners. In *Palestinian Walks*, Shehadeh explores the effects that such a cataclysmic change had on his thinking and way of life. Now that some concrete forms of constriction of Palestinian space had attained quasi-legal status, his vocation of collecting lengthy legal documentation seemed to lose its point. Yet even while describing the pain of losing the battle for Palestinian space in a legal sense, Shehadeh skillfully transformed his life's work to another sphere. *Palestinian Walks* represents a turn from a preoccupation with space to a defense of Palestinian place through eloquent description of personal history, landscape, and a renewed sense of being. The turn to values is the signal to the reader that the discussion, formerly confined to legal definitions of Palestinian space, now involves place. This is not to say that Shehadeh has given up the struggle for Palestinian space. The separation barrier came after the Oslo Accords and signals a continuing requirement to address needs for both space and place in the West Bank. Shehadeh's recent work, however, is an important step forward in recognizing the distinction between space and place and in granting the importance of a shared sense of place.

Shehadeh's final trek in *Palestinian Walks* is a poignant account of how Palestinian and Jewish Israeli senses of place might come together in mutual recognition of the other. In his sixth walk, Shehadeh was picking his way along paths that formerly were unobstructed, when he suddenly came across a young Israeli near a seasonal creek, or wadi. He noticed two signs of danger: the man was smoking a water pipe, and he had a gun next to him. Taken aback but saying nothing, Shehadeh decided to leave immediately by crossing the brook. He accidentally dropped his hat into the water, however. The Israeli called out, "You've dropped your hat."[13] Shehadeh tried to retrieve it, but the Israeli was quicker and came up with the hat. The Israeli began a conversation with Shehadeh. As described in the book, the two people spoke of many deep issues dividing Palestinians and Jewish Israelis. The surprise, however, is found in the values they shared in appreciating the landscape and especially in the fact that they ended up smoking together. It is a small thing, really, but Shehadeh's account gives a palpable sense of hope through the shared value of place.

Shehadeh's turn to a shared sense of place in *Palestinian Walks* suggests a way forward in the Israeli-Palestinian conflict. Certainly place depends on a modicum of space, but place is an imaginative value that may grow through mutual recognition by the relevant stakeholders in the region. As Sayyid Qutb puts it, "In the shelter of this idea [of place], the peoples of all races, colors, and territories can associate as people of one homeland [Ar. *watan wahid*]."[14] Qutb is speaking in the context of shared Arab values, but because the concept of place is plastic and malleable, it offers the opportunity to share values across other boundaries. The recently formed group "Two States, One Homeland" shows that a renewed concept of place offers this opportunity even across Israeli-Palestinian boundaries.[15]

Sari Nusseibeh, a professor of philosophy and a former president of Al-Quds University in Jerusalem, devotes a chapter of his book *What Is a Palestinian State Worth?* to a discussion of shared moral values as a possible solution to the Israeli-Palestinian conflict.[16] Nusseibeh's family has a long history in the Jerusalem area, having settled there over a thousand years ago. Like Shehadeh, he shares a deep sense of place and attachment to the area. Nusseibeh suggests that sharing universal values may help find a way toward a solution to the conflict. He warns against behaving according to norms scripted solely by the group in which one finds oneself. Nusseibeh establishes a distinction between values as reflective of who one is as an autonomous human being and values that simply reflect what one is supposed to think by virtue of being a member of a particular group, whether that is "Arab" or "Jew."[17] If one believes that group identity rigidly dictates what one should do, one remains merely a puppet in that group entity's hands; but if one is truly autonomous, one has the potential to transform values in common enterprise with others.

Nusseibeh suggests a thought experiment. "Imagine," he begins, "an ancient society developing in a fertile river valley."[18] The inconsistency of the flooding of the river causes the people to attempt to placate God for the sake of their well-being. They develop the notion that God requires them to sacrifice the lives of each family's firstborn child in order to stem the river's flood. They comply with what they perceive to be God's wishes, even though they intensely mourn the loss of their children. Nusseibeh notes that these events are distant from us in time and space. They contain enough moral relativity that we would not judge the people's acts of child sacrifice the same as murder in the modern sense. However, we would still draw on a sense of shared values in order to judge the case as immoral. He writes, "But surely it also would be wrong to suspend our moral judgment altogether, telling ourselves that sacrificing our children can under some conceivable circumstance (such as on instruction from God) be the moral thing to do."[19]

That Nusseibeh begins the thought experiment with the word "imagine" is striking, because child sacrifices actually occurred in the ancient Levant, Middle East, and Mediterranean Basin.[20] Echoes remain in the Hebrew Bible in a number of places, with the most obvious example being Abraham's near sacrifice of his son Isaac. This particular echo reverberates through Islam as well, where Abraham's son Ishmael becomes the potential sacrificial victim. Child sacrifice is a powerful image from humanity's shared past. Its contemplation shows us that in many ways our modern ethical intuitions are more similar to one another than different and that our interpretations of ancient sacred texts must remain open to contemporary judgment and transformation.

Nusseibeh applies the thought experiment to the contemporary world, a news story from the West Bank city of Hebron. In December 2008 a group of masked men, determined to evict an Arab family of about twenty people from their home, set fire to the house while the family was inside. The act was in retaliation for Israeli authorities evicting Jewish settlers from a building that the settlers had taken over in 2007. Journalists were on the scene when the fire was set. Neither Arab neighbors nor the Israeli army responded to the emergency. The police would arrive late. It was up to the journalists. They acted morally and rescued the family, although the house was destroyed. The violence of the act prompted the Israeli press to call it a "pogrom" and elicited an expression of outrage from many, including the Israeli prime minister.

Nusseibeh appeals in this contemporary example to a sense of shared values. Everyone condemned the actions of this particular group of Jewish Israeli settlers. Nusseibeh defines "settlers" as "Israelis, including new immigrants, who have established urban colonies in the territories occupied in 1967, with or without government assistance."[21] He then asks whether individuals who acquire the property of being a settler must become enslaved by that group's definition, so that they escape personal responsibility for their actions. Like Shehadeh, Nusseibeh holds that settlements are illegal under international law. Yet beyond the legal question, in terms of place, he argues that being a settler need not mean being a person who hates Palestinians. One is responsible for one's own behavior and can be called to account for heinous crimes, not absolved of them because of membership in a group. Nusseibeh also cites a number of cases of Palestinian excesses, in which members of Hamas and Fatah committed crimes in the name of their respective groups and exhibited "beastly passions."[22]

Nusseibeh points to what philosophers sometimes call the merely "provisional reality" of group identities such as the State of Israel, the Palestinian Authority, the settlers' movement, Hamas, and so on.[23] He notes that while we often think of these as the "grand players" in the Israeli-Palestinian conflict, they are also "meta-biological entities."[24] Nusseibeh appeals to the real dangers of essentialism, arguing that the metabiological is provisional and ought not to be taken as ultimate. If we think of a person as delivered at birth to the address marked on a preaddressed envelope that constitutes her life, with her destiny prescribed by external commitments as formulated by her group, the person may lose faith in her ability to control her life.[25] The world becomes a grim unfolding of events beyond her control. Nusseibeh takes the existentialist view that we do not arrive here with preexisting addresses. He argues that we should grant ourselves the privileges of imagination and freedom and, therefore, the power to redefine the world around us. Nusseibeh's antiessentialist argument forms a component of a larger compatibilist argument for freedom. Freedom becomes a necessary condition for a solution to the Israeli-Palestinian conflict, and its conceptual elaboration provides a context for moving forward. The mutual acknowledgment of common moral values joins the appreciation of aesthetic values in our quest for plural solutions to the conflict.

Chaim Gans, a professor of legal, moral, and political philosophy at Tel Aviv University, shares Nusseibeh's sense of the importance of freedom and individual autonomy. Yet, in arguing for a carefully defined and restricted form of Zionism, Gans defends the value of group identity. Borrowing Nusseibeh's terms, we can see that Gans is concerned to retain the importance of metabiological values for the Jewish people. Gans frames the debate in terms of a distinction found in political science between ethnocultural and civic nationalisms. Gans defines ethnocultural nationalism as an ideology according to which "groups sharing a common history and culture have fundamental and morally significant interests in adhering to their culture and in sustaining it for generations."[26] Civic nationalism, on the other hand, is the contrasting ideology that holds that citizens of a state have an interest in sharing one homogeneous national culture. Civic nationalism tends to embrace many of Nusseibeh's universal values, such as democracy, distributive justice, and economic growth.[27]

While Gans recognizes some features of civic nationalism in the historical ideology called Zionism, he admits that Zionism is basically a form of ethnocultural nationalism. Gans seeks a form of Zionism that is just and defensible in light of valid, competing Palestinian values and aspirations. His book *A Just Zionism: On the Morality of the Jewish State* is an effort to defend Zionism in a carefully circumscribed fashion. Gans' distinction between ethnocultural and civic nationalism has a counterpart in the intellectual tradition of Israel's Arab neighbors. Adeed Dawisha, in *Arab Nationalism in the Twentieth Century*, defends an Arab form of ethnocultural nationalism and shows that it has been a strong force in Arab history. He traces the path of ethnocultural nationalism (Ar. *al-qawmiya*) through twentieth-century Arab history and shows its confrontation with *al-wataniya*, nationalism based on state sovereignty.[28] Although Arab ethnocultural nationalism has failed thus far to bring together nations in a lasting union, Dawisha shows its deep and abiding attraction to Arab people. Comparison of Gans and Dawisha shows that any defense of ethnocultural nationalism, whether Zionist or Arab, constitutes a pluralist project because ethnocultural nationalisms must remain irreducibly many as defined and lived by their respective groups.

Nusseibeh points out the danger of collectivist thinking that forces individuals to engage in immoral behavior for the benefit of the group. Gans recognizes the danger but suggests that ethnocultural nationalisms may take more benign forms as "individualist" rather than "collectivist." He writes,

> There are ethnocultural nationalists who are individualists. They believe that many individuals have interests in adhering to their culture and in sustaining it for generations because their culture constitutes an important component of their identity, because it constitutes the world where their endeavors will leave their mark, and because to a large extent their welfare depends on whether or not their culture flourishes.[29]

When Gans speaks of preserving cultural identity and maintaining the welfare of individual people within that culture, he is drawing attention to values that invoke the concept of place. Like Nusseibeh, he supports a two-state solution, one in which each group may find values appropriate to its individual members.[30] Gans includes the important component of Jewish cultural value in his discussion of the moral and aesthetic dimensions of place. Gans argues that two conditions must obtain in order for a Jewish ethnocultural nationalism to be morally acceptable. First, it must give equal consideration to similar demands made by other nations. In the present context, this refers to the Palestinians. Second, it must be based on the interests of the individuals that make up the group, and it must give moral precedence to those individuals.[31] This means that an acceptable form of Jewish ethnocultural nationalism may not engage in the kinds of behaviors that Nusseibeh also condemned, where individuals lose their autonomy and allow the group to dictate immoral acts to be performed by its individual members. Such acts, Gans notes, go against the original motivation and impetus of the Zionist movement, which was characterized by the experiences of Jewish people during the hundred-year period from the middle of the 1800s to the middle of the 1900s. These experiences produced a need for individual Jewish people to escape persecution, humiliation, and physical danger. Gans takes pains to limit Zionism by proscribing forms that would elevate Jewish collectivism over the individuals that constitute it or forms that value a Jewish nation over all other values. For example, Gans holds that Jewish Israelis have a special obligation to conciliate both their non-Jewish fellow citizens and their Palestinian and Arab neighbors. The obligation to recognize a plurality of values leads to a discussion of the Jewish right to establish a nation in Palestinian space in the first place.

Gans argues that the Jews did have a right to return to their historical homeland—which happens to coincide with Palestinian space—but that this right has to be carefully circumscribed. He links the right to the events of 1880–1945 and finds it ultimately grounded in a foundational sense of Jewish identity. He writes, "I will argue that the historical rights argument, in conjunction with the horrendous scope and nature of the persecution in the 1930s and 1940s, provided justification for establishing Jewish self-determination in the Land of Israel."[32] The first thing to note in commenting on Gans' argument is the introduction of the term "Land of Israel" (Heb. Eretz Israel). This term suggests two things, one having to do with space, and the other with place. First, it denotes space that is equivalent to Palestine.[33] Gans deals with this problem by suggesting that the context of the term as stated "in the Land of Israel" does not mean that Jewish Israelis may establish hegemony over the *whole* of the Land of Israel, only that they may do so *in* the land. Gans acknowledges that Palestinian and Arab opposition to the establishment of the State of Israel was justified. Jewish Israelis must conciliate their neighbors by allowing Palestinians to pursue freely the same kind of ethnocultural values that Jewish Israelis themselves wish to pursue. For Gans, this implies, in the real space-time continuum that constitutes Israel and Palestine, that two states should be effectuated for at least the immediate future.

The term "Land of Israel" invokes the cultural concept of place because it derives from biblical usage and plays an important role in the formation of Jewish self-identity. A necessary component of the inquiry into place and space is to explore in a critical way the historical contexts of the term "Land of Israel" and its semantic cousins, terms like "Promised Land" and "Sacred Place." Such a study explores, on the Jewish side, use of the terms in the Hebrew Bible, the Mishnah, and the Talmuds and, on the Muslim side, in the Qur'an and the Hadiths. The goal of such an inquiry is to recognize the concept of place as it informs the Israeli-Palestinian conflict through religious and cultural values. Raja Shehadeh, for example, expresses joy that Ramallah, his hometown, is not mentioned in the Bible and that Jewish Israelis have not therefore seen an immediate attachment to this particular place. He decries the "mythologization" of the places mentioned in the Bible and the constricting effect that has had on Palestinians who reside in those places. A critical examination of the concept of the Land of Israel in its religious and historical contexts could go some way toward fulfilling Shehadeh's desire to clarify the role of concepts like promised land and sacred place in Israel and Palestine. In the Mishnah, for example, ownership of land forms the legal foundation of social life. Even money is reducible to land. It could be the case that interpretation of the Land of Israel as God's promise to Israel rests as much on a legal paradigm as it does on mythologization in the modern, theological sense used by thinkers like Rudolf Bultmann.[34] In other words, Jewish attachment to the land may depend on values that lie deep in history, values that remain unrecognized in their origin and complexity. That possibility could be significant because the concept of place could then be used to justify a modicum of space for both peoples, Jewish and

Palestinian. Jewish reliance on the Bible would then take on a richer nuance and a firmer basis, even though Shehadeh's sentiment remains a valid expression of the Palestinian sense of constricted space.

As noted above, Gans argues that the Jewish right to self-determination, even if given in a particular geographical location, does not form a basis for the right to territorial sovereignty over the whole of the Land of Israel. According to Gans, the Jewish right to self-determination in some part of the Land of Israel is valid, however, for three reasons. First, the Land of Israel was the formative territory of the Jews, the place where they began to consider themselves a people. Second, Jews have retained an emotional attachment to the place, an attachment that has endured through the centuries. Finally, the Land of Israel represents a constitutive part of Jewish identity.[35] Gans circumscribes the right of the Jews to the Land of Israel, however. He writes, "If it is deemed appropriate for the Palestinians to allow the Jews to select the site of their self-determination in Palestine, then they should be given territory in compensation for the territories they have lost or at least be compensated financially by the other nations of the world."[36] The theory of global distributive justice would seem to demand both the primary right of the Jews to select a site of national self-determination in a historical territory—even though they stopped living in the territory sometime in the past—and the right of the Palestinians to actualize their own self-determination in the same land that they have continuously occupied for many centuries. Gans argues that it would be impossible to actualize both rights if the theory of global distributive justice remained on the plain of the ideal or, in terms of the place/space distinction, if the attempt were made to implement both rights solely in terms of competition for a single space.[37] Space in the region is, after all, finite. Gans' goal is to formulate a practical solution in terms of place—that is, a remedial right or justification for the establishment of the Jewish homeland in the Land of Israel that would at the same time compensate the Palestinians for their losses and provide the conditions for Palestinians to actualize their own ethnocultural and national aspirations for self-determination. Gans argues that Jews have a special moral obligation to understand Arab and Palestinian opposition to Jewish return to the Land of Israel and to contain it by way of conciliation. He adds that the nations of the world, especially Germany and the European nations, are morally obliged to assist in such conciliation and to compensate Palestinians for the price that they have paid.[38] The latter suggestion has merit in that it could identify those European nations that were colonial powers in the region and help them heal the effects of colonialism, while aiding Germany with the legacy of its role in the Holocaust.

The Jewish remedial right to self-determination in the Land of Israel is based on the historical events that led up to and included the Holocaust (Heb. *shoah*). Gans writes,

> It was not until the 1930s that the persecution of the Jews became serious enough to create an incontrovertible necessity for the Jews to realize their right to self-determination in Palestine. . . . It is the Nazi rise to power and the Holocaust that followed which ultimately rendered the persecution of Jews shocking to the extent that it demanded an urgent solution.[39]

The ideology of the National Socialists included the claim that Jews were not fully human beings. In terms of the place/space distinction, the Nazis recognized that, like any other sentient being, Jews required space in which to live, move, and work. Yet, by attempting to erase Jewish humanity, cultural life, and achievement, the Nazis thereby denied Jews the right to a sense of place. The attack on Jewish place is much in evidence in accounts of Jewish experience in the Holocaust. Primo Levi, for example, describes in *Survival in Auschwitz* the Nazi assault on Jews' having a right to any sense of place in this world. It is appropriate to discuss those aspects of the Holocaust that might have a bearing on the Jewish sense of place. Such a discussion can help clarify the relationship between Jewish Israelis and Palestinians in the Land of Israel as both peoples seek an authentic place.

Levi begins *Survival in Auschwitz* by noting that the premise "every stranger is an enemy" is common among people and nations. He calls it a "latent infection," however, and argues that when carried rigorously to its logical conclusion, it leads to the Lager, the German term for concentration or extermination camp.[40] The treatment of strangers has relevance today in thinking about the Israeli-Palestinian conflict, because the duty to treat strangers hospitably is thoroughly grounded in obligatory laws of all three religions of the book: Judaism, Islam, and Christianity. Some lessons about hospitality are implied in Shehadeh's example of his smoke with the Jewish Israeli settler. Duties toward the stranger are made in terms of the Jews' own history in the following passage from the Hebrew Bible: "[The LORD spoke to Moses:] 'When a stranger resides with you in your land, you shall not wrong him. The stranger who resides with you shall be to you as one of your citizens; you shall love him as yourself, for you were strangers in the land of Egypt: I the LORD am your God.' "[41] This passage from Leviticus is found in the context of God giving Moses the statutes for organizing a flourishing society. The speech is given in a long series of ordinances handed down to Israel. Its substance has legal and ethical implications in Jewish history that remain as viable contenders today in the public space of ideas.

Islam also enjoins specific duties to strangers. In the hadith called *Sahih al-Bukhari*, the Prophet Muhammad said, "Whoever believes in God and the Last Day, let him honor his neighbor; whoever believes in God and the Last Day, let him honor his guest as he is entitled."[42] Muhammad set a limit to such duties, which is accurately reflected in the contemporary concerns of Shehadeh,

Nusseibeh, and Gans: "And it is not lawful for a guest to stay with his host for such a long period as to put him in a critical position."[43] A balance must be sought between hospitality and imposition. In a number of hadiths, Muhammad echoes the Jewish belief that originally the people of God were strangers in the land and it is thus incumbent upon one to treat strangers hospitably.[44]

Gans argues for a Jewish historical right to live in the Land of Israel, but with the condition that Jewish Israelis recognize Palestinian rights to live in the same land and with compensation to the Palestinians for those parts of the land that they lost. It can be seen that the concept of place in Levi's book offers a number of relevant ways to understand the relationship between the Holocaust and the Land of Israel.

Levi is himself a Holocaust survivor. Packed with people of all ages in the train on the way to Poland, Levi learned that the destination of the journey was Auschwitz. Feeling relief that they were headed toward "some place on this earth," he did not realize that Auschwitz would turn out to be what has since been called an anti-place or anti-world.[45] Only later did Levi learn that Auschwitz was known as *anus mundi*, the anus of the world. Levi's writings reverberate with a sense of loss of place. As one of those who survived the initial selection on the railway landing at Auschwitz, a process in which five hundred people were simply "swallowed up by the night," Levi found himself on a vortex toward "the bottom." He writes, "Imagine now a man who is deprived of everyone he loves, and at the same time of his house, his habits, his clothes, in short, of everything he possesses: he will be a hollow man."[46]

The items that Levi mentions are markers of one's place in the world. The German guards took pains to remove as many of these markers as possible and to assault the personal dignity of their prisoners. Richard Rubenstein, in *After Auschwitz*, describes the treatment of prisoners in the camps as "excremental assault."[47] The normal acquisition of modest possessions, markers of place, was replaced with an assault on normal human behaviors of morality and decency. Promiscuity was enforced by regular orders to strip off one's clothing. Rules were enacted that demanded cleanliness and continence while at the same time places and times for evacuation of the bowels were highly restricted. Thousands of prisoners, for example, were expected to go to a single latrine at a particular time. The time-space problem was exacerbated by a diet and living conditions that promoted diarrhea and dysentery. Levi gives an example of excremental assault when he describes the enforced ritual of carrying the latrine bucket from the barracks to the latrine, occurring about twenty times a night. It was impossible to keep the contents of the bucket from sloshing onto one's feet. Then one had to return to his bunk and sleep with one's feet next to his neighbor's face. Levi writes that no matter how repugnant the duty of carrying the bucket may have been, "it is always preferable that we, and not our neighbour, be ordered to do it."[48] Auschwitz dehumanized its prisoners before they were led to their deaths by gas, disease, malnutrition, or other forms of brutality and violence.

Levi suggests that, in spite of the attempts at the Lagers, it is impossible to take away a person's humanity completely while that person is still alive. He describes one incident when he was sharing the heavy load of a soup kettle with a fellow prisoner. The men walked one behind the other, a pole on each shoulder, burdened with the hundred-pound kettle hung precariously between. While walking in this way, Levi forgot himself and began to teach his friend a little Italian by way of the poet Dante. He recited, "Think of your breed; for brutish ignorance/Your mettle was not made; you were made men,/To follow after knowledge and excellence."[49] Jean, his Alsatian companion, begged Levi to repeat the passage. Levi writes:

> How good [Jean] is, he is aware that it is doing me good. Or perhaps it is some-
> thing more: perhaps, despite the wan translation and the pedestrian, rushed com-
> mentary, he has received the message, he has felt that it has to do with him, that
> it has to do with all men who toil, and with us in particular; and that it has to do
> with us two, who dare to reason of these things with the poles for the soup on
> our shoulders.[50]

The optimism expressed here, while real, is in tension with other passages of *Survival in Auschwitz*. Hope does not really take hold until the Lager itself dies, with the onset of the Russian offensive coming from the east. It is only at that point that the remaining prisoners may again begin to assume the human role of helping one another rather than simply looking out for themselves. It is only then that they begin again to see fellow prisoners as human beings instead of simply competitors for the scarce resources needed for survival in Auschwitz. In robbing their victims of their very lives in the extermination camps, the camp overlords removed the victims' right to their normal human allotment of space and time. Yet, in attempting to rob their prisoners' humanity, they also attacked those values that are formative of each human being's sense of place in the world.

The linkage of the Holocaust to the right of Jewish self-determination in a homeland of historical significance to themselves is established not by a sim-ple cause-and-effect relationship between the Holocaust and the State of Israel. Rather the linkage is established as a remedy for the lack of place and space that the destruction of European Jewry caused during the last century. The rem-edy continues to be needed, but it also affects the Palestinians adversely. It is now the case that Palestinians, too, require a remedy. The remedy begins with acknowledgment of the need for a Palestinian place within the space of Israel-Palestine. Such a remedy is possible in the form of sharing space and granting unique place to one's neighbor. Violent incidents, campaigns, and wars that mar the relationship of Jewish Israelis and Palestinians are not a normal mode of existence, even if their frequency makes them appear so. People attempt to live out their everyday lives in the places they call home, even if ravaged by violence and surrounded by the signs and symbols of conflict. Common people, with their attachments to place and their need for a modicum of space, give specification to the minimum requirements that are needed to find a better way moving forward.

When Jewish Israelis call the land of Israel "the promised land," they invoke deep historical concepts of both space and place. The establishment of the State of Israel in 1948 meant that a defined object, a state, would come into being—that is, take its place—in a particular area that was the former British Palestinian Mandate west of the Jordan River. Palestinians disputed both the newly established place and the occupation of the space. Yet Palestinians and Jewish Israelis share a sense of place in terms of the aesthetic, moral, and cultural values that they ascribe to the region. The task here has been to inquire into Jewish and Palestinian concepts of place and space in order to clarify conceptual attachments that the people have developed over time. This in turn allows people to increase their understanding of their own and their neighbor's perspectives, see the historical forces that have brought them to the present situation, and suggest a way forward through mutually shared concepts of place.

This chapter has joined Palestinian hope for autonomy and love of homeland with Jewish historical experience and aspiration for safe haven in a post-Holocaust world. The juxtaposition of Holocaust accounts with expressions of Palestinian memory provides a striking contrast in perspective. Deeper comparison of these diverse accounts suggests necessary conditions for fulfilling the hopes of peace-loving Palestinians and Jewish Israelis. The argument leads along premises toward a pluralist conclusion of multiple places within the space that is Israel and Palestine. It is not that the Bible and the Holocaust have a simple *causal* relation to the establishment of the State of Israel. Rather, valid but competing Palestinian and Jewish desires for place give rise to the necessity to *correlate* aspirations under a new, pluralist vision.

NOTES

1. Quoted in Sayed Khatab, "Arabism and Islamism in Sayyid Qutb's Thought on Nationalism," *Muslim World* 94, no. 2 (April 2004): 220.

2. Yi-Fu Tuan, *Space and Place: The Perspective of Experience* (Minneapolis: University of Minnesota Press, 1977).

3. See, e.g., Raja Shehadeh, *Palestinian Walks: Forays into a Vanishing Landscape* (New York: Scribner, 2007).

4. See, e.g., Chaim Gans, *A Just Zionism: On the Morality of the Jewish State* (Oxford: Oxford University Press, 2008).

5. Tuan, *Space and Place*, 12.

6. Shehadeh, *Palestinian Walks*, 44.

7. Ibid., 1.

8. Tuan, *Space and Place*, 9.

9. Quoted in Gans, *A Just Zionism*, 33.

10. Shehadeh (*Palestinian Walks*, xiv–xv) quotes Twain's *The Innocents Abroad* and Thackeray's *Notes of a Journey from Cornhill to Grand Cairo*.

11. Ibid., xv.

12. Raja Shehadeh, *Occupier's Law: Israel and the West Bank* (Washington, DC: Institute for Palestine Studies, 1985).

13. Shehadeh, *Palestinian Walks*, 186.

14. Khatab, "Arabism and Islamism," 220.

15. Two States, One Homeland reflects mutual recognition of historical, religious, and cultural ties to the land through its mission statement. See http://alandforall.org/en.

16. Sari Nusseibeh, *What Is a Palestinian State Worth?* (Cambridge, MA: Harvard University Press, 2011), 93–123.

17. Ibid., 95.

18. Ibid., 97.

19. Ibid.

20. See Jon D. Levenson, *The Death and Resurrection of the Beloved Son: The Transformation of Child Sacrifice in Judaism and Christianity* (New Haven, CT: Yale University Press, 1993).

21. Nusseibeh, *What Is a Palestinian State Worth?*, 101.

22. Ibid., 103.

23. The concept "provisional reality" comes from the Indian philosophical school of Advaita Vedanta and is a translation of the Sanskrit *vyavaharika*.

24. Nusseibeh, *What Is a Palestinian State Worth?*, 104.

25. The preaddressed envelope example is from Agnes Heller.

26. Gans, *A Just Zionism*, 3.

27. Ibid., 9.

28. Adeed Dawisha, *Arab Nationalism in the Twentieth Century: From Triumph to Despair* (Princeton, NJ: Princeton University Press, 2003), 219.

29. Gans, *A Just Zionism*, 18.

30. Nusseibeh, *What Is a Palestinian State Worth?*, chap. 5; Gans, *A Just Zionism*, chap. 4.

31. Gans, *A Just Zionism*, 19.

32. Ibid., 25.

33. The Land of Israel is defined in many ways. Even the biblical descriptions admit of many interpretations. In Gans' use, and for our purposes here, we may define it as the same area as British Mandatory Palestine, or present-day Israel, West Bank, and Gaza.

34. Bultmann explored the concepts of mythologization and demythologization in *Jesus Christ and Mythology* (New York: Scribner's, 1958).

35. Gans, *A Just Zionism*, 37.

36. Ibid., 39n23. Financial compensation may not be sufficient, given the Mishnaic principle mentioned above that money is reducible to land.

37. Ibid., 45.

38. Ibid., 50.

39. Ibid., 47.

40. Primo Levi, *Survival in Auschwitz: The Nazi Assault on Humanity*, trans. Stuart Woolf (New York: Simon and Schuster, 1993), 9; originally published as *Se questo è un uomo* (1958).

41. Lev. 19:33–34 (New Jewish Publication Society of America Tanakh).

42. Quoted in Ashia Stacey, "Treating Guests the Islamic Way" (2014), *The Religion of Islam*, http://www.islamreligion.com/articles/10662/treating-guests-islamic-way/.

43. Ibid.

44. *Sahih Muslim*, *At Tirmidhi*, *Ibn Majah*, and *Ahmad*, quoted in Ashia Stacey, "Who Are the Strangers" (2011), *The Religion of Islam*, http://www.islamreligion.com/articles/4303/who-are-strangers/.

45. Emil L. Fackenheim, *To Mend the World: Foundations of Post-Holocaust Jewish Thought* (Bloomington: Indiana University Press, 1994; first published in 1982).

46. Levi, *Survival in Auschwitz*, 25.

47. Richard L. Rubenstein, *After Auschwitz: History, Theology, and Contemporary Judaism* (Baltimore: Johns Hopkins University Press, 1992; first published in 1966).

48. Levi, *Survival in Auschwitz*, 62.

49. Quoted in ibid., 113.

50. Levi, *Survival in Auschwitz*, 113–114.

PART V

THE EMOTIONALLY EMPLACED BODY

Exile as "Place" for Empathy 15

Ilana Maymind

Historically, exile has been a political act that has various philosophical and psychological ramifications. In the Roman world, exile was a substitute for physical death.[1] Adorno argues that exile is a "life in suspension" as a result of being placed in the diasporic conditions of estrangement. For Adorno, "it is part of morality not to be at home in one's home,"[2] since being in exile makes one a perpetual stranger and sharpens one's ethical stance. The idea of being a stranger leads to the significance of the issue of empathy. In this chapter, I discuss Shinran and Maimonides as I maintain that the focus in some of their writings demonstrates the effects of exile as "place" for empathy. I further propose a link between empathy and ethics by viewing empathy as a measure of genuine ethical concern.

The choice of focus on Shinran and Maimonides is not predicated merely on their being contemporaries, though divided by vast geographic distance, but is informed by their respective statuses within their communities. In addition, by choosing these thinkers, I aim to problematize a tendency to view Eastern and Western thought as existing in the unrelated milieus that continue drawing the boundaries between the familiar and the unfamiliar as impenetrable. This comparison attempts to decrease this perception.

While philosophy and consequently philosophers are often treated in terms of "a continuation of Plato's enterprise," which is the life of a withdrawal from everyday social life, viewing any thinkers and their thought outside of their respective environments means overlooking that some of their views are directly affected by these environments. Any thinker's thought cannot be fully understood if it is abstracted from the history of his or her life as a whole. Rather than viewing Shinran and Maimonides as Plato's "cave philosophers," we can note that their thought demonstrates direct applicability to human lives. In the cases of Shinran and Maimonides, their thought cannot be fully comprehended if their respective exiles are not taken into account. In both cases, their life conditions resulted in the creation of either "hybrid" or new identities that allowed them to view certain issues from the position of empathic insiders/outsiders.

As a result of their displacement from their familiar environments, both thinkers had to reinvent their own identities. The "hybrid identity" of Maimonides was a result of his belonging to multiple communities: his own Jewish community and the Islamic community in which he became embedded. Shinran's identity was reinvented as well when, following expulsion from the monastic community, he entered the community of the common people and broke the monastic tradition by starting his own family. For him, exile meant being defrocked and expelled from Japan's capital, the nation's intellectual and religious center, and returning to secular life. In this process of being stripped of his ordination, Shinran's exilic identity underwent a change as he lost his religious name and was given a new name as a layman, a name he refused to own.

For Maimonides, his new life conditions stimulated an increased emphasis on Jewish communal life and the endorsement of the commandments (religious law) as a means to his continual existence fully embedded and involved in the culture of his host land. For Shinran, they meant a complete and unconditional embrace of the teachings of the Pure Land and particularly of the practice of the Buddha Amida.

Since Jews in Maimonides' time never wrote their autobiographies, Maimonides did not address his own experience. Thus, everything that is known about him comes from his other writings and letters. Likewise, Shinran did not leave any notes or a personal account of his experience of exile. The influence of their displacements from their respective communities becomes apparent through their writings. Their writings demonstrate that this displacement—from the Andalusian Jewish community of his childhood and youth for Maimonides and from the monastic community of Kyoto for Shinran—produced an empathic and tolerant approach to other human beings, enhanced by their experience of the embodied knowledge of their new surroundings and new community members. The goal is to demonstrate that their biographical experiences, which have informed their thinking, resonate with conditions of exile and diasporic living in pluralistic societies that define the lives of many individuals, communities, and societies in the twenty-first century. Let us briefly turn to their respective environments before we attempt to tackle the elusiveness of the idea of empathy.

Japanese Environment

Shinran's life and writing fall within the Kamakura period (1185–1333), which directly followed the Heian period (794–1185). The Kamakura period was a time of much devastation and suffering. During this period the scholarly communities of Buddhist monks suffered a decline because their focus on the educated elite failed to address social concerns. The first shogunate (military) government was established in 1192, and the Japanese warriors, rather than the court nobles, took control of the government. In addition to many social and cultural changes, this period was characterized by an unusual number of natural disasters, such as typhoons, epidemics, fires, and earthquakes. The Kamakura period represented the crisis of the age, the so-called degenerate age (*mappō*), characterized by increased distance from the teachings and practices of the Buddha.

The Pure Land tradition was a direct response to these hardships and human uncertainties. Already enjoying some popular support among the nonelite in the earlier Heian period, in the Kamakura period the Pure Land tradition took a critical stance toward the decline of the preceding Buddhist traditions into monastic formalism, sectarianism, and a focus on individual liberation. Remaining connected to the larger Mahāyāna principles the Pure Land tradition did not negate its principle of the nondichotomous relation between self and other. In effect, the Pure Land tradition became an admixture of a Mahāyāna conception of enlightened wisdom and the karmic nature of human existence. While the traditional Buddhist view of karmic existence builds on the principle that performing good deeds counters the negative influence of evil deeds and hence improves conditions for rebirth, the Mahāyāna tradition, while accepting the principle of karmic causation, maintains that bodhisattvas perform good actions and practices and accumulate merits that become transferred to human beings. In other words, bodhisattvic practices are undertaken with the goal of liberation of all beings.

All the teachings of the Pure Land tradition pivot around the Buddha Amida (Skt. Amitabha), a bodhisattva Hōzō (Skt. Dharmakara) who attained the state of Buddhahood. Making forty-eight vows, Amida Buddha established a Pure Land as the land of happiness (Jōdo). His most important is the Eighteenth Vow, or Primal Vow (*hongan*)—the vow of birth through the recitation of the name of Amida Buddha (*shōmyō nenbutsu*). This vow expresses the desire to free all beings from the weight of karmic evil. In the Pure Land tradition, the recitation of the name of the Buddha Amida nullifies one's karmic evil and revokes karmic causation. Hence, any human attains the potentiality of enlightenment. Shinran was particularly attracted to the nondiscriminative nature of this tradition.

Shinran

Shinran became a Tendai monk at the age of nine and studied on Mount Hiei. During his studies Shinran was an ordinary temple monk (*dōsō*), exposed to the Tendai system's major doctrines as well as Pure Land thoughts of such Tendai masters as Ennin, Ryogen, and Genshin. In addition, he was influenced by a prevalent religious consciousness in society known as the "veneration of

Prince Shotoku." Traditionally credited with the formal adoption of Buddhism in Japan, Shotoku (574–622) was seen as a manifestation of the bodhisattva of compassion, Avalokiteśvara (J. Kannon). At the age of twenty-nine, Shinran left Mount Hiei and, after a period of spiritual turmoil, joined Hōnen and his Pure Land movement.

Hōnen—the founder of the Jōdo, or Pure Land, school of Buddhism—established the popular independent movement of Pure Land teaching, advocating belief in the power of Amida Buddha's Eighteenth Vow and the recitation of Amida's name as the sole means for birth in the Pure Land. Hōnen's teachings challenged the prevailing Tendai view of Pure Land thought by articulating the *nenbutsu* practice as "exclusive *nenbutsu*" (*senju nenbutsu*), as an independent and self-sufficient path of Buddhist practice. Hōnen's teaching questioned the Tendai school's focus on the significance of merit transfer and self-power (*jiriki*). However, as his teaching of the exclusive *nenbutsu* spread throughout the country, old temples at Mount Hiei and in Nara tried to prevent the further dissemination of this practice. In his teaching practices Hōnen never differentiated between monks and laypeople, men and women, or aristocrats and common folks. This lack of differentiation was perceived as a challenge to the traditional Buddhist institution because it ultimately ensured everyone's access to the sacred. Hōnen's approach was seen as a "religious democratization."[3] Already in 1204 the priests of Mount Hiei appealed to the chief abbot to abolish the exclusive *nenbutsu* practice.[4] As a result, Hōnen and his main disciples, including Shinran, were exiled from Kyoto to different remote parts of Japan. Shinran's tenure with Hōnen was short, for he never saw Hōnen again after being exiled.

Shinran's period of exile fell between 1207 and 1235, during which he lived in the harsh environment of Kokufu in the Echigo District and broke the monastic tradition by marrying and raising a family, calling himself "neither monk nor layman." After Shinran's exilic ban was lifted in 1211, he chose not to return to Kyoto and the monkhood but stayed in Echigo for two more years. He then moved with his family to Kantō, still a somewhat rural area, perhaps benefiting from its proximity to the libraries where he began writing his *Kyōgyōshinshō* (Teaching, practice, faith, and realization).

The exilic period was the most significant time in Shinran's life in relation to the crystallization of his thought. During this period, as he became further disillusioned with both Buddhist institutional power and institutionalized societal power, Shinran continued self-consciously exploring human nature, with all its passions and instincts. In his postscript to *Kyōgyōshinshō*, Shinran wrote:

> The emperor and his ministers, acting against the dharma and violating human rectitude, became enraged and embittered. As a result, Master Genku [Hōnen]—the eminent founder who had enabled the true essence of the Pure Land way to spread vigorously [in Japan]—and a number of his followers, without receiving

any deliberation of their [alleged] crimes, were summarily sentenced to death or were disposed of their monkhood, given [secular] names, and consigned to distant banishment. I was among the latter. Hence, I am now *neither a monk nor one in worldly life*. For this reason, I have taken the term "Toku" [stubble-haired] as my name.[5] (Italics mine)

By saying he was not a monk, he divorced himself from the temporal power of the Buddhist tradition in Japan, and by saying he was not a layperson ("nor one in worldly life"), he distanced himself from the nobility and warriors as well. These words clearly articulated his political views as well as his displeasure with the lack of ethical treatment of Hōnen's followers.

The exposure to farmers, hunters, fishermen, and other working people made Shinran more appreciative of a nondualistic principle that did not view the religious life and lay life as two separate realms. Shinran further reconceptualized the doctrine of merit transference. In his interpretation, merit transference not only entailed individuals to send out their merits but could also be a manifestation of the compassion sent to others by the already enlightened Amida Buddha. He further reinforced the idea of "other power" (*tariki*) by negating the value of self-power (*jiriki*). This reconceptualization grew out of his own inability to attain enlightenment by the traditional Tendai principle of accumulating merits through one's own efforts. Becoming sensitized to the inadequacy of one's own efforts, he viewed self-power in terms of rational calculation (*hakarai*) as merely egotistic self-focus devoid of compassion for other beings.

One of Shinran's most important concepts is *shinjin*, a concept that defies a precise translation. Its approximate translation is "entrusting faith," and it implies a "true, real, and sincere heart and mind."[6] For Shinran, the practice of *shōmyō nenbutsu* was much less significant than attaining the sincere mind (*shinjin*). It is sincerity and spontaneity that Shinran emphasized, not any form of rational calculation.

Cognizant of life's challenges and his attention to those afflicted by negative karmic effects,[7] Shinran did not use the terms "good" and "evil" to describe people's actions but viewed karmic "evil" as "suffering and the awareness of suffering."[8] Shinran's early works, although lacking sophistication of *Kyōgyōshinshō*, already demonstrated a humanistic focus driven by his compassion for all beings. For instance, in *Kangyo-amidakyo-shuchu* (Annotated Amitayur-dhyana sutra), composed in 1217, he cited a passage from *Le-pang-wen-lei*, written by Tsung-hsiao in 1200, in which Tsung-hsiao discussed the rebirth of the animal slaughterer. In medieval China, by the standards of that time, the animal slaughterer was considered unable to die a peaceful death. Shinran reflected on this story by arguing that it is entirely *possible* for a butcher to be saved through Pure Land faith. Here we can see a significant element of Shinran's Pure Land theory, which he would call *akunin-shōki* (literally, the wicked person as the true opportunity).

The notion of *akunin-shōki* matured during Shinran's period of exile, when he became most intimately familiar with the hardships of daily labor that he shared with his neighbors. This cognizance of human weakness and wickedness (one's own and that of others) led him to realize the absolute or eternal truth of the Buddha Amida's Eighteenth Vow, which was explicitly directed toward those whose karmic situation made it impossible for them to reach the place of enlightenment by their own efforts. For Shinran, that karmic situation was in fact shared by everyone living in the degenerate age of *mappō*.

In a *Kyōgyōshinshō* chapter on faith (admittedly one of the most important chapters in *Kyōgyōshinshō*), Shinran reflects and acknowledges the difficulty of overcoming human inclinations, including a propensity for violence and greed. Shinran refers to the Buddha's compassion in this passage:

> When there is sickness among the seven children, although the father and the mother are concerned equally with all of them, nevertheless their hearts lean wholly toward the sick child. Great King, it is like this with the Tathāgata. It is not that there is no equality among all sentient beings, but his heart leans wholly toward the person who has committed evil.[9]

Shinran's work demonstrates carefully argued religious logic largely informed by his views on human nature, including human imperfections. Human nature, prone to weakness and wickedness, exhibits an inability to know Buddhist reality (to be reborn and hence to attain enlightenment) through one's own efforts. In Shinran's thought, this inability became an equalizer among all human beings, regardless of their wealth, social status, education, or heredity.

It would be incorrect to argue that Shinran's reform of Buddhist practice started only during his exile. Exile, however, helped him crystallize certain of his contentions that resulted in some radical changes. Shinran's own experience of exclusion from a monastic community and his refusal to be merely a layman either resulted in the need to reinvent his identity and increased his sensitivity to the issues of inclusion. His firsthand familiarity of exile enlarged his awareness of the arbitrariness of judgments about good and evil and contributed to his amplified compassion for all sentient beings. While he remained committed and devoted to his ideals, this experience further informed his thought and his commitment to ordinary men and women. The ordinary people who followed Shinran's teaching were spared anxiety over salvation and continual rebirth. This angst was alleviated with the relocation of the center of agency to the Buddha Amida.

Jewish Environment

In Jewish tradition, God's intentions encompass the expectation of human righteousness and ethical behavior. The question of fulfilling God's expectation is directly linked to one's religious and ethnic identity. The preservation of religious and ethnic identity arose in biblical times. The Babylonian exile demonstrated the hardships of survival in the conditions of displacement but also demonstrated a number of factors that influenced the successful resistance to the pressures of assimilation and preservation of one's religious and cultural identity.

Preservation of the Jewish tradition was affected by its history of persecution. The history of Jewish displacement influenced the need for counteracting these adverse conditions by further strengthening ethnic and religious identity. From the time of the loss of their native land and their separation from the central institution of the temple, Jewish survival depended on the caprice of local rulers. Subjected to discrimination, expulsion, and massacre, the Jewish people developed a keen sensitivity to danger. As Jews became scattered, the commandments assumed a central role in preserving Jewish existence by giving the Jewish people norms and obligations to follow.

In medieval Muslim Spain, Jews enjoyed a period of relative peacefulness under the rule of the Almoravids (1054–1147), a confederation of Berber tribes. In 1125 the Almohads, rival Berber tribes who advocated the "Unity of Allah," rebelled against the Almoravids in the Atlas Mountains. The fighting between these tribes lasted until 1147 and ended with the victory of the Almohads. By the early 1150s the Almohads had conquered a wide area of North Africa as well as the western portion of Muslim Spain, including Córdoba. By 1160 the Almohads had expanded their control, covering vast territories that included Tunisia and Tripoli. Ten years later the Almohads had completed their conquest of Muslim Spain. By that time the Almohads had forced conversion on all non-Muslims, and previous protection of minority religions (*dhimma* status) was lifted.

Maimonides

Moses Maimonides was born in 1138 in Córdoba, Andalusia, which was then a major Arabic metropolis. When the Almohads conquered Córdoba, the relatively safe Andalusian environment fell apart and Jewish lives dramatically changed. Some information on the treatment of the Jews during this time can be gleaned from a letter written by Maymun b. Yusuf, the father of Maimonides, in 1160: "Overwhelmed with humiliation, blamed and despised, the seeds of captivity surround us and we are submerged in its depth."[10] Unable to live under these conditions, Maimonides' family left Córdoba in 1148. As his family wandered from place to place in Andalusia, Maimonides became an exile and a refugee at an early age. In 1160, Maimonides and his family settled in Fez, Morocco, where they stayed for about five years. In 1166, Maimonides and his family finally came to Fustat (Old Cairo) after a brief stay in Alexandria.

These wanderings from place to place influenced Maimonides' ability to integrate various influences and later were manifested in his intellectual versatility and testified to his "cosmopolitan" nature. Perhaps this ability was enhanced by the fact that, even before his exile, Maimonides' life was embedded in the Islamic culture of Muslim Spain (Andalusia), characterized at that time by a peaceful coexistence of Muslims, Jews, and Christians. Although his ability to adapt to a new environment was developed prior to his final exile in Egypt, his life under Islamic dominance made him well aware of a certain inherent duplicity.

While still wandering from Andalusia and not settled in any permanent place, Maimonides started writing his *Commentary on the Mishnah*. In his conclusion to the *Commentary*, he wrote, "My heart is often burdened by the troubles of the time and what God has decreed for us with regard to exile and wandering the world from one end to another."[11] *Commentary on the Mishnah* was Maimonides' preparatory work for his *Mishneh Torah* (Repetition of the Torah), his major compilation of comprehensive law code.

Maimonides' life significantly improved when he moved to Egypt in 1166. The Fatimid dynasty that ruled Egypt at that time was spared the Almohads' fanaticism. In Fustat, Maimonides became integrated into Egyptian society and involved with the day-to-day life of the Egyptian Jewish community. There the boundary between the Jewish community and the other communities was largely demarcated by the commandments and the requirement to adhere to them. Maimonides did not necessarily translate this legal separation into strict relational boundaries and did not erect any impenetrable boundaries between his existence as a Jewish leader and an Islamic thinker.

Maimonides' participation in public affairs demonstrated his concern with the lives of the Jewish community. For instance, in 1169 he became actively involved in obtaining funds for the Jewish prisoners from Bilbays who had been captured in the Crusades. He sent letters to Jews throughout Egypt asking for contributions to pay out ransom fees demanded by the crusaders for these prisoners. Maimonides' commitment to his community was not limited to writing letters and listing his name as a signatory; he also served as the campaign's treasurer, overseeing the distribution of the obtained funds.

In 1171, Egypt was conquered by the Ayyubids, a Muslim dynasty of Kurdish origin. Shortly after Saladin became sultan over Egypt, Maimonides was elected the head of Egyptian Jewry—*ra'is al-yahud*. Navigating between Jewish and Islamic communities, Maimonides exercised the highest judicial authority by appointing chief judges and having broad communal responsibilities. In addition, he functioned as a respondent to legal inquiries from Jewish communities in Egypt and elsewhere.

Given the political and institutional standing of his position, Maimonides was thrown into a struggle with the dominant and well-established local power.

Here we note a certain resonance with Shinran's situation. While Shinran voiced his objections in terms of embracing a different approach to religious practices, Maimonides also did not always go along with the rules of the prevailing establishment. A case in point is his refusal to collect funds for the support of halakhic scholars.[12] Perhaps this explains why, despite Maimonides' integration into the society and his role as *ra'is al-yahud*, he held that position for only two years, from 1171 to 1172. He did not regain the position until later in his life, serving from 1196 to 1204.[13]

In Egypt, Maimonides' commitment to the Andalusian halakhic tradition remained firm. This commitment was tested between 1189 and 1191 when Maimonides argued against some of the prevailing views held by the Babylonian geonim—presidents of the Babylonian Talmudic Academies. A head of the yeshiva in Baghdad, Samuel ben Eli, did all in his power to discredit Maimonides' rulings by ruling himself that it was permissible to sail on the Sabbath in the Euphrates and the Tigris. A parallel can be seen in Maimonides' commitment to those whom he considered his Andalusian "teachers" and Shinran's loyalty to Hōnen. In both cases, an approach chosen by these two thinkers respectively was not in line with the prevailing view of those in power.

While Shinran directly acknowledges his debt to "seven patriarchs," Maimonides' debt to his predecessors appears to be less straightforward and depends on whether the debt is related to his halakhic works or to his philosophical writings. He acknowledges that his thought was influenced by Aristotle, though read through the eyes of Alexander, Themistius, and Ibn Rushd (1126–1198). He articulates his reverence for these thinkers in *Eight Chapters*, his introduction to *Commentary on Tractate Avot*.[14]

Naming Aristotle (or those who explicated his writings) would have been dangerously unprecedented, but even the reference to the "ancient and modern philosophers" as a guide for his explanation of the commandments was already revolutionary. Maimonides further challenges authority by adding, "Hear the truth from whoever says it."[15] It is truth that matters, not whether it comes from the mouth of a given sage. Holding his "teachers" in high esteem does not translate into Maimonides' complete agreement with their views. In analogy, but also in contrast, with Shinran—who interpreted (or in some cases translated) the words of his "seven patriarchs" in a slightly different vein than intended by them—Maimonides offered his own objections to some of the views of the sages as well as the views of those whom he called his teachers, highlighting his ability to think beyond what was already accepted.

Similarly to the writings of Shinran, in which he further democratized and radicalized Hōnen's teachings, Maimonides' writings exhibit certain "heretical" features. Nonetheless, even those writings, which were infused with a highly provocative perspective, never strove to undermine but, rather, empathically focused on ensuring the preservation of Judaism and the Jewish people.

Like Shinran, Maimonides espoused certain opinions that contradicted established norms. He explicitly and implicitly challenged the conventional understanding of Judaism. Similarly to Shinran, Maimonides did not have any institutional support that could have helped legitimize the transformations he envisioned. Neither did Maimonides claim any divine inspiration, nor, contrary to Shinran, did he back up his claim by referring to the thinkers before him. In his introduction to the third part of his philosophical magnum opus entitled *The Guide of the Perplexed*, Maimonides writes: "I followed conjecture and supposition; no divine revelation has come to me to teach me that the intention in the matter in question was such and such, nor did I receive what I believe in these matters from a teacher."[16]

Maimonides' possession of a heretical streak should not be mistaken for an intention to undermine the centrality and the significance of the commandments. While he recognized that complete adherence at times might not be feasible, he considered following the commandments as being imperative to preserving Jewish heritage. The possible inability for a complete devotion to the commandments necessitated certain creative reinterpretations. Maimonides was acutely aware of the contradictions and stipulations that originated from the conditions of exilic life. His *Mishneh Torah* was, in effect, an instrument of sustainability of one's existence in exile. By contextualizing specificity of the conditions and putting *Mishneh Torah* into language accessible to everyone, he converted it into a mechanism central to the construction of a viable diaspora. Maimonides transformed the Talmudic elliptic style, with its variety of overlapping arguments, into comprehensible material and a functional tool for continual survival.

Maimonides' approach to intolerable conditions and imposed conversion can be gleaned from some of his direct thoughts in his "Letter on Forced Conversions" (Iggeret ha-Shemad).[17] In this letter he privileges human life and states that the only clear case in which the Jew should die rather than transgress is when he or she is under condition of being forced to violate the commandments that prohibit idolatry, adultery, and murder. Maimonides asserts that, in other cases, the Jew must take into account the purpose for which the transgression is being forced upon him or her and whether the transgression will occur in private or in public. Maimonides makes a clear distinction between the matters of the heart (inner feelings) and outer exhibitions (any actions that one is required to perform in order to survive). He exhibits a high sense of tolerance when he advises Jews to confess the Islamic creed rather than die. Yet when Jews are forced to transgress, they should do it to the smallest extent possible and aim to leave that place as soon as it becomes possible.

In this letter Maimonides combines an allowance for compromise (to ensure survival) with an argument against complacency. Despite his empathic approach, Maimonides transcends the immediacy of suffering and provides a nuanced perspective. Typical of his style, Maimonides does not aim to offer clear guidelines for acting under duress; on the one hand, he shows leniency; on the other, he encourages Jews not to stay in the environment that is conducive to coercion. He combines his love for the Jewish people and anxiety for their personal safety with his concern for the Jewish community's continual existence.

Maimonides' *Epistle to Yemen*, written in 1172, is a further testimony to his commitment to the Jewish community. He concludes this epistle by noting that despite having concerns about his own safety after making his views public, he is convinced that "the public welfare takes precedence over one's personal safety."[18] Maimonides' diasporic personality is that of a person who shared the fate of those to whom he addressed his writings, which provides him with language that speaks directly to his audience.

Throughout his life in Egypt, Maimonides always considered himself an Andalusian. despite being displaced from Andalusia. His life in exile, as his writings demonstrate, was dedicated to preserving Judaism, to "save the Jewish world from the halakhic and spiritual ruin he had experienced.[19] His goal, however, was never to claim the impossibility of coexistence with other traditions; rather, he believed in that coexistence with the distinct particularities remaining intact.

Empathy

Recalling that I suggested that exile is conducive to the increased ability for empathy, I turn now to empathy as an important concept in relation to our capacity to gain a grasp of the content of other people's minds. It also has been seen as important in relation to our faculty to identify with others and to respond to them in an ethically appropriate way. I focus here on empathy as understood by Edith Stein (1891–1942), a student of Edmund Husserl (1859–1938). In her 1916 doctorate on empathy, Stein addressed not only what empathy means but also its problematic character. While she follows Husserl that empathy is "the basis of intersubjective experience" and "the condition of possible knowledge of the existing outer world," she emphasizes the embodiment of empathy by pointing out "the expressive dimensions of bodily movement and of speech."[20] Stein argues that empathy is "the experience of foreign consciousness in general, irrespective of the kind of the experiencing subject or of the subject whose consciousness is experienced."[21] In her view, empathy is a shift of intentional focus to the recipient's viewpoint without loss of self-awareness. Emphasizing the intersubjective and relational dimensions of empathy allows one to understand others but also to increase one's self-understanding.

In some cases, empathy becomes affected by emotional contagion or emotional infection. Precisely because there is the danger of confusing empathy with emotional contagion or emotional infection, it is important to keep in mind the significance of the differentiation between self and other. Emotional contagion is a process that is relatively unreflective, unintentional, and hence largely inaccessible to one's awareness. It is usually driven by a self-oriented perspective and results in one's assessing the other according to one's own perceptions. A self-oriented perspective errs on the side of misrecognizing that in actuality one's own response to a set of circumstances is rarely an indication of another's reaction. In actuality, self-oriented perspective leads to personal distress when, by seeing everything as related to self, one loses track of the fact that the experience is actually someone else's, not one's own. Empathic distress in effect nullifies empathy to the other because all attention becomes focused on the self, and the focus is now placed on the means to alleviate one's own pain and discomfort.

Because of its self-oriented perspective, empathy is more likely to extend to kin group members than to strangers from another land or tribe. Being in exile limits this self-oriented perspective because, as Adorno expressed, exilic conditions are characterized as "an incomprehensible" and one might be less tempted to project one's own experience as universally applicable to everyone.

In her discussion of empathy, Stein differentiates between our experience of our own pain as a primordial, or firsthand, experience and our experience of another's pain as nonprimordial, or secondhand, experience. However, she argues that the *awareness* of the pain of others is primordial for us. For Stein, empathy is an "embodied experience" rather than merely abstract or theoretical. I suggest that exile provides the embodied experience conducive to an enhanced sense of empathy.

In her later works, Stein posits that individual consciousness can be understood only as a result of external impacts and influences, and she places much more emphasis on the importance and impacts of one's community.[22] She develops an account of social acts as "a third form of social relation" in which social acts are intermediary between empathy and collective intentionality. Mutual communication among human beings is the means of establishing communities that are characterized by the integration of the individuals on the basis of the cognitive, the intentional, the normative, and the phenomenological dimensions. These dimensions cannot be considered in isolation from each other but, rather, must be considered in relation to one another. According to Stein, humanity is "one great individual,"[23] and community its best representation.

I suggest that exile further sensitizes one's sense of empathy to extend beyond the familiar without reducing the identification with the members of one's own group. From a Buddhist viewpoint, however, empathy might be a natural state of being with others. If we take into account the Buddhist concept of interrelatedness, we recognize that each self is embedded in a sharing meaning with others. In this case, exile reinforces the sense of empathy by bringing an increased awareness of life's travails.

What is the relation between empathy and ethics? According to Hume, our empathic feelings toward someone affect our judgment of one's actions and provoke our desire for justice. Empathy is instrumental for the development of our capacity to make moral judgments by increasing our sensitivity to moral rules and the ideals of justice. Exile can be a means of familiarizing oneself with diverse and distant cultural and religious groups and developing "a broader and more consistent capacity to empathize."[24] Invoking Adorno again, I recall his words that "it is part of morality not to be at home in one's home,"[25] and exile certainly increases the likelihood of not being "at home in one's home." Empathy is a measure of genuine ethical concern. However, empathy is not a condition for ethical response but a *possibility* for it. In other words, empathy increases potentiality for an ethical involvement. This ethical involvement in the case of Shinran and Maimonides may be observed through some of the themes addressed in their writings.

Michael Slote argues that empathy provides the "cement of the moral universe" and foregrounds moral approval.[26] Reflecting on the notion that empathy can be a means of moral approval, we should not go so far as to suggest that the writings of Shinran and Maimonides exhibit moral approval; rather, they exhibit the absence of moral *disapproval*. Their respective exilic conditions enabled them to distinguish between self and other without assessing this distinction in any moralistic terms. For Shinran this is observed in his conceptualization of *akunin-shōki*, whereas for Maimonides it is exemplified in his articulation of the approach to conversion. In addition, their need to reinvent their own identities resulted in an empathic understanding of the complexity of the identities and ethical needs of others.

With this in mind, I suggest that Shinran's and Maimonides' writings demonstrate that exile heightened their sense of empathy and as a result further sensitized their respective approaches to ethics. Their writings implicitly exhibit the key components of empathy, and their approach intertwines affect and cognition rather than building only on either one of these components of empathy. As Lawrence Hatab has observed, empathy is "a mode of disclosure that generates ethical import."[27] For Shinran and Maimonides, this mode of disclosure is in their writings.

Empathy is one of the significant concepts that served both Shinran and Maimonides as a means for their empathic identification with their newly acquired communities. Some of Maimonides' writings demonstrate that a sense of empathy is his ability, in Stein's terms, to "enter the foreign consciousness" affected by his own experience of displacement. That ability, while enhanced by his sense of duty to his own community, is intensified also by his appreciation and respect for the other. Like Maimonides' writings, Shinran's teachings are testimony to his own empathy.

Exile as "Place" for Empathy

Despite their differences, Shinran's and Maimonides' tolerance and empathy arose, not only from their intellectual musings, but also from their need to contend with these issues personally. It is their respective exiles that provided them with a "place" for empathy but also allowed them to show resolve rather than capitulation of their values and to challenge a perception of powerlessness and fearfulness often associated with those who are placed in adverse or unfamiliar conditions. In some instances, their capacity for empathy enhanced their ability to compromise without sacrificing their values. Their respective conditions of exile allowed them to develop empathic feelings, not only toward the people who shared their immediate experiences or to the members of their own community, but also toward the people who shared the experiences of life's hardships. To say that their experience of exile attuned their sense of empathy only for those who were like them is to limit empathy to empathy contagion and to see them as exercising a self-oriented perspective. The idea of emotional identification cannot be reduced to the narrowly conceived similarity in one's experience. Emotional identification in their case reflects their nuanced approach to what can be considered morally acceptable.

However, we should not reduce their approaches to mere similarities, and we should be careful not to overlook differences that inform their views. Their focus on empathy for human beings carries differing undertones. Shinran, driven by a sense of compassion that became heightened by his exilic conditions, advanced teachings that included acceptance of the disenfranchised and the disadvantaged. He emphasized overcoming life's problems from within oneself, viewing the world of *mappō* as fundamentally "unsaveable." This approach remains within the parameters of traditional Buddhism.

Shinran's focus on the individual rather than on social transformation contrasts with Maimonides' approach. Maimonides stressed the communal, social, and political commitments related to the covenantal (obligatory and promissory) relationships that typify Judaism. To claim, however, that Maimonides was concerned with the survival of the community at the expense of the individual would be incorrect. His emphasis on the commandments as the underlying ethical system testifies to his commitment to Judaism but also to his concern for the community's preservation. Yet, out of his sense of empathy, he is capable of taking into account any extenuating circumstances that might require an adjusted approach.

Exile heightened Maimonides' sense of empathy, coupled with his concern for justice and ethics. As a leader of the Jewish community and a liaison between that community and the Muslim rulers, Maimonides was acutely aware of the intricacies involved in this setting. Despite his ability to learn from and appreciate an unfamiliar environment, his own experience of exile made him intensely mindful of the dangers of being swallowed by a surrounding alien culture, and it strengthened his aspirations for the preservation of the community and its traditions. In some cases his ideas involved disagreement with other members of the Jewish community, but more often than not those ideas encompassed critical awareness of the dangers of outside forces.

While Shinran was not embedded in a similarly complex and conflictual environment that required balancing between different cultural and religious systems of thought, his firsthand experience of being exposed to the corruption of the ruling powers (shogunate) and also to the complacency of the monastic community similarly augmented his sense of ethical compassion. His exposure to his own culture's inadequacies heightened his empathy for ordinary folks whose lives were directly affected by these failings. Although he was not faced with the loss of Buddhism per se (contrary to Maimonides' concern that Judaism might become absorbed into Islam), he was critical of the prevailing Tendai system of thought and was convinced that the True Pure Land tradition was more inclusive and accepting of all beings. At the core of the thought of these two men was a similar concern with the well-being of humans.

Shinran's exile, unlike that of Maimonides, did not result in aspirations and concerns of retaining a distinct theological community but pointed to his hope of transforming and democratizing the prevailing Tendai tradition. If viewed superficially, his take on adherence to a tradition can seem diametrically opposed to that of Maimonides. Yet this is not completely accurate, because Shinran aimed not to get rid of the Tendai tradition, which in itself incorporated some ideas of Pure Land thoughts, but to further strengthen this thought within the existing tradition by challenging its status quo. His implicit desire to transform the tradition does resemble Maimonides' service to his coreligionists when he is similarly willing to challenge the existing state of affairs. However, it would be misleading to claim that his concerns for his fellow human beings included a direct call for any reformation of the political structure, which is absent in Maimonides' thought as well. Like Maimonides, Shinran was personally aware of the political repercussions of challenging the prevailing religious system. An expectation for ethical treatment was inherently linked to concern for inclusion but also to concerns for safety and the provision of unthreatening and humane conditions.

The thought of Shinran and Maimonides, two exceptional men who, even in conditions of adversity, were capable of focusing on larger concerns for others, reminds us that empathy and tolerance are notions that will never become obsolete. The cultivation of these qualities will always be imperative to humanity's well-being. Exile teaches us to look empathically beyond our own group by warning us that "within an embrace of particularity lies the danger of tribalism, where a myopic fixation on one's own group can obscure or cancel out the dignity and humanity of other groups."[28] This is not to say that one's cultural and religious heritage is to be forsaken and replaced but to say that one's culture has a finite presence capable of accepting other cultures. Shinran and Maimonides in their exile were directly exposed to the other, which taught them empathy and acceptance of difference.

NOTES

1. See Jo-Marie Claassen, *Displaced Persons: The Literature of Exile from Cicero to Boethius* (Madison: University of Wisconsin Press, 1999).

2. Theodor Adorno, *Minima Moralia: Reflections on a Damaged Life* (Brooklyn, NY: Verso, 2006), 87.

3. James W. Heisig, Thomas P. Kasulis, and John C. Maraldo, eds., *Japanese Philosophy: A Sourcebook* (Honolulu: University of Hawai'i Press, 2011), 238.

4. Hōnen founded Jōdo Shinshū in 1175. Shinran became his disciple in 1201.

5. Shinran, *The Collected Works of Shinran* (hereafter cited as CWS) (Kyoto: Jōdo Shinshū Hongwanji-Ha, 1997), 1:289.

6. CWS, 2:206.

7. See Ronald W. Neufeldt, ed., *Karma and Rebirth: Post Classical Developments* (New York: State University of New York Press, 1986).

8. Heisig et al., *Japanese Philosophy*, 239.

9. CWS, 1:133.

10. Norman Roth, *Jews, Visigoths and Muslims in Medieval Spain: Cooperation and Conflict* (Leiden: Brill, 1994), 119.

11. Moshe Halbertal notes that these words were written in Maimonides' *Commentary on the Mishnah*, conclusion to *Seder Taharot* [Laws of purity]. See Moshe Halbertal, *Maimonides: Life and Thought* (Princeton, NJ: Princeton University Press, 2014).

12. Halbertal, *Maimonides*, 43–47.

13. See Martin Gilbert, *In Ishmael's House: A History of Jews in Muslim Lands* (New Haven, CT: Yale University Press, 2010).

14. Moses Maimonides, *Eight Chapters*, in *Ethical Writings of Maimonides*, ed. Raymond L. Weiss with Charles Butterworth (New York: Dover, 1975), 60.

15. Ibid.

16. Moses Maimonides, *The Guide of the Perplexed*, trans. Shlomo Pines (Chicago: University of Chicago Press, 1963), 2:416.

17. Moses Maimonides, "The Epistle on Martyrdom," in *Crisis and Leadership: Epistles of Maimonides*, texts translated and notes by Abraham S. Halkin, discussions by David Hartman (Philadelphia: Jewish Publication Society of America, 1985), 24–25.

18. Moses Maimonides, "The Epistle to Yemen," in *Crisis and Leadership*, 131.

19. Halbertal, *Maimonides*, 23.

20. Alasdair MacIntyre, *Edith Stein: A Philosophical Prologue, 1913–1922* (New York: Rowman and Littlefield, 2006), 84.

21. Edith Stein, "On the Problem of Empathy," in *The Collected Works of Edith Stein, Sister Teresa Benedicta of Cross, Discalced Carmelite* (Washington, DC: ICS Publications, 1989), 3:11.

22. See Edith Stein, *Philosophy of Psychology and Humanities*, trans. Mary Catherine Baseheart and Marianne Sawicki (Washington, DC: ICS Publications, 2000).

23. Edith Stein, *Finite and Eternal Being: An Attempt at an Ascent to the Meaning of Being*, trans. Kurt F. Reinhardt (Washington, DC: ICS Publications, 2002), 507.

24. Lawrence J. Hatab, *Ethics and Finitude: Heideggerian Contributions to Moral Philosophy* (Boston: Rowman and Littlefield, 2000), 263.

25. Adorno, *Minima Moralia*, 87.

26. Michael Slote, *Moral Sentimentalism* (Oxford: Oxford University Press, 2010), 13.

27. Hatab, *Ethics and Finitude*, 150.

28. Ibid., 203.

Sprouts, Mountains, and Fields   16

SYMBOL AND SUSTAINABILITY IN MENGZI'S MORAL PSYCHOLOGY

Carl Helsing

故苟得其養, 無物不長; 苟失其養, 無物不消.
Hence, given the right nourishment there is nothing that will not grow,
and deprived of it there is nothing that will not wither away.

—Mencius

Mengzi scholarship widely agrees on the central importance of the heart of compassion (惻隱之心 *cèyǐn zhī xīn*) and the four seeds (四端 *sì duān*) in Mengzi's moral psychology.[1] These concepts serve as the basis for Mengzi's arguments concerning the goodness of human nature and help define his thought in contrast to that of other classical Chinese thinkers. Despite the wide agreement regarding the importance of the heart of compassion and the four seeds, important differences exist in scholarship regarding exactly how human emotion functions in Mengzi.[2] This chapter builds on these previous investigations while also providing an alternate interpretation of Mengzi's moral psychology: I view the image of the seed (端 *duān*) as a key metaphor that structures Mengzi's understanding of emotion. The image of the seed is not simply an image but provides a technical and systematic understanding of emotional-moral experience.[3] In the first part of this chapter, I discuss the image of the seed, its components as a metaphor, and its relationship to moral behavior. I demonstrate how the metaphor structures emotional experience and how this structure then functions in the image of Ox Mountain. I then examine how Mengzi nourishes the heart of compassion and I raise three mechanisms for guiding emotional response.[4]

In the second half of the chapter, I use Mengzi's model of moral psychology to discuss how healthy emotional activity depends on two important factors: a healthy social environment and a sustainable material environment. I demonstrate how Mengzi relates healthy emotional development to a healthy social environment, and how a healthy social environment depends on a sustainable relationship between human society and natural resources. I show how the well-field system integrates these concerns, providing the necessary material conditions for nurturing human relations while maintaining sustainable material consumption. In Mengzi's view, I argue, a healthy human society requires a nourishing yet sustainable relationship with adequate material resources. A healthy social atmosphere, in turn, helps nourish the seeds of human compassion. This view of moral psychology extends beyond previous inquiries by discussing the relationship of human emotion with material conditions and sustainability. This develops our understanding of Mengzi's philosophy and expands the idea of moral psychology in general.

Mengzi's Moral Psychology

Mengzi's view of human nature is most famously stated in 6A1, in the course of his debates with the philosopher Gaozi. Mengzi regards human nature as "good" because human nature has a tendency toward becoming good. His word choice here is important: *shàn* (善) means "good" but with the connotation of "friendly," "gentle," or "well-intentioned." This concept of good is not connected to concepts of metaphysical or ontological good: it is a concept of good based in human interaction and human relationships. Being good is understood in terms of how we relate to other people and how we treat them.

In terms of becoming good, all persons possess four important emotional "hearts" (心 *xīn*) that lead to moral behavior:

> The heart of compassion, all people have it. The heart of shame, all people have it. The heart of reverence and respect, all people have it. The heart of right and wrong, all people have it. The heart of compassion [leads to] benevolence; the heart of shame [leads to] rightness. The heart of reverence [leads to] ritual. The heart of right and wrong [leads to] wisdom. Benevolence, rightness, ritual propriety, and wisdom are not welded to us from outside, we firmly have them, we [simply] do not think![5]

Mengzi explicitly indicates four specific principles or impulses that are key to emotional-moral development: compassion, shame, respect, and a sense of right and wrong.[6] As implied by the passage, these four emotional responses must be cultivated and nourished in order to manifest moral behavior: the heart of compassion results in the expression of benevolence; the heart of shame results in performance of duty; the heart of respect results in ritual observance; and the heart of right and wrong leads to wisdom.

In a crucial parallel passage (2A6), Mengzi refers to these four qualities as seeds or sprouts (端 *duān*):

> The heart of compassion is the seed of benevolence; the heart of shame is the seed of rightness; the heart of courtesy is the seed of ritual; the heart of right and wrong is the seed of wisdom. People have these four seeds just as they have four limbs.

This term *duān* is complex. As an adjective it can mean "upright"; as a noun it can mean "end," "tip," or "cause"; and as a verb it can mean "to hold level."

In this passage it can be translated as seed, seedling, sprout, or principle. The etymology suggests something standing upright like a growing plant that has a sprout-like beginning and a process of fruition. This image provides a beautiful suggestion for Mengzi's process of emotional-moral development: emotional feelings emerge outward into the world and grow into moral activity, in the same manner as a seedling develops into a fully grown plant. I suggest that this image—of the growing seed or sprout—is a key metaphor in the text that organizes Mengzi's understanding of emotion in multiple spheres of human activity.

Mengzi's discussion with Gongsun Chou in 2A6 provides more precise detail of the emotional-moral process. Mengzi states that "all people have a heart [that does] not endure the suffering [of other] people." He illustrates this claim in 2A6 with the image of the child about to fall into a well. Mengzi states that at such a sight any person will have "a heart of fear, distress, and compassion" (怵惕惻隱之心 *chù tì cè yǐ zhī xīn*). This is a complex combination of feelings but might be expressed as "feelings of fear, distress, and compassion." From the passage, it appears that these feelings occur simultaneously, which is important for our understanding of how emotion shapes experience.

First, the emotional experience arises as part of our general experience and is inseparable from our experience. This helps explain Mengzi's claim in 6A1 that morality is an "internal" part of human nature. This does not mean that moral knowledge is innate; rather, it means we are born with emotional capacities that function within our living environments.[7] This does not mean our morality is externally determined by our environment; it means our moral actions emerge as responses to emotions generated within an environmental context. Second, the terminology for "suffering" is *rěn* 忍, which very strongly relates to emotional suffering. The character is composed of a knife above a heart and is used frequently to describe situations of emotional distress or emotional burdens. So Mengzi here is stating that no person has a heart that actively seeks to witness the emotional suffering or distress of others.

These two points suggest a strong place for the role of empathy in learning to develop healthy emotional response. Mengzi in fact uses the term *cè yìn* 惻隱, which has dual meanings of "anguish" and "compassion." These two meanings indicate the central role played by empathy and suggest a tentative model: an empathetic feeling of emotional distress occurs in response to the emotional suffering of others, and this can lead to benevolent action. Thus, the person feeling distress about the child falling into the well does not require moral calculus or more complex moral reasons for action: the feeling of distress is sufficient reason to act.

This supports Mengzi's basic claim regarding compassion and benevolence: empathetic experiences of suffering can lead to expressions of benevolent action. The heart of compassion responds to suffering by creating an empathetic feeling of suffering. This empathetic feeling of suffering provides the basis for further action, which must be expressed outwardly and brought to completion in the form of successful action. We see support for this process in the imagery of 2A6, where Mengzi states:

> All people have these four seeds in themselves; know/understand everyone can expand and then fill them! Like a fire beginning to burn, or a flowing spring. If they can fulfil this, it will be sufficient to protect the four quarters. If they cannot fulfil this, it is not possible even to serve their parents.

Mengzi uses two terms, expansion (擴 *kuò*) and fulfilment (充 *chōng*), that continue the analogical relationship between natural development and emotional expression. The term *kuò* 擴 means "expand, enlarge, stretch," and *chōng* 充 means "fill, be full, supply." The image of the fire corresponds to the initial feeling of an emotional impulse; the seed, or root, of the impulse ignites, and then we have the capacity to respond to this impulse; the image of water corresponds to the spreading of an emotional impulse into a fully grown moral expression. These images reinforce the idea that, for Mengzi, morality is a combination of emotional impulse followed by proper action.

This process results in what we might regard as a model of emotional-moral expression: moral behavior is a combination of certain emotional impulses and their resultant beneficial behaviors.[8] An empathetic feeling of compassion occurs in response to the experience of suffering. This causes a desire or motion to "resolve" the situation, which in turn leads to benevolent actions. Mencius does not specify exact criteria for what counts as benevolence, but he often describes benevolence in terms of sharing material resources, clothing the elderly, feeding the young, and protecting those in need. The action is considered successful or fully extended when it adequately resolves the situation.[9]

Benevolence is both pragmatic and ideal: in the moment of crisis the benevolent action functions pragmatically to alleviate the problem of suffering. Benevolence is also a moral ideal in the sense that it is understood as the desirable or ideal manner of resolving human suffering. And for Mengzi it is also natural, for the empathetic feeling of suffering prompts the moral agent to act compassionately with benevolence.

Ox Mountain and Nourishing Emotion

How does this theory of moral-emotional expression correlate with Mengzi's discussions of emotional development? We can consider the image of Ox Mountain and the parallels between the sprouts and trees of the mountain and the human emotions necessary for moral behavior. Mengzi invokes the image of Ox Mountain to help defend his position against Gaozi regarding the good-ness of human nature, but the image also presents parallels between emotional development and agricultural sustainability:

> The trees of Ox Mountain were once beautiful. [But] because they were next to a large country, axes and hatchets cut them down. How could they become beautiful? With their daily and nightly resting place, with the moisture of the rain and dew, they were not without the births of little sprouts [萌 *méng*]. But ox and sheep followed and [grazed] on them. That is why it is eroded [washed out] there. People see it is eroded and think it never had timber. Is this what the nature of the mountain is like?[10]

This metaphor is then used for a direct comparison with the nature of human moral expression: just as a bare mountain is mistakenly thought to lack any vegetation, the human heart devoid of emotional expression can be mistak-enly thought to lack any benevolence and rightness. Mengzi explicitly regards damaging the human heart-mind as a process similar to overfarming the trees on the mountain:

> And so for those who are living, how can they be without the heart of compassion and rightness? The manner of one who loses one's virtuous heart is the same as the axes cutting on the trees: [after] day after day [of] being cut, how can it [the mind] become beautiful?[11]

If we view the shoots and sprouts of vegetation on the mountain as analo-gous to the four hearts or seeds of human emotion, this analogy suggests that we give special attention to caring for our emotional impulses and nurturing their healthy expression. If we live in an environment where our emotional impulses are constantly attacked, cut short, or otherwise responded to with hos-tility, how can those same moral impulses develop into expressions of benevo-lence? The implication here is clear: if we do not allow our emotional responses to develop in a healthy environment, then we risk creating an environment devoid of benevolence (仁 *rén*) and rightness (義 *yì*). Fully manifested actions of benevolence and righteousness would be analogous to the fully grown trees on Ox Mountain.

This view also suggests that we should be particularly concerned with devel-oping nonviolent methods of emotional regulation. The images of chopping and cutting are directly analogous to "cutting short" the emotional expressions of benevolence and rightness, which perpetuates a cycle of inhibiting empathy and the expression of empathy. Benevolent action, as a natural outgrowth of an empathetic impulse of suffering, cannot be forced. The text reveals this in the cautionary tale about a man from Song:

> Do not be like the man from Song. There was a man from Song who grieved because his [corn] sprouts were not long, so he pulled them up. [Making them]

like bristled grass, [he] returned home. Speaking to his people, he said: "Today I feel tired, I helped the corn grow long." His son hurried and left to inspect it, but the sprouts were all withered and dead. There are few under heaven who do not [try to] help their sprouts grow long. There are [also] those who believe it without profit, they do not weed their crops. Those who help it grow long, they pull up (and wipe out) the plants. Not only is following this without any advantage, but it also kills them![12]

This concern regarding force echoes Mengzi's earlier debate with Gaozi in 6A1 regarding human nature. Mengzi explicitly rejects Gaozi's notion that morality is a process of forcing conformity with external standards. Gaozi claims that moral cultivation is analogous to shaping cups and bowls from the wood of the willow tree: human nature must be shaped into benevolence just as wood must be carved and shaped into cups and bowls. Mengzi views this approach as damaging to human nature and to morality. This position echoes concerns voiced by Confucius in *Analects* 2.2:

> Lead the people with administrative injunctions and keep them orderly with penal law, and they will avoid punishments but will be without a sense of shame. Lead them with excellence and keep them orderly through observing ritual propriety and they will develop a sense of shame, and moreover, will order themselves.[13]

In this light, attempting to force human behavior to conform to standards of benevolence will instill resentment and distrust, simply by trying to forcefully shape human behavior. Perceived violence will also inhibit the heart of compassion; the application of force creates emotional resistance to empathy; the application of violence or force directly inhibits the ability to feel compassion or empathy for others.

Emotion and Cognition: Guiding Emotional Growth

Knowing how force and violence affect the heart of compassion raises a serious question: How do we encourage empathy? In 6A7, Mengzi suggests that differences in human behavior may result from trapping or submerging the heart-mind (其所以陷溺其心者然也 *qí suǒ yǐ xiàn nì qí xīn zhě rán yě*). In terms of our discussion here, this means when the heart-mind is suppressed or ensnared by other desires, its ability to respond empathetically to the suffering of others is diminished. Other interests or targets of desire distract the heart-mind and prevent it from extending benevolence. Mengzi states:

> Benevolence is the heart of [being] human, righteousness is the path of [being] human. The road is his dwelling but he does not bring it about, [he] loses his heart but he does not seek it, how sad! People lose their chickens or dogs [and] they know to seek them! Lose their heart [and] they do not know to look for it.

The path of learning and questioning is nothing else, to seek the lost heart and be cured![14]

This passage suggests that empathy can be encouraged in part by leaving space for empathy. It is equally important that moral agents, especially those in positions of power, place themselves in situations where they can be exposed to the suffering of others. Mengzi implies this in his conversations with King Xuan in 1A7. When the king responds to the sight of an ox about to be sacrificed, he experiences distress and compassionately spares the animal. He offers a sheep in its stead, but he refuses to see the sheep prior to the sacrifice. Mengzi claims that King Xuan must extend his benevolence to the people. Mengzi cites the example of King Wen, who practiced benevolence toward his family and successfully extended benevolent actions toward his kingdom. In 1B4, Mengzi also calls for kings to conduct the "Tour of Inspection" and the "Report on Duties." These imperial rituals require the king to tour the lands to inspect the population and understand the state of affairs in the kingdom. I suggest that Mengzi raises these rituals at least in part to bring the ruler into greater contact with the subjects. Doing so increases the likelihood that the ruler will experience an empathetic response to the suffering of the people, which helps the ruler extend benevolent action to the people.

This example raises related questions: How do we guide or direct our benevolent actions? How do we use our capacity for reason in conjunction with our emotions? Mengzi states that every heart-mind shares a capacity for reason (理 *lǐ*) and rightness (義 *yì*). Reason and rightness present two modes of reflective or cognitive activity that can assist emotional development. A third mechanism occurs in the form of the heart of affirmation and negation (是/非 *shì/fēi*).

The idea of reason (*lǐ*) can be understood as logic, measurement, or correct arrangement. In this sense it may be a means of guiding emotional response. Benevolent actions may at times be simple in nature, as with the direct response to the distress of the child or the sacrificial animal, but at times benevolence will require understanding complex situations. This is certainly the case as Mengzi describes the various tasks related to benevolent rule: benevolent governance requires proper management of natural resources, understanding crop cycles, knowing proper court procedure, managing official pay, and even knowing the correct method for a ruler to issue a summons to court. Reason means we can know how much is too much and how little is too little. We can set boundaries, make limits, and draw comparisons. We can judge how far or fast we need to run to save the child from falling into the well. We can measure the fields necessary to produce sufficient grain to feed the elderly and the young. Reason occurs not in isolation but in conjunction with the emotional processes that push life forward.

The idea of rightness (*yì*) has its origin in the correct performance of ritual action: the image depicts a figure approaching the ritual sheep with a ceremonial knife.[15] In a broader sense rightness is both the knowledge of what is correct and the capacity for acting in a correct manner. It is both the moral norms and the performance of those norms. This means rightness may be more or less in the forefront as the situation demands: saving the child from the well may involve less reflective thinking about what is right, but it certainly involves acting in a manner regarded as correct. Conversely, appropriate land management involves both extensive knowledge of what is thought to be correct as well as the capacity to practice those ideals or standards. In either case our ideals function in conjunction with our capacity for reason. We can aim toward ideal images, we can discuss our ideals, and we can examine our attempts to reach them. We can recognize better and worse ways of doing things. Reason and rightness combine pragmatic actions with meaningful ideals. Both help us embody those ideals through meaningful action. Both function to support the healthy development of human relationships.

Mengzi also claims all hearts share a capacity for *shì/fēi* (right and wrong, or so and not-so). According to Mengzi, the heart or seeds of "right and wrong" lead to wisdom. Mengzi does not elaborate on the topic of *shì/fēi*, but I suggest that his inclusion of *shì/fēi* as one of the four hearts or seeds may point to a complex combination of emotional and cognitive activity. We find affirmations of "right" pleasing and the presence of "wrong" displeasing. We regard things as correct or incorrect. Our collected impressions of right and wrong compound over time with experience and eventually resolve into cognitive maps or frameworks that help us understand experience. This does not mean that knowledge is merely emotional or that meaning is simply emotive. It means that our feelings about rightness and wrongness inform our interpretations of information and our moral norms. These phenomena point to an emotional component of knowledge, but they also point to a cognitive element of emotion.

Mengzi's ideal of sagely emotional-moral development culminates in "the heart that cannot be stirred" (2A2). This ideal refers to the particular ability of the sage to maintain constant benevolence even in the face of malnourishing conditions. The sage does not waver from the path of benevolence but harnesses all his or her energy for the sake of completing benevolent activity. A heart that cannot be stirred does not mean a heart that lacks emotional activity. A heart that cannot be stirred means a heart that cannot be misdirected from fulfilling benevolence—that is, a heart that is not distracted by petty concerns or by unhealthy objectives. This means exercising care toward oneself and others so as to sustain one's energies and not damage one's capacity for empathy and benevolence. Doing so ultimately culminates in the ideal of flood-like *qi*:

This is spirit [*qi*]: it is very great, it is very strong. Being nourished by what is right while [being] without harm or injury, it fills up the idle [spaces] between heaven and earth. This is spirit: it blends with rightness and the Way; without it there is hunger. It is such that it gathers with a life of rightness; it is not the righteousness of attacking and conquering. If there is no contentment in the heart, there is starvation.[16]

Mengzi and Environmental Psychology

Now I will examine Mengzi's discussions of land management and consider how they relate to our model of emotional-moral expression. I suggest that Mengzi's proposals work toward creating a sustainable, flexible model of human society. Mengzi seeks to balance the material and emotional needs of a population with the sustainability of the local agricultural system. His proposals for land usage and land management function as regulatory mechanisms that help sustain a kind of homeostasis between human society and the surrounding environment. Consider the following passage regarding the kingly way:

Do not violate the farming seasons [and] there will be more crops than can be successfully eaten; do not [put] numerous nets in the still waters [and] there will be more fish and turtles than can be successfully eaten; use the axes and hatchets in the forests in the right seasons [and] there will be more lumber than can be successfully used. If the crops, fish, and turtles cannot all be successfully consumed [if they cannot be overeaten], if the lumber cannot all be successfully used [if it cannot be overused], this allows the people to care for the living and mourn the dead without dissatisfactions or regrets. This is the beginning of the way of kings.[17]

The passage continues:

In the five-mou homesteads plant the mulberry trees, and those of fifty years may wear silk. In raising poultry, piglets, dogs, and swine, do not neglect their seasons [for breeding], and those of seventy years may eat meat. In the hundred-mou fields, do not rob them of their [times for planting], and families with numerous mouths [to feed] will not go hungry. In schools pay careful attention to the order of lessons, through repetition causing obedient and respectful conduct, and white-haired [elders] will not bear heavy burdens in the roads. When persons of seventy [can] wear silk and eat meat, when the numerous people are neither hungry nor cold, even if one is not a king he will have it [the kingly way].[18]

Mengzi's proscriptions here regulate human activity by providing both limitations and proscriptions: Mengzi prohibits the ruler from interfering with busy times in the fields (most likely a problem when waging war against neighboring territories), but he also prohibits overconsumption of natural resources. These regulations have several important effects. First, they aim at creating a sustainable relationship with the surrounding environment. Human society cannot flourish if natural resources are overconsumed (thereby creating a shortage) or underutilized at the right times (thereby also creating shortages). Second, these regulations help promote a flexible human society: the excess products of human activity can be stored in times of surplus and used during times of shortage. This maintains the basic material conditions for human activity. Third, these regulations aim at creating conditions necessary for fulfilling human emotional activity. The central human demands of caring for the young and the elderly require basic material resources. These resources allow human beings to fulfil their feelings of obligation toward their family relations, and they create a sense of satisfaction with life itself. Here we see the direct relationship between Mengzi's proscriptions of land usage and moral psychology: any population requires the right kinds of material sustenance for nurturing a benevolent state. Benevolent action can grow from the seeds of the sensitive heart, but creating an environment or society that provides key material resources allows human beings to most effectively fulfil their emotional relationships with others. This is not in any way a call for a material society; rather, it is simply acknowledging the manner in which material needs are important for fulfilling our social obligations. What Mengzi recognizes here is that our sense of fulfilment often relates to our ability to act on our emotional impulses in ways that create benevolent action. Seeing this occur in the different relations that define our lives leads toward a sense of fulfilment and completion and an overarching satisfaction with life.

Another important element of Mengzi's proscriptions for land usage is the manner in which he champions the good of the general population. Although he generally finds himself engaged in dialogues with kings, dukes, and other rulers, his actual proscriptions explicitly state that success as a ruler should be defined in terms of a flourishing population. In this manner Mengzi deftly appeals to the ambitions of Warring States feudal lords while directly arguing for the well-being of the people under their rule.

This leads us to the final image in this chapter, the model of the well-field system. My argument here is that this system integrates all concerns at this point: it includes Mengzi's model of moral psychology, his concerns with nurturing and guiding emotional development, his concern with creating a sustainable human economy, and his concern with redirecting local rulers' attentions toward the good of their people.

D. C. Lau notes that the term "well-field" originates from the division of land into nine plots with a central plot relegated to the central administrator.[19] The design for this series of divisions resembles the character *jǐng* 井, or "well."

One square *li* [a unit of distance] is one *jǐng* [nine plots of land]. Nine *jǐng* give one hundred *mǔ* [mou], with the center for the public field. Eight families each have one hundred *mǔ*, [and] together they work the public field. The public work finished, only afterward can [one] venture to tend private affairs. In this manner the countrypeople will be set apart. This is the general outline.[20]

First, the well-field land arrangement creates an environment where the central ruler and the subjects interact together: the location of the central plot promotes interaction between the ruler and his subjects. These interactions help encourage empathy and compassion from the local ruler toward his subjects. Mengzi explicitly directs rulers to interact with their subjects, to see their suffering, and to be in positions where they can respond empathetically with benevolent action. The position of the central plot does not ensure this, but it at least creates the possibility.

Second, the well-field system helps maintain a kind of homeostatic equilibrium between human society and natural resources. Presumably the central plot regulates human activity by monitoring consumption and production; measurements can be taken and regulations can be devised that meet the particular local needs of the unit. The central plot can be adjusted as needed, based on local changes, and can store excess in times of surplus and distribute that same surplus in times of need.

Third, the well-field system utilizes reason and rightness to help regulate human activity, but it does so in a nonviolent manner. Just as the man from Song should not pull his rice plants in anticipation of their growth, so should the wise king not force his people to action through violence. Mengzi calls for education and the establishment of schools, which provide the people the intellectual tools for learning to measure and regulate their own fields. While Mengzi is working within the confines of the feudal system, he finds methods for extending the mechanisms of the feudal institutions to a broader population.

Fourth, this system encourages interaction between social divisions. Mengzi is keenly aware that ruling feudal lords are guided by their ambitions for their own self-perceived greatness and do not sufficiently interact with their subjects. Mengzi calls for rulers to act with benevolence toward their subjects, to tour their countries and view local conditions, and to extend their own successes and joys to those around them. Mengzi also utilizes the well-field system as a means for guiding interactions among the general populace: all people are called upon to meet the shared needs of the *jǐng* unit and then to assist each other in the cultivation of their own private plots.

Ultimately, this arrangement reflects a general cosmological conception of power in ancient China: a central source of power emanates outward, transforming the surrounding environment and organizing the world.[21] This model is present in the well-field system and in Mengzi's own model of moral psychology. What makes this noteworthy in Mengzi is that it unites his theories of moral psychology with his models of governance and land management; in moral psychology this means cultivating an environment where experiences of empathy can develop into expressions of benevolence. In terms of governance, this means creating an environment that sustains human activity and allows human activity to express itself in acts of benevolence and kindness. In terms of land management, it means creating a community where people interact and mutually care for others.

The presence of this model in the thought of Mengzi is not unexpected: the general Confucian project relies on creating a positive presence that emanates outward and creates social transformation. What makes Mengzi's version of this model unique and interesting is the manner in which he regards cultivation of all parts as necessary for the whole. While the central element is key in providing the impulse of activity, whether it be the moral impulse of moral psychology or the proper regulations of land usage, Mengzi is clear that all parts require proper nourishment. In this manner Mengzi again champions the people while appealing to the ambitions of the rulers.

My interpretation of Mengzi's arguments in this chapter suggests that healthy emotional development considers issues of material sustainability. Mengzi suggests that a certain degree of human flourishing occurs when people possess sufficient material means to care for their families, and successful policy must balance providing resources while avoiding overconsumption. The relationship between moral psychology and a nourishing environment provides a basis for engaging contemporary discussions on poverty and mental health. Health sciences and sociology have demonstrated repeatedly over the past century a significant relationship between conditions of material duress and mental and emotional suffering. There are significant debates surrounding the nature of the relationship between poverty and mental health, but recent research indicates that poverty directly detracts from cognitive function.[22] In this sense, any theory of moral psychology should also take into account how social and material environments influence emotional and cognitive health. Similarly, the problems of overconsumption and sustainability are crucial for contemporary societies. It remains to be seen if we can regain equilibrium between our human activity and our use of material resources. Whereas the conflicts of the Warring States era endangered the resources necessary for the survival of kingdoms, we live in a time where overconsumption threatens global ecological stability. Given these similarities, I can only hope that engaging Mengzi's philosophy provides additional resources for cultivating compassion and benevolence today.

NOTES

Epigraph: D. C. Lau, trans., *Mengzi Mencius* (London: Penguin Classics, 2005), 165.

1. "Moral psychology" is a very broadly understood term. I understand the term in reference to earlier Mengzi scholarship (discussed briefly below), which often considers

Mengzi's claims regarding the moral nature of the emotions. More recent scholarship also considers the relationship between affective (emotional) and cognitive (reflective or rational) elements of human activity. I also draw from Martha C. Nussbaum's discussions of moral psychology, which I first encountered in her work *The Therapy of Desire* (Princeton, NJ: Princeton University Press, 1994). Nussbaum investigates the idea of philosophy as therapy as it occurs in Hellenistic thought, but she also proposes understanding ethics through an analogy with medicine. Nussbaum combines three important ideas in proposing a therapeutic model of philosophy: (1) a diagnosis of disease, understood in terms of both individual beliefs as well as social factors, that prevent people from living well; (2) a tentative and open-ended model of human nature that provides a basis for making proscriptive recommendations; and (3) a conception of proper philosophical procedure that leads to the development of healthy norms (ibid., 28–29). Nussbaum's discussions of Hellenistic thought do not perfectly agree with contemporary discussions on Chinese thought, but her approach of viewing philosophy as a therapeutic treatment of human suffering corresponds well to the Warring States' philosophical discussions on human virtue and the breakdown and restoration of social harmony.

2. Cf. Angus C. Graham, *Disputers of the Tao: Philosophical Argument in Ancient China* (Peru, IL: Open Court Publishing, 1989), 132; David B. Wong, "Is There a Distinction between Reason and Emotion in Mencius?," *Philosophy East and West* 41, no. 1 (1991): 31–44; and Emily McRae, "The Cultivation of Moral Feelings and Mengzi's Method of Extension," *Philosophy East and West* 61, no. 4 (2011): 587–608. Graham locates Mengzi's morality in the heart-mind's capacity for rational reflection on the emotions and for "judging the relative importance of the various appetites and moral inclinations." Wong argues against separating reason and emotion and demonstrates how emotions perform important roles in framing moral situations and recognizing reasons for moral action. McRae discusses the nature of moral extension (至 *zhi*) in Mengzi and suggests that moral extension can be aided by rational reflection on our emotional states.

3. See George Lakoff and Mark Johnson, *Metaphors We Live By* (Chicago: University of Chicago Press, 2003). The view of metaphor in this chapter is based on Lakoff and Johnson's view of cognitive metaphor. According to this view, metaphor is more than simply a symbolic representation of an idea; metaphor provides a symbolic structure to experience by integrating collective impressions and organizing them in a symbolic form. Each metaphor possesses an internal consistency because of the manner in which the impressions are identified as possessing similar features, and these features are then coordinated together in the metaphorical image. Metaphors convey meaning precisely because they structure experience; in this manner they synthesize prior experience into a meaningful form while also providing the structural basis for extended meaning to other situations. This means that all metaphor is in some way a process of evaluation and judgment; some element of experience is prioritized and regarded as similar across individual experiences.

4. Wong and McRae both reject the dichotomy between reason and emotion. In "Reason and Emotion," Wong discusses what he refers to as the cognitive capacities of emotion, which he explains by reference to Ronald de Sousa's theory of emotional framing. In this theory, according to Wong, emotions create an emotional framing of experience by drawing attention to the salient features of an experience. In this manner emotions help filter experience and create the conscious framework necessary for any cognitive engagement. See Wong, "Reason and Emotion," 33. See also Ronald de Sousa, *The Rationality of Emotion* (Cambridge, MA: MIT Press, 1987).

5. Mengzi 6A6. This and subsequent translations are my own. My translations attempt to mimic the syntax of the classical Chinese, in an effort to help keep some of the "feel" of the original passages. I also use brackets to indicate where I insert words that are understood in the classical Chinese or that are not explicitly present in the text. This method is less fluid but perhaps useful for analysis or criticism.

6. I suggest that this is not an innate, content-specific understanding of right and wrong but, rather, a desire or direction toward affirming and negating. As Zhuangzi is keen to observe, people are quick to approve or disapprove, bounding off like crossbow bolts, and then cling to their ideas of right and wrong. See Burton Watson, trans., *The Complete Works of Zhuangzi* (New York: Columbia University Press, 1968), 36–37.

7. Wong, "Reason and Emotion," 31–44.

8. I realize this claim may appear controversial. It does not mean that all emotions are valid emotions for Mengzi. What this claim does mean is that empathetic experiences of suffering can lead the moral agent to act in benevolent ways to alleviate said suffering. It means that feelings of shame can lead the moral agent to act in ways that conform to *yì*, or rightness. It means that feelings of reverence can be cultivated to lead the moral agent to follow the ritual forms of behavior, and these ritual forms should exist for the sake of maintaining healthy relationships. And it means that feelings of affirmation and disapproval can lead the moral agent to investigations of what is right and wrong, culminating in wisdom.

9. I want to make explicit here the idea that this process of emotional-moral expression relies on the successful expression of the emotion and its completion or resolution as a particular action. Mengzi regards the impulse as innate, as part of our nature, which is why he regards morality as "internal." But truly benevolent action requires expression and successful completion. Mengzi's use of "internal" here is to draw attention to the emotional impulses that require healthy development. "Internal" is not meant to refer to Western debates between idealism and empiricism.

10. Mengzi 6A8.

11. Ibid.

12. Mengzi 2A2.

13. Roger T. Ames and Henry Rosemont Jr., trans., *The Analects of Confucius: A Philosophical Translation* (New York: Ballantine, 1998), 76.

14. Mengzi 6A11.

15. Ames and Rosemont, *Analects of Confucius*, 53–55. These ritual ideals, and ideals in general, are often presented as the norms of the ancient sage-kings. This cultural framing may occur partially as an appeal to tradition and partially as an accepted rhetorical device.

16. Mengzi 2A2.

17. Mengzi 1A3.

18. Ibid.

19. Lau, *Mencius*, 99.

20. Mengzi 3A3.

21. Aihe Wang, *Cosmology and Political Culture in Early China* (Cambridge: Cambridge University Press, 2000). Wang traces the emergence of the *sìfāng* 四方 cosmology and its evolution into the *wǔxíng* 五行. Centrality is a key feature of the *sìfāng* model.

22. Anandi Mani, Sendhil Mullainathan, Eldar Shafir, and Jiaying Zhao, "Poverty Impedes Cognitive Function," *Science* 30 (August 2013): 976–980.

The Place of the Body in the Phenomenology of Place

EDWARD CASEY AND NISHIDA KITARŌ

Lara M. Mitias

In the twentieth century, Nishida Kitarō and Edward Casey stand out as being distinctly describable as philosophers of place. For both philosophers, place is phenomenologically and ontologically fundamental and irreducible. For both, "space" and "time" are abstractions from the more primordial "place," and place is of inestimable value because it overcomes, or subverts, our apparent dualities, as it also makes them possible. In different ways, Casey and Nishida encourage recognition of the significance of place and a return to place. Casey's monumental work on the nature and fate of place urges a "renewed sense" of place and our "getting back into place," while Nishida's philosophy of the logic of *basho* (place) aims to overcome problems created by subject-object dualisms and a false sense of self.

In this chapter, I begin with Casey's exposition of place to show the nature and significance of our places, and then I explore how Nishida's logic of *basho* and "active intuition" can help us understand what it means to "get back into place." For both Casey and Nishida, embodiment is of central importance to place. Casey says that we get back into place through our own lived body, and Nishida's later development of *basho* and pure experience in active intuition involves a turn to the historical somatic individual. It is my view that, in both accounts of place, the lived and living body must be considered the quintessential place and not just a protoplace or a place in a minimal sense, as Casey suggests.

Recognizing the body-mind complex as our most fundamental place, determinant of all our places and placements, is significant for theories of the self's social and personal construction. This recognition also serves as a practical heuristic for understanding our own selves and experience, as well as those of others, and can aid us in the intentional transformation of our places and placements, helping us understand what it is to "get back into place."

Lived and Living Places

For Casey, our place-specific living is fundamental. As he describes it, *being-in-the-world* is, in fact, the concreteness of *being-in-place*, or being in the place-world itself.[1] Throughout his extensive work on place, Casey returns to the Archytian axiom that "to be is to be in place" and that "place is the first of all things."[2] As he elaborates, "Places are not so much the direct objects of sight or thought or recollection as what we feel *with* and *around*, *under* and *above*, *before* and *behind* our lived bodies."[3] We are embedded in place and are originally emplaced as embodied.

In Casey's exposition, an originary grounding in "place" has been overcome by modernity's abstractions of "space" and "time," leading to many forms of postmodern displacements. The meaningfulness and felt value of our emplacement, the value of our being-in-place, has been supplanted by abstractions of aspects of fragmented experiences of place and by ideas of places as simple locations or sites. Abstracting time from place, we are left with a disembodied space existing apart from the irreducible coordinately constitutive activities of our sociocultural, historical, and environmental *place*.

Casey emphasizes two essential qualities of places: that they are embodied and that they enactively gather. I will show that, given the nature of place and these two qualities of place, the mind-body complex is our most fundamental place.

Embodied Places

Unlike space or time considered abstractly or conceptually, places are essentially embodied. We are, Casey says, "bound by body to be in place." The lived body is the "dynamic bond to place" and is the material condition for the possibility of the place-world, while itself being a member of that world.[4] Lived bodies require places and places require lived bodies: "Just as there are no places without the bodies that sustain and vivify them, so there are no lived bodies without the places they inhabit and traverse. . . . Bodies and places are connatural terms. They interanimate each other."[5]

Relating his phenomenological projects, Casey says that while imagination projects us into what *might be*, and memory returns us to what *has been*, place ushers us into what *already is*: namely, the environing subsoil of our embodiment, the bedrock of our being-in-the-world." It is one's immediate place, or emplacement, that is essentially significant, he says. This placement is constantly shifting and complexly constituted. For Casey, place does not serve "as a mere backdrop for concrete actions or thoughts"; rather, "place itself is concrete and at one with action and thought."[6]

The Gathering of Places

Casey proposes that places are "eventmental"—that is, they are "happening not only in space but in time and history as well."[7] He describes the "eventmental" character of places as "their capacity for co-locating space and time (even as they deconstruct this very dyad)."[8] This, he says, is both an "*in-gathering* effected by the body as the crux of nature and culture" and "a still more general and pervasive *gathering-with* that occurs by virtue of the very power of emplacement to bring space and time together in the event" (italics mine).[9] This gathering is "the turning point of space and time, the pivot where space and time conjoin in place."[10] Space and time are only dimensions of place and are "experienced and expressed *in place by the event of place*."[11] It is essential to note that the in-gathering aspect of the eventmental character of place is effected by the body, because the body (mind-body complex) co-locates space and time. The body is the essential turning point, or the very real pivot where these dimensions conjoin in place.

This *gathering* activity of places is the second of the two essential traits of place. Places, Casey says, gather experiences, histories, languages, thoughts, and animate and inanimate entities. He notes this is not an amassing but a coordinate arrangement. Places are configurative complexes of things: "Place is the generatrix for the collection, as well as the recollection, of all that occurs in the lives of sentient beings, and even for the trajectories of inanimate things. Its power consists in gathering these lives and things, each with its own space and time, into one arena of common engagement."[12]

Thus, in contrast to spaces, places are determinantly filled and are in co-constituting actively gathering relations. Places essentially involve their constituents, and the furniture of place, what takes place at that place, or what is *taking* place, is essential to that place. Places are thus not static locations but are *lived* as embodied and are also *living*, as actively incorporating. A model of "place" as merely site, location, or container cannot actively gather. It is only as places of *habitus*, and as places of inhabitance, that places can *gather* and are most significantly "places" as such.

So although our places are commonly denominated or designated, they are constantly changing over time, and their constitution is essential to their essence at any time. Any place at any time is a unique and distinct place, affectively and effectively "idiolocal," as things take place. And unlike our spaces, our places involve times and carry histories. Places are not only eventmental but also social and historical (and, especially, personal). They are absorptive and co-constituting, emplacing other places and placements; and places incorporate their pasts.

Embodiment as Emplacement

As Casey insists, "We should think of culture, ethnicity, gender, class, etc., as furnishing *dimensions* of a place beyond its exact location in geographic space and chronometric time. . . . They act as indwelling forces that contribute to a place its non-physical and non-geographic dimensions."[13] To be sure, Casey very briefly notes these "dimensions of place" only a few times in his work. But by emphasizing the platial nature of the lived and living body, we can shift our attention to the inestimable significance of these local and regional vicissitudes in phenomenologies of "place." Because of the co-constitutive gathering activities of bodies and places, these dimensions of place are more than indwelling forces that contribute nonphysical and nongeographic dimensions—they both determine and are determined by our experiences of places and placements.

Casey says that we are never without placed experiences and that we not only are *in* places but also are *of* them: "We are ineluctably place-bound." We are "placelings," he says, adding, "Our very perceptual apparatus, our sensing body, reflects the kinds of places we inhabit. . . . [P]lace . . . is as primary as the perception that gives access to it."[14] The co-constitution of place and perception indicates an ultimate primacy of the lived body as fundamentally cultural and social.[15] But it is not just the sensing body that is central to experiences of being in places and of them; it is its role *as a place* that is encultured and is both social and historical, with an ongoing particular form and as a coordinate activity of space and time, mind and body, subject and object. This place is a gathering of the constructed self, of our past places and placements, and a locus of current emplacement and lived places.

While embodiment is central to Casey's understanding of emplacement, the body, for Casey, is not a "place," properly speaking. In his analysis, the lived body and the landscape are coeval dipolar parameters that serve as the pivot and the inner and outer boundaries of place. They are, "at the very least, the bounds of places," and emplacement is a function of the differential interplay between these inner and outer boundaries of place.[16] But as the locus of any place and source of any possible placement, the lived and living body is genuinely the central pivot of any "place" and not just its inner boundary. This body must share in the nature of place.

Casey describes the body as being a "micro-place" and a "proto-place."[17] He says that we can be *here* in the living body and that *here-there* relations exist within the body. According to Casey, the very existence of a *here-there* relationship indicates that the body, "taken as a single intact entity, is itself a place—if it is the case that anything that exhibits a here-there structure counts as a place in some minimal sense."[18] Since the indexical "here" requires an embodied locus, all places, having a here-there structure, are dependent on the here-there structure of the body. Thus, our lived and living body is a place in more than a minimal sense. It is not merely requisite for place; it is the preeminent place.

Why Body as Place?

Coordinately co-constructing in creative advance, places essentially incorporate their contents—cultural, social, and historical; things, people, and events—and coevolve all other places as co-constituting fields of activity. All places, as such, are emplaced and emplacing, embedding and enveloping. We—or our individual body-mind matrices, or our psychophysical and social selves—are emplaced and are emplacing in this place. Our lived and living body serves as our own place, giving us access to any place and also taking place as part of any place.

Our awareness and bodily sensations are felt as located in places in our body and mind (as here or there) as given in an extensive and intensive awareness. It is in this place that inner and outer, subject and object, space and time, can be coordinately conjoined or separated. This is the place of the gathering of contradictory but coordinate co-constitutive dualities. As a locus of orientation, this place is central to the delineation of any place as such; and our embodiment as a locus of indwelling enables inhabitance of any other place.

Our constantly changing place always revolves around this constantly current and particular place, and, as Casey notes, we cannot get wholly outside of this place.[19] We cannot escape our mind-body place as our interface with the world, nor can we escape our ensuing placements, and the real effect of the particularities of our embodiment on our experience cannot be understated. We are anyplace only in and through our unique embodied place, and this place is significantly determinant of all other places and placements and of what takes place. Our vicissitudes and our actual relative categorical form—as naturally informed and informed by others—are of the utmost significance in this process, and ensuing placements are incorporated into our current place.

A renewed understanding of places as lived and living, along with the following recognition of the platiality of our embodiment, encourages us to acknowledge the climatic and environmental particularities that lived and living places have and experience and to foreground these in our accounts of place. The unique changing peculiarities of the place of the self-aware organism both determine and are an expression of any particular place, and the particular lived and living body is an extended locus of climate, culture, and history.

Because our emplacement is grounded in our embodiment, we must recognize the influences of our places and placements and the lasting impact of negative experiences of place and placement in our current embodiment. As we incorporate places we have been and what has taken place, we incorporate our past placements and may forever carry these with us as part of our self. They may detract from our abilities and knowledge of the world as certainly as they enable it. We may be unable to overcome these co-constitutions of person and place. We also cannot, to any great degree, escape our particularities of form and our vicissitudes—our gender, the color of our skin, the shape of our face, the size of our body, or our abilities or the condition of our mind or body. We cannot escape the coloring of places by our own place and as co-constitutive of our places.

Our bodies and minds are experienced as platial, as lived and living, and we inhabit them as the basis of all further inhabitances and emplacements. We live *in*, *through*, and *with* the conditions and variations of our embodiment and not just *as* its conditions and variations. We know our embodiment as a place of shifting feelings, internal and external, corporeal and noncorporeal. Recognizing the platial nature of the mind-body can contribute to our understanding of others as likewise being uniquely placed and as being places of *habitus* and a very real affective and effective indwelling.

The centrality of place to person can also bring our attention to problems of placement and displacement. We may be in-place or displaced (physically, socially, or otherwise) both within a place and with respect to other places or placements; and we can be in place or displaced with respect to others, as to our own selves, and with respect to our own mind and body. We place and displace others in a myriad of ways, and recognition of the significance and nature of place, and especially that of the mind-body place, can bring our direct attention to the variety and details of our forms and relations of placement.

Getting Back into Place

As a place of inhabitance and indwelling and as the locus of embodiment and gathering, the particular lived and living body is central to any other place or placement. The climate and environment of this place determine and are determined by any other climate. If place is phenomenologically and ontologically primordial and irreducible, then it is our embodiment—as a place of inhabitance and dwelling, enabling and gathering these emplacement relations—that is central to our being-in-place and, therefore, to our getting back into place. It is our *way* of embodiment or indwelling, our mode of inhabiting our place, that is essential (and not just contingent) in determining our places.

Casey notes that on journeys travelers often seek displacement. Not to keep moving on and being responsive to change at every step is to risk being bound to a false and limited ego, to have a sense of "being stuck-in-place."[20] And in many ways we are always striving to improve and change our places. Even more than seeking a form of displacement through traveling, much of human history and individual action has been aimed at not only making a better place but just finding a place when another place becomes untenable—or when a place changes, just trying to re-place oneself in place.

We are always reorienting ourselves in places as they are constantly changing, as are our placements, how we are placed by others, how we place others, and so how we order and understand and act within the world. With a renewed sense of place, and especially of the place of the body-mind, we can consciously reflect on this inescapable place and its placements in a transformative way. Understanding embodiment as emplacement encourages us not only to reconsider the value of our places but also to intentionally reorder our places and placements.

How to "Get Back into Place"

The road to getting back into place is itself a route of renewed sensitivity to place, affording a refreshed sense of its continuing importance in our lives and in the lives of others. That sense and sensitivity offer a viable alternative to being and feeling out-of-place.[21]

Casey notes the fragility of our being in-place and its value, as well as the ease of displacement.[22] We are alienated, he says, "so lost in space and time as to be displaced from place itself." He argues that we can draw on the resources of reemplacement and cohabitancy with and in the world and can return resolutely to place. He describes getting back into place—or re-placing places as aesthetically vivid places—as potentially redemptive. In this regard, he says that we can get inspiration from landscape painters who get back into place by a transformation of place, as in a finished painting. He says that the result is redemptive for the place as it finds new pictorial depths, as well as for the artist and our own selves as spectators. By these methods and likewise by narrational journeys to and between places, we can begin to get back into place. Such work "reminds us that we are not altogether without resources in our placelessness."[23]

Casey then asks if re-placing is just a matter of re-minding: "Does getting back into place mean getting back into mind?" Although this is tempting, he says, we should resist the lure. Our revived intimacy with places "need not be mental," and "the introspection of self-contained mind . . . must be supplemented, and in many cases supplanted, by the exteroception of the environing place-world and by the intermediation of the body."[24] But, as we will see with Nishida, these cannot truly be separated. There is no "self-contained mind."

The mental cannot be supplanted by the bodily, nor can it avoid being supplemented by the body. Any clear division between internal and external is as disrupted by the lived and living body as it is made possible by it. We are intensively and extensively aware. We have an inexpressible interior sense, an intense sensitivity, and an exterior sense of other forms and of our own external form conjoined.

Casey says that we get back into place by the very way in which we are always already there—by our own lived body[25] and with the recognition that the body is not an object but a lived and living body, a subject integrated with its immediate environment, for "place integrates with body as much as body with place."[26] Discussing wilderness, Casey writes:

> As the felt surface of land (or sea), it links up with my own bodily surface. The two porous surfaces, one belonging to the circumambient world and the other to my *corps propre*, intertwine and become at once co-experiential and co-essential. My lived body rejoins a wild place . . . as the flesh of one takes in the flesh of the other. As I come to know it from within, such a place, despite its wildness (or rather, just because of its wildness) becomes "flesh of my flesh."[27]

The place of the body and the place wherein it is emplaced are primordially co-constituting as one *takes place* along with things *taking place*. Such co-constitutive activity denotes a sharing of place, and, as argued here, it is only as my body itself serves as a place that it can be ontologically commensurate with the places in which it is emplaced. Because the flesh of the world intertwines with my flesh, any epistemology or ontology of place requires this source place of our own living environment.

Every place, Casey says, has its own "operative intentionality" with which it "elicits and responds to the corporeal intentionality of the perceiving subject."[28] This is also true of that "proto-place," as Casey describes it, of the embodied self. We respond to ourselves and are aware of ourselves as psychophysical individuals and as both subjects and objects. We recognize our places and placements and codetermine them. We have our own operative intentionality eliciting and responding to our own corporeal intentionality. Because of this relation, it is only by way of the lived body with its requisite mind that we may remake our relations to place, or get back into place, and "affirm both members of all these divisive dyads [of space and time, body and mind, etc.] and thereby live our lives in an intimacy neither simply mental nor merely physical but altogether placial."[29]

Recognizing that the mind-body complex serves as a place of *habitus* and inhabitance that may be reordered or re-placed, we can renew our connection to places by dwelling in a different manner, beginning with our own indwelling. In this way, we may be able to reconnect to place and find ourselves more "at home" in any place. Such a sufficient being-in-place may be associated with a realized state of corresponsiveness with and within places that might be enactively realized, overcoming the irrevocable displacements of modernity. Nishida's logic of *basho* and his conception of action-intuition may serve as a guide for cultivating a sense of being-in-place by enabling a constantly fluid connection with our constantly changing places and can even give us clues to overcoming the negative influences of our past places and negative platial constructions.

The Place of Non-oppositional Nothingness

Nishida's aim in developing the logic of *basho* was to overcome what he perceived as insurmountable difficulties in Western epistemology. Prior to the division of subject and object is our actual emplacement, making possible both the bifurcation and the unification of opposites in a self-contradictory identity. Nishida calls the logic of *basho* a concrete logic because it is based in our lived experience, and he argues that only such a logic can be the basis for the development of object logic.

At the start of his 1926 essay "Basho," Nishida explains that the idea of *basho* is a very simple one. Relata and any possible relations must have a place that envelops and enables the development of such relations. Only such a place can allow incorporative becoming as the unity of this formative and dynamic contradiction. The ultimate *basho* allows for the unification of disparate and correlative dualities of time and space, subject and object, active and passive, being and nonbeing, internal and external, and so on in a dialectic of reversing negation and becoming by way of this dialectical constitution in a self-contradictory identity.

Nishida's original development of *basho* explicates the true *basho* as a nonoppositional nothingness, an emptiness at the ground of being and its oppositional nothing. He explains the true *basho* of absolute and non-oppositional nothingness as the consciousness that enables but is also beyond our phenomenal consciousness with its shifting contents. In his later development of the *basho* of action-intuition, this becomes distinctly dynamic, and the historical somatic self both expresses and becomes the expression of the self-determination of the world as a dialectical universal. This essential *basho* is the historical and somatic individual as the locus of action-intuition:

> Our very thinking is a historical action. We are aware in the place that is at the same time Created and Creating. Accordingly, our self is historical and somatic. Otherwise, this is nothing but a thought self [not the thinking self]. . . . We grasp the True Self in the place where we negate the abstract conscious self and become one, body and mind.[30]

The absolute present, or place of nothingness, is the place of the True Self where mind and body are one. This is realized in action-intuition, where action and intuition are in a dialectical unity with the historical world of becoming.

Nishida's Concrete Paradoxical Logic

For Nishida, the contradictory identity of space and time of the self-forming world is the dynamic form of contradictory identity that makes possible both change and conscious life. Time and space are not independent forms but only dimensions of the self–transforming matrix of space-time. He says that the only way we can conceive of a self-conscious individual is in terms of this dynamic form of contradictory identity.[31]

As the self-determination of the absolute present in the form of the contradictory identity of the many and the one, the spatiotemporal world is the historical world. It is a coordination of space and time in an existential integration that is nonfinite and subject to constant creation. Nishida says that both awareness and individuality have this structure of the absolutely contradictory identity of the many and the one, as this is the logical form of the self-transforming matrices that are conceived as our physical, biological, historical, and self-conscious worlds: "It is in the historical world-time of the absolute present that the monads form the individual expressions of the world." These monads, or individual expressions, "are both self-originating and co-originating in the matrix of the absolute present." It is this concrete paradoxical logic of the transforming matrices of our worlds that necessitates and makes possible our response of *poiesis* to place and our placement.[32]

> Concrete logic sees the true individual as active in the dimension in which it sees things in the form of *poiesis* and acts from so seeing, as contradictory identity of the many and the one. This is precisely the dimension of an individual's concrete involvement in the historical world. The various acts of our individual selves must be conceived in this way. They must be conceived as the self-determinations of the world seen as a living space, as it were.[33]

The Development and Unity of Pure Experience and Action-Intuition

The concreteness of Nishida's logic of self-contradictory identity is grounded in something universal—namely, the form of the absolutely present becoming of the self-transforming matrix as a particularized expression:

> The idea of "Place" was made concrete as "Dialectical Universal" and the position of "Dialectical Universal" was made direct as the position of "active intuition." . . . What was defined as the world of "direct experience," "pure experience" and

so on, now has come to be thought of as the world of Historical Reality. It is the very world of action-intuition, the very world of *poiesis* that is the world of pure experience.[34]

This is described by paradoxical logic as seen from the form of thinking of the historical self-conscious self as transformed and transforming, created and creating. As expressive expressions of this matrix, the historical somatic individual is a transforming transformation of the self-transforming matrix. Action-intuition is an intimate and unobstructed connection to the self-transforming matrix in continuous coordination. Nishida writes:

> Acting-intuition is a contradictory self-identity; it is the self-identity of opposites, such as temporal and spatial, [epistemological] subject and object. Such self-contradictory movement of the present in turn entails that the present, while moving, does not move. It means the self-determination of the eternal now. It is a self-contradiction wherein the one is the many and the many is the one.[35]

The self-contradictory identity realized in action-intuition as pure experience, or absolute presence, is concretely embodied. As a formative subjectivity, the free and volitional conscious self always expresses the objective world within itself, for it is an expression of the world. For Nishida, this coordinate relation enables shared states of enactment with the world and others in a natural sympathetic coalescence. This can be in the form of *poiesis*, or pure experience, realized from the emptying of the self.[36] This is not an absence or mindlessness but a fully present unity of mind and body and realization of a true self. And, at its limit, this entails both an active aesthetic intuition and a realization of nondifference of self, other, and world in an absolute presence of becoming. "Compassion," Nishida says, "always signifies that opposites are one in the dynamic reciprocity of their own contradictory identity."[37]

Although action-intuition is common to ordinary experience itself in the sense that pure experience is present in immediacy as the ground of all possible consciousness, it can be cultivated and is realized in the self-determination of the absolute present in a fluidly correlative activity. The creative process has "the form of self-contradiction in that we take the other as our self and simultaneously see our self in the other."[38] This coordinated realization is both given and to be achieved and is both ordinary and extraordinary experience.

Nishida says that when we abandon the standpoint of thought and enter into the internal unity of the whole person, we become the act itself. At this level, object and act are one. In such a place, our object logic fails and nothing is nameable because of an immediate interexpressivity that is pure awareness or a foundational presence of the self-contradictory identities of space and time, mind and body, inner and outer, active and passive, and so on. This coalescent becoming is exemplified as artistic intuition and creation as well as scientific engagement and religious intuition, where "there is neither inner nor outer, neither I nor other."[39] This unity of pure experience does not differ in kind from other experience but differs only in its unity.[40]

Seeing as Making and Being Made in the Making

Our historical life is expressive as the self-determination of the world in this dialectical becoming of the created and the creating. The embodied self is the essential *basho*, the ultimate *basho* where this takes place. Nishida discriminates the world of biological life from the world of true life, saying that biological life is also a world of active intuition where historical nature sees by making, but "true life, as the affirmation of absolute negation, as the continuity of discontinuity, is a formative act."[41] In this act, what is environmental becomes instrumental; and as the body becomes a tool, the world becomes one's body. Nishida writes: "The body is a thing and is that which is seen from the outside. While being a bodily existence, we also possess the body as tool. In saying so, I do not mean that the body disappears. [I mean that] the body becomes that which sees. The body becomes formatively active and creative."[42]

At the extremity of possessing the body as a tool there is a separation of self from body, Nishida says, and we become simply a seeing self. It is on this basis that we can think of something like the conscious "I."[43] He emphasizes that the self is not a cogito, however. It is essentially active and transactionally productive.[44] It is necessarily embodied. The self is by its very nature simultaneously incorporating and acting; and Nishida constantly emphasizes that it is both made and making (even in seeing) and is made in this making. He illustrates this in terms of works of artistic intuition, combining both subjective activity and objective result, for the artist is also acted upon by the artwork. "The artwork is realized from a mutual interaction—or reciprocal transaction—of subjectivity and objectivity."[45]

We are simultaneously created and creating as the self-determination of the historical and dialectical world. We are thus not simply bound by the world of objects, and so we can consider ourselves free. According to Nishida, historical nature continually forms itself *via* active intuition and through the *technē* of our individual historical bodies as we become one with the world in this true experience of enactment as *poiesis*. Culture is the continuity of such historical self-development through contradictory identities, and we exist in such a world as bodies that are expressions of this world in acts of expression.[46]

The Pulse of Historical Life

Things become expressions of historical life as we are creative, and here they are not simply seen. Because things are expressions of life in the historical world, "we see the self in the thing, regard the thing as the self, and think of the I and the thing as one."[47] Nishida repeatedly emphasizes that our body is a thing seen in the historical world and is a tool, as well as being that which sees. It is as a *basho* of self-contradictory identity that one can be truly creative. Our acting is an act of expression, and we see things only through acting. In this action-intuition, the self does not disappear or become a thing, but it becomes a true self or a creative element. Nishida emphasizes that this does not mean that the body or self disappears; rather, it is the returning of true life to itself: "The casting-off of body-and-mind does not simply mean becoming empty. The world becomes expressive to the I, who as a creative element sees with the body. Things appear as expressions of life. Only upon such a standpoint, he says, can we say that expressions move the I."[48]

The self becomes truly creative in an enactive intuition, which is not the loss of self or body in a simple unity with the object or events. Intuition is the self-identity of the mutually opposed and is established as the self-determination of the world.[49] In this, the self does not stand opposed or apart from the world but instead becomes "an operative element of the creative world." The true self of the artist, Nishida says, lies in the work, and the body becomes that which actively sees and is at work. When we truly live with the body, he says, we truly see things through acting, and "the world becomes one's own body." Nishida adds that "those who truly create and truly see are only those in whose pulse historical life flows."[50]

For Nishida, the origin of the artist's productive act is when the bodily self becomes active as a creative element and the flow of historical life permeates the body.[51] Both the world and historical somatic individuals are the self-expression of historical life, and intuiting is the permeation of historical life through our body.[52] This is not merely a passive observation or condition but is enactive. It is with the acting-intuition of the historical life of the instrumental-bodily self that the world of artistic ideas can be seen:[53]

> When our self becomes a creative element, things become expressions of life. This is an instance of what I mean when I say that the world becomes instrumental and becomes the self's body in the region where we possess things as tools. Although one may think that the bodily self disappears therein, the historical-bodily self does not disappear. Instead our bodily self becomes active as a creative element and the flow of historical life permeates our body. Herein lies the origin of the artist's productive act.[54]

For both Casey and Nishida, place is much more than location. Places gather and enact, and they enable collocated coordinate and incommensurate dualities. Given Casey's phenomenology of place and Nishida's concrete logic of *basho*, the body-mind must be recognized as preeminently platial. The history, form, and climate of this place enables and codetermines all experiences of place, environment, and climate. This is the source and the locus of the inhabitance of any place. This is the actual place where the dualities of space and time, mind and body, subject and object, and so on are collocated in an active becoming, and the only place where these can be abstracted or appear separated.

Classifications and placements, as well as displacements of many kinds from psychological to physical, determine and delimit the place and/or placement of a present self. We should recognize to what degree our places and our placements (social, categorical, etc.) are delineated unavoidably from our particular embodiment. Our irreducible place, the place that grounds us in place, is our current place and what has taken place. Through this renewed sense of the place of the body (and mind), we can become more conscious of our lived and living places and our placements and of the places of others. Also, to some degree perhaps, we can intentionally change our ways of placing and being in place, our *habitus* and our mode of dwelling.

Conceiving embodiment as emplacement enables recognition of the centrality of place to person and brings our attention to problems of our displacement—physically or socially, within and with respect to our places and one's own mind-body place. Philosophies and practices of enlightenment offer remedy to the fixity of our places and what has and is taking place. Practices to change the habits of body and mind can encourage a state of creative coordination and can help counter some of the negative aspects of the constructed self, imbued by past places and placements, and of our *habitus* and ways of inhabitance that may negatively define oneself or limit one to repetition or reaction.

Realizing being in no-place, one retrieves a common place of being in emptiness. Here, there is room for affective reception and spontaneity or self-placements (and placements of others). An effectively correlative placement, or being-in-place, can be considered as fully taking place or (re)making one's place and so also other places. An efficacious placement with respect to mind and body can be associated with a state of relative enlightenment or perhaps even pure experience, conducive to a constructive being-in-place and genuinely feeling in-place.

As it is developed in action-intuition, "Nishida philosophy" (the logic of *basho*) allows us to focus on the most relevant place to our emplacement. Our places radiate outward from our own motile place that enables all places and is codeterminant and cocreative with all other places. We can get back into place by cultivating this foundational becoming structure of action-intuition as our own historical and somatic self in an inclusive dialectical relationship with the world in a sympathetic coalescence and resonance.

Due to the constantly changing nature of places and our many irredeemable postmodern displacements, such an actively inclusive and groundless grounding place as a source for our sense of being-in-place becomes ever more essential. It is not enough to realize the significance of our places as spectators of artwork or to consider narrations of journeys—these are mental prompts—and even if one is not physically displaced, with time's advance we can never return to the same place. Moreover, we are, as Casey emphasizes, by nature and necessity motile beings and are always changing places.

Our own body-mind complex, with its particular characteristics and vicissitudes must be the source of any being or feeling in-place, giving us the potential to be "at home" in any place. Nishida's later philosophy especially, with its emphasis on the historical and somatic individual and the true self, gives us some insight into the possible cultivation of a stability of our sense of place and hints at a way to get back into place that might counteract our displacements. It is precisely because of the correlativity of persons and places and the platial nature of the body-mind that our being or feeling in-place, and our making of place, begins *here* and always *now*, with *this* place.

NOTES

1. Edward S. Casey, *Getting Back into Place: Toward a Renewed Understanding of the Place-World* (Bloomington: Indiana University Press, 1993), xviii.
2. Ibid., 319.
3. Ibid., 313.
4. Edward S. Casey, "How to Get from Space to Place in a Fairly Short Stretch of Time: Phenomenological Prolegomena," in *Senses of Place*, ed. Steven Feld and Keith H. Basso (Santa Fe, NM: School of American Research Press, 1997), 24.
5. Ibid.
6. Casey, *Getting Back into Place*, xiii.
7. Ibid., xxv.
8. Casey, "How to Get from Space," 38.
9. Ibid.
10. Ibid.
11. Ibid., 39.
12. Ibid., 26.
13. Casey, *Getting Back into Place*, xxv.
14. Casey, "How to Get from Space," 19.
15. Casey, *Getting Back into Place*, 322.
16. Ibid., 29.
17. Ibid., 56, 104, 52.
18. Ibid., 52.
19. Ibid., 125.
20. Ibid., 308.
21. Ibid., 310.
22. Casey, "How to Get from Space," 34.
23. Casey, *Getting Back into Place*, 310.
24. Ibid., 312.
25. Ibid., 310.
26. Casey, "How to Get from Space," 29.
27. Casey, *Getting Back into Place*, 210.
28. Ibid., 29.

29. Ibid., 314.

30. Matteo Cestari, "The Knowing Body: Nishida's Philosophy of Active Intuition (*Kōiteki chokkan*)," *Eastern Buddhist*, n.s., 31, no. 2 (1998): 205.

31. Kitarō Nishida, *Last Writings: Nothingness and the Religious Worldview*, trans. David A. Dilworth (Honolulu: University of Hawai'i Press, 1993), 52.

32. Ibid., 58.

33. David A. Dilworth, Valdo Humbert Viglielmo, and Agustín Jacinto Zavala, trans. and ed., *Sourcebook for Modern Japanese Philosophy: Selected Documents* (Westport, CT: Greenwood Press, 1998), 68.

34. Cestari, "The Knowing Body," 181.

35. Kitarō Nishida, "Logic and Life," in *Place and Dialectic: Two Essays by Nishida Kitarō*, trans. John W. M. Krummel and Shigenori Nagatomo (New York: Oxford University Press, 2012), 170–171. The bracketed interpolation is Nishida's.

36. Kitarō Nishida, "Basho" [Place], *Nishida Kitarō zenshū* 4 (1949): 253.

37. Nishida, *Last Writings*, 107.

38. Dilworth et al., *Sourcebook*, 45.

39. Yoshihiro Nitta and Hirotaka Tatematsu, eds., *Japanese Phenomenology: Phenomenology as the Trans-cultural Philosophical Approach* (Dordrecht: D. Reidel, 1979), 8:246.

40. Kitarō Nishida, *An Inquiry into the Good*, trans. Masao Abe and Christopher Ives (New Haven, CT: Yale University Press, 1990), 7.

41. Ibid.

42. Nishida, "Logic and Life," 146.

43. Ibid., 123.

44. Dilworth et al., *Sourcebook*, 41.

45. Ibid., 40.

46. Nishida, "Logic and Life,"123.

47. Ibid., 145.

48. Ibid., 146.

49. Ibid., 144.

50. Ibid., 141.

51. Ibid., 149.

52. Ibid., 147.

53. Ibid., 158.

54. Ibid., 149.

Putting the Dead in Their Place   **18**

Kathleen Higgins

Place would seem to be a notion that does not apply to the dead. They have left us and, in doing so, left space as we know it. And perhaps precisely for this reason, survivors are burdened by a felt need to find a place for those who have died. Survivors seek to find both literal and figurative places for the dead. Successful efforts to situate the dead, I will argue, benefit the bereaved in a variety of ways. The employment of literal places in commemorating the dead is a widespread phenomenon, and while this can facilitate recovery from the distress of bereavement, such efforts are not without their ironies. The deeper challenge of locating the dead is a matter of finding a place for them in one's ongoing life, and when this challenge is met, this aspect of grief work strengthens, rather than weakens, the bonds between the living and the dead.

Where Are They?

Once when I was discussing the phenomenon of loss with philosopher Timothy Gould, he told me that the overwhelming question one keeps asking oneself is straightforward: "Where are they?" Anyone who has experienced the loss of a close family member or friend understands, I suspect, what Gould meant.

One of the disorientations of bereavement is a disturbance in one's confidence in the space-time continuum. The fabric of the world seems to persist intact, but the person has vanished from it. But how can one assimilate this? One might latch onto false comparisons. The person's absence may feel much as it does when the person steps out of the room or goes to work or some such thing. If the person isn't here, he or she must be elsewhere. But this returns us to the question, "Where?" To acknowledge that the person has simply disappeared from our reality is to accept the idea of beings popping in and out of the very space-time continuum, a notion that is fundamentally rattling.

If Kant is right that we can intuit things only by assigning them a place within time and space, we should not be surprised that we are intent on locating the deceased somewhere in the space-time continuum. And this seems to be precisely what we do when manifesting the "search behavior" that is typical of the early stages of grief. Search behavior is the expectation of seeing the deceased loved one and the persistence in this effort despite continual failure. Saint Augustine movingly describes search behavior in his account of the death of a close friend: "My eyes were restless in looking for him, but he was not there. I hated all places because he was not in them."[1]

Expecting to see a person whom one is in the habit of seeing is hardly surprising. But in bereavement, one does not simply quit looking when the sought person fails to appear. Sartre observes that the unsuccessful search for a person amounts to an encounter with something else—the palpable presence of the person's absence. He describes a case of this sort:

> I have an appointment with Pierre at four o'clock. I arrive at the café a quarter of an hour late. Pierre is always punctual. Will he have waited for me? I look at the room, the patrons, and I say, "He is not here." . . . I myself expected to see Pierre, and my expectation has caused the absence of Pierre to happen as a real event concerning this café. It is an objective fact at present that I have discovered this absence. . . . Pierre absent haunts this café.[2]

Sartre's example also draws attention to the spatial character of being haunted—one encounters the absence of a person as a presence, and thus as a presence in a place. But quite often the place is not a determinate place. Although the bereaved person does not manage to locate the loved one anywhere, uncannily he or she encounters the deceased everywhere, though (to use Sartrean terms) "in the mode of not being there." The person's absence is bizarrely present everywhere one looks. This sense of absence as a presence is one of many reasons, I suspect, for the widespread conviction that a dead person may become a ghost, still "in" this world but here in an eerie, disturbing way.[3]

The compulsion to try to locate dead loved ones may explain, in part, the widespread belief that the deceased can turn into ghosts. It may be psychologically more palatable to believe that a dear one shows up as a ghost, even a hostile one, than to accept that he or she is so completely erased as to be no longer even intuitable. A ghost, though out of place in one sense, at least sometimes appears in places that we know. Or perhaps the idea of a ghost that shows up erratically helps normalize the notion of popping in and out of time and space. The effort to locate the person may also account for the tendency to envision heaven and hell as "above" and as "under the earth," respectively. Although not places that we can visit (Dante's masterpiece notwithstanding), heaven and hell represent locations where we can think of the dead as having gone.

The Remains of the Dead and Literal Places

But the dead do not simply disappear, and this complicates survivors' psychological efforts to situate them. Because they leave behind physical remains, literal place becomes an issue. Where should one put the remains, and how should they be disposed of? Human societies ubiquitously specify ritual ways of answering these questions. As historian Thomas Laqueur observes in his cultural history of dealing with remains, "Death and the dead have always mattered everywhere in important, defining, and broadly similar ways" and that this is a "civilizational ground zero."[4] It is striking that even Mozi, despite his strenuous objections to the ostentatious funerals encouraged by the Confucians, took for granted the importance of having funerals (albeit simple ones), and he concurred with the reigning view among his contemporaries that the failure to assure burial for corpses was a mark of abominable rulership.[5] Laqueur indicates Diogenes as holding an exceptional view; the ancient Cynic "wanted his body tossed over the walls into a no man's land, with no attention to the placement or posture of the corpse, and left there to be eaten by beasts." But Diogenes is certainly an outlier. Laqueur concludes, "This wish has been viewed, almost universally, as insane."[6]

Precisely how it matters depends on the specific society, but place matters when it comes to remains. Even in those that practice sky burial, where the aim is not to put remains in a final "resting place," place is nonetheless a concern, since a location where birds of prey are present is essential to carry out ritual requirements.[7] In some societies the movement of the corpse from one specific context to another is prescribed. A very large percentage make use of elaborate scripted behaviors that involve a phase of intimate physical contact with the corpse by close kin before disposing of the remains; in some cases the corpse is kept present in the family circle for an extended period of time before being disposed of.[8] Some also practice double burial, in which the remains are buried in a temporary grave and then moved to a permanent burial place later on, often after the flesh has decomposed. Another mortuary pattern is a period during which the remains are exposed, sometimes on a platform that has been built for this purpose, and then buried subsequently.

Cremation does not eliminate concern about physical place. Cremations often occur at a culturally specified location, and cremains are often interred. Where they are scattered, sometimes a specific place for scattering is ritually prescribed or preferred (as the River Ganges is for many Hindus). And if a specific place for scattering is not determined by custom or the explicit request of the deceased, the bereaved have to decide on a place, which many do with great care.

Burial, perhaps most obviously, demands concern with places, for it situates the remains at a specific site. Many societies also place importance on the orientation of the grave, thus linking the spatial arrangement of the corpse with the spatiality of the physical world and the symbolism attached to it.[9] The definitive location of the buried cadaver affects the relationship of survivors to the place. A burial site provides survivors a place to visit, to commune with the dead (whether or not one takes this idea literally). The burial location can become a site of pilgrimage,[10] and it provides a sense that the deceased still has a place in the world.

The practice of dedicating literal places to the dead serves a number of functions that benefit bereaved people (whether considered individually or as groups). Marking a place for the dead helps restore a sense of normalcy after the disruption of our sense of security in things continuing in space and time. It serves to reassert some continuity of the person with something that resides in the physical world and that we can locate. The remains retain an aura of association with the person even if deprived of agency, and to place them in a particular physical location is reassuring. Even though the remains are palpably *not* the person, it is also comforting in that it allows a surrogate physical contact with the person, which is soothing at a juncture when one is deprived of it. Perhaps these considerations help explain why so many cultures develop rituals of extensive intimate contact with the body of deceased loved ones (though evolutionary psychologists such as Claire White would emphasize that such contact provides veridical evidence that the person is no longer a living agent).

Physical places can also play a role in survivors' efforts to act on behalf of the dead. These literal locations for the dead provide a dedicated precinct for enacting gestures of love and respect for them. Because the place has become associated with the person, literally tending to the place (e.g., laying a wreath) is a way of honoring the deceased person. The association with the deceased also makes site a designated place for the absence of the person to be felt as a presence. This presence of absence serves as a way of feeling connected to the person, albeit often in a sad way.

Physical sites associated with the dead can also function as "ritual spaces" for attending to and addressing the deceased and, when availed of these, can help mitigate the guilt feelings that so often affect the bereaved. Commonly, bereaved individuals feel that they have failed and continue to fail the deceased. Such survivor guilt arises for many reasons. The most straightforward cause of survivor guilt is the feeling survivors have that they should have been able to prevent the death or that their actions or choices in some way contributed to the circumstances of death. Many, including Eric Lindemann, have pointed out the tendency of the bereaved to find ways in which they contributed to the death of a loved one, even when this requires considerable ingenuity.[11] Perhaps this is partially motivated by a felt need to overcome the overwhelming sense of powerlessness that arises when a loved one dies. If one is to blame, it might seem, one is at least not completely ineffectual.

Survivor guilt is intensified by the fact that every move toward becoming accommodated to the new situation tends to be experienced as an act of disloyalty. A bereaved person often feels guilty for any thought or feeling that is not focused on the deceased and the loss. Distraction from the loss is often followed by a feeling that one is unfeeling, that one has done the equivalent of betraying the deceased. Moreover, any act that alters anything the deceased has done (be it as simple as moving a pair of shoes that the deceased had taken off) can seem a gesture of violation. The bereaved person often engages in a very real struggle between efforts to adjust to the new situation and the perceived obligation to devote one's full agency to responding to the death of the other (sometimes by acting vicariously on that person's part, sometimes by keeping the person in one's own and other people's minds).

The death of a loved one can also provoke a sense that an injustice has been done to the deceased, which provokes a motive to find a guilty party, even if that party is oneself. Caring friends of the bereaved may attempt to convince the person that guilt feelings are inappropriate, but this often does not help the bereaved overcome the guilt. It is at least as likely to make the person feel isolated in these feelings and thus to cause further distress.

Strikingly, Xunzi recognized the tendency of bereaved people to feel at fault. This is one of his arguments for claiming that codes establishing appropriate rituals are valuable because they do help preempt a sense that one has not done enough on behalf of the dead.

> Everyone is at times visited by sudden feelings of depression and melancholy longing. A loyal minister who has lost his lord or a filial son who has lost a parent, even when he is enjoying himself among congenial company, will be overcome by such feelings. If they come to him and he is greatly moved, but does nothing to give them expression, then his emotions of remembrance and longing will be frustrated and unfulfilled, and he will feel a sense of deficiency in his ritual behavior. Therefore, the former kings established certain forms to be observed on such occasions so that men could fulfill their duty to honor those who deserve honor and show affection for those who command affection.[12]

One can make the argument that like specific rituals, specific sites for making gestures honoring and tending the dead also encourage the sense that, in the context, one is doing right by the dead, that one is doing what one can do and focusing one's attention directly on the deceased person.

As sites of action for sheltering the dead (tending to their remains and honoring them and their legacies), such places help the living to reassert relationships of caring and close connection with the deceased. By providing a space in which the person's absence can be felt as present, such spaces provide the living with a focus for communicative gestures directed toward the deceased person, satisfying a desire that may otherwise be frustrated.

Definite sites associated with particular dead individuals can also reassure the living that a beloved person will not be forgotten. Perhaps this is especially so when the place has some marker to draw the world's attention to the person whom it has lost. Burial sites, especially when individually marked, draw attention to a person's having lived, and grave markers literally present the person as making a mark on the very landscape that surrounds us. The force of these gestures becomes clear also in its absence, as for instance the pathos of the anonymous burial of those whose remains cannot be identified or the indignity of being crammed into a pauper's grave in Great Britain, which Laqueur associates with the rise of the modern civic cemetery and its capacity to underscore differences of social standing.[13]

Laqueur associates the rise of the modern cemetery, which replaced the churchyard as the preferred burial site among Christian Westerners, with the triumph of the bourgeoisie. The churchyards kept the dead within the community of the living and within a particular community of religious membership. By contrast, civic cemeteries were "self-consciously planned landscapes . . . that could be anywhere and mean anything and belong to anyone," at least anyone who had the means.[14] They provided "a space in which one could mourn and remember in whatever fashion one could afford in the company of a veritable museum of styles and even bodies."[15]

And this draws attention to one of the ironies that can afflict efforts to find a literal "place" for the dead. Although aimed at securing a respectful place in which one can focus one's sense of connection with the dead, more this-worldly concerns associated with status can divert attention back to relative social positioning vis-à-vis the living. Of course, it is not only the placement of a person's remains that can direct attention to social prominence. The level of pomp and circumstance associated with a funeral reflects the person's relative standing, and sumptuousness incommensurate with that standing is regarded as improper in many contexts, as the attitudes of both Confucians and seventeenth-century Londoners attest.[16] However, the placement of remains and the way in which that placement is marked or outfitted can emphasize social stratification (as it has done in many modern Western cemeteries), not one's connection with the person who has died. Laqueur thinks this irony is endemic to the modern Western world's approach to death; a cultural shift has occurred, from viewing a person's death as marking "a time for reflection on the transience of earthly glory" to viewing the death as an "occasion to exult in it."[17]

The irony of focusing on the literal place for depositing the remains of the dead is that the result can be less attention in the minds of the living to the role the person who has died might continue to play in their lives, and more attention is diverted into what might be construed as the pettier aspects of relationships among the living. Class consciousness can also intrude in cases in which grave decoration is left largely up to family members. Disputes over the appropriateness of personal effects deposited at graves and clashing sensibilities of families with loved ones in proximate graves can make graves into sites of power struggles with other people as opposed to places for reflection and recollection.[18]

A second irony that may arise from too much focus on literal places for the dead is a magnification of cognitive dissonance. Dissonance arises in connection with human remains because they are seen as both the beloved person (the one who is "laid to rest") and *not* the beloved person. It is difficult to have a consistent reaction to remains for this reason, and the difficulty may be exacerbated when attention is focused on the literal location of interment. This is not to say that it is inappropriate to continue to associate the remains with the person (even if the alternative is psychologically possible). As I have already suggested, it may be comforting and emotionally significant for a bereaved person to engage in physical gestures of tending the deceased, even if those gestures are functional only in symbolic terms. But there may be a danger of fetishizing the physical location of the remains, at least for some people. (The British mother who erected a life-size realistic statue of her son on his grave and claimed that it comforted her to hug it, for example, may be such a person.[19]) Focus on a literal place for a late loved one might amount to a gesture of denial in the face of reality, a fetishizing of the remains of the person, or a form of concretizing wishes that cannot be fulfilled.

A third possible irony of emphasis on physical sites for the dead works in the opposite direction. This is the possibility that memorializing markers facilitate forgetfulness, not memory. Robert Musil, in his witty essay "On Monuments," points out that the ostensible aim of establishing a permanent memorial or monument to the dead is to "conjure up a remembrance," and yet "there is nothing in this world as invisible as a monument." A monument "repels attention." Monuments "elude our perceptive faculties," a feature that Musil terms "a downright vandalism-inciting quality." Part of the explanation of their invisibility is their characteristically monochrome character.[20] But they also fail in their efforts because "anything that endures over time sacrifices its ability to make an impression." Musil is skeptical that monuments succeed in making us remember. He concludes his essay, "Why then, matters being the way they are, are monuments erected precisely for great men? This seems to be a carefully calculated insult. Since we can do them no more harm in life, we thrust them with a memorial stone hung around their neck into the sea of oblivion."[21] Clearly, the intent of survivors who mark a loved one's grave with a headstone is typically not to surrender them to oblivion, and marking the headstone with the person's name is an antidote to this possibility. In any case Musil is describing public monuments, and graves are usually not the sites on which such memorials are constructed. But situating remains in a "final resting place" may similarly fend off attention, even among those who would have cause to notice (i.e., the bereaved), even if they happened to be in the vicinity (which in modern industrialized societies cannot be assumed).

In the case of contemporary cemeteries that have strict decorating restrictions and standardized headstones, the difficulty of noticing any particular site of interment seems to be intentional. The uniform marking of burial sites in cemeteries may be a deliberate effort to stress the equal enormity of the death of any person, or it may be aimed at encouraging reflection on our common status as mortal, both of which may be worthy gestures. However, it does not necessarily help a bereaved person to feel that the unique loss of a particular person has been addressed. The felt need to do this may prompt another kind of effort to associate a deceased person with a particular place through makeshift shrines, often at the site of death. Such sites may enable the loved ones who erect them to play an ongoing role of maintaining and adding to the site, and in this sense it may make them feel that they are tending to the dead. However, such shrines seemed to be geared toward calling the public's attention to the loss, a gesture that offends some members of the public and may not be condoned by the authorities who control the (usually public) sites on which they are erected. To this extent, such displays again give the dead a "place" in the public sphere, but a place that is likely to be contested. In general, insofar as burial sites are geographical locations, they are always subject to transfer of control by the living. If we give the dead sites on our geopolitical map, they can be pawns to our geopolitics at every political level.

A Place in One's Life

The greatest irony would be to imagine that we can resolve the problem of placing the dead by way of physical location. Disposing of the remains of our loved ones is not the end of our relationship to them. Indeed, the optimal place that the dead can come to occupy is not that of being out of sight. It is a matter of their coming to have a meaningful place, in their new status, in our ongoing lives.

Our relationships are decisive for who we are, and our selves have been damaged by the loss of someone who is close to us. We cannot reconstruct the self that has been damaged without taking the deceased into account. And this requires absorbing the fact that we must relate to them differently from the way we did in the past. As those who have spearheaded the "continuing bonds" movement in bereavement psychology tell us, when we are bereaved, we need to place our relationship with the deceased person on a new footing.

Among the ways that we can relate to a deceased person in this fashion is to consider the person's perspective when making decisions and to assimilate aspects of the person's outlook into our own repertoires. In these ways, the deceased person plays the role of guide and, for those in particular relationships, that of an ancestor.[22] The deceased loved one is often felt as an implicit audience for the survivor's activities, an indication that the living person continues to envision the deceased person's point of view and refer to it in shaping further conduct. Although it involves considerable work of creative imagination on the part of the living person, such active relating can involve honoring, deferring to, and even negotiating with someone who is dead. It can result in finding new meanings in the relationship.

The relationship one has to the dead can be a very "live" relationship, in a nondelusory sense. Richard Russo indicates that in his novel *Everybody's Fool* he takes the physical "movement" of the remains of the dead as a metaphor for a less material but no less literal kind of movement:

> The soil beneath where so many people lay interred has begun to erode, and so when you go to visit Grandma and you stand before her headstone, you have no guarantee anymore that Grandma's still there. She may have moved down the slope a way. So the dead in this book are on the move, which is another way of suggesting of course that they are not fixed in there, any more than they're fixed in our memories. They have more to say to us when they're gone if we're the sort to listen.[23]

While literal places and spaces can serve facilitative roles, they do not on their own ensure a place for the dead in our lives. But to the extent that the living person remains open and responsive, relationships with the dead can continue to develop. We cannot know what we are to the dead, if such a notion is even coherent. But we can keep learning and cherishing what they are to us, and in doing so we make and maintain a place for the dead.

NOTES

My thanks to Edward Casey, Karsten Struhl, Vrinda Dalmiya, and other members of my audience at the Eleventh East-West Philosophers' Conference (2016) for their helpful comments on this chapter.

1. Saint Augustine, *Confessions*, trans. Frank J. Sheed (Indianapolis: Hackett, 1993), 59.

2. Jean-Paul Sartre, *Being and Nothingness: A Phenomenological Essay on Ontology*, trans. Hazel E. Barnes (New York: Simon and Schuster, 1956), 40, 42.

3. Cf. Randolph M. Nesse, "An Evolutionary Framework for Understanding Grief," in *Spousal Bereavement in Late Life*, ed. Deborah S. Carr, Randolph M. Nesse, and Camille B. Wortman (New York: Springer, 2005), 195–225. Nesse takes it as a given that searching behavior "gives rise to belief in ghosts" (210).

4. Thomas W. Laqueur, *The Work of the Dead: A Cultural History of Mortal Remains* (Princeton, NJ: Princeton University Press, 2015), 31.

5. See *Mozi*, trans. Philip J. Ivanhoe, in *Readings in Classical Chinese Philosophy*, ed. Philip J. Ivanhoe and Bryan W. Van Norden (New York: Seven Bridges Press, 2001),

66, 67n, 85. Cf. Mo Tzu, "Basic Writings," in *Basic Writings of Mo Tzu, Hsün Tzu, and Han Fei Tzu*, trans. Burton Watson (New York: Columbia University Press, 1963), 40–41, 76–77. Mozi presents, as an argument in favor of impartiality on the part of the ruler, that even during a dreadful epidemic, when large numbers of people are dying, the impartial ruler would bury his people when they die, while the partial one would be unreliable.

6. Laqueur, *Work of the Dead*, 110.

7. Artist Anjolie Ela Menon told me that an acquaintance from a group that practices sky burial described the considerable distress experienced over not doing right by the dead when birds did not appear in a place as expected, as a consequence of changing habitat.

8. Cf. Claire White, "Not Just Dead Meat: An Evolutionary Account of Corpse Treatment in Mortuary Rituals," presentation at the Psychology Department of the University of Texas at Austin, April 29, 2016.

9. See the discussion of the necrogeography of the churchyard and the traditional east-west alignment of the graves of the faithful in Laqueur, *Work of the Dead*, 123–133.

10. Sometimes it is an unwelcome site. The fear of Osama bin Laden's grave becoming a pilgrimage site was allegedly a motivation for the sea burial he was given by the US Navy.

11. Eric Lindemann, cited in Maurice Lamm, *The Jewish Way in Death and Mourning* (Middle Village, NY: Jonathan David, 2000), 142–143.

12. Hsün Tzu, "A Discussion of Rites," in Watson, *Basic Writings*, 109.

13. Laqueur points out that British pauper funerals were considered so degrading in the eighteenth and nineteenth centuries that even exceedingly poor people scrimped to be able to join societies that provided burial benefits. See Thomas W. Laqueur, "Bodies, Death, and Pauper Funerals," *Representations* 1 (1983): 110.

14. See Thomas W. Laqueur, "Spaces of the Dead," *Ideas* 8 (2001): 5, 11.

15. Ibid., 16.

16. Laqueur, "Bodies, Death, and Pauper Funerals," 113.

17. Laqueur, *Work of the Dead*, 361. See also Laqueur, "Spaces of the Dead," 6.

18. Tracy Chevalier's novel *Falling Angels* (New York: Dutton, 2001) focuses on a conflict between the disparate tastes and sensibilities of two families who have loved ones buried in adjacent graves.

19. The case is described as follows in the *Daily Mail*: "SOLIHULL: A life-size effigy of Danny Pedley, his arm resting casually on his gravestone, is an arresting sight at Widney Manor Cemetery, Bentley Heath. Danny is wearing a grey, green and white Nike track-suit—as he did in life, according to his mother Debbie. 'The resemblance is uncanny, it looks more and more like him every day. The statue was made in China and cost £8,000. I go to the grave everyday to change his hat and give him a little kiss,' she says. Danny was diagnosed as having small cell lung cancer on Christmas Eve 2008. He died aged 27 last January, just six days after marrying his long-term girlfriend, Stacey, 26, mother of his two children, Lacey-Leigh, seven, and Mason, four." Bel Mooney, *Daily Mail*, March 18, 2011, http://www.dailymail.co.uk/news/article-1353815/Colourful-poundland-graveyard-shrines-British-councils-trying-wipe-out.html.

20. Robert Musil, "On Monuments," in *Posthumous Papers of a Living Author*, trans. Peter Wortsman (Hygiene, CO: Eridanos Press, 1987), 60–61.

21. Ibid., 64, 65.

22. Dennis Klass, Phyllis R. Silverman, and Steven L. Nickman, eds., *Continuing Bonds: New Understandings of Grief* (Washington, DC: Taylor and Francis, 1996). See also Nico H. Frijda, *The Laws of Emotion* (Mahwah, NJ: Lawrence Erlbaum, 2006), 289.

23. Richard Russo, interviewed by Steve Inskeep, *NPR Morning Edition*, May 5, 2016.

Contributors

Roger T. Ames is Humanities Chair Professor at Peking University, a Berggruen Fellow, and professor emeritus of philosophy at the University of Hawai'i. He is a former editor of *Philosophy East and West* and the founding editor of *China Review International*. Ames has authored several interpretative studies of Chinese philosophy and culture: *Thinking Through Confucius* (1987), *Anticipating China* (1995), *Thinking from the Han* (1998), and *Democracy of the Dead* (1999) (all with David L. Hall), and most recently *Confucian Role Ethics: A Vocabulary* (2011). His publications also include translations of Chinese classics: *Sun-tzu: The Art of Warfare* (1993); *Sun Pin: The Art of Warfare* (with D. C. Lau, 1996); *The Analects of Confucius* and *The Chinese Classic of Family Reverence: A Philosophical Translation of the "Xiaojing"* (both with Henry Rosemont Jr., 1998 and 2008, respectively); *Focusing the Familiar: A Translation and Philosophical Interpretation of the "Zhongyong"* (2001); and *Dao De Jing: A Philosophical Translation* (with David L. Hall, 2003). Almost all of his publications are now available in Chinese translation, including his philosophical translations of Chinese canonical texts.

Meera Baindur is an associate professor at Manipal Centre for Philosophy and Humanities, Manipal Academy of Higher Education, India. She has a doctoral degree in the interdisciplinary area of environmental philosophy from the National Institute of Advanced Studies, Bangalore. Earlier, she stayed with village communities in the Himalayas for a few years, working at a grassroots level on environmental and sustainability issues. During this time, she also pursued traditional studies in Indian philosophy and yoga. Her research interests include environmental philosophy and humanities, conceptualization of nature in Indian thought, gender, and religions. Her recent work focuses on Indian philosophical concepts related to body, gender, ritual and aesthetic traditions, and place. She is currently working on a study around landscape deities and ecological practice in the Himalayas, rituals, and cultural geography.

James Buchanan is a university professor and the executive director of the Edward B. Brueggeman Center for Dialogue at Xavier University. Prior to founding the Brueggeman Center in 2003, he held the Besl Family Chair in Ethics/Religion and Society at Xavier, the Carolyn Werner Gannett Chair in Humanities at the Rochester Institute of Technology, and the Endowment for the Humanities Chair in Ethics at Hamilton College and was a member of the founding committee for the Hong Kong University of Science and Technology, where he was also a professor. The Brueggeman Center sponsors conferences on critical issues of globalization, interfaith, comparative ethics, refugees, and environmental sustainability. The students from the Brueggeman Fellows Research Program have done research in more than sixty countries worldwide. Buchanan is a recipient of many awards, including the Building Bridges Award, the Eternal Light Award, and numerous humanitarian awards for work in intercultural understanding. He has delivered more than three hundred lectures and seminars in over forty countries and publishes in ethics and comparative ethics, global systems, biotechnology, and interfaith understanding, including *Changing Nature's Course: The Ethical Challenge of Biotechnology* and the forthcoming *Wagers into the Abyss: Ethics in an Age of Global Systems*.

Steven Burik is an assistant professor of philosophy at Singapore Management University. He holds a PhD in comparative philosophy from the National University of Singapore. His research interests are mainly in comparative philosophy, continental philosophy (Heidegger, Derrida), Chinese philosophy (Daoism), and critical thinking. Among his works are *The End of Comparative Philosophy and the Task of Comparative Thinking* (2010), a coauthored textbook in critical thinking, and articles in various journals and books, including *Philosophy East and West* and *Comparative and Continental Philosophy*. He is currently working on an edited volume (with Ralph Weber and Robert W. Smid), tentatively titled *Comparative Philosophy and Method: Contemporary Practices and Future Possibilities*, which brings together leading scholars' thinking about the methodology used in comparative philosophy.

Carl Helsing completed a PhD in philosophy at Southern Illinois University, where he studied the history of Western philosophy, classical Chinese philosophy, and Buddhism. His research interests include Zhuangzi, Confucianism, moral psychology, theories of language, and cognitive metaphor. His scholarship explores these topics and their intersections with literature, poetry, politics, and public health. Helsing has taught at the Nanjing Foreign Language School, the Johns Hopkins Center for Talented Youth, and Southern Illinois University. He currently lives in the foothills of North Carolina and teaches philosophy and religion classes at High Point University.

Michael Hemmingsen is an assistant professor of philosophy at the University of Guam. He completed his doctorate at McMaster University, Ontario, and holds an MA in philosophy and a master's in international relations from Victoria University of Wellington, New Zealand. His research interests include non-Western and comparative philosophy, intercultural moral conflict (with a particular focus on colonial contexts), environmental philosophy, ethics, social and political philosophy, and critical theory (with a focus on the Frankfurt School). He has published papers on topics such as wealth redistribution, the nature of value in environmental philosophy, and Deleuzean and Vedantic interpretations of Spinoza's substance monism.

Peter D. Hershock is the director of the Asian Studies Development Program (ASDP) and an education specialist at the East-West Center (EWC) in Honolulu, Hawai'i. His work with ASDP over the past twenty years has centered on designing and conducting faculty and institutional development programs aimed at enhancing undergraduate teaching and learning about Asian cultures and societies. As part of the EWC Education Program, he has collaborated in designing and hosting international leadership programs and research seminars that examine the relationships among higher education, globalization, equity, and diversity. Trained in Asian and comparative philosophy, he has focused his research work mainly on using Buddhist conceptual resources to reflect on contemporary issues of global concern. His books include *Liberating Intimacy: Enlightenment and Social Virtuosity in Ch'an Buddhism* (1996); *Reinventing the Wheel: A Buddhist Response to the Information Age* (1999); *Chan Buddhism* (2005); *Buddhism in the Public Sphere: Reorienting Global Interdependence* (2006); *Changing Education: Leadership Innovation and Development in a Globalizing Asia Pacific* (edited, 2007); *Educations and Their Purposes: A Conversation among Cultures* (edited, 2008); *Valuing Diversity: Buddhist Reflection on Realizing a More Equitable Global Future* (2012); *Public Zen, Personal Zen: A Buddhist Introduction* (2014); and *Value and Values: Economics and Justice in an Age of Global Interdependence* (edited, 2015).

Kathleen Higgins is a professor of philosophy at the University of Texas at Austin. She has also been a frequent visiting faculty member at the University of Auckland. She has published a number of books: *Nietzsche's "Zarathustra"* (2010); *The Music of Our Lives* (rev. ed., 2011); *A Short History of Philosophy* (with Robert C. Solomon, 1996); *A Passion for Wisdom* (with Robert C. Solomon, 1997); *Comic Relief: Nietzsche's "Gay Science"* (2000); *What Nietzsche Really Said* (with Robert C. Solomon, 2000); and *The Music between Us: Is Music a Universal Language?* (2012), which received the American Society for Aesthetics Outstanding Monograph Prize for 2012. She has edited or coedited several other books on such topics as non-Western philosophy, Nietzsche, German idealism, aesthetics, ethics, erotic love, and the philosophy of Robert C. Solomon. She has been a visiting fellow at the Faculty of Psychology and Educational Sciences of Katholieke Universiteit Leuven, a visiting fellow of the Australian National University's Philosophy Department and Canberra School of Music, and a resident scholar at the Rockefeller Foundation's Bellagio Study and Conference Center.

Marion Hourdequin is an associate professor of philosophy at Colorado College, where her research and teaching center on environmental philosophy, ethics, and comparative philosophy. Her current research projects focus on climate ethics and climate justice, the social and ethical dimensions of ecological restoration, and relational approaches to ethics. Hourdequin is the author of *Environmental Ethics: From Theory to Practice* (2015) and a coeditor (with David G. Havlick) of *Restoring Layered Landscapes* (2016). Her work has been published in a variety of journals, including *Environmental Ethics, Ethics and the Environment, Philosophy East and West*, the *Journal of Chinese Philosophy*, and *Ethical Theory and Moral Practice*, and she serves as an associate editor for *Environmental Values.*

Naglis Kardelis is an associate professor at the Department of Logic and History of Philosophy at Vilnius University, Lithuania, and the head of the Department of Contemporary Philosophy at the Lithuanian Culture Research Institute in Vilnius. He is the author of two books—*Vienovės įžvalga Platono filosofijoje* (The insight of unity in Plato's philosophy; 2007; in Lithuanian) and *Pažinti ar suprasti? Humanistikos ir gamtotyros akiračiai* (To know or to understand? The horizons of humanities and natural sciences; 2008; in Lithuanian)—as well as numerous scholarly studies and articles in the fields of classical Greek philosophy, classical literature, comparative philosophy, and contemporary continental philosophy. He has translated four Platonic dialogues from Greek into Lithuanian— *Timaeus* and *Critias* (both 1995), *Phaedrus* (1996), and *The Apology of Socrates* (2009)—as well as translating, from Greek and Latin into Lithuanian, a number of texts from the corpus of Christian classics. His research interests include the philosophy of classical antiquity, contemporary continental philosophy, and comparative philosophy.

John W. M. Krummel is an associate professor in religious studies at Hobart and William Smith Colleges in Geneva, New York; an assistant editor of the *Journal of Japanese Philosophy*, the editor of *Social Imaginaries*, and the president of the International Association of Japanese Philosophy. He has a PhD in philosophy from the New School for Social Research and a PhD in religion from Temple University. His dissertation at the New School was on Heidegger and

Kant, and his dissertation at Temple University was on the dialectic of Nishida. He is the author of *Nishida Kitarō's Chiasmatic Chorology: Place of Dialectic, Dialectic of Place* (2015). His writings on various topics have appeared in a variety of journals, including *Auslegung, Dao, International Philosophical Quarterly, Existentia, Philosophy Today, Vera Lex,* the *Journal of Chinese Philosophy, Research in Phenomenology, Philosophy East and West, Anarchist Developments in Cultural Studies, Social Imaginaries, Diaphany, Studia Phaenomenologica, Continental Philosophy Review,* and the *European Journal of Japanese Philosophy,* as well as in *Portland Monthly Magazine* and in several books as chapters. He has also translated several works from Japanese or German, including *Place and Dialectic: Two Essays by Nishida Kitarō* (2011). His research interests include continental philosophy, phenomenology, Heidegger, Schürmann, Kant, Nietzsche, Buddhism, Dōgen, Kūkai, Japanese and Kyoto School philosophy, Nishida, Nishitani, Ueda, Dostoevsky, Mishima, comparative philosophy/religion, nihilism, imagination, philosophy of religion, anarchism, and mysticism, among others. He was born and raised in Tokyo in a bilingual family.

Justas Kučinskas earned a master's degree in the history of philosophy from King's College London. He completed his doctoral studies of philosophy at Vilnius University in 2017 and is in the process of defending his PhD thesis titled "The Principle of Balance in Arvydas Šliogeris' Philosophy" ("Pusiausvyros principas Arvydo Šliogerio filosofijoje," in Lithuanian). Kučinskas is the author of a number of research articles redefining the perception of Arvydas Šliogeris' philosophy in Lithuania. Currently he serves as a member of the board at ISM University of Management and Economics and is also a member of Lithuanian Council of Higher Education. His nonacademic interests include the practice and teaching of natural movement, as well as hosting and facilitating conversations that matter while being an active member of an international Art of Hosting community.

Ilana Maymind holds a PhD in comparative studies from Ohio State University and is currently a lecturer at Wilkinson College of Arts, Humanities, and Social Sciences at Chapman University. Her work primarily focuses on East-West comparative religious thought, and she is interested in issues of transition, displacement, and exile. She has written a number of articles and papers in edited collections and journals, including "Learning from the Past: Exile and Ethics," in the book *Perspectives on Culture, Values, and Justice* (2015); "A Comparative Case Study: Memory, Law and Morality," in the *Journal of Indian Philosophy and Religion* (2013); and "On the Concept of Self-Hatred: A Misnomer," in the *Journal of Jewish Identities* (2016). Maymind is a regular contributor to the book review section of the *Journal of International and Global Studies.* In addition, she is an associate editor of the *Journal of Bioethical Inquiry's* Faith

and Ethics section and is part of the advisory member team for Cambridge
Scholars Publishing.

Lara M. Mitias currently serves as an associate professor of philosophy at Antioch
College, where she teaches Asian philosophies, along with various courses in
Western philosophy. She received her doctorate from the University of Hawaiʻi
at Mānoa in Asian and comparative philosophy. She has taught more than thirty
different courses in philosophy—including logic, metaphysics, social and political philosophy, and philosophy for children (P4C)—and courses on death. The
many independent study courses she has taught include Indian Philosophy of
Language and On Happiness. She has two published articles, "Desiring the
Past" and "P4C: Process, Perspective, and Pluralism for Children."

Michael Warren Myers holds a PhD in comparative philosophy from the
University of Hawaiʻi and is currently a professor emeritus of philosophy at
Washington State University, where he taught for twenty-seven years. His publications have focused on two areas of study: philosophy of religion and military/
political strategies for peace. His *Brahman: A Comparative Theology* appeared
in paperback in 2016, and *The Pacific War and Contingent Victory* in 2015. He
has written numerous articles and book reviews for *Philosophy East and West* and
other journals and contributed to a Festschrift in honor of B. N. K. Sharma, the
late doyen of Madhva Vedanta in India. Myers published his dissertation as *Let
the Cow Wander: Modeling the Metaphors in Veda and Vedanta* in the monograph series of the Society for Asian and Comparative Philosophy (University
of Hawaiʻi Press). He contributed four hymns translated from the Ṛveda to
the textbook *Reading about the World* and a chapter, "Ethical and Religious
Perspectives on Living Together," to the book *Toward a Peaceable Future*. Myers
is a graduate of the Galilee International Management Institute's 2017 summer
program "The Israel-Palestine Conflict: Understanding Both Sides." His work
on shared existence in Israel-Palestine sums up the problems and possibilities of
a lifelong commitment to religious pluralism.

Takahiro Nakajima is a professor of Chinese philosophy and comparative
philosophy at the Institute for Advanced Studies on Asia, the University of
Tokyo. After completing his studies at the Graduate School of Humanities at
the University of Tokyo, he worked for that university (1991–1996, 2000–present) and Ritsumeikan University (1996–2000). He is the editor in chief of the
International Journal of Asian Studies and is currently interested in comparative research on Confucianism in East Asia and how to write the history of
Chinese philosophy. He has received prizes such as the twenty-fifth Watsuji
Tetsurō Culture Prize (2013) and the first Nakamura Hajime Prize (1993). He
has been a visiting scholar or professor at EHESS, Princeton University, IKGF

at Friedrich-Alexander-Universität Erlangen-Nürnberg, New York University, University of Paris 8, the Harvard-Yenching Institute, and the Marcel Granet Institute at the University of Paris 7. His publications include *Language qua Thought* (2017), *Zhuangzi and the Happy Fish* (coedited with Roger T. Ames, 2015), *Philosophy of the Evil* (2012), *Praxis of Co-existence: State and Religion* (2011), *The Zhuangzi* (2009), *Philosophy in Humanities* (2009), and *The Reverberation of Chinese Philosophy: Language and Politics* (2007).

Bindu Puri is a professor of philosophy at the Centre for Philosophy, School of Social Sciences, Jawaharlal Nehru University, and its chairperson. Her main interests in philosophy are in political, moral, and contemporary Indian philosophy, and she is a leading scholar on the thought and practice of Mahatma Gandhi. Puri has published extensively in edited anthologies and philosophical and interdisciplinary journals and has authored two books: *Gandhi and the Moral Life* (2004) and *The Tagore-Gandhi Debate on Matters of Truth and Untruth* (2015). She has also edited five books, including *Mahatma Gandhi and His Contemporaries* (2001). She has coedited *Reason, Morality, and Beauty: Essays on the Philosophy of Immanuel Kant* and *Terror, Peace, and Universalism: Essays on the Philosophy of Immanuel Kant* (both with Heiko Sievers, 2007), as well as *Living with Religious Diversity* (with Sonia Sikka and Lori G. Beaman, 2016). Most recently Puri delivered the annual M. K. Gandhi Lecture on Peace and the Humanities for the Mahatma Gandhi Peace Council of Ottawa (2017) and the Johnson and Hastings lectures at Mount Allison University.

Rein Raud is a professor of Asian and cultural studies at Tallinn University and a visiting professor at the Free University of Berlin. He graduated from Japanese studies at St. Petersburg University in 1985 and defended his doctorate in 1994 at the University of Helsinki, where he worked as a professor of Japanese studies from 1995 to 2016. He served as president of the European Association of Japanese Studies from 2011 to 2014. Raud has published numerous articles on Japanese classical literature and philosophy, notably on the thought of Dōgen, and has also published translations of many of the texts he studies. His books on cultural theory include *Practices of Selfhood* (with Zygmunt Bauman, 2015) and *Meaning in Action: Outline of an Integral Theory of Culture* (2016). He is also an acclaimed and award-winning author of fiction, with three novels translated into English.

Britta Saal completed her studies of fine arts in 1996 and her MA in philosophy, German literature, and modern Japan studies at Heinrich Heine University Düsseldorf in 2004. She held a scholarship from the Japan Foundation in 2005–2006 and was in Japan for ten months. In 2012 she completed her PhD in intercultural philosophy at the University of Bremen; her thesis was an intercultural critique of modernity. Between 2004 and 2013 she was a research assistant and an assistant professor at the East Asian Institute/Modern Japan at Heinrich Heine University Düsseldorf. Since 2013 she has been a member of the editorial staff of the German-language journal *Polylog: Zeitschrift für interkulturelles Philosophieren* and is working freelance. She is an active participant at international conferences, and since 2015 she has been doing philosophy with elementary school children in various institutions in Wuppertal. She also gives talks and teacher trainings in this field. In 2016 she worked with Thomas Jackson and the staff of the Uehiro Academy for Philosophy and Ethics in Education at the University of Hawai'i at Mānoa. In this context, she initiated what she calls a Children's Polylogue—a philosophical exchange between children from Wuppertal and the Waikiki Elementary School in Honolulu. Her main research interests lie in intercultural philosophy, philosophy in Japan, philosophy in Africa, philosophy and place/space, postcolonial theory, and philosophy with children.

Joshua Stoll is a PhD candidate at the University of Hawai'i at Mānoa. His current research is directed at criticizing some assumptions in the philosophy of mind that underlie the epistemological and conceptual problems of other minds by emphasizing the value-laden and unprincipled nature of our situated and embodied interactions. In particular, he focuses on critiquing the philosophical starting point of emphasizing the epistemic and logocentric functions of mind as being precisely the sort of starting part that gives rise to the aforementioned problems. Emphasizing experiences of situated embodied engagements between individuals, he argues that our interactions with each other are deeply dependent on pragmatic improvisations, more so than on concerns for accurately representing what's on each other's mind. He has presented his research at several conferences, including "The Science of Consciousness" conferences in 2015 and 2016, the 2015 Australasian Society for Asian and Comparative Philosophy Conference, the 2016 Society for Asian and Comparative Philosophy Conference, and the 11th East-West Philosophers' Conference (2016).

Albert Welter is a professor of East Asian Buddhism and intellectual history at the University of Arizona and an honorary professor at the Hangzhou Academy of Social Sciences. He received his MA and PhD from McMaster University. His previous publications include *Monks, Rulers, and Literati: The Political Ascendancy of Chan Buddhism* (2006), *The "Linji lu" and the Creation of Chan Orthodoxy: The Development of Chan's Records of Sayings Literature* (2008), and *Yongming Yanshou's Conception of Chan in the "Zongjing lu": A Special Transmission within the Scripture* (2011). Welter is also a coeditor of (with Jeffrey Newmark) and a contributor to *Religion, Culture, and the Public Sphere in China and Japan* (2017). His latest publication is the study and translation of a seminal text on the administration of Buddhism in China, entitled *The Administration of Buddhism in China: A Study and Translation of Zanning and the Topical Compendium of the Buddhist Clergy* (*Da Song Seng shilüe* 大宋僧史略) (2018). He is currently working on a research project on Hangzhou Buddhist culture funded, in part, by the Khyentse Foundation.

David B. Wong is the Susan Fox Beischer and George D. Beischer Professor of Philosophy at Duke University. He has written essays on contemporary ethical theory, moral psychology, and classical Chinese philosophy, including "Cultivating the Self in Concert with Others," in *Dao Companion to the Analects* (2013), ed. Amy Olberding; "Emotion and the Cognition of Reasons in Moral Motivation," *Philosophical Issues* (2009); "Cultural Pluralism and Moral Identity," in *Personality, Identity, and Character: Explorations in Moral Psychology* (2009), ed. Darcia Narvaez and Dan K. Lapsley; "The Meaning of Detachment in Daoism, Buddhism, and Stoicism," *Dao* (2006); and "Is There a Distinction between Reason and Emotion in Mencius?," *Philosophy East and West* (1991). His essay "Early Confucian Philosophy and the Development of Compassion" appears in *Dao* (2014), as do commentaries on the essays and responses from Wong (2015, 2017). His books are *Moral Relativity* (1984) and *Natural Moralities: A Defense of Pluralistic Relativism* (2006). He coedited *Confucian Ethics: A Comparative Study of Self, Autonomy, and Community* (with Kwong-loi Shun, 2004). *Moral Relativism and Chinese Philosophy: David Wong and His Critics*, edited by Yang Xiao and Yong Huang (2014), is a book of critical commentaries on *Natural Moralities* and contains responses to each of the commentaries.

Index